P9-DCZ-362

The Tragedy of
EUROPEAN LABOR

The Tragedy of EUROPEAN LABOR 1918-1939

By ADOLF STURMTHAL

COLUMBIA UNIVERSITY PRESS
New York

COLUMBIA UNIVERSITY PRESS, NEW YORK

First printing 1943
Second printing with a new Preface, 1951

This study was made possible in part by funds granted by Carnegie Corporation of New York. That Corporation is not, however, the author, owner, publisher, or proprietor of this publication, and is not to be understood as approving by virtue of its grant any of the statements or views expressed therein.

MANUFACTURED IN THE UNITED STATES OF AMERICA

To the memory of

HELENE AND OTTO BAUER

PREFACE TO THE SECOND PRINTING

THE time is probably approaching when the history of European labor during and after World War II ought to be written. Indeed, there is some danger in delay; memories fade (and memories are probably at this time the only record of much of this history), and in the fast-moving kaleidoscope of the postwar scene history is no doubt being assiduously rewritten to fit later insights and necessities. Pending this major piece of history writing, however, a few significant trends perhaps deserve immediate, though brief, attention, particularly as they refer to the main developments outlined in this book.

The end of hostilities in Europe has been followed by a major attempt to unify the trade-union movement in those countries in which it has traditionally been split according to political philosophies. This effort was the result of a number of factors: the Socialist-Communist division, sharply accentuated by the Russo-German pact of 1939, had lost a good deal of its acerbity after June, 1941, when the Communists once again changed their "line" and became the most enthusiastic advocates of resistance to Hitlerism; under the Nazi occupation the labor groups—Socialists, Communists, and Catholics—coöperated wholeheartedly in the "Resistance"; after June, 1941, the Communists developed a new stage in their United Front policy, which was intended to bring about the merger of all anti-Nazi unions, clearly in the hope of dominating the united organizations; lastly and less significantly, the German Labor Front, despite its objectionable basic features, had demonstrated what powerful means of action—financial and otherwise—a unified labor organization might have at its disposal.

The attempt to merge Socialists, Communists, and Catholics in one trade union organization was made in six Continental countries: Austria, Belgium, France, Germany, Holland, and Italy. The results are significant.

From the outset, unification failed in three countries among the six. To facilitate the merger of the unions, the Dutch Social Democratic party allied itself with religious groups holding socially advanced views and thereby clearly marked its intention of opening its doors wide to non-Marxians or anti-Marxians. It even dropped its old name and called itself the Party of Labor. Nevertheless the religious unions refused to merge with the Socialist-led movement and maintained the division of Dutch trade unionism. In Belgium, the Socialist-led unions, which had in the past followed somewhat the British pattern and had been collectively affiliated with the Belgian Labor Party, now separated from the party in the hope that this move would make it possible for the Catholic unions to merge with them. This hope was not realized. Similarly, the French Christian Unions rejected without hesitation the invitation to join the Confédération Générale du Travail (C.G.T.).

In Italy, the attempt was at first successful. Unified trade unions were established to combine workers of differing social and political views. Yet from the outset each unified union was, so to speak, a federation of differing political groups, which maintained a sort of existence as well-organized factions within the union and strove to gain control over the entire body. At the Congress [of unions] the various factions submitted resolutions designed primarily to test their relative strength within the "united" organization. The membership of the Executive Committee of the Confederation was carefully divided among the various factions according to their numerical representation at the Congress as demonstrated in the vote on the resolutions submitted. Even in this first stage, the so-called unity barely concealed the division of the organization over political and social issues. Each of the factions, needless to say, represented a political party.

Even this "sham unity" did not last very long. First the Catholics (1948), then the anti-Communist wing (1949) of the Socialists and the Republicans broke away. One group of the Republicans merged with the Catholics, another is engaged in an attempt to remain independent. Without too much difficulty, it is possible to see in this threefold division a reflection of the threefold split of Italian socialism into the pro-Communist Nenni group, the right-wing Saragat Socialists who are coöperating with the Catholics in the government, and the independent Socialists led by Romita and Silone.

Germany and Austria thus offer the only examples of successful attempts at unification on the basis of "nonpartisan" labor action. But closer examination would indicate that in these countries, too, political groups contrive to exist within the unified trade unions. The official publication of the Austrian trade union confederation, in its reports on discussions of the governing bodies of the confederation, carefully indicates the political affiliation of each speaker. A rough system of proportional representation for the various political factions in the governing union bodies is used in both countries.

"Political" unionism, it would seem, remains the fate of European labor, for better or for worse. It "fits" Europe clearly in the same sense in which, according to Selig Perlman, "pure and simple" trade unionism "fitted" American labor.[1] In its philosophy, as well as in its methods, European labor remains intensely "political," at least in the usual meaning of the term.[2] Thus, in most countries the unions continue to coöperate closely with particular political parties and to rely largely upon them for the satisfaction of some major demands. Among these parties the Socialists, the Communists, and the Catholics continue to be the most important.

In these respects the over-all picture does not show any basic alteration, but the relations of the political parties with which the unions are allied have undergone considerable and significant

1 The past tense has been used since Perlman himself has recently described "pure and simple" unionism as a "museum piece." See Selig Perlman and A. S. Knowles: "Unionism in the Postwar Period" in T.C.T. McCormick, ed., *Problems of the Post-war World,* New York, McGraw-Hill, 1945, p. 41.

2 This does not coincide with the way I have used the term "political" as opposed to pressure-group activity. I designated by the expression "political" a content of action rather than its form. An organization would be engaged in "political" action regardless of whether it runs its own candidates or not, if it has a sense of statesmanship, a feeling of responsibility for the entire community, and a concern with the broader issues that confront the nation in which it operates. From this point of view, the time-honored issue of labor's independent political action becomes a rather insignificant, pragmatical question for which different countries find different solutions.

changes. The most notable are concerned with Socialist-Communist conflict.

The liberation of Continental Europe from German occupation was accompanied by a semirevolutionary trend, although neither of the major advancing armies favored a fully revolutionary development. The result was an impressive growth of the Socialist and Communist movements and, on the whole, closer coöperation between the two. To a large extent this reflected the wartime alliance of the Soviet Union with the Western powers. A series of well-known events profoundly disturbed the Socialist-Communist harmony: the absorption of the Socialist parties in Eastern Europe by the Communists; the radical divergence of the attitudes taken by Socialists and Communists toward the Marshall Plan; the rapidly growing tension between the Soviet Union and the Western nations.

This evolution has been clearly reflected in the international organization of the unions. At the height of the wartime alliance in World War II the old International Federation of Trade Unions (I.F.T.U.) appeared more and more anachronistic. Not only had it lost, by the advance of the Nazis, its strongest battalions on the Continent, it had also excluded the trade unions of the Soviet Union on one hand and the C.I.O. on the other, each representing vital elements in the chain of resistance to the Axis powers. By almost irresistible pressure the Russians and their friends succeeded in forcing the reluctant British trade union leaders—who held key positions in the international trade union movement—to abandon the I.F.T.U. In its stead was set up a new organization, the World Federation of Trade Unions (W.F.T.U.), which united all major labor organizations of the world except the American Federation of Labor. The basis of the W.F.T.U. was Socialist-Communist cooperation. As soon as this was endangered, the W.F.T.U. was doomed.

After prolonged negotiations the unions of the West finally left the W.F.T.U. and established in December, 1949, the International Confederation of Free Trade Unions (I.C.F.T.U.). With this step the division between Socialists and Communists was reestablished. Indeed, in some ways it was more complete than ever before.

During the interwar period the Socialist movement was divided into two main currents, the reformist Right Wing and the Marxian Center. These were in some ways the continuation of pre-World War I divisions of the Socialist movement. While the Communists had absorbed most of the former extreme leftist groups, the Right Wingers continued the traditions of the Revisionists, and the Marxian Center more or less continued those of the old Radicals. In particular, the leaders of the Center maintained consistently that the Socialist-Communist split was only a passing phenomenon and that the reunification of all currents in one large Socialist party was the indispensable condition for the final victory of socialism. As long as the division persisted, one wing would emphasize the immediate tasks at the expense of the future, and the other would sacrifice present-day interests of the workers for the sake of their future victory. Only a united movement, combining the best features of both Reformists and Communists, could provide for the proper distribution of emphasis between the immediate and the future tasks of the movement and thus ensure victory.

It is, perhaps, the most significant fact in the recent evolution of Socialist labor in Europe that this faction has, for all practical purposes, ceased to exist. Its main leaders (Leon Blum, Otto Bauer, Friedrich Adler) have disappeared, and postwar events seem to have convinced the great majority of the European Socialists that the reunification of the movement is neither desirable nor possible. The Socialist-Communist split is being accepted as permanent.

Perhaps the most widely accepted analysis of this change of attitude is that it is impossible for the Socialists to unite with the Communists on the basis of a loyal understanding. The violence and trickery employed against the Socialists of Eastern Europe, both before and after their merger with the Communists, and the gradual disappearance of the Socialists from the leadership of the united party seem to have finally convinced most of the Socialists that Moscow demands submission rather than loyal coöperation. Tito's rebellion against the Kremlin greatly accentuated the feeling that true unification was impossible, as did the growing conviction that communism is not only a method of social transformation, but also a means of national oppression.

The policy of the Marxian Center had been based upon the conviction that the objectives of Socialists and Communists were identical and that the divergence concerned merely the methods of achieving the common end. This belief seems to have been shaken on two counts. Socialism was to be a free society with a controlled economy—yet more than thirty years after the great Russian Revolution the Soviet dictatorship shows no signs of relaxing its iron grip. Also, instead of being a brief transitory phase in the development of socialism in Russia, the dictatorship of the proletariat seems fiercely resolved to remain as a dictatorship over the proletariat. On the other hand, democratic socialism, perhaps warned by the example of the Soviet dictatorship, is setting its sights considerably lower than in the past. For a whole period at least it is aiming at what has been labelled a mixed economy, combining a substantial nationalized sector of the economy with another sector left to private enterprise. The Socialist-Communist split, it becomes increasingly clear, concerns not only methods, but also objectives.

This growing realization of the gulf separating Socialists and Communists is furthered by the greater emphasis which Western Socialists are placing upon democracy and civil liberties. Not that Socialists at any time failed to realize that their ultimate aim was a society of democracy and fully developed civil liberties, but a number of Socialist parties—particularly the French and the Austrian—had at times expressed the view that a temporary dictatorship of the proletariat would become inevitable since the bourgeoisie would not give in without unconstitutional resistance to a Socialist majority engaged in constructing the bases of a new society. Such unconstitutional resistance on the part of the bourgeoisie (the 1926 Linz program of the Austrian Socialists pointed out, for instance) would compel the Socialist majority to resort to dictatorial methods for a period of transition. The experience of Nazi oppression and probably even more the struggle against the establishment of a Communist dictatorship has changed the Socialist attitude to one of unconditional allegiance to democracy and civil liberties. This does not necessarily imply that a Socialist party would never be willing to associate itself in time of war or civil war with emergency measures which might temporarily suspend civil liberties or democratic rights. That change implies, instead, a shift in emphasis, so far as the education of the party members is concerned, to an unconditional belief in the value of democratic methods.

This shift has been accompanied by a rapid, perhaps not very profound but nevertheless significant, re-examination of Marxian theory. Differing in this respect from British Labour, Continental Social Democracy has been deeply imbued with the spirit of Marxism. Unlike American journalists, the Continental Socialists have never identified Marxism and communism, but have rather disputed the Communists' claim to be the true descendants of Marx and Engels. The Socialists have described themselves, rather than the Communists, as the true disciples of Marx. Indeed, fear of Communist vituperation often compelled Socialists to profess publicly a belief in Marxian theories which they did not hesitate to criticize privately. The postwar years have produced the first open signs of a change of attitude. Leaders of the German Social Democratic party, once a stronghold of real or professed belief in Marxism, have publicly admitted that the party has opened its doors to Marxians and non-Marxians alike. Although the intellectual productivity of the Socialist movement since the end of the war has not been very great, its intellectual activity has indicated a readiness to revise and re-evaluate accepted notions, which contrasts strongly with the prewar dogmatism. There is, in particular, great emphasis on "voluntarism" as opposed to the "inevitability" of the prewar version of Marxism, on human choice among alternative courses of action, and consequently on moral and humanitarian values. Indeed, one of the significant intellectual developments is the search of the Socialist movement for its ethical, humanitarian, and often religious sources. The stronger the opposition to the Communist belief that the end justifies the means, the greater the emphasis on the moral value of Western civilization.[3]

[3] Adolf Sturmthal, "Democratic Socialism in Europe," *World Politics,* III, No. 1 (October 1950).

As a result, the Socialist-Communist opposition has become much sharper than it has been at any time since the beginning of the Popular Front period in the 1930s. The main issue in the battle between the two is the control of the trade union movement; the principal battlefields are France and Italy.

West of the line from Lübeck to Trieste which divides Europe into two halves, democratic socialism is in almost full control of the labor movement—with two major exceptions—France and Italy. In these two countries the trade unions are divided along politico-philosophical lines, and the Communists are in control of the majority of the unions. It is here that the great, and in many ways decisive, battles between socialism and communism are being fought. On their outcome a good deal of the future orientation of European labor is likely to depend.

Northwestern Europe—Great Britain, Scandinavia, and in some respects Belgium and Holland—is the stronghold of democratic socialism. It is at the same time the outstanding example of the reformist current in European labor whose leadership has passed more and more into the hands of British labor. Full employment, the nationalization of certain parts of industry, and a more equal distribution of income by means of taxation represent the main planks of British Labour's policy. Similar ideas are guiding the activities of most other labor movements of Western Europe.

These and related policies have brought a number of new issues to the fore. The labor parties of Northwestern Europe are government parties. The policies of the administration are worked out in close coöperation with the unions, but the labor parties represent vastly larger parts of the electorate than do the unions. What is the status of unions under such conditions? While they are closely associated with the government they must at the same time retain a large measure of independence from it. Has a permanent form yet been found for this peculiarly ambiguous relationship of intimacy and independence?

A similar problem arises in the nationalized industries. Nationalization has been to a large extent the result of union pressure. The unions feel a certain sense of responsibility toward the nationalized enterprises. But, at the same time it is the duty of the unions to represent their members' interests as against those of the enterprises themselves. Two main patterns have evolved in Western Europe in the attempt to solve this contradiction: the British "public corporation," with a board on which former trade unionists represent the spirit of labor without being delegated by labor; the French tripartite board, in which delegates of consumers, the government, and the union are supposed to coöperate in such a way that out of the clash of interests a wise compromise emerges.

Full employment has placed the unions in a strategic position favorable to a rapid increase of money wages. If the unions were to take full advantage of their opportunity, inflationary tendencies would inevitably result. Once again, labor is confronted with a difficult choice torn as it is among its national responsibility and its loyalty to its membership; its political responsibility and its pressure group tradition. I have used these terms in the pages that follow.

Basically, this dilemma is part of the normal life of democracy. The conflict between group interests and the interests of the community at large is inevitable, not only in a class society, as the traditional Marxian view leads one to believe, but in any social organization with a developed division of labor, and perhaps even one with different temperaments and inclinations. It is the everyday business of democracy to find compromises for such issues which will be acceptable to the majority of its citizens. Perhaps it is not excessive to say that democracy is firmly established only when conditions and traditions are such as to make compromises continuously possible between group and community interests.

Any theory of the European labor movement must take into account the fact that European labor has grown up in a society in which the tradition of democratic compromise has been conspicuously lacking—moreover, in a society in which clear lines of demarcation separated class from class. The feudal tradition of a strictly hierarchical society allocated to everyone a distinct status. Every effort was made to impress on each subject a sense of this status, its rights and even more its duties and its relative place in the social structure. The worker in industry did not need much education in class consciousness. It was impressed upon him by the powers that be and by his daily experience. It was this social and political disqualification, far more than his economic exploitation, which shaped the European worker's mind. Almost fully insulated from the life of the upper classes, he was the object of politics. Whether or not governments were friendly or unfriendly toward the worker, they always represented a different class and did not conceal this fact either by their hostility or by their patronizing benevolence.

Socialist unionism thus essentially only articulated the class division and an awareness of the social hierarchy which the worker experienced. But, undoubtedly, the separation was accentuated by this awareness of his place in society and of its structure. The growth of Socialist unionism, the power which it acquired, particularly after the turn of the century, and the gradual progress of democracy made this existence of what was almost a nation within a nation a serious issue for society. The continued existence of this bloc within society to which other blocs were sharply opposed presented a problem somewhat similar to that which monopolies create for a competitive market economy. The use of the power contained in this bloc in the way pressure groups are inclined to employ it, threatened to become incompatible with the functioning of democracy. Indeed in the great depression which sharply intensified the opposition of the power blocs, democracy, where it was not firmly established, broke down in a wave of totalitarian dictatorships.

The great task to be performed was that of reintegrating this power bloc into society. But this could no longer be done on the basis of the place which labor formerly held in the social hierarchy. Labor was demanding a far higher place. The new status of labor in society has become the basic social issue of the West. The Russian Revolution shows the explosive qualities of this problem. The British Labour government is an example of an attempt to solve the problem within the framework of Western democracy. It requires for its success that the power bloc which claims leadership in society acquire not only the qualities, but also the sense of responsibility, which go with leadership. The pressure group must transform itself into a real political party. It must concern itself with all the great issues which confront society. It must be willing to integrate the particular interests of the group which it represents with the general interests of the community. If democracy is to survive, labor must not only accept, but must formulate for itself the compromises that democratic government requires.

It is in this light that the postwar issues of Western Europe, and labor's attempts to solve them, must be examined. Has labor acquired the maturity and the statesmanship which its new power in society requires? Much more may depend upon the answer to this question than the success or failure of labor in Western Europe. Success may mean the revival of Western Europe, giving new meaning and a new lease on life to the civilization of the Old World. Failure would throw Western Europe into social disorganization, which would seriously impair its power of resistance and its chances of survival.

No doubt these considerations could not be applied to the American scene without substantial qualifications and modifications. The belief that American labor is in some way following, with a certain time lag, the example set by British labour has little foundation in fact. It overlooks the tremendous differences between the social and political history of this country and that of the Old World (and clearly also the significant differences among the various European labor movements). Indeed, it might be said with at least equal justification that in some respects European labor is following the example set by the brethren on this side of the Atlantic.

I am referring particularly to the complex of union activities to which Professor Perlman has given the label of "control of job opportunities." With political democracy as firmly established in many countries of Western Europe as anything can be in the twentieth century, European unions have devoted increasing attention to the problems of "economic democracy"—the participation of the unions in the determination not only of wages, but also of job opportunities and working conditions. The French Joint Shop Committees (Comités d'Entreprise) reflect this trend as much as does the emergence of the "closed shop" issue in Great Britain and some recent developments of labor relations in Scandinavia.

It is perhaps a symbol of these developments that coöperation between the unions of the United States and those of Western Europe has reached an intensity which few would have believed possible twenty years ago. It is sufficient to read Samuel Gompers's unhappy reflections on his meetings with European labor leaders during World War I to measure the distance which labor has traveled on both sides of the Atlantic.

ADOLF STURMTHAL

Annandale-on-Hudson, New York
December 20, 1950

PREFACE

THE catastrophe that engulfed European democracy has found a great many historians. There is no lack of books that tell the dramatic story of the last decade. Much less attention, however, has been devoted to the decline and fall of European labor, although the destruction of the trade unions and the socialist and communist parties on the continent of Europe is no less spectacular and politically significant an event than the downfall of European democracy. It seems to me, moreover, that it is impossible to understand what happened in Europe without reference to the fate of its labor organizations, which were, as they have never been in the United States, the strongest of all democratic forces.

The root of the breakdown of European democracy is its failure to integrate the social groups with their conflicting interests into a functioning industrial society. This failure, heralded by the first brief post-war depression and the rise of Fascism in Italy, became universal during the great slump of the early thirties. The crisis of European democracy was a social crisis. It expressed the disintegration of a society which failed to solve its vital economic and social problems.

Most of the European labor organizations were strongly committed to the defense of democracy. It had enabled them to grow into a powerful social force and to develop institutions that were among the highest achievements of European civilization. But they failed in their decisive test. They were not able to stem the progressive disintegration of democracy and to offer a rallying point for the reconstruction of a democratic society. The defeat of democracy on the continent of Europe is due no less to this failure of labor than to the breakdown of democratic capitalism. Labor was strong enough seriously to interfere with the smooth working of the existing institutions of society, but it was neither sufficiently strong nor sufficiently constructive to rebuild society. It is this stalemate of conflicting social forces which, I believe, is the essence of democratic disintegration. The bulk of this book is intended as proof of this thesis.

The material presented here is in many respects fragmentary. It deals with a period which, while of vital significance by itself, is only part of the life of the European labor organizations. Obviously, it is impossible to understand what happened in 1918 and thereafter without reference to previous developments. The brief remarks I have made about this part of the past are, as I well know, too scanty to be of great help. Any other treatment, however, would have required so much space as to make the volume inaccessible to most readers.

No less conspicuous are the lacunae in the geographical area covered. Since I was more concerned with trends and problems of significance to European labor as a whole, I was compelled to neglect a great many organizations, important as they were from other points of view. Moreover, I decided from the start of the work to exclude from its scope the Soviet Union. To treat Soviet labor adequately would have required a book by itself. I have endeavored, of course, to discuss the tremendous influence which the Soviet Union has exerted on labor in the rest of Europe.

Any well-informed observer will find that I have neglected to mention or to discuss a great deal of what to him might appear of the greatest importance. I have no apology to offer but the obvious one that I am presenting a theory of the political labor movement in Europe and that I have looked at its history from the point of view of this theory.

This essay is intended as a contribution to the discussion of a topic whose bearing upon the future of the social and political institutions of the world is being more and more widely recognized. For the specialist interested in certain aspects of labor problems, it will be of little value in view of the large scholarly literature in the field. There are also in pıint authoritative discussions of the labor movement of individual countries for parts of the period with which this book deals. I believe, however, that a more general survey, such as this one, may be of use, and I hope that my efforts to present a theory of the decline and fall of European labor may justify this particular presentation.

The key to this theory is the distinction between pressure-group action and political activity. I am using this latter term in a special sense. It refers not simply to the actions of a political party; it is intended to mark democratic leadership, initiative, and responsibility for the nation as a whole as distinguished from the narrow outlook of a pressure group. From the point of view of this classification, a political party may be considered as a pressure group if it does not make an effort to integrate the interests of its group with those of the community of which it forms a part. It is also possible, though less likely, on the other hand, that what would commonly be called a pressure group, might deserve to be rated as a political party.

The problems for the functioning of democracy to which the existence of pressure groups in our sense of the word may give rise, have to my knowledge hardly been explored. This approach seems to me, however, the vital one as far as labor in a modern democracy is concerned.

Another term used in a way not quite familiar to many American readers, is "middle class." In the terminology of European labor and European democracy, with their traditions of the struggle against feudalism, the middle class is what Americans would call the upper class, the employers, or the bourgeoisie. What Americans refer to as the middle class is then the lower middle class in Europe. Other terminological difficulties will, I hope, be overcome with the aid of the context in which they will appear.

Professor Joseph A. Schumpeter's new book, *Capitalism, Socialism, and Democracy* (Harpers, New York, 1942) was published after this book was already in print. Professor Schumpeter's volume contains, as its last part, a historical sketch of socialist parties. The seventy pages which Professor Schumpeter devotes to this survey form the nucleus of a fascinating analysis of socialist movements. Unfortunately, it ends at the very moment when the most burning question of all arises, namely why the socialist parties in Europe failed so utterly. Some of the elements for the explanation of this catastrophe are contained in Professor Schumpeter's masterly analysis, but hardly in such a form as to satisfy the reader's legitimate curiosity.

I am grateful to the Carnegie Corporation of New York, and especially to Mr. Charles Dollard, for grants which enabled me to complete this study. Professor Charles A. Gulick, Jr., and Mr. Alexander Gerschenkron of the University of California and Professor P. F. Brissenden of Columbia University have helped me greatly with their criticism and numerous suggestions. Henry C. Fleisher, Alberta Curtis, Edna Albers, Eleanore Levenson and Elizabeth J. Sherwood (the latter of Columbia University Press) have assisted me in editing this manuscript. I owe the greatest debt of all to my wife; without her unfailing assistance this book would hardly have been completed.

A. S.

Bard College, Annandale-on-Hudson, New York
December 20, 1942

CONTENTS

Part V. FASCISM ON THE INTERNATIONAL SCENE

Part VI. OUTLOOK

PART I

Why Labor Failed

Chapter 1

PRESSURE GROUP OR POLITICAL ACTION

1.

"WHAT *happened to German labor was the result of the unions' mixing too much with politics. We American labor leaders are now more decided than ever not to take part in the political game.*" This was the conclusion of a leading official of the American Federation of Labor with whom I talked in the spring of 1938. It was the opinion of a man particularly concerned with the international connections of the American trade unions. We had discussed the danger of war in Europe, the victory of Hitlerism in Germany, and the dissolution of the German trade unions. My American friend was visibly disturbed by events in Germany, but his attitude was more that of a spectator than that of a man who feels that his own cause is endangered. The lesson which he drew from the fate of German labor was only the reaffirmation of the time-honored anti-political theory of the American trade unions.

In this book, I shall try to prove that this anti-political bias which my labor colleague represented was wrong in every respect. It is hardly necessary to point to the fact, obvious by now, that even the most non-political attitude could not have saved European labor from destruction by fascism, since a totalitarian dictatorship does not tolerate the existence of any independent organization, be it only an Association of Stamp-Collectors. I intend to show that European labor, far from "mixing too much with politics," was not sufficiently politically minded and hesitated to accept real political responsibility commensurate with the political and social pressure which it exercised. It was this fact, more than anything else, which caused the downfall of European labor and, at the same time, of democracy, since both perished by the same processes. Democracy could not prosper without the active participation of labor, and on the other hand, labor could not be crushed without the simultaneous destruction of democracy. I shall demonstrate that the labor organizations across the Atlantic had too much the character of pressure groups and were not enough concerned with the fate of the community of which they formed a part for democracy to function smoothly, and for labor itself to prosper. Finally, I mean to show that blindness to the peculiar problems which the existence of large labor pressure groups created for democracy was common, with very few exceptions, to all factions of European labor. The bitter feuds within the working class organizations, between Socialists and Communists, reformists and radicals, had little reference to the basic weaknesses of European labor's actions—the lack of real political participation and constructive thinking on basic social problems.

This I want to show because I hope that it will explain in part the catastrophe which has engulfed European labor and freedom. I firmly believe that, in spite of superficial differences, similar problems for democracy have arisen in the United States as a consequence of the rapid growth of labor organizations during the last decade; similar problems and therefore similar dangers for labor and democracy. The lessons of the European experience are, with modifications in many details, applicable to America. This is not the lesson of political isolationism which the old-fashioned labor leader, engrossed in his traditional routine, might be eager to draw, but exactly the opposite: that labor has to face its political responsibility as a powerful part of the nation if democracy and free labor organizations are to survive.

2.

In order to defend the thesis outlined above, it will be necessary, first of all, to show to what extent both European and American labor organizations partake of the nature of pressure groups. A pressure group, as distinguished from a political party, is directly concerned only with a narrow range of problems, namely those immediately affecting the interests of its membership. American unions have avoided, in most cases, taking a stand on problems that are not related to wages and hours, rights of collective bargaining, social insurance, and a few other social issues. They rarely express any opinion on problems of agriculture, or of education, and unless a serious crisis develops, they have very seldom taken a stand on questions of foreign policy. And even if they do, no action is undertaken to impress their views on such problems upon the policy makers.

Compared with American unions, the European labor organizations might seem at first glance to have been deeply engrossed in political action. The leading European labor organizations were political parties, mostly Socialist, to a smaller extent Communist. They took part in elections, held government offices, formed governments. They stood for a political program which demanded not merely full political rights and higher material and cultural standards of living for the industrial workers, but also a full Socialist reorganization of society.

All this, however, was largely surface activity. Scraping below it, we would find, well hidden in the maze of political action but determining its content, the same pressure-group mentality that is characteristic of American labor. For most Socialists, during the entire period between the two wars, and most Communists after 1923, Socialism was a distant objective which had little influence upon present-day action. Their actual objective was the defense of the interests of industrial workers in much the same way as the American unions represent the interests of their members. They realized that their Socialist program could be carried out only after labor had achieved full power. Their immediate activity was thus restricted to immediate demands which fell into two types: social demands as advocated by and for the trade unions, and democratic demands as proclaimed by all democratic elements, labor and bourgeois alike. These were their real objectives until the day should come when, with full power in their hands, they could create a Socialist society. To all intents and purposes, therefore, the labor parties acted as pressure groups.

This can be clearly drawn from a significant remark of Keir Hardie, the leading British Socialist of the time, at a conference of the British Labour party in 1907. Reporting on the party activity in the House of Commons, he said, "Questions of foreign affairs, education, the welfare of subject races, militarism (that sinister foe of progress) . . . have been dealt with by members of the Party speaking for their colleagues. . . . These things, however, have been merely incidental to the *real* work of the Party." Although this statement was made seven years before the outbreak of the First World War, it still held true during most of the twenty years between the two world wars.

What really distinguished European labor, in this respect, from its counterpart in the Western Hemisphere was the *method* of pressure group activity, or—to use a current American term—the technique of lobbying. Here again, the differences appear to be much greater on the surface than they are in actuality. Compared with the American methods of lobbying, the European methods were more direct. The American labor lobbyist is outside of parliament. Before every election, the American unions examine the record of the candidates, endorse some, and oppose others, according to the established rule of "rewarding labor's friends and punishing its enemies." This technique has been quite successful. Some unions, in particular the railroad brotherhoods, have a well-deserved reputation for having "pull" in Congress. Certain Congressmen are considered mouthpieces of organized labor groups. But they are not members of organized labor parties; they belong to the traditional political organizations of the country. This is typical American pressure-group policy. A pressure group endeavors to influence those in control, to move them in certain directions. It works on the outside, while the political parties are in the center of the political scene. A pressure group feels responsible only for the welfare of the particular group or faction it represents. Political thinking and political action, as these words are used in this context, are directed toward furthering the interests of the whole society into which particular interests are to be integrated. As pressure groups, the American unions are satisfied with influencing those in the seats of power, within the limited scope of their interests.

In the case of the European labor parties, the situation was not as clear and obvious as in the United States. The Socialist and Communist parties were represented in the parliaments and they strove to increase their representation. But increased representation meant little more to them than increased pressure upon the legislature as policy-maker in favor of the immediate interests of their members, rather than a chance to carry out constructive policies of their own. Unfortunately, the labor parties, though thinking and acting as pressure groups, were political parties and as such were called upon to form governments, either through a revolutionary process, as was the case in Central Europe in 1918, or according to the rules of parliamentarism. When confronted with governmental responsibilities, the narrowness of the range of problems for which labor offered constructive solutions became apparent. This lack applied to practically all labor parties throughout the fateful twenty years between the two world wars, although frequent reference to the Socialist objectives of the movement—in words rather than in deeds—tended to obscure this conspicuous narrowness of scope of the parties' real interests.

As one example among many others, I refer to the actions of the German labor movement in the first few months after the revolution of November, 1918. The bulk of the decrees enacted by the Socialist Council of People's Commissars concerned trade-union demands and suffrage reform, disregarding basic economic and political issues. Throughout the whole period of the great depression, the European labor parties, with one or two conspicuous exceptions had a social but no economic policy. They strove to defend wage rates and unemployment benefits as well as they could, but they had no constructive program for dealing with the economic crisis itself. Although later evolution tended to lead the labor organizations slowly beyond the pressure-group state, even as late as 1936 the French Popular Front stressed social reforms at the expense of foreign affairs, at a time when foreign issues obviously were of decisive significance.

Fear of the responsibility involved in political power was a dominant trait in European labor politics. This lack of self-confidence found its expression in many forms, some of which will be described in this book. At this point, it will be sufficient to refer to the almost ridiculous abdication of the German revolution in 1918 in favor of the imperial authorities. The new rulers of Germany did not even dare to demobilize the defeated army and to organize the new armed forces of the Republic. Their self-distrust compelled them to call in the officers of the Imperial Army for both of these vital jobs.

Thus, though organized as large political parties, the European labor organizations did not act as such. In their spirit and their outlook on politics, and in the scope of their interests, they were pressure groups much like the American unions. The labor organizations on the two sides of the Atlantic differed in the forms and techniques of action, rather than in the content of their action.

3.

Little attention has been paid, even in the United States, to the problems which the organization of strongly coherent social groups creates for the smooth working of democracy. There is, to be sure, a long series of democratic struggles against private monopolies running through American history. The successes and retreats of the anti-monopoly movement can almost be used as a measure of the relative strength of the popular democratic forces. European democracy has been less alive to the dangers of concentrated wealth, partly perhaps because the strongest democratic force in Europe, the Socialists, regarded organized capitalism as an evolutionary step toward a Socialist order of society, and, therefore, welcomed the advance of monopolies. But the problem of concentrated power is no longer merely that of private monopolies and private wealth; it is also that of the power wielded by pressure groups and coherent and well-organized social classes.

The formation of such groups was one of the main characteristics of the social evolution of the last half century. Adam Smith's laissez-faire world was peopled by small independent businessmen of about equal wealth. Thomas Jefferson dreamed of a "simple society composed largely of freehold farmers and small-town mechanics." [1] But our real world has developed into a system of large scale businesses existing next to small ones, and into a network of organized pressure groups. Democratic government does not rule over small and weak atoms, but is exposed to the stresses and strains of conflicting social groups.

As long as labor organizations were small and powerless groups of trade unions or Socialist propagandists, their existence interfered hardly at all with the smooth functioning of democratic government. But the history of European labor furnishes many examples of the problems for democracy created by the growth of labor organizations.

It is difficult for Americans to realize that the European labor movement was a huge social force. In fact, many Americans who speak about "putting down labor" or "keeping labor in its place" do not realize the strength of labor in their own country. The labor parties across the Atlantic were powerful mass organizations. At the time of the International Socialist Congress in Vienna in 1931, the parties represented there counted more than six million dues-paying members, with some more outside the ranks of the international movement, in such organizations, for example, as the strong Norwegian Labor party. In addition, the European Communist movement had hundreds of thousands of members at this same time, mainly in Germany, France, and Czechoslovakia. Numerically, the strongest Socialist parties existed in Great Britain, Germany, Austria, Belgium, and Sweden. The total parliamentary vote of the Socialist parties in the last elections preceding the International Congress in 1931 amounted to no fewer than 26 millions, almost precisely the popular vote for President Roosevelt in his third-term election. More than 1,300 Socialists sat in the parliaments of European democracies. Some 360 daily newspapers spoke for the labor movement, and to all these figures the Communists added their considerably smaller numbers.

In the United States it is legitimate and necessary to distinguish

[1] Charles A. Beard, *Public Policy and the General Welfare*. New York, Farrar & Rinehart, 1941, p. 127.

between Socialists and Communists on one hand and the labor organizations on the other. In Europe trade unions and political labor organizations were so intimately tied up with one another that they appeared as a unit. In many countries they rose together; everywhere they fought as one army and perished together. The fact that there were political labor organizations in Europe does not imply, of course, that they were more than pressure groups, since the labor parties acted as the political mouthpieces of the trade unions.

It is true also that large parts of the European working class remained outside the ranks of the Socialist and Communist movements. Large groups were unorganized, and others belonged to non-Socialist organizations of various types. Nevertheless the Socialists, to a lesser degree the Communists, and the trade unionists connected with them represented a sufficiently large proportion of the European workers to hold a strong lead over the labor organizations connected with the middle-class parties. In the light of the figures quoted above, it will become clear to what extent the labor movement affected the democratic life of Europe.

Organizations of this size represent a social force of significant influence. Moreover, the labor organizations had a stronger cohesion than most other pressure groups. Socialists and Communists developed, in many countries, a comradeship of intense emotional appeal. The memory of oppression borne in common during the heroic age of the movement formed a strong tie among later generations of party members. They felt too that they were defending not merely their own interests and those of the working class, but also right against wrong, the coming age of brotherhood against the dark forces of evil. They were convinced that they represented not only material demands, or even a party program, noble as this appeared to them, but a *Weltanschauung*, a creed, a way of life and looking at life, better than that of any other group.

All this did not make for compromises between labor and nonlabor forces. Opposing economic interests can often be reconciled with ease, particularly in times of prosperity and in rapidly developing countries. But it is difficult to accomplish a reconciliation between good and evil, or between hostile and mutually exclusive ways of life. Tolerance is possible as long as each side admits that there is another side to a question. Good, however, cannot tolerate evil, and one way of life cannot exist as long as another takes up the space (its *Lebensraum*) in which the first wishes to live. In view of all this, the readiness of labor to compromise was a sign of its pressure-group thinking, and of the insignificance in practice of its own philosophy.

Cohesion was increased, again, by the excellent organization of most Socialist and Communist parties. The industrial worker, employed in factories and subjected to the stringent discipline of modern factory life, was easily trained in the requirements of mass organization. The enthusiasm of the Socialist idea, the fellowship of his co-workers, gave him the necessary impetus. No wonder that some of the Socialist and Communist parties were marvels of organization. Perhaps the most outstanding example was the famous Viennese Social-Democratic party, with a half million dues-paying members in a city of fewer than two million inhabitants, with thirty or forty thousand men and women at the call of the party at any time, and with its tremendous network of affiliated organizations for every activity from armed defense to stamp-collecting and hiking.

Pressure groups of such size, emotional impetus, internal cohesion, and precise organization are bound to create serious problems for democracy. Democratic government was confronted not with a diffuse mass of citizens, but with an organized power almost equal to that of the civil authorities. The Executive Committee of the German Social-Democratic party (Sozialdemokratische Partei Deutschlands), sitting in the center of a web of organizations stretching all over the country, with an income of many millions of marks and with hundreds of local administrative offices, was a second government rivaling the official one.

If the mere growth of labor pressure groups was sufficient to interfere with the smooth functioning of democratic government, these problems took on increased seriousness when the labor parties and the social forces opposed to them became almost equal in strength. This situation, described by the Austrian Socialist leader Otto Bauer as a "balance of class forces," prevailed in most countries of Western, Central, and Northern Europe during the period between the two world wars. The middle class was no longer strong enough to govern freely according to its own ideas, against the powerful opposition of labor, while labor was not yet strong and politically mature enough to take over the reins of government.

As a government by a majority against a minority, democratic government functions best when there is a large and unified majority. A narrow majority, or a majority split internally, does not permit strong government, able to carry out long range policies or basic reforms. When a "balance of class forces" exists, democratic government therefore becomes weak. It requires continuous compromising for a majority and a minority almost equal to it in strength to carry on parliamentary government.

Some of these difficulties will appear strange to Americans, used as they are to the working of a presidential democracy, in which the problems of a majority government as they exist in a parliamentary democracy are unfamiliar. Still, whenever a clash arises between the President and the majority of Congress, even the presidential democracy shows signs of paralysis. Moreover, it would be erroneous to think that a balance of class forces can exist only in the form of two hostile parties or party blocs of approximately equal strength. This is one form, but only one of many, in which this situation may present itself. A balance of class forces can exist when a president's policies are rejected or stalemated by strong social groups whose representation in Congress is not very strong; or when a Congress is dominated by one party which is confronted with an opposition whose power is based upon strong social forces and institutions in the country. This is the essence of pressure-group success. A presidential democracy is, therefore, not in itself sufficient protection against the dangers for democracy inherent in a "balance of class forces."

With one or two exceptions the necessary compromises were achieved in Europe, even under the balance described, as long as national incomes were increasing. The post-war depression of 1920–21 was sufficient to destroy Italian democracy. The great depression of the early thirties changed the situation radically in the rest of Europe. The rapid and extreme reduction of the national income no longer allowed for easy compromises. The issue of the social conflicts now was the distribution of sacrifices rather than of advantages. The labor organizations no longer fought to obtain for their members a share of increasing wealth, but rather to stave off attacks upon the standards of living of the working class. The full strength of labor organizations was turned against the efforts of the employer to recoup on wages and salaries the continued reductions of profits. Actually however, labor was barking up the wrong tree. For the decline in business returns did not permit employers to maintain the pre-depression wage rates. The real enemy of the working class was not the employer, who, in most cases, had only the alternatives of reducing production costs or closing down altogether. The real snag lay in the economic and financial policy pursued by the government, such as the orthodox financial and monetary policies which were the holy tradition of laissez faire. The dangers for the working class could be resisted only by constructive political action against these policies, not by mere pressure-group methods.

European labor was not politically mature enough to play a political and constructive part in this emergency. The working-class organizations were strong enough to make life difficult for many employers, and to delay and hinder wage reductions that were unavoidable as long as the governments pursued orthodox monetary and financial policies. But labor was incapable of showing a way out of the depression. It is possible that labor would not have been strong enough to obtain a real leadership even if it had realized its task; but the essential fact was the failure of labor to understand that it could win only by constructive political action.

The conflict between the exigencies of orthodox financial and monetary policies and the resistance of labor to these was a political one. Labor made a hopeless effort to win by pressure-group means. The working class was bound to lose, but its defeat threatened the very existence of democracy, for the prolonged struggle paralyzed democratic government and gave fascism a splendid opportunity.

Whenever a balance of class forces exists, the smooth functioning of the democratic machinery depends upon the political wisdom of both sides engaged in the struggle. If democracy is to survive, both parties in balance must recognize that neither side, being of approximately equal strength, can hope to defeat the other, and that continued and ruthless social warfare will endanger the democratic system under which they live. Unless a way out is found, the large mass of the population not vitally engaged in the issue, but suffering under the prolonged social warfare, will clamor for a strong government that can keep down both opponents and establish social peace, be it at the price of totalitarian dictatorship. This analysis may help to explain the rise of fascism in Italy, Germany, and Spain.

Although Europe provides the most conspicuous examples, the problems for democracy created by a balance of class forces tend to develop also in the United States. Since the rapid growth of American trade unionism in the last decade, a balance of class forces seems to be evolving under which the labor unions may be strong enough to prevent the smooth working of the present social system, but not strong and not constructive enough to supersede it by another. European experience points toward the dangers of democracy implied in such a social stalemate.

This does not mean that whenever a balance of class forces exists, fascism becomes inevitable. A great deal depends upon conditions that vary from nation to nation, from the strength of democratic tradition down to the particular electoral system in use. But everywhere a balance of class forces means a possibly fatal strain upon the strength of democracy and, perhaps, a challenge to its ability to perpetuate itself. In Germany, and in Italy, where a tradition of democratic self-government was lacking, the result was the victory of fascism. In Britain, where even members of pressure groups think as members of a community and not merely as partisans in a struggle the outcome of which the government as a superior force will finally determine, democracy survived and labor's defeat did not involve the destruction of democracy.

The chances of democratic survival are considerably strengthened, however, if both sides in a great social conflict are aware of the political implications of their actions. This means, on labor's part, full understanding for the alternatives before labor, once a "balance of class forces" has been reached. To continue the traditional pressure-group policy would mean endless conflicts out of which neither labor nor its counterpart can emerge as definite victors; with the possible result that, driven to despair by continuous strikes, lock-outs, and perhaps a situation approaching civil war, large parts of the population would clamor for the strong man who could hold down both labor and its enemies and restore social peace.

The alternative is real and responsible political action by labor. This does not necessarily mean that labor must organize as a separate political party; indeed, the formation of a political party is not enough. Labor must be willing to accept the responsibilities of leadership and must be conscious of the interests of the entire nation rather than of the industrial working class alone. In other words, labor must either submit to the necessities of the existing social order or transform it by taking the initiative for constructive action. It is this constructive effort which I designate by the term "political action."

Nothing is more dangerous to democracy than a social stalemate, a paralysis of one regime without any hope for the rise of another. The price for the neglect of political thinking and political action, once labor has grown to full strength, is fascism.

Chapter 2

FROM REVOLUTIONARY PARTY TO PRESSURE GROUP

1.

IRWIN ROSS tells an amusing story of a labor mediator who has a particular method for dealing with any employer who complains that the union in his plant is run "by a pack of reds." " 'Red, you say?' the mediator would ask. 'What kind of Red? Are they Communists or Socialists or Socialist Laborites, or are they Trotzkyites or Lovestoneites? And if Trotzkyites, of what faction? Or perhaps they are anarchists? Or perhaps syndicalists?' " By this time "the employer is completely baffled," Ross reports, "and is usually ready to admit that his adversaries are not Reds after all." [1]

To the average citizen most of the internal conflicts of the radical movements appear as tempests in a teapot and, perhaps, as harbingers of the decline of social radicalism. Conflicts of this kind, however, accompanied the rise of the labor movements in Europe from their beginning to the present day. Some of these internal divisions greatly influenced the fate of the European working class. These must be traced in at least broad outline in order to show how the labor parties developed into the pattern of pressure groups rather than as political parties.

In their earliest phase, in the seventies and eighties of the last century, the Continental labor groups were revolutionary sects. They had a revolutionary philosophy which had as its main tenets that reforms of the capitalist society in favor of the working classes

[1] Irwin Ross, "Labor Mediators," *Harper's Magazine*. CLXXXII (May, 1941).

would be insignificant and merely temporary, and that a permanent improvement of the workers' lot required the overthrow of capitalism and the establishment of socialism. Accordingly the early Socialist parties regarded their own efforts for reform merely as preparatory moves for an armed revolution which was the real objective of the party. Philosophy and policy thus were in basic harmony.

The suppression of Socialist activity by many of the European governments and the difficult economic situation following the great crisis of the early seventies greatly contributed to the maintenance of the revolutionary temper of the movement. Toward the end of the century the political and economic situation changed favorably for the working class. Economic conditions improved, allowing for great advances in working-class conditions and rapid progress of social insurance systems. Government pressure ceased, or at least diminished considerably, except in czarist Russia. The early radicalism of the Socialists began to give way to new ideas. The end of capitalism seemed further away than it had seemed when the movement sprang up. The development of military techniques—in particular the invention of the machine gun—as Friedrich Engels pointed out,[2] made revolutionary upheavals against well-armed regular troops seem increasingly difficult. Reforms of a social and even political nature, on the other hand, appeared much more probable than in the seventies. Rising national wealth enabled the working class to obtain important concessions. In the semifeudal Central European countries liberal middle-class groups strongly advocated democratic reforms, and an alliance between them and the Socialists seemed to promise a democratization of Germany and Austria in the near future. Would it not be better, the Reformists or Revisionists asked, to postpone or abandon the hopeless revolutionary dreams and to concentrate upon the prospects of immediate advantage to the movement?

The struggle between Radical revolutionaries and Reformists reached a climax in the strongest and most successful Socialist party of the world, that of the German Social Democrats. In the "battle of the Titans" at the German party conference in Dresden in

[2] In the Introduction to Karl Marx, *Class Struggles in France,* written March 6, 1895.

1903, August Bebel and Karl Kautsky, the Radical leaders, defeated the right-wingers, and shortly afterwards the International—the alliance of all Socialist parties of the world—endorsed the Radical victory at the Congress in Amsterdam in 1904.

This was perhaps the most fateful event of pre-World War socialism. Out of the Reformist defeat emerged the pressure-group mentality of European labor. The two possible ways for labor to take political action were lost at that time. One of these would have been coöperation with progressive middle-class groups for democratic aims. This was prevented by the Radical victory. The alternative was to strike a revolutionary blow for democracy or for socialism; this was impossible not only because of the military strength of the governments but also because even under Radical leaders the Socialist parties were developing into great electoral machines rather than into revolutionary shock troops. Thus, no serious activity for political objectives was possible. The main attention of the labor movement was focused upon trade-union problems, to the neglect of basic political and even economic issues. It would be interesting to speculate as to what might have happened if the Reformists had carried the day in the 1903 conference.

The British Labour party came into being during the same period that saw the rise of the Reformist tendencies on the Continent and was completely lacking in the radical spirit of the early Continental movement. The party was founded and controlled by trade unions and was intended from the beginning to be an instrument for pressing most effectively their demands in Parliament. The Socialist groups within the movement were small minorities eager to please the unions and to win them over for political action and for socialism by showing the effectiveness of parliamentary activities for the achievement of trade-unionist aims. Trade unionism thus formed the core of the party.

2.

From the turn of the century until the end of the First World War, the European Socialist movement, under its cloak of a revolutionary party, was thus a mere parliamentary instrument of trade unionism. Its real activity was restricted to trade-unionist problems, its constructive action to questions of wages and hours, social insurance, tariff problems, and, at the most, suffrage reform. The struggle against militarism, for a democratic foreign policy, and for the prevention of war, important as it was, was "incidental" to the main work of the party.

The revolutionary struggle for socialism was abandoned by all but a few Socialists on the extreme left. But the great majority did not seriously inquire how its Socialist aims could be reached by non-revolutionary methods. The Reformists felt that the everyday activity of the movement would slowly change the character of the social system so that it would somehow gradually be transformed into a Socialist order. By concentrating upon its immediate tasks the party would thus, in a distant future, attain its major objectives. With this forecast, the Radicals were in profound disagreement. They were convinced that at some crucial stage the bourgeois classes would resist further Socialist advances and that the decisive battle would probably have to be fought with revolutionary means. But the question of how the party, now organized as a tremendous vote-getting machine and led by parliamentary and trade-unionist experts rather than by military men or revolutionary adventurers, could effectively engage in an armed revolt, remained unanswered. The Radicals felt that the future would provide the answer. In the meantime, the movement would go ahead in its daily work of attracting the entire working class, and of creating a situation in which the overwhelming majority of the population would oppose the small capitalist minority.

Thus, no program for the transformation of society by non-violent democratic means was ever thought out or adopted by the Socialist movement. Deeply engrossed in its pressure-group activity, the party "wasted" little time on theoretical problems of this type. It kept intact its old program of a full-fledged Socialist society next to its statement of immediate aims, but no bridge joined them. The Socialist movement had a philosophy, but no policy to implement its basic creed. Its real trade-unionist activity, it was believed, would eventually lead into socialism.

In this state of mind the labor movement entered the First

World War. The patriotic upsurge in which most of the internationalist creed of the party was engulfed did little to make the movement more aware of its political and economic aims. Only toward the end of the war did the Socialist parties in the Allied countries coöperate with progressive middle-class groups in formulating plans for the League of Nations and an International Labor Organization. The gulf between the pressure-group mentality of the movement and its final Socialist objectives, in other words the lack of a political and economic policy as distinct from mere trade-union demands, continued to exist. In this condition, the European labor parties faced the stormy post-war world.

3.

In 1914 the Socialist parties were minority groups with little influence upon the real major decisions. In 1918 labor was on the threshold of power. An evolution which might have taken a quarter of a century had been telescoped into a few years by the war. But the mental growth of the movement had not kept step with its rise in influence. German labor was still primarily a pressure group when the breakdown of the Hohenzollern empire forced political control upon the Socialists. British labor had little understanding of the basic economic and international issues when, a few years after the war, a labor leader became prime minister of Great Britain.

The lack of a constructive Socialist program on issues outside the realm of labor's traditional pressure-group activity became painfully patent once labor was in political control, as a few examples above have shown. From the pages that follow it will be seen how labor permitted and encouraged the representatives of the old regimes to continue in their functions outside the narrow range of labor's pressure-group interests. This is the essence of the history of the German revolution of 1918–19 and of the German Republic's congenital weakness. In the next stage labor, though depending to a lesser extent upon the personnel of the preceding regimes, took over the policies of sympathetic middle-class groups. British, and later German, labor became the most ardent advocates of economic laissez faire, combining it in a highly contradictory fashion with trade-unionist demands for government interference in the restricted field of labor laws and social insurance.

The great depression marked the climax of labor's pressure-group era and the beginning of a slow revision of labor action. Out of the catastrophical defeats of labor during this stringent period emerged the first effort to develop a Socialist economic program for a transition from capitalism to socialism. Still, in the field of international affairs, European labor remained dependent upon progressive middle-class political ideas and hampered by its own pressure-group aims until its very end. The spectacle of the French Popular Front engaged in social reforms while Europe was about to burst into flames demonstrates the strength and persistence of labor's pressure-group thinking at this late stage. The history of European labor during this period between the two wars is the story of the decline and downfall of European democracy. The rise of fascism was primarily determined by the failure of Europe's strongest democratic force to fulfill its constructive task.

Chapter 3
LENINISM

I.

ONE division in the ranks of European labor must have special discussion, not only because of its great historical consequences but also because it furnishes the main example of a philosophy and organization directed against the pressure-group tendencies of the movement. This is the example of Leninism.

With the outbreak of the First World War, the old divisions of the European labor movement gave place to new and even more bitter divergences. The pre-war conflicts between reformists and radicals related to the question of coöperation with middle-class parties and the issue of a gradual transformation of the social system versus a violent revolution. Now it was the attitude toward the war that tore European labor asunder.

The great majority of the labor leaders and their followers on both sides of the trenches became ardently nationalistic. Their opponents labeled them with bitter scorn "Social Patriots." There were German "Social Patriots," French, British, and even Russian "Social Patriots." A minority within each of the various Socialist parties was pacifistic; they described themselves as "Internationalists" because they felt that they had remained loyal to the anti-war stand of the international labor movement. Actually, much of this internationalism was but a form of pressure-group policy, concentrating upon trade-union demands and disregarding the political issues.

A third group, small in numbers, headed by Rosa Luxemburg and Karl Liebknecht in Germany and by Lenin in Russia, disagreed with both Social Patriots and Internationalists. They accused the first of having betrayed socialism in favor of nationalism, and criticized the Internationalists for missing a great opportunity for a social revolution. In Lenin's view it was the Socialist's duty to use the war and the post-war crisis to further the advance of a Socialist revolution. Since a military defeat would shake the foundations of the existing social and political regime, the revolutionary Socialists should strive to bring about the defeat of their own country. Developing this theory to its logical conclusion, Lenin propagated the slogan of "turning the imperialist war into a civil war."

Lenin's opposition to the great majority of the European labor movements went back much further than 1914. Since the turn of the century Lenin and the Bolsheviks had been engaged in a conflict with the rest of the Russian Social Democratic party. His opponents, the Mensheviks, regarded the Central and Western European Socialist parties with their mass organization as the model to be followed in Russia. Lenin favored restricting the party to a small group of well-trained men, "professional revolutionists," who would furnish the direction for the large mass of the working class.

Lenin's theory was determined not only by the particular conditions of czarist Russia, which prevented the successful organization of large Socialist parties after the Western European pattern, but even more by his fear that a mass party would tend to become a trade-unionist party. In his view the workers, if left to themselves, would develop only a "trade-unionist" consciousness. It required a few highly trained leaders, imbued with the right spirit, to make the workers understand and strive for socialism.

Lenin might thus be considered the first critic of labor's tendency to develop into a pressure group, abandoning its wider political outlook and aims. Two conclusions could be drawn from this criticism, a revolutionary or a reformist conclusion. Political, as opposed to pressure-group action, could be carried on either in connection with a revolutionary method or on the basis of a gradual transformation of the social system. Lenin favored the revolutionary method. This combination was perhaps merely a historical accident, as it would have been equally possible to combine pressure-group criticism with a policy of gradual and deliberate transformation of the capitalist society. But the fact that Lenin, who criticized labor's pressure-group mentality, also favored revolutionary action associated these two elements of his policy so closely that they appeared inseparable.

The gradual ascendancy of Leninism over other forms of opposition to labor's pressure-group attitude is reflected in the history of the international labor organizations during and shortly after the war.

2.

Small groups of those Socialists who opposed the war policy of their governments met twice during the war in the little villages of Zimmerwald and Kienthal in Switzerland. They were united in rejecting Social Patriotism, but apart from this major point considerable differences existed among them. The majority of those who took part in the conferences were pacifist Internationalists, who favored immediate peace on the basis of "no victors, no vanquished." Lenin and Zinoviev, the leaders of the minority, considered this pacifist formula ridiculous. To expect that imperialist powers would accept such a policy was in Lenin's view sheer nonsense. Indeed, Lenin had no desire for such a peace, since he hoped that continued war would end in revolution. As Lenin stated in an article which he wrote in 1915 in his exile in Switzerland, to explain the policy which he would follow if his party should win power during the war: "We would propose peace to all belligerents on condition that all colonies and all oppressed, enslaved and dependent nations receive their freedom. Under their present governments, neither Germany nor England nor France would accept this condition. As a consequence of their refusal we would be forced to prepare and wage a revolutionary war."

At the two conferences held in Zimmerwald and Kienthal Lenin was in a hopeless minority. Apart from the Bolsheviks only small groups from other countries supported Lenin, while the German Spartacists refused to associate themselves with him. Lenin was practically isolated, and his lieutenant, Zinoviev, wrote bitterly that the conference "did not want to declare open war upon opportunism." To the majority of the conference Lenin's proposals were obviously of little significance. The underground reports of the Spartacus group about the conference, covering almost four printed pages, contained barely two sentences referring to Lenin and his supporters. Yet this small group was the nucleus of the future Communist International.

As a matter of fact Lenin was already planning to create a new, a Third, International, about the time when the Zimmerwald movement began. Rosa Luxemburg, whom Lenin consulted, rejected this plan, although she agreed with him in considering that the Second International was dead forever. Rosa Luxemburg had taken sides with the Mensheviks against Lenin at the time of the party split.[1] She realized that Lenin, following his conception of organization, would set up a new International as a "general staff of the world revolution," a numerically very small organization which would control the international working class. Rosa Luxemburg foresaw that such a system would end in a bureaucratic dictatorship over the Communist parties in the different countries, in the same way that Lenin's principles would lead to the control of the party in each country by a small bureaucratic clique. She favored setting up a new International, but to balance the influence of Lenin she suggested that the new organization be created only after large parts of the working class had abandoned their Social Patriotic leaders.

Rosa Luxemburg held steadfastly to this opinion even after the Russian revolution. The Communist International was created against her advice.

Lenin's victory in November, 1917, and the successful resistance of the Soviets to counter-revolutionary armies and foreign intervention increased Lenin's prestige immensely. The great strike wave which swept over Central Europe in January, 1918, and later the mutiny in the French Black Sea navy were largely due to the powerful impression which the Russian revolution made upon the war-weary working class abroad.

This state of mind favored Lenin's plan to set up a new Inter-

[1] Rosa Luxemburg, "Organisationsfragen der russischen Sozialdemokratie," *Neue Zeit,* XXII, Pt. II (July, 1904), pp. 484–92, 529–35.

national and prevent the immediate reconstitution of the Second International after the war. The Russian Communists' refusal to take part in international gatherings together with "Social Patriotic traitors" blocked the efforts to reconstitute an all-inclusive International. The international labor movement was split from top to bottom by passionate discussions about the attitude to be taken toward the Russian dictatorship.

In this atmosphere an international Socialist meeting held in Berne, Switzerland, in February, 1919, had little success. Several parties refused to take part in the meeting. The thorny question of the German Socialists' share in the war guilt was adjourned by a diplomatic maneuver, but the conflict between friends and foes of the Russian Revolution prevented any real agreement. The right-wing leaders proposed a resolution criticizing by implication the Russian Revolution. The leftist majority of the French Socialists, the German Independents, the Austrians, Spaniards, and Norwegians, declared that in their opinion the Social Patriots had no moral standing to criticize the Bolsheviks. The left-wingers did not deny that there might be reasons for criticism, but they preferred to postpone judgment since they desired to "reserve free entry into the International for the Socialist and Revolutionary parties of all countries conscious of their class interests."

Further meetings called to reconstitute the Second International ended in the same deadlock. Finally, at a congress which met after many delays in Geneva in July, 1920, a group of right-wing dominated parties decided to carry on alone as a continuation of the Second International. The main groups were the British Labour party, the German Majority Socialists, the Belgian, Dutch, Swedish, and Danish Social Democratic parties and a small French splinter group. The secretariat of the International, which had been in Brussels before the war, was transferred to London and James Ramsay MacDonald was elected secretary. The transfer from the Continent of the headquarters symbolically expressed the fact that British labor had become the spiritual leader of the reformist groups united in the Second International after the war. The leftist groups of the Berne Conference, on the other hand, formed their own group, the so-called "Viennese Union" which was sometimes labeled the "International Two and a Half" because of its position between the Second and the Third International.

Lenin bitterly criticized those internationalists who stood for a peace of reconciliation, yet he won power under the slogan "peace, bread, and land." He had believed that the next revolution in Russia would be a middle-class revolution, although one in which the workers would play a decisive part. Under his rule the middle class in Russia was expropriated and a full-fledged Socialist regime set up.

These contradictions Lenin found justified in his belief that an international Socialist revolution was impending. He thought that the peace treaty with Germany would be a mere scrap of paper and that socialism could be established in Russia not because Russian conditions warranted it, but rather because a victorious German revolution would soon destroy the peace treaty and come to the aid of the weak and undeveloped Russian working class.

Lenin was convinced that the war would lead to revolution, at first in Central Europe, then in Western Europe, and the situation called for a party able to make use of the revolutionary situation at the end of the war. The Communist International was set up to create such parties. Whether they would be numerically strong or not, made little difference to Lenin. The Russian Revolution had shown that a few leaders who knew the laws of revolutionary action could control the masses in a crisis.

On January 24, 1919, Moscow summoned the revolutionary working-class groups of all countries to a conference to be held in Moscow for the purpose of organizing a new International. The call was an answer to the organization of the Berne Conference, which was scheduled to meet on January 27. A tentative platform for the proposed Third International set out the main objectives of the new organization. The main task of the working class, the platform said, was the immediate seizure of power and the abandonment of "false bourgeois democracy" in favor of a dictatorship of the working class to be used for the "systematic suppression and expropriation of the exploiting classes."

The congress met on March 2, 1919. Rosa Luxemburg had been

assassinated a few weeks before, but her demand to postpone the founding of the International was expressed by a delegate of the German Spartacus group. This was rejected and the decision was made to create a new International. The few foreign delegates present—whose claims to represent organized parties were in many cases doubtful—enthusiastically applauded the passionate appeal of the representative of the almost non-existent Austrian Communist party in favor of the constitution of the Third International. A manifesto was adopted proclaiming the principles of revolutionary communism and calling the Communists to fight the Social-Patriotic "hangmen" of the working class and "the hazy, fickle, and irresolute center." The Zimmerwald movement was declared to be liquidated and "all that was really revolutionary in it goes over to the Communist International."

If this first congress was a rather poor gathering as far as numbers and scope of representation was concerned, the second congress, which met in 1920, showed that the new International exerted powerful influence over the Socialist working class on the European Continent and in other parts of the world.

At the time of the first congress a world revolution seemed "palpably near" to the Communist leaders, as Clara Zetkin, a leader of the German Communist party, put it. The Hungarian and Bavarian Soviet Republics came into being shortly after the first congress, Austria was due to follow, the Communists thought, and the Balkans were in a state of ferment. When the second congress met in July, 1920, the first revolutionary wave had died down. The Hungarian and Bavarian Soviets were defeated, the Austrian middle-class republic was stabilized, the Communist parties in the Balkans had passed the peak of their power. Yet apart from the fact that the Bolshevik leaders refused to face the situation realistically and persisted in regarding a revolution as imminent even where counter-revolution was in progress, there were many reasons for Communist optimism. Italian, Bulgarian, and Norwegian Socialists, in addition to the small German Communist party, had joined the Comintern. More important was the fact that the big German Independent party had sent delegates to express its wish to join the Comintern, that the French Socialists had sent a delegation consisting of Marcel Cachin and L. O. Frossard to Moscow to obtain information on conditions of affiliation, and that a powerful movement in favor of the Comintern was in progress in Czechoslovakia under the leadership of the former Social Patriot Smeral. A considerable part, perhaps a majority, of the Socialist workers on the Continent were prepared to accept the leadership of the Third International.

Thus encouraged, the Communist leaders confidently expected a new revolutionary wave in Europe and they redoubled their efforts to destroy the Socialists' hold over the working class by a direct assault. By 1923 the failure of their revolutionary hopes and the "strategic retreat" of the "New Economic Policy" in the Soviet Union forced a change in tactics upon the Comintern. But between 1919 and 1923 Leninism was on the offensive.

3.

The Leninist struggle against all non-Communist labor groups was so fierce that it forced them all together for their mutual protection, pressure-group parties and constructive reformists alike. This was true in the individual European countries, as well as on the international scene. The Viennese Union, an international association of non-Communist, internationalist labor groups, was compelled to come to terms with the remnants of the pre-war Second International, although the latter had been branded Social-Patriotic traitors by the Internationalists of the Viennese Union. In the campaign against the non-Communist labor groups, Moscow stressed the issue of revolution versus reform, rather than the issue of trade-unionist versus general political action. As a result, it was the former, rather than the latter issue which dominated the internal discussions of the labor movement. Tremendous energies were wasted in endless dissertations on the respective merits of a proletarian dictatorship and a democracy at a time when the growing strength of the middle class had destroyed any prospect of a successful proletarian revolution. The far more important issue, constructive political action versus trade-unionist pressure-group activity, was almost everywhere disregarded. As a matter of fact, fear of the Communist "guardians of the revolutionary tradition" tended to hinder whatever germs of a constructive new departure may have still existed within the Socialist movement.

Leninism was an effort to overcome "pure trade unionism" by an organizational device which would enable the Communists to lead the working class into revolutionary struggles. As long as the prospects of an immediate proletarian revolution in Europe seemed bright, the Communists regarded political action as their prime weapon and trade unionism as a subsidiary instrument of the proletarian revolt. With the abandonment of an immediate revolution around 1923, much of the criticism of "pure trade unionism" was discarded, even among the Communists, and the Communists themselves engaged in pressure-group activities of the same type as those of their Socialist opponents. For many years the main difference between Communist and Socialist pressure-group action lay merely in the size of the demands made. When Socialists asked for a 10 percent increase in wages, the Communists would feel it their revolutionary duty to ask for 20 or 25 percent. The sterility of Communist pressure-group thinking became patently clear during the first Popular Front regime when their total economic wisdom was limited to the slogan: "Soak the Rich!"

Still, during the brief period from 1918 to 1923, the Communists were engaged in a life or death struggle against labor's pressure-group attitude. Using the victory of the Russian Revolution as their main propaganda item, the Communists succeeded in attracting considerable parts of the European, particularly the Continental, working class. At some periods they probably controlled, directly or indirectly, more than half the organized workers of the Continent. Following the Leninist scheme in Russia, they endeavored to insure the supremacy of political over pressure-group action within the Communist movement by a peculiar system of organization on the pattern of the Bolshevik party.

In 1920 and 1921 the stabilization of the Bolshevik regime led to a tremendous growth of the Communist parties. This tendency, from the Leninist point of view, was dangerous for the political spirit of the Communist movement. Unless the leadership could be removed from the influence of the new masses of party members, trade-unionist thinking might be imposed upon the party heads. In the famous "Twenty-one Conditions" for admission to the Communist International,[2] Moscow endeavored to set up a system of organization which by protecting the party leadership against control by the followers would secure the supremacy of political over trade-unionist pressure-group thinking. The actual party leadership was to be organized in a secret committee, unknown not only to the police but also to the ordinary members of the party. This secret committee would control the party, and through it all other working-class organizations in which party members could succeed in obtaining influence.

An organizational device was thus supposed to remedy the lack of political maturity of the labor movement. This scheme was successful in Russia, but it proved a complete failure in Western and Central Europe. Leninism, outside Russia, was twice defeated; the first time when, after 1923, the great majority of the workers in Western and Central Europe rejected the revolutionary and dictatorial methods of Bolshevism in favor of the evolutionary and democratic tactics of the Socialists; and again when, in spite of the Leninist scheme of organization, the Communist parties, after 1923, developed into pressure groups, differing from the Socialists merely by the size or extravagance of their demands. The first defeat was due to the progressive stabilization of the middle-class forces and the economic reconstruction of Europe. But the second, even more decisive, failure was intimately tied up with the futile efforts of communism to disregard the basic differences between the labor movements in Russia and the rest of Europe and to press both into the same Russian pattern.

In Russia the Leninist scheme of organization, with its highly trained political leadership and a relatively small number of well-selected and controlled members, was very well adapted to the conditions and the state of mind of the working class. A small minority was alive to the political problems of Russian labor, and another small, though more numerous, group understood the need

[2] On the "Twenty-one Conditions," see F. Borkenau, *World Communism: a History of the Communist International*. New York, Norton, 1939, p. 197; also Arthur Rosenberg, *A History of Bolshevism from Marx to the First Five Years' Plan*. London, Oxford University Press, 1934, p. 146.

for trade-unionist action. It was not too difficult, under the circumstances, for the political leadership to control the not very large trade-unionist group. The permanent and ruthless czarist oppression made every trade unionist realize that the success of his own struggle depended upon a democratization of the political system. The trade unions themselves were thus ready to admit the supremacy of political action.

Outside Russia, however, under the conditions of Europe in the early twenties, Leninism came into contact with labor organizations of tremendous size and well-established traditions, which enjoyed the advantages of political democracy. The millions of organized trade unions and their well-established leaders rejected control by a political party, however close it might be to the industrial working class. The trade unions did not admit that the success of their own efforts to improve the living conditions of their members depended upon the achievement of political successes by the Communist party. Whatever modest political wishes the trade unions might have, the Socialist party was willing to fulfill. In resisting what was called Communist control of the unions, the labor leaders fought for their right to continue as pressure groups; and the fact that political control would have meant control by a revolutionary, dictatorial party with a leadership independent from its members, facilitated trade-union resistance and delayed the progress of labor's political maturity.

The lesson of the Leninist failure in Central and Western Europe should have been plain to any Marxist. It was that no device of organization could defeat the powerful economic and social forces which had turned the labor organizations into pressure groups. Political maturity depended upon the recognition by labor that its interests required institutional changes in society. Not before the facts had demonstrated to the large working masses themselves the extent to which their immediate interests required basic reform, could labor develop into a genuine political movement.

PART II

The Failure of a Revolution

Chapter 4

HERMANN MÜLLER, PARADIGM OF THE GERMAN WORKER

1.

THE date is June 28, 1919. In Versailles the Peace Conference is meeting, with Georges Clemenceau acting as chairman. It is the climactic moment in the life of the Conference: Today the German representatives are to sign the Peace Treaty.

Around a great horseshoe-shaped desk the leading statesmen of the victorious powers are assembled. Next to Clemenceau sit Woodrow Wilson and Lloyd George; Orlando of Italy; the Japanese representative; Vandervelde, the Socialist foreign minister of Belgium; and many others. The Germans are still absent. The vanquished are kept apart from the victors. They have practically been prisoners since their arrival in Paris.

For many weeks Germany has refused to sign the "Diktat" of Versailles. The first Socialist chancellor of Republican Germany, Philipp Scheidemann, preferred to resign rather than to put his signature on the document which he felt would enslave Germany. The trade-union leader, Gustav Bauer, who succeeded Scheidemann as chancellor, and his foreign minister are prepared to bow to what they consider the inevitable. The foreign minister in particular is a realist. Germany is defeated and must submit to the victors' demands. These are the facts—all the rest, all the thundering moral protests of the German Nationalists, are empty phrases, the foreign minister thinks; and for phrases he has no respect. Facts alone count, not moral ideas.

The door opens and the German delegates appear. A tall Teuton towers over the heads of his colleagues. He is dressed in black, which accentuates his pale face and his giant stature. He looks a bit like the guardsmen, hand-picked tall fellows, whom the Prussian king Frederick I once selected for his personal guard. The foreign minister advances to sign the document. He is offered a fountain pen, a special gift of a French city for the occasion. But the German refuses. Out of his own pocket he takes his own pen, a very common one wrapped in paper; it will fit the occasion, he thinks. He bends over the parchment and with steady fingers he signs his name: Hermann Müller.

Of all European labor leaders probably none has played a more fateful role in history than Hermann Müller, foreign minister and twice chancellor of the German Republic. None is more qualified than he to personify the lack of constructive thinking on the part of the German workers; it is for this reason that he is sketched here. Müller-Franken—the name of his constituency was added to distinguish him from other Müllers in the German Reichstag—was by no standard whatsoever a remarkable man, except in one respect: in his very mediocrity he was the most faithful representative of the most predominant type of German worker. Intelligent, reliable, bitterly opposed to disorder and lack of discipline, he was also skeptical toward new ideas and completely lacking in political imagination. All these positive and negative qualities he shared with the skilled German workmen.

German Social Democracy under Müller was a faithful reflection of its leader. The party became the most reliable of the pillars on which German democracy rested, but in its failure to act as a creative force it was also one of the main causes of the decline of German freedom.

Like most German Socialist leaders Müller began his political career on the Radical left of the party. Prior to 1913, when the Socialist machinery lay under the absolute rule of the veteran leader August Bebel and his theoretical adviser Karl Kautsky, men of the right wing were rarely admitted to the party executive, the all-powerful "Partei-Vorstand," whose control of the huge network of Socialist organizations constituted a sort of Socialist parallel to the Reich government.

Until the end of the war Müller was just a cog in the party machinery, loyally following the strange evolution that led most of the Radicals in the movement to become ardently nationalist once the war had broken out. In his case the conversion was very conspicuous. Müller had been sent by the party during the critical pre-war days in 1914 to learn the designs of the French Socialists, so that Socialist action on the two sides of the Rhine might be harmonized. Queried by his French colleagues on the attitude of the Germans, he declared that either they would vote against the government's demand for the appropriation of war credits or abstain from voting at all—but certainly they would not support the government's war policy. The German Socialists would, according to him, express in parliamentary routine their opposition to the war.

Returning to Germany just in time to take part in the vote, Hermann Müller joined his colleagues in supporting the government! The majority had decided, and Müller submitted without protest.

From this moment on, the former German Radicals abandoned all pretense of maintaining their earlier radicalism. They became moderate progressives, social and political reformers rather than revolutionists. Then the break-down of the empire in November, 1918 placed them in power. Müller, now a member of the Central Committee of the Soldiers' and Workers' Council, supported the cautious and hesitant policy of his party, which stressed a narrow range of reforms, principally dealing with the suffrage of the workers and certain time-honored trade-union demands. With the resignation of the first regular Republican government, Müller began his rapid rise in public affairs. He became foreign minister in 1919 and chancellor of the Republic in 1920. When Friedrich Ebert, elected president of the Republic, slowly began to lose his grip on the party, Müller became the Socialists' political leader, while his friend Otto Wels controlled the party machine. To quote an old saw, he was leader because he followed the masses. The skilled German worker, mainstay of German Social Democracy, trusted Müller because in his leader he found his prototype. The tragic failure of German labor, involving the destruction of German democracy, was caused not so much by betrayal on the part of the leaders as by the shortcomings of the German worker himself. The leaders, it is true, shared these shortcomings with their followers and were thus incapable of making up for the meagerness of constructive thought.

From 1919 almost to the end of the Republic, the Social Democratic party was the strongest political organization in the country. It was natural, therefore, that the party should control the government several times under the Republic. True, the Socialists were at no time in sole control, except for the first few months after the revolution; accordingly they were never completely free to carry out their own ideas in unadulterated form. But even taking into account this restriction upon their action, the Socialists as the leading party of the government were under obligation to direct the policies of the cabinet. It is in this respect that they failed most conspicuously. For this failure Hermann Müller's responsibility was great.

Readiness to adopt constructive policies and to effect basic institutional changes was a quality in which Müller and his colleagues were utterly lacking. Although a government leader, he acted more as the representative of a sectional group than as the political head of the nation. As a result the great and powerful Social Democratic party lost the initiative in most social and economic questions to the Catholic Center party, and in foreign policy to Gustav Stresemann, head of the capitalist German People's party. This was largely inevitable, owing to the later internal situation of the German Republic; many of the key positions, such as the presidency and the control of the army, had fallen to Hindenburg and other enemies of the democratic system. But the Social Democrats blindly felt at ease in this situation, and Müller did little to avail himself of the opportunities for leadership provided by his position.

The crucial test for Müller and his party came after the general elections of May, 1928, had brought a Socialist victory. By far the strongest party in the Reichstag, the Socialists were the leading group in the new parliamentary majority. Müller was chosen chancellor, and with three other Socialists in key positions—Rudolf Hilferding as minister of finance, Karl Severing as minister of the interior and Rudolf Wissell as minister of labor—labor dominated the cabinet. The economic situation being favorable at the moment, the cabinet took hold under comparatively good auspices.

At the inception of its career, however, an incident occurred of symbolic rather than factual significance. During the election campaign the Socialists had made effective use of a slogan directed against the public expenditure involved in building a naval cruiser of the famous "pocket battleship" type. "Food for school children versus the armored cruiser" was the Socialist cry that resounded throughout Germany. But the campaign was hardly over when Müller's new cabinet decided to carry on the construction of the battleship begun under the preceding government. President von Hindenburg and some of the middle-class parties represented in the cabinet had enforced this decision and Hermann Müller felt that the question of Socialist representation in the government, which was at stake in the issue, was worth the expenditure of a few million marks.

It was a decision highly characteristic of Müller. For him the symbolic and sentimental implications of the decision counted for little. He established a mental balance sheet on which there was no place for moral values. On the debit side was the battle cruiser, and on the credit side the advantages which the Socialist ministers would be able to obtain for the working class. Comparing the two sides and finding a net gain for the working class, he considered the problem settled. He was sincerely surprised to see that many party members and Socialist voters felt differently and protested vocally against what they considered a betrayal of promises given during the election campaign.

This was only the beginning of his difficulties. The great depression made itself felt earlier in Germany than elsewhere and it soon became obvious that only drastic methods could bring relief. But Hermann Müller and his chief economic adviser, Rudolf Hilferding, refused to depart from tradition in handling the crisis. With a stubbornness worthy of a better cause they defended the currency against the dangers which any economic experiments might have entailed. To a large extent this policy was determined by the panicky popular fear of a currency inflation akin to that which had ravaged Germany after the war. No German who had lived through those frightful years of starvation and social disintegration could have been expected to embark light-heartedly upon changes in the monetary system. Many now familiar devices of monetary manipulation were as yet unknown. Not until deflation became unbearable, did the demand for a new monetary policy become insistent.

It was significant that the decisive impetus for such experiments came from outside the ranks of the Socialist movement, whose own leaders were among the most inflexible conservatives in economic policy. Even when finally Socialist university professors and a small group of trade unionists called publicly for new methods to overcome the depression, the Socialist leaders remained unmoved. Unable to imagine that new policies might have any virtue, the chancellor followed the well-established line of laissez faire, permitting the depression to "run its natural course." He was anxious to help the employed worker defend his wages and the unemployed obtain decent relief within the limits set by the financial distress, but at no time did he work out a general policy to attack the crisis itself. Müller's attitude during these fateful years in which the Nazi rise to power began was an outstanding example of pressure-group thinking: protection of the working class within the framework of a policy which was in no way determined by constructive Socialist thought.

Oddly enough, the Radical Marxist tradition, still alive in Hermann Müller and other right-wing leaders, increased their stubborn support of laissez faire. The belief that "capitalism cannot be reformed" was part of the Marxist credo, designed at the beginning of the Socialist party to separate it from all middle-class reform movements. Capitalism was supposed to follow its own laws; only a Socialist revolution, overthrowing the old order and laying the basis for a new society, would permit banishment of the evil social consequences of the old system. The obvious implication of this theory was a belief in revolutionary rather than democratic methods, but even when the Socialist movement accepted democracy it did not completely abandon the basic ideology or its original theory. Capitalist governments had to be administered, according to this view, within the traditional framework of capitalist economy. The laissez faire doctrine that an economic crisis must run its natural course without government interference was considered one of the "natural" laws of capitalism. Thus Hermann Müller's passivity had the support of Radicals, who otherwise held him in deep distrust.

Müller did not live to see the victory of Nazism. A sick man when he resigned as chancellor in March, 1930, he devoted his last strength to the struggle against Hitler. He died a year later, almost to the day, on March 20, 1931, before the final great assault upon the German Republic began. His last public appearance before the representatives of the international labor movement took place a few months before his death, at a meeting at Castle Wyden in Switzerland to celebrate the anniversary of a secret congress of the German Social Democrats held there in 1880. The sickness which was to cause his death was already upon him. Did Müller then foresee that in a short time his party would once again be forced to meet secretly, as it had done fifty years before?

Chapter 5

THE SOCIALISTS AND THE REVOLUTION

I.

THE afternoon of November 9, 1918, found the German Social Democratic leader, Friedrich Ebert, installed in the Chancellory in Berlin. In Vienna, Emperor Charles discussed the terms of his abdication with the leaders of the Austrian Social Democrats. The revolution which had begun in March, 1917, in Russia, was spreading toward the west. In the vast territory extending from the Rhine to the easternmost boundary of the Communist revolution in Asia, the old regimes were breaking down. A new world was being born.

Labor was the strongest among all the revolutionary forces. It was considered the main force for peace, and the masses were longing for the end of the war. The breakdown of military authority carried with it that of the employers, whose control had been superseded by the military during the war. The workers were left in charge of the factories. The old middle-class parties, associates or supporters of the former ruling powers, shared in the failure of the old regimes. In large parts of Central Europe the Socialist movement was the only remaining organized force.

This force, however, was far from being homogeneous. During the war, as we have seen, three currents emerged within the labor movement. The Majority Socialists, who advocated support of the government during the war, were headed in Germany by Ebert and Scheidemann. The center group, expressing mainly pacifist and internationalist tendencies, was represented in Germany by the

Independent Socialists whose leaders were Karl Kautsky, Haase, Wilhelm Dittmann, and Eduard Bernstein. Karl Liebknecht, Rosa Luxemburg and Franz Mehring were the main spokesmen of the extreme left. They had created their own organization, "Spartacus," which rejected not only the "social-patriotism and chauvinism" of the Majority Socialists, but also the "petty-bourgeois" pacifism of the Independents. Karl Liebknecht proclaimed that "the chief enemy is at home."

The extreme left was small in numbers in Germany, and when the Berlin Workmen's and Soldiers' Councils met to elect the first republican government of Germany, they chose three representatives of the Majority Socialists and three of the Independents. In a proclamation addressed to the German people, the new government announced: "The government emerging out of the Revolution, whose political leadership is exclusively Socialist, sets itself the task of realizing the Socialist program." The revolution, however, was by no means Socialist in character; it was first of all pacifist and democratic. Most Majority Socialists were more anxious to continue the process of democratization, begun toward the end of the war under the imperial government, than to embark upon what they themselves considered dangerous Socialist experiments. Although elected to the Council of People's Commissars by Workmen's and Soldiers' Councils, the Majority Socialists had little interest in the Councils and wished to establish a parliamentary democratic regime. The Councils were regarded as the instrument of a dictatorship of the Bolshevist type, although they were dominated by Majority Socialists in most cases and could thus have served democratic purposes as well, and the Majority Socialists were categorically opposed to Bolshevism.

Not only did the Majority Socialists fear that Bolshevist experiments might lead to armed Allied intervention, which Germany, exhausted by the war and disorganized by revolution, could not resist; but a Bolshevist system in Germany, Ebert and Scheidemann were convinced, would prevent or delay the resumption of peacetime production and expose Germany to the famine and misery from which Russia was suffering at the time. They preferred that socialism be introduced in Germany by cautious and gradual reforms which would not interfere with essential production. The first task, according to the Majority Socialists, was to call for a democratic Constituent Assembly, stabilize democracy, and end the revolutionary period as soon as possible.

The Independent Socialists were in a peculiar situation after the outbreak of the revolution. Their party had split from the Majority Socialists early in 1917 over the issue of Socialist policy toward the war. The divergence no longer existed, and in many issues of the day the leaders of the Independent party were close to the left wing of the Majority Socialists. But the Independent leaders had to take into account the left wing of their own party, headed by the so-called Revolutionary Shop Stewards (Revolutionäre Betriebs Obleute) of Berlin who had prepared a Socialist uprising in October, 1918. The plans of the Shop Stewards failed to materialize, but the results of the November revolution did not satisfy them. They continued to advocate a Socialist state based on the exclusive rule of the Councils. Torn between the right-wing leaders and the Shop Stewards, the Independents were unable to follow any clear line. They vacillated between the Majority Socialists and the extreme left, Spartacus.

Luxemburg and Liebknecht, the leaders of Spartacus, realized that the German Republic was to be a middle-class state and that the masses agreed with the Majority Socialists. They believed, on the other hand, that disappointment was inevitable and that it would offer a revolutionary party an opportunity for carrying out an eventual proletarian revolution. The immediate task of Spartacus was therefore to organize and prepare for the decisive day. Within Spartacus, however, the leaders found themselves of a minority opinion. Muddle-headed revolutionists, opposed to any sort of discipline or cool reasoning and unfamiliar with the traditions of the labor movement, had entered the organization en masse. Luxemburg and Liebknecht were overruled by the left wing of Spartacus in much the same way as the Independent leaders were under constant and often irresistible pressure by the Independent left wing. During the revolutionary period Russian influence seems to have favored the confused revolutionists as against

Rosa Luxemburg, who rejected Lenin's ideas concerning a party dictatorship over the proletariat.

The Majority Socialists, therefore, had tremendous advantages over Independents and Spartacus. They had the support of most workers and soldiers and their internal unity allowed them to act, while the Independents were often condemned to passivity through lack of unanimity. The decisive issue—progressive middle-class Republic versus Socialist opposition and preparation for a proletarian revolution—was never clearly presented to the German working class.

2.

The Majority Socialists were the leaders of the Council of People's Commissars, and after the withdrawal of the three Independent members at the end of December, 1918, the Majority Socialists governed alone. The activity of the Council of People's Commissars was therefore a clear expression of Majority Socialist philosophy.

The decrees of the Council dealt with two groups of problems, social reform and electoral reform. The traditional demands of the trade unions, and the standard demands of the old Social Democratic party with regard to a democratization of suffrage, were realized within a few weeks' time. Nothing, on the other hand, was done with regard to the economic system of the country. Nor was the democratization of suffrage implemented by a democratization of the army or of the administration and the judicial system of Germany. The social reforms were merely grafted on to the existing economic system, and the suffrage reform hardly affected the structure and composition of the administration.

Among the most obvious economic reforms which were advocated by workers or peasants were the nationalization of the coal mines and the distribution of the large estates of the east Elbian landowners. With the flimsiest excuses, the Majority Socialist leaders refused to carry out these popular demands, although they were by no means specifically Socialist in character. Some of the Independent Socialists urgently suggested the formation of a new democratic army, but the Majority Socialists coöperated from the beginning with the former Imperial High Command in demobilizing the troops and failed to prepare for a new army. When the government needed military support against Spartacus, Ebert saw no alternative than to call in the officers of the Imperial Army. Lacking in self-confidence, the Majority Socialist leaders looked anxiously for assistance from the officers and the civil service of the former regime. The fact that they did not realize their program of Socialism could be justified under the circumstances. Their truly decisive failure was the inability to establish a genuinely democratic regime.

The Majority Socialists made the experiment, doomed to failure, of building a democratic system upon an anti-democratic army, civil service, and judiciary machinery. Not even the educational system was radically changed. Apart from the social reforms —which again had no economic foundation—the reforms introduced by the Council of People's Commissars were similar to a change in the name of a business firm, without any transformation of the business routine.

The want of decisiveness on the part of the Majority Socialists was the cause of friction between them and the Right-Wing Independents, who sensed rather than realized the serious weaknesses in the actions of the government. The issue of a Socialist revolution separated Majority and Right-Wing Independents on the one hand from Left-Wing Independents and Spartacus on the other, and in this issue the government had the backing of the overwhelming majority of the working class against Spartacus and the Left-Wing Independents. At a Congress of the Workmen's and Soldiers' Councils of the Reich, held in December, 1918, the Majority Socialists were backed by about 350 out of the 450 members of the Congress. The Right-Wing Independent leaders supported the government against the combination of Spartacus and the Independent Left Wing, who held about a hundred seats at the Congress.

3.

Of all sins of omission committed by the Majority Socialists, none was as fatal as their neglect to set up a new, democratic army. The fact that the workers, tired of warfare, were by no means enthusiastic about once again becoming soldiers, does not excuse the government, since at the same time and under similar circumstances the Austrian Social Democrats succeeded in building a democratic and pro-labor military force.

A conflict between the government and a mutinous group of so-called revolutionary sailors found the government completely unprepared, from a military point of view. The sailors arrested some members of the government, not for political reasons, but simply to extort money, and Ebert called in a detachment of the old army that had not yet been demobilized. The soldiers were not successful in quelling the sailors, and finally the government had to accept the terms of the mutineers. Yet, the action of the government in sending a general of the Imperial Army against what the workers considered a "revolutionary detachment" aroused many workers against the government and caused the Independent members of the Council of People's Commissars to resign. Although in agreement with the Majority Socialists about the issue of an immediate Socialist revolution, the Right-Wing Independent leaders accused the Majority Socialists of betraying democracy to the leaders of the former regime.

The Spartacus people believed their play for power was fast approaching. At the end of December, 1918, they constituted themselves a Communist party. Against the advice of Rosa Luxemburg and Karl Liebknecht, they decided not to take part in the elections for the Constituent Assembly to be held on January 19. The majority of the delegates to the party congress fanatically believed that they could forestall the elections by a revolt. They were not even discouraged by the fact that the Revolutionary Shop Stewards, the main link between Spartacus and the great mass of the workers in Berlin, rejected association with a party dominated by the unruly and muddle-headed men who refused to follow Luxemburg and Liebknecht.

Nevertheless, the Shop Stewards and even the Independents coöperated with Spartacus in calling for mass demonstrations against the removal of the leftist Independent police president of Berlin, Eichhorn. Neither the Independents, nor most of the Shop Stewards, intended to use this issue as a starting point for an armed revolt against the Majority Socialist People's Commissars, but the Spartacus group thought they would do so. The latter took up arms —and found themselves hopelessly isolated. Nonetheless, with fanatical devotion to their cause, they refused to abandon the struggle, and occupied the building of the Majority Socialist newspaper *Vorwärts,* valueless from the military point of view but of symbolic significance to Spartacus.

The government appointed the Majority Socialist leader, Gustav Noske, commander in chief. Although in the meantime some military detachments had been formed by Majority Socialists workers, Noske relied mostly upon the Free Corps, created by former imperial officers. They were eager to help the Majority Socialists, not for the sake of the party or of democracy, but to crush the revolution. A defeat of Spartacus, they thought, would be the first step toward the return of the old regime.

The government's fault was not so much in resisting Spartacus, but rather in using anti-democratic and anti-labor troops for that purpose, for no one could doubt the real intentions of the Free Corps. After the defeat of Spartacus, Free Corps officers murdered in cold blood Luxemburg and Liebknecht, who had been arrested after the fighting was over. A mistaken sense of honor had led the two Spartacus leaders first to support Spartacus in a venture which they condemned as foolish and then to stay in Berlin after the defeat of Spartacus. The atrocious murders clearly demonstrated the hatred of the Free Corps for the left.

Spartacus was defeated, but the real victor was the Free Corps, rather than the Majority Socialist government. This was clearly demonstrated by the subsequent rapid development of the Free Corps and the declining influence of the Workmen's Councils in Germany. It was not really the middle-class Republic that emerged victorious against the leftist threats, but the anti-democratic forces that had come to the rescue of the Republic. In this sense January, 1919, marked the beginning of the counter-revolution in Central Europe.

4.

In Bavaria alone did the authority of the labor movement continue to increase until April, 1919. This was due largely to the fact that the new Bavarian prime minister, Kurt Eisner, succeeded in maintaining coöperation among the three wings of the labor movement and in gaining leadership of all three of them—although the Majority Socialists were far stronger than his own Independent Socialist party and the Communists combined.

Kurt Eisner,[1] son of a Jewish industrialist, was one of those moderate labor leaders who joined the Independent Socialist party to express their protest against the war guilt of the German government and the war policy of the Majority Socialists. After being released from prison, where he had spent several months for his part in an anti-war strike in January, 1918, he became the outstanding leader of the Bavarian working class when the revolution broke out. He succeeded in winning the support of a peasant party under the blind peasant apostle Gandorfer, and on November 7, 1918, Eisner and Gandorfer proclaimed the Bavarian Republic. The Majority Socialists accepted the accomplished fact and entered the revolutionary government which Eisner formed. While the Berlin government eagerly sought the support of the representatives of the former regime, Kurt Eisner demonstrated its responsibility for the outbreak of the war. He endeavored to establish a truly democratic state, based upon workmen's, soldiers' and peasants' councils. Willingly or unwillingly, the Bavarian Majority Socialists continued to serve under the leadership of the Independent Socialist Eisner, despite the fact that his party was but a small minority compared with the large organization of the Majority Socialists. But Eisner was more than a mere party leader,

[1] About Kurt Eisner, see Robert Michels in *Archiv für die Geschichte des Sozialismus und der Arbeiterbewegung,* XIV (1929), 364 ff.

he had become representative of democratic, peace-loving Bavaria, and his constructive policy and personal prestige made him the most powerful man in the country.

At the International Socialist Congress in Berne in 1919, Eisner and the French Socialist Pierre Renaudel together submitted a resolution demanding the speediest possible repatriation of the war prisoners. Eisner declared that Germany was bound in honor to contribute to the reconstruction of the war-torn regions of France. This work could not be done by war prisoners, he said, but only by voluntary coöperation of German workers and intellectuals. Nationalist propaganda in Bavaria accused Eisner on his return from Berne of having opposed the liberation of German war prisoners. Within less than a month after his return, Eisner was assassinated by Count Arco-Valley, a German Nationalist whom his fellow nationalists later rewarded with a well-paid job.

The Majority Socialist leader, Johannes Hoffmann, succeeded Eisner as premier of Bavaria. Unfortunately Hoffmann lacked not only Eisner's authority but also his ability and constructive statesmanship. Adventurers of the same type as those who had staged the January revolt in Berlin moved into control of some sections of the Majority Socialist party. While this party practically ruled Bavaria, some of its own officials aided in the formation of the Munich Soviet Republic to replace the Socialist led government. The leftist confusionists completely failed to realize that the existing government was based upon the workmen's councils and was thus itself a form of Soviet government, although no dictatorship.

By April 7 the new Soviet government of Bavaria had obtained control over Munich without meeting any resistance. This new regime was even more farcical than the leadership of Spartacus in Berlin which had overruled Karl Liebknecht's and Rosa Luxemburg's objections. A simple threat from the Hoffmann government was sufficient to force the Soviet leaders into retreat after they had come to power. At this point, however, a sense of solidarity and honor induced the official Communist party to take over the leadership of the Soviet Republic. Although the party had previously looked askance at this poor imitation of the Russian revolution, it now tried in vain to organize resistance against the advancing government troops. The Free Corps, which the Reich and the Bavarian governments sent against Munich, quickly overcame the insurgents, and by the beginning of May the government troops took the city itself, killing hundreds of people. Hoffmann remained premier, but even more than Ebert and Scheidemann he abandoned real control to the counter-revolution, in this case to reactionary groups within the strongly monarchist Bavarian People's party. Bavaria was the first of the German provinces to complete the cycle from revolution to counter-revolution. While labor in Berlin at least slowed down the advance of the reaction, Bavaria by May, 1919, was the stronghold of all the forces bent on destroying democracy in Germany. The country became fertile soil for all sorts of conspiracies aiming at the overthrow of the Republic and the destruction of organized labor. One of the many hundreds of conspiratorial groups, practically unknown at the time to anyone outside a narrow circle, was the National Socialist Workers' party, which counted as Number 7 among its twenty-odd members a young volunteer of the Bavarian army during the World War, Adolf Hitler.

5.

With the defeat of Spartacus in Berlin and of the Soviet Republic in Munich, the first phase of the German revolution came to an end. At about the same time, the Hungarian Soviet Republic led by Bela Kun was defeated. This government had been created jointly by Socialists and Communists into whose hands the democratic Premier, Count Michael Karolyi, had resigned authority; it had undertaken to defend the pre-war frontiers of the country against the Central European allies of the victorious Entente: Czechoslovakia, Yugoslavia, and Rumania. In November, 1918, a democratic republic had been set up to create sympathy for Hungary among the Western democracies. When this hope was disappointed and the French insisted upon the cession of former Hungarian territory, the Magyars pinned their hope on Russia, whose armies were victoriously resisting Allied intervention and white counter-revolutionaries. The Hungarian Soviet was thus primarily an instrument to realize nationalist hopes, but the armies of Czechoslovakia and Rumania, supported by the French, crushed them. In the van of the victorious Rumanians, the counter-revolutionary government of Admiral Horthy took possession of Budapest to start the first great wave of white terror in Europe in retaliation for the red terror of the Soviets.

Austria followed a course midway between those of Germany and Hungary. The Austrian Social Democrats were much more politically minded than the Germans, and far more realistic than the Hungarians. Apart from Czechoslovakia, Austria was the only descendant of the old autocratic Hapsburg Empire which made a success of democracy. For this the Austrian Social Democratic party under the able leadership of Otto Bauer, Friedrich Adler, Karl Seitz, and Karl Renner could claim full credit.

In pre-war Austria the permanent conflicts among the various national groups compelled the Austrian Social Democrats—both German and Czech—to engage in constructive political action at an early stage. For, as long as the problems of the dissatisfied national groups within Austria were unsolved, public attention was diverted from social issues. To make pressure-group policy successful, the Social Democrats were therefore compelled to try to solve the minority conflicts first. This gave them practice in dealing with political problems and led them to a deeper understanding of such issues than most other labor parties acquired.

During the war the Social Democratic party suffered the internal conflicts common to practically all Socialist parties in countries engaged in the war. Victor Adler, the founder of the party, Seitz, and Renner headed the Social-Patriotic wing of the party; Friedrich Adler and Otto Bauer headed the internationalist group which corresponded to the German Independents.

Friedrich Adler was a professor of physics at Zürich, Switzerland, and entered upon a political career only a few years before the outbreak of the war. He was appointed secretary of the Social Democratic party in Austria and was engaged mainly in its international work. A convinced internationalist, he saw in Social Democratic support for the war the breakdown of his most cherished ideas. He became the leader of a small opposition which remained faithful to the internationalist program of the party, while his father, Victor Adler, headed the Social-Patriotic majority.

The Austrian premier, Count Stürgkh, ruled the country in a dictatorial fashion, without convoking Parliament. Friedrich Adler believed that the working class ought to be called upon to resist with revolutionary means the dictatorial regime; since the party refused to do so, Adler decided that he himself would set an example of resistance. In October, 1916, he shot and killed the premier.

For weeks he had prepared his deed, carefully choosing as his target the man who would best give his action full meaning in the minds of the masses. His speech at the trial, a quiet and well-reasoned statement of his democratic and internationalist faith, resounded throughout Austria. He was condemned to death, but the temper of the working class was such that the emperor did not dare permit the sentence to be carried out. During the last days of the monarchy workers demonstrated everywhere in Austria, carrying huge banners asking for the release of "our Fritz," and finally forced the emperor to sign a pardon. When Friedrich Adler left prison, he was the most powerful man in post-war Austria.

Soon afterwards, he was elected president of the Soldiers' and Workers' Council and chairman of the Social Democratic group in Parliament. The Russian Bolsheviks hoped that he would take the leadership in the newly formed Austrian Communist party, which with his prestige at its service, might have become the leading working class party in the country. Friedrich Adler was made honorary commander of the Russian Red Army, streets in Russia were named for him, he was even elected honorary president of the Russian Soviets. Despite this flattery Adler refused to abandon the Social Democratic party, in which the internationalists had obtained control at the end of the war. When the Bolsheviks, disappointed, withdrew one after the other the honors they had given him, he published an open letter to Trotsky stating the democratic and internationalist ideas which had inspired his action but kept him separated from the Communist movement.

Thanks mainly to Adler's attitude, the Austrian working class kept its unity, and the Communist party remained a small minority group. The existence of the Hungarian Soviet Republic gave the Austrian Communists a certain prestige for some time, but from the defeat of Bela Kun in 1919 until 1934 the party never succeeded in winning any grasp upon the Austrian working class. The Communists did not elect a single member to Parliament, nor any representatives in any important city council. To "Austrianize" a Communist party, that is, to reduce it to insignificance, came to be a catchword in Moscow.

On October 30, 1918, a Provisional National Assembly of "German-Austria" was formed, composed of deputies of the former imperial parliament who represented German-speaking constituencies. The assembly elected a government consisting of members of the three major parties—the Christian Socials, the Pan-Germanists, and the Social Democrats. For the first time in history, the Socialists entered the Austrian government. In its early stages the Austrian revolution had a nationalist complexion. Little Austria, all that remained of the former Austro-Hungarian Empire after the victorious national revolutions of the Czechs, Yugoslavs, Poles, and Italians, did not believe in its own independent existence and wished to join the German Reich. Black, red, and gold, the colors of the democratic revolution of 1848, dominated the streets of Vienna. Soon, however, the revolution took a Socialist turn as the army and the authority of the old regime broke down. A new army had to be formed, and the Social Democrats succeeded in staffing it with industrial workers. The new *Volkswehr,* as the army was called, was thus under Socialist leadership and able to stave off both reactionary and Communist attacks upon the new regime. The Austrian revolution, controlling the military forces of the nation, met successfully the decisive problem which the Germans had failed to solve. For as long as the army remained under the influence of the Socialists, Austrian democracy was safe against enemies from within. Moreover, the formation of the new army immensely increased Socialist prestige.

On November 12, the republic was proclaimed. Intending soon to merge with the young German Republic, the new regime had first to solidify the bonds among the German-speaking people of the former Hapsburg Empire. Two obstacles soon became apparent: the new Czechoslovakian authorities refused to hand over the Sudeten German districts to Austria, and the peasants in the Austrian provinces, who had welcomed the Republic, now wanted to dissociate themselves from Socialist Vienna. Indeed, the peasants went so far as to claim their independence. The Viennese government hoped that by assuring representation in the government to the Christian Socials and Pan-Germans, which were mainly peasant parties, as well as to the industrial and urban Social Democrats, the tendency toward disintegration of Austria could be overcome. In the end the Peace Conference rejected the Austrian demand for the *Anschluss,* the unification of Austria and Germany; the national revolution remained abortive.

Events in Hungary and Germany changed the trend of the Austrian revolution toward social objectives. When, in the spring of 1919, the Hungarian Soviet Republic was proclaimed and a proletarian dictatorship was established in Munich for a short time, Communist propaganda for an Austrian Soviet Republic reached its peak. The Communists claimed that, thanks to the proletarian character of the army, internal resistance to a dictatorship of the industrial workers could be easily overcome. Austria, they said, would form the link between revolutionary southern Germany and Red Hungary. The Hungarian embassy in Vienna, particularly after a victory of the Hungarian Army over the Czechs in May, 1919, became the center of tireless Communist activity dedicated to attaining this revolutionary goal.

The Austrian middle-class parties at the time were almost impotent, and the task of defending Austrian democracy thus fell to the Social Democrats. They did not believe that Austria could withstand the opposition of the victorious Allied powers to a proletarian dictatorship economically or by armed force. Moreover, while the Austrian cities were under the control of the working class, the peasants in the provinces would have fought against a dictatorship of the industrial workers. Austria had no food or coal; consequently the very life of the Austrian population depended upon imports from abroad. The Austrian Army could not fight with any chance of success against the neighboring nations, who might have attacked a Communist Austria in the same way that they had invaded Communist Hungary. In view of these facts, the Socialists succeeded in convincing the Austrian masses of their economic and military weakness against possible attacks by the victorious powers, although the workers felt that they were stronger than their Austrian middle-class opponents. As a result, the Communists never gained any considerable following; Communist revolts, sporadic and doomed to failure, were overcome by the *Volkswehr* without much bloodshed and without assistance from reactionary forces, as was the case in Germany. After the downfall of the Hungarian Soviet government in the summer of 1919, Communist propaganda in Austria petered out.

Thus democracy was saved from its enemies on the left while at the same time the unity of Austrian labor was preserved. The elections held in February, 1919, gave the Socialists 69 seats out of 159 in the constituent National Assembly, making them the strongest party, followed by the Christian Socials and the small Pan-German group. The Social Democrats were the democratically elected leaders of the Republic.

Their influence, however, was not based exclusively or even primarily upon their number in Parliament. The control of the army, the continuing revolutionary tension among the working class, the immense moral authority of the Socialists, and the political unity of the industrial workers were far more important. Within the Christian Social party the peasants outweighed the reactionary representatives of the cities. The Social Democrats allied themselves with the Christian Socials, forming a government of industrial workers and peasants in which the Socialists clearly predominated. The Social Democratic leader, Seitz, was elected president; the Social Democrat Karl Renner, chancellor; and Otto Bauer, foreign secretary. Social Democrats controlled the important ministries of war and interior. A democratic constitution was adopted; far-reaching social reforms were carried through within a few months.

6.

Germany, Austria, and Hungary produced three different types of labor action in roughly similar revolutionary situations. The Hungarian experience proved that a proletarian dictatorship in Central Europe was doomed to fail because of the overwhelming military strength of the victorious countries. Britain and France had been unable to crush the Russian Bolshevik revolution because it extended over the entire continent and was defended by the workers and even by the peasants, who felt that a counter-revolutionary victory would deprive them of whatever gains they had won in November, 1917. Perhaps an equally powerful bloc could have been created by simultaneous proletarian revolutions in Germany, Austria, and Hungary; but many factors prevented any such development. Most German workers refused to risk a war against what they considered hopeless odds for the sake of a proletarian revolution, and the bulk of the peasant population would have refused to support a campaign for a workers' dictatorship. Nevertheless, the Central European revolutions had a historic task. They could have created the basis for democratic regimes, established democratic administrations, set up armed forces to guard democratic ideals, destroyed the semifeudal big-landed estates, expropriated the former ruling dynasties. This was essentially a reformist task, though it required revolutionary methods. Such a task could not be performed successfully by trade-unionist pressure groups whose outlook was restricted to certain superficial reforms which did not affect the underlying economic and political structure. Unfortunately for democracy, the decisive Central European labor party, the German Majority Socialists, still clung to the status of a pressure group.

Chapter 6

THE STABILIZATION OF THE MIDDLE-CLASS REPUBLIC

1.

ON March 13, 1920, Reichswehr troops under the political leadership of a little-known Nationalist named Wolfgang Kapp mutinied and marched into Berlin. The republican government led by the Majority Socialists was unable to find loyal troops to defend the capital; it fled to Stuttgart in Southern Germany. Thus, a year and a half after the democratic revolution, the old regime dared to raise its head again. Failure of the *Putsch* was due partly to luck, more to the faith of the workers in their new democracy.

Basically, the Kapp *Putsch* symbolized the Socialist failures either to establish a democratic regime which would prove durable or to lead it successfully. The army created by the revolution was openly hostile to democracy and labor. In the economic field all efforts—mainly those taken by the Socialist minister of economy, Rudolf Wissell—to exert government control over industry and to introduce economic planning had failed. Exasperated because even the Socialist leaders showed scant interest in his suggestions, Wissell had finally resigned. In the domestic field the new regime thus produced little after the initial social reforms. One exception however was the adoption of a new constitution. It was a basic law which fulfilled all the dreams of progressive democrats; but under its liberal cloak the old economic and political institutions of the empire nevertheless continued to exist.

In their foreign policy the German Socialists were no more

successful. Their line lay roughly midway between pacifism and nationalism, yet was satisfactory neither to the pacifists nor to the nationalists. Philipp Scheidemann, the first Socialist chancellor of the Republic, refused to sign the "Diktat of Versailles," but Gustav Bauer, another Majority Socialist, headed the government which assumed that heavy responsibility.

The same inner contradiction was visible in the Socialists' attitude toward the former regime. Their concept of national honor, and their coöperation with officers and civil servants of the imperial regime, prevented the Majority Socialists from exposing the former regime's share in the war guilt or its responsibility for the misery caused by military vanquishment. The party rejected a policy akin to that of the Jacobins during the French revolution, who successfully combined the struggle for national freedom with implacable action against the supporters of the former regime. Such a policy would have required revolutionary internal changes which the Majority Socialists rejected. A full pacifist line involving anti-militarism seemed no more acceptable to the party, as it would have deprived Germany of all means of resistance to the victorious powers and, particularly, their protégés to the east of the Reich, who were eager to extend their frontiers at the expense of Germany. The Majority Socialists followed a policy of moderate nationalism which the Nationalists criticized as contemptibly weak and the pacifists regarded with suspicion. The Nationalist youth of Germany was taught to despise the Socialist traitors and weaklings who had "stabbed in the back" the German army "undefeated in the field," as the propaganda phrase went. The pacifists on their part held the not unjustified suspicion that the government was secretly supporting the nationalistic Free Corps, which emerged during the conflicts between Germany and her eastern neighbors over the new German boundaries and were a nucleus of all armed reactionary conspiracies against the Republic. The Socialists' timid and vacillating foreign policy thus satisfied no one. The Nationalists turned toward those right-wing parties which openly stated their nationalist objectives. The pacifists preferred the Independents to the Majority Socialists.

The failure of the Republic under Socialist leadership to

develop a clear-cut foreign policy was a serious shortcoming, but this might have been of less consequence if the new regime had been more successful in fulfilling the social hopes of the working class. True, Germany was a poor country, bled white by the war. The first decrees of the Council of People's Commissars had realized vast social reforms, and it was difficult, if not economically impossible, to go beyond them. Yet when many workers grew dissatisfied with the new regime, it was because of its failure to fulfill social rather than economic demands. The workers expected that in the new Republic, which they felt was their own creation, they would have a preponderant influence over both the administration and the economic life. Unfortunately for their hopes, the republican administration was only a slightly altered hand-me-down from the imperial regime, and in it the Workers' and Soldiers' Councils were mere debating societies with little influence. In the factories the newly established councils of the workers proved to have no more influence than had the trade-union delegates before the war. The sharing of economic control, which the government had promised the workers, failed to materialize; indeed, mounting currency inflation tended to enhance big business's control of economic life. Unrest thus grew among the workers, unrest which the government crushed in the name of law and order. Although the middle class had reason enough to be grateful to the government, big business and its followers among the middle classes, frightened by the mood of the working class, turned increasingly during 1920 toward the reactionary parties.

In this atmosphere some of the reactionary leaders thought that the cards were in their hands. The Reichswehr mutinied. Fortunately for the Republic, Kapp had few contacts with the Nationalist mass organizations and found little support from their best-known leaders, who thought that the hour had not yet struck for overt counter-revolution. A powerful general strike defeated the *Putsch* within four days. For once the working class acted in concert, Communists, Independents, Majority Socialists, and Catholic workers joining in the strike. Countered by a united working class, the badly prepared, premature offensive of the reactionaries broke down, Kapp resigned, and the workers won a splendid victory.

The episode jolted the progressives. Moreover, it gave the government and the labor parties another opportunity to correct some of the mistakes committed since November, 1918. The Socialist led trade unions suggested that a labor government be formed consisting of representatives of Socialist and Catholic trade unions, Majority Socialists, and Independents. Such a government might have been able to clean the Republic's house, oust its enemies from leading positions, and purge the Reichswehr of active opponents of democracy. But the Independents defeated this really progressive move. The Independents' left wing was under considerable Communist influence, and that of romantic revolutionaries; to "appease" these left wingers, the right-wing Independent leaders submitted in order to maintain the unity of the party—which served only to keep it practically paralyzed. The Independents' refusal to concur checked the trade-union proposal.

Another government was formed by the Weimar coalition, consisting of Majority Socialists, Democrats, and Catholic Center party, with the Majority Socialist Hermann Müller as chancellor. The Socialist Reichswehr minister, Gustav Noske, during whose control the monarchist conspiracy had been hatched, resigned. His name had come to be, even among many Majority Socialists, a symbol of ruthless persecution of the left and indifference to the activities of rightist enemies of the Republic. Noske's resignation was the only leftist success consequent upon the defeat of the Kapp *Putsch,* although the working class, Socialist and Catholic, had proved to be the only reliable and active support of democracy. Yet in the end the workers suffered most. Waiting for some evidence that the government was carrying out its promise to stem reaction, the workers in the industrial district of the Ruhr continued the general strike after Kapp's defeat; the Communists supported the continued strike in the hope of enforcing far-reaching revolutionary demands. The Reichswehr, which had just mutinied against the government, was now sent to crush the workers, and again it asserted its power. The army remained the real victor of the battle.[1]

[1] General Von Watter, sent against the "Red" army in the Ruhr district, reported, according to the London *Times* of April 5, 1920: "Troops are advancing along the entire line, killing hundreds of Spartacists." On the same day, the Berlin correspond-

Because the new coalition government did nothing to crush anti-democratic forces in the Republic, the final outcome of the Kapp *Putsch* was thus a defeat of labor. The workers were deeply dissatisfied with the Majority Socialists. They showed their feeling in the general elections of June 6, 1920, in which the Majority Socialists lost almost half their votes to the Independents, while the two middle-class parties of the Weimar coalition lost in roughly the same proportion to Nationalist and Monarchist parties. Constantin Fehrenbach, a leader of the Catholic Center party, succeeded the Socialist Hermann Müller as chancellor of the Reich. His government included representatives of the German People's party, the political organization of big business, which was hardly reconciled with the republican system. For the first time in the history of the Republic, the labor parties remained outside the government; and this situation continued, with two brief interludes, until 1928.

The Socialist parties were defeated. Now the struggle for the defense of the Republic was on in earnest. Its outcome depended to a large extent upon the results which the German Republic would obtain in its foreign policy.

2.

German labor could expect little help from the French and British workers. For, although labor had become increasingly radical in France and England during the war and the post-war crisis, nationalist enthusiasm following in the wake of victory strengthened the rightist parties. It is true that the French Socialist party increased its membership about tenfold from 1918 to 1919, reaching the record figure of 180,000 in 1920, while the trade unions (Confédération Générale du Travail, C.G.T.) grew from about 800,000 members in 1918 to 2,500,000 in 1920.

---

ent of the London *Times* wrote: "It is militarism that is guiding the tied hands of Herr Mueller and his colleagues." Cf. Crook, *The General Strike* (Chapel Hill, University of North Carolina Press, 1931), p. 523. General Von Watter previously had recognized the Kapp government, immediately upon its formation, and had endeavored to prevent the general strike in the Ruhr, contrary to the orders of the Republican government in Stuttgart.

Similarly, the British Labour party increased its membership from 2,500,000 in 1917 to 3,500,000 in 1919 and to 4,400,000 in 1920. These advances, however, were more than balanced by the increased strength of the right, as the general elections in both countries proved.

At the elections of December, 1918, the British Labour party elected 57 members to Parliament, only a slight gain compared with the pre-war strength of the "Parliamentary Labour party," the British term for the labor group in Parliament. Lloyd George and his Liberal-Conservative coalition retained full control over the House of Commons. After the "sacrificial, if conventional, national patriotism" of the workers during the war "that might well have shamed certain war profiteers," labor felt that it was given a very "raw" deal by the government. The holding of the elections at a time when the war fever was still high and so many soldiers were unable to go to the polls, embittered the workers. Under the British election system the fact that the middle-class parties were united against labor had a disastrous effect upon labor representation in the House of Commons. Although it polled 22 percent of the total vote, the Labour party obtained only 10 percent of the members elected. Such outstanding leaders as James Ramsay MacDonald, Philip Snowden, and Arthur Henderson lost their seats, thereby depriving the party of its best spokesmen in Parliament. The election campaign was conducted by the Lloyd George coalition under the slogans of "Hang the Kaiser" and "Make Germany Pay." As long as this spirit of hysterical patriotism and vindictiveness prevailed, labor was practically powerless in Parliament.

The French Socialists fared even worse than the British. Premier Georges Clemenceau won a sweeping victory in the general elections of November 16, 1919, with the Socialists routed all over the country. Having lost 70 seats in the Chamber of Deputies, they returned much weaker than before the war. Thus, the "khaki elections" in England and the "élections bleu-horizon" in France considerably weakened the influence of labor in the victorious nations at a time when Central European labor urgently needed its support. Not for the last time in the post-war history of

European labor did this unevenness of the political evolution in Western and Central Europe become a major cause of labor's setbacks.

Moreover, the labor movement had no really independent international policy. Basically the Socialist movement in the victorious countries backed the Treaty of Versailles, and the necessary changes were to be accomplished within the framework of this treaty. When at Frankfurt, in 1922, representatives of the French, Italian, and Belgian Socialists, of the British Labour party, of German Majority and Independent Social Democrats met to discuss the reparations problem, they reaffirmed the principle of reparations. The major demand of the Conference was "the cancellation of all war debts and the limitation of reparations to the compensation of the civil population for the material damage suffered by it in the war zones." At no time could the Austrian Social Democrats obtain international Socialist support for a proposed change in the treaty, such as self-determination for Austria, whose population urgently requested permission to join a democratic Germany.

Only in 1931, when Hitler threatened the very foundations of Europe, could the German Social Democrats cause the Labor and Socialist International to give a solemn promise that the Socialist parties "will, when they capture power, gradually and peacefully revise the (Peace) Treaties so as to secure for all nations equal rights within the peaceful community of nations, the right of self-determination within a pacified Europe, and protection and cultural autonomy for national minorities."

In all essentials, therefore, the Socialists followed the foreign policy of their respective governments. They shared with them the belief—based upon nothing but wishful thinking—that a combination of the existing nations in an international body such as the League of Nations could secure peace. Thus the Socialists of the Allied countries defended the Peace Treaties, while in the defeated nations the labor organizations joined the non-labor groups in demanding a revision of the Treaties. Characteristically the British Socialists—in agreement with their own middle class—were far more pro-German than the French or Belgians. The difference between Socialist and conservative foreign policy was only a matter of degree; the Socialists were eager to compromise over issues disputed by the victorious and defeated nations, while the conservatives frequently remained stubbornly hostile to sacrifices for the sake of international understanding.

An almost painful piece of evidence showed how far personal relations even among Socialists were affected by the political differences of their nations. In 1929 a Conference of various Socialist organizations was held in London to discuss once again the reparations problem. When the morning session was over and the delegates were about to disperse for their luncheon, the chairman, MacDonald, came with outstretched hands toward the German delegates and inquired anxiously whether someone had taken care of them and would show them to a good restaurant. Satisfied that all had been done to facilitate the stay of the Germans in the British capital, he left the room without so much as saying good day to the French and Belgian Socialists. It is true that in the preceding morning session, Philip Snowden had roundly accused the Belgians and French of "talking the same language as Poincaré," the protagonist of a strong anti-German policy. Snowden overlooked, of course, the fact that his pro-German stand was no less fully in agreement with governmental opinion in Great Britain.

The lack of a forthright Socialist international policy was not due to cowardliness. It required courage in France or Belgium, shortly after the war, to advocate even those small changes in foreign policy which French and Belgian Socialists favored. For many years Léon Blum was the victim of darkest calumnies because he opposed the Ruhr occupation. The real root of the failure of the Socialists to follow an independent line in international affairs was their pressure-group attitude. Beyond the range of general resolutions against war and against imperialism, which it was claimed could only be overthrown by the establishment of a Socialist regime, the Socialists had never endeavored to develop a foreign policy with a foundation of realism rather than of wishful thinking. The utopian traits in President Wilson's League of Nations thus found a sympathetic response among the

Socialists, unprepared as they were for a realistic analysis of international problems.

Weakness and lack of constructive thought thus combined to reduce the effectiveness of the support given the German Socialists by international labor, which could not help to solve the financial worries of the German Republic, nor prevent the Ruhr occupation, in spite of heroic efforts on the part of Léon Blum. Only after Poincaré's policy of revenge and oppression had failed and the United States and Britain had begun to favor an understanding with Germany, could French and British labor move to inaugurate an era of coöperation. Before the first British Labour government and Herriot's cabinet in France—the latter backed by a measure of collaboration between Socialists and progressive middle-class parties—superseded the old policy of revenge, German democracy had already passed through years of danger.

The harsh treatment of the Republic on the part of the Allies and the rapid currency inflation which after 1920 reduced the standard of living of the lower middle class, the professionals and the workers, created a situation favorable to anti-Republican movements.

The Republican parties lost popular support to the benefit of a whole network of more or less openly fascist movements whose basic strength came from the Free Corps and the romantically nationalistic youth movements. After the downfall of the Munich Soviet Republic, Bavaria had become the hotbed of these rightist organizations, and from there they spread to Northern Germany. They received new blood when the Free Corps, fighting against the Bolsheviks in Latvia and Estonia, were forced to leave these countries upon the withdrawal of the Bolshevik troops. The so-called racist movements became the main channel for the passionate protest of the lower middle class, intellectuals, youth, peasants, and civil servants against the inflation. By clever propaganda the racist movements turned this social movement into a campaign against the "Marxists," the Republic, the Jews, and the Allied Powers.

Political murder was one of the main weapons of the Free Corps. Leftist leaders like Kurt Eisner, Karl Liebknecht, and Rosa

Luxemburg had been killed in the early days of the Republic. Now there developed a new series of political assassinations, with the victims exclusively men of the left or of the Republican parties. In June, 1921, Gareis, a Socialist deputy in Munich, was murdered. His death was followed, two months later, by that of the leading Catholic politician, Mathias Erzberger, a member of the Reich government. In June, 1922 another member of the government, Walther Rathenau, the outstanding figure of the Democratic party, was killed for the threefold crime of being a progressive Democrat, a Jew, and perhaps the most gifted statesman of post-war Germany. Rathenau's murder profoundly aroused the working class. Its main answer consisted of a reorganization of its political forces.

The constantly threatened split of the Independent Social Democratic party had been finally achieved by Zinoviev, the president of the Comintern, at the party conference in Halle, in October, 1920. The majority of the Independents joined the communist party, the minority continued a separate existence. There was little, however, that separated the Right-Wing Independent leaders—Dittmann, Hilferding, Breitscheid, and Crispien—from the Majority Socialists. Their disagreements belonged to the past. Confronted with the racist threat, Right-Wing Independents and Majority Socialists agreed that the defense of democracy was the vital task of labor. Besides, a left wing had developed within the Majority Socialist party whose point of view was practically identical with that of the Right-Wing Independents.

Spurred into action by the shock of Rathenau's assassination, the remaining Independents agreed to merge with the Majority Socialists and to form the Social-Democratic party of Germany. Had this been done in 1919, the course of the German Revolution might have been deeply affected and German democracy been stronger than it actually was. Welcome as the fusion of the two parties was, it was hardly sufficient as a single force to prevent the victory of racist nationalism in 1923.

3.

The influx of the majority of the Independent party in 1920 gave the German Communist party a powerful impetus. Even after the defeat of a Communist uprising in Central Germany in 1921 and the resignation from the party of its president, Paul Levi, the German Communist party remained a strong mass movement. Between 1921 and 1923 it gained millions of new supporters. When, on January 11, 1923, Allied troops marched into the Ruhr district to punish Germany for its allegedly willful failure to pay reparations, the hour for a Communist offensive seemed to have struck.

The "passive resistance" with which Germany answered the Ruhr occupation and the complete breakdown of the currency created a revolutionary situation. Prices reached astronomical figures and wages lagged far behind. Trade-union funds vanished almost overnight, so weakening the unions that they were unable to resist when the eight-hour working day was abolished.

The working class was in a revolutionary mood. Any faction willing to stake everything on one daring move not only could have counted upon the support of its own followers, but would also have found new recruits among the millions of lower-middle-class people fluctuating among the various extremist movements, eager to express their dissatisfaction with the state of turmoil existing in the country.

The Communist party rapidly gained at the expense of the Socialists, while the middle-class parties lost many followers to the racist movements on the extreme right. For a time the Communists were probably even stronger in numbers than the Socialists. Yet, the Communist party, strangely blind to the revolutionary outlook, missed its opportunity. After 1922 the Communist International had abandoned hope for an immediate revolution. Brandler, Paul Levi's successor in the leadership of the German Communists, believed that mere peaceful evolution would lead to the establishment of a workers' government in which would be included Communists, Socialists, and Catholic trade unionists. The transition to a dictatorship of the proletariat could then, he thought, be achieved by constitutional means; revolutionary attempts might spoil this prospect. As a matter of fact, workers' governments were set up in Saxony and Thuringia, but in the Reich a different course of events followed.

During the summer of 1923, while the Communist party remained paralyzed, the masses showed unmistakable signs of revolutionary temper. A leftist group within the Communist party urged prompt and drastic action to meet the situation, but Moscow, and under its pressure the German leader Brandler, refused to believe that the time for decisive steps had come. Even the resignation of the reactionary Chancellor Cuno, due to the failure of passive resistance in the Ruhr and the chaos throughout the country, was insufficient to rouse the Communists from their self-imposed torpor. Clinging to their belief that the period of revolutionary action was past, they persisted in denying the existence of a revolutionary crisis in Germany. Belatedly, in October, when the disappointed workers had reached the stage of apathy, the Communists began to organize an insurrection. Armed Communist groups were formed in all sections of the Reich. According to the Communist plan, Saxony and Thuringia, with their leftist Social-Democrat and Communist governments, were to be the nuclei of the uprising. The final decision was to be made in Moscow, but the leaders of the Comintern, unable to make up their minds, several times postponed the revolt. Each time couriers were sent to all the important centers to inform the Communist leaders of the postponement. Then Brandler learned that the Social Democratic ministers in Saxony refused to embark upon what they considered an adventure, not justified by the situation in the Reich. Brandler called off the insurrection once and for all, but, owing to a mistake, his order failed to reach Hamburg in time. There, a few hundred Communists, isolated from the rest of the country, attacked police stations throughout the city and succeeded in seizing many. This half-hearted action resulted in utter defeat. The Hamburg uprising simply petered out when no one joined the armed Communist corps, and in the rest of the country the Communist leaders themselves prevented their supporters from coming to the aid of Hamburg.

The complete indifference of the Hamburg workers, among whom were many Communists, proved that the Saxon Social Democratic leaders had been right. If a few months before the working class had been waiting for a signal to revolt, the delay and the first signs of stabilization of economic life had turned the revolutionary tension into apathy. In addition, the Communists, acting as if they were out to prepare a conspiracy rather than a popular mass movement, had done very little preparatory political work. It has frequently been suggested that the Communist leaders themselves were not only hesitant about the date of the rising, but also reluctant to commit themselves definitely to a *Putsch*. Karl Radek, sent from Moscow to direct the German Communist party, found it in a state of despair and dissolution, unable to cover the defeat by a rear-guard battle in the form of demonstrations and local strikes.

The Reichswehr, marching into Saxony and Thuringia to oust the labor governments and dissolve the armed Communist groups, met no resistance. The Communist party was declared illegal without a hand being raised in its defense.

After the Communist defeat, it was the turn of the extremists on the right to try to profit from the crisis in the country. On November 8, 1923, Adolf Hitler organized his famous "beer-garden *Putsch*" in Munich. He hoped to win the support of the counter-revolutionary ministers who had governed Bavaria since the downfall of the Munich Soviet Republic. With their aid he planned to march against Berlin. The Bavarian government, however, had similar plans of its own and did not wish to submit to Hitler's leadership. This split among the reactionary and fascist forces saved the Republic from a great danger. When the future Fuehrer of Germany met serious resistance where he expected co-operation, his world broke down and he took to flight. Soon afterwards, the stabilization of the German mark and the influx of foreign, primarily American, capital, brought about economic progress in Germany; and political stability followed in its wake.

Not labor, but capitalist prosperity eventually saved the German Republic.

4.

The surprising blindness of the German Communists in the face of what was probably their greatest chance of success cannot be understood without consideration of the Communist evolution after 1919.

After the defeat of Spartacus in Berlin and of the Munich and Hungarian Soviet Republics, Communist hopes turned toward the Russian Red Army. When the Polish Marshal Pilsudski embarked upon a campaign of conquest in the Soviet Ukraine, the Red Army, after a long retreat, took the offensive. In August, 1920, the Russian troops were at the walls of Warsaw.

Communist prestige at this moment was at its peak. Working-class organizations in all countries prevented Allied transports of arms and ammunition from reaching Poland, which, the workers felt, was engaged in a war of aggression against Russia. British labor was particularly successful in its fight against the English interventionists.

Eagerness to save British capitalist interests in Russia was regarded as the main motive of those who wanted—as one speaker of the Labour party conference in Southport in July, 1920, put it —"to send the boys of the working classes to fight for their capital." The Conference threatened a general strike against British intervention in the war. A special National Labor Conference attended by more than a thousand delegates, endorsed the formation of a "Council of Action" already decided upon by unions and party, and authorized the Council to call a general strike. British conservatives angrily protested against this "undemocratic" pressure on the government, but there was no intervention in Russia after this threat.

In Russia the victories over Poland, together with the signs of effective working class sympathy with the Soviet Union, led to the belief that the Red Army could be effectively used in spreading the revolution in Europe. Moscow dreamed of the revolutionary armies' breaking the chain of conservative countries between the Soviet Union and Germany, marching towards the Rhine, and extending the proletarian dictatorship from the shores of the Pacific Ocean to the Franco-German frontier. From a war of defense, the Russo-Polish war developed into a military attack in the service of Bolshevist world revolution.

In the Balkans, the news of the Russian advance created a state of high tension. The Communist parties there, weakened by peasant desertion as a consequence of recent agrarian reforms and subject to terroristic oppression as enemies of national freedom, made renewed progress.

The Communist offensive failed however. In the summer of 1920 the tide of war turned against the Russians. With the aid of an Allied military commission under General Weygand, the Polish troops forced the Russians back. The Red Army began to disintegrate and the Soviet Union was forced to sign the Peace Treaty of Riga, which submitted to Polish rule about six million people of races closely linked with the population of the Soviet Union.

The effects of the Russian defeat were felt all over Europe. In all countries bordering on Russia, from Finland to Rumania, conservative forces were considerably strengthened. The Socialists were forced out of the Polish government, which they had joined at the moment of danger. Special laws were passed against the Jugoslav Communists, who were deprived of their parliamentary representation. In Hungary, now that the danger of foreign Communist advance seemed averted, the old feudal regime reëmerged out of the terroristic dictatorship which until then had been considered necessary to stave off Communist danger.

Thus, toward the end of 1923, social and political conditions all over Central and Eastern Europe were approaching a stage of stabilization. Russia herself had embarked upon the New Economic Policy, moderating her extremist war communism. Disappointed in his hope for the success of a Communist revolution in Europe, Lenin felt, in view of the rising unrest of the peasants and the revolt of the sailors of Kronstadt, that a strategic retreat had become necessary, which he hoped would be only temporary. Greater freedom was thus granted to the peasants and the small business men, while the international policy of Moscow abandoned its short-range revolutionary objective to gain a double purpose. Moscow was anxious, first, to forestall any new intervention in Russia, and therefore wished to establish closer contacts with labor in Western and Central Europe so as to have friends in case of need. Second, the Comintern acknowledged the fact that without the support of a majority of the working class the Communist parties could not hope to succeed in their revolutionary efforts in any crisis that might develop in the future. It set out to win such support.

The Communists decided to exploit for their own party ends the ardent desire of the working class for a unified labor movement. Real unity between Socialists and Communists "must of course be rejected with utmost firmness," as the Fourth Congress of the Communist International declared in December, 1922. But offers for united action were considered by the Communists excellent opportunities for "unmasking the betrayal" of the working class by the Social Democrats. If the Socialists rejected a Communist United Front proposal, the Communists accused them of subordinating vital working-class interests to the Socialist struggle against the Communists. If United Front proposals were accepted, the Communists proceeded to raise more and more extremist slogans until the Socialists eventually rejected them, thus permitting the Communists to criticize the Socialists for their failure to agree to Communist suggestions. As Karl Radek put it at the Fourth Communist World Congress: "The road to the United Front is a much harder one than our tactical motto of 1919, 'smash everything up'; it is much easier and pleasanter to smash everything up, but if one is not strong enough to do so, and if this road (that is, the United Front) is necessary, we must walk along it . . . in the firm belief that this road will not lead us but the Socialists to perdition . . . with the conviction that we shall be able to stifle them in our embrace."

No immediate revolutionary demands were to be raised by the Communist parties according to the Comintern instructions. Their main task was to win the confidence of the working class so that it would be amenable to Communist control when the next revolutionary crisis arose, in the meantime helping to prevent foreign counter-revolutionary intervention in the Soviet Union. When the revolutionary crisis arose in Germany, in 1923, the Communist party, engaged in the strategic retreat ordered by Moscow, "missed the boat."

The Communist failure in 1923 was thus a result of the general Communist retreat in Europe. But as a consequence of the defeat of 1923, the abandonment of revolutionary action, originally a "temporary strategic maneuver," became a permanent feature of Communist policy. This evolution found its reflection in the changing relationship between Radicals and Leninists within the Communist International.

In the first years after their victory, the Leninists, as will be remembered, had succeeded in bringing many Radicals under their control. The split of the German Independents and of the French Socialist party into a pro-Moscow majority and an anti-Moscow minority was the crowning triumph of Leninism over radicalism. This victory, however, was more superficial than Moscow thought. Even within the Comintern, the Radicals remained what they had been. Moscow succeeded in imposing the Leninist scheme of party organization upon the Radicals, but this did not alter the fact that most Radicals continued to prefer extremist propaganda to action, the "purity" of the party to contact with life, and "theoretically" sound though sterile formulas to effective compromises. Grumblingly, the Radicals submitted to the "temporary" retreat to moderate slogans when Lenin in 1921 used his full authority to make the Comintern adopt his policy. When the turn to the "United Front" slogan and collaboration with Socialists became a more permanent feature of Communist action, the Radicals grew more and more restive, but still Moscow was strong enough to control the Comintern. The moderate course was continued, but against growing Radical opposition.[2]

A new leadership under Ernst Thälmann was appointed for the German Communist party. Practically the whole leadership of the French Communist party revolted against what was regarded as unbearable meddling by Moscow with the internal affairs of the

[2] Cf. p. 31.

party. L. O. Frossard, who had led the majority of the French Socialists into the Communist party, resigned and created an intermediary group between Socialists and Communists, the so-called "Socialist-Communist Union." Other groups were expelled from the Communist party for having "overstepped the limits of the 'united front' and made deals with Socialists and other parties," during the elections of May, 1924.

New internal conflicts arose as a consequence of the Communist about-face, and these were aggravated by the struggles within the Russian Communist party, where Stalin, Trotsky, and Bukharin were aspiring to Lenin's heritage. These conflicts heightened the crisis of the Comintern stemming from the failure of the United Front policy and from the progressive stabilization of Europe. Less and less could the Comintern be regarded as a means for furthering a proletarian revolution in Europe. Instead, Stalin began to value the support of Communism abroad in his struggle against other pretenders for Lenin's succession. To have this support, he increasingly adapted Communist policy to Radical desires.

It is, therefore, only partly true that world communism became a mere appendix to the Russian Communist party, an instrument in the hands of those in control in Moscow. Such control was exercised only in matters of the personnel of the party leadership and its international policy, vital to Moscow. In domestic affairs, the Communist parties were increasingly permitted to follow a Radical course, widely at variance with Leninism. From 1928 to 1934—the beginning of the Popular Front period—communism was the heir to pre-war radicalism—talking big and doing little.

5.

The "United Front" line culminated in a great effort to gain entrance into the trade-union movements. The Communist attitude toward the Socialist led trade unions, organized in the so-called Amsterdam International, the International Federation of Trade Unions, was never completely clear. Although a special Red International of Trade Unions (Profintern) had been set up in Moscow, many Communists remained inside Amsterdam unions, with the intention, of course, of "boring from within," overturning the old leadership of the unions, and finally leading them into the Communist Red International. According to Zinoviev, Moscow had hoped at first to "break through the enemy (that is, the Socialist) lines by a frontal attack and quickly win over the trade unions." However, Zinoviev admitted, it was disappointed in this hope. "The Social Democrats in places grew stronger, in trade-union work as well as in the political field." And so Zinoviev concluded that "We must fight with them (the Socialists) more slowly, by more difficult, roundabout means. . . . It is necessary to decide at once that we must prepare our foundation in the masses, that we must organize our propaganda of 'trade union unity' on an international scale, that we begin at once to arrange meetings all over the world on this subject, that we prepare the soil, and then begin our negotiations."

It is obvious that in this speech, delivered in July, 1924, at the Fifth Congress of the Communist International, Zinoviev thought of the slogan "trade-union unity" as a means, not so much for achieving unity, as for outmaneuvering the Socialists. Yet, there was a difference between the demand for "trade-union unity" and mere "United Front" on the political field. It is hard to guess what might have happened if negotiations between Amsterdam and the Profintern had rendered possible real trade-union accord. It cannot be excluded that in such a case the maneuver might have ended in a sincere, although possibly temporary, understanding. The new policy was a queer mixture of maneuver and of a certain readiness to agree to real unity if by chance it should come about as a consequence of the Communist campaign.

Amsterdam, however, refused to enter into any negotiations with Moscow. The International Federation of Trade Unions cooperated with the unified Labor and Socialist International while "strictly preserving its equality and independence," but laid down certain conditions for negotiations with the Russian unions, the most important of which was independence of the unions from the Communist party and the Soviet government. These conditions were of course rejected by Tomsky, the leader of the Russian unions, and there the matter rested.

In a few countries, particularly in England, the Communists approached the Socialist led trade unions with some success. By 1924, the British unions formed a left wing within the Amsterdam International, in opposition to the Continental union leaders, and the Russian question was the main point at issue. The British succeeded in forcing passage of a resolution asking for continued consultations with the Russians. In addition, the moderate J. H. Thomas was succeeded as president of the I.F.T.U. by the leftist and pro-Russian British trade-union leader, A. A. Purcell; another British left winger, J. W. Brown, was elected one of the three secretaries, to serve along with Jan Oudegeest of Holland and Johann Sassenbach of Germany. As a consequence of the resolution for consultations with the Russian unions, letters were exchanged between Amsterdam and Moscow concerning the basis for Russian affiliation with the I.F.T.U.; but the Continental unions decided that a joint conference—which the Russians desired as a preliminary to affiliation—could be held only after the All-Russian Council of Trade Unions had "intimated" its desire for affiliation.

The British, having been outvoted on this decision, met with Russian delegates in April, 1925, and set up an Anglo-Russian Committee to promote international unity. Thus the British unions accepted coöperation with Communists just when the British Labour party was categorically rejecting the British Communist party's demand for affiliation. In Britain this divergence could be explained by differences in personnel, the unions being under leftist control while the party was dominated by MacDonald and his right-wing friends.[3] It is more difficult to explain Moscow's willingness to coöperate with the British trade-union leaders, whose organizations after all were the backbone of the Labour party, but who apparently did nothing to help the Communists in their desire to enter the party. Moscow, it has been claimed, was willing to sacrifice the insignificant British Communist party to win the sympathy of the mass organizations of British labor. The British unionists, on the other hand, were little interested in the British Communist sect, but were filled with sympathy for Russia, partly out of opposition to the British Conservatives—who

[3] Cf. p. 106.

were deadly enemies of the Soviet government—partly because the unions believed that the Russian market would offer a chance for the revival of British industry.[4]

The Continental Socialists and unionists were disturbed by their British colleagues' aid to what the Continental leaders regarded as Communist maneuvers. When delegates of the English Independent Labour party suggested a joint Socialist-Communist conference for the purpose of "exploring the possibilities of the formation of an all-inclusive International" in the political field, the executive of the Labor and Socialist International felt very much relieved by Zinoviev's answer, "No, a thousand times no," even before the Labor and Socialist International could consider the suggestion of the I.L.P. In the political field, the Communists favored, according to Zinoviev, "unity among the working class, but unity based on Communism, on Leninism."

Fortunately for the Continental unions, the defeat of the general strike in Britain in 1926 put an end to leftist rule in the British unions. The solidarity of the Continental unions during the strike and the financial aid given afterwards to the British Trade Union Congress, tightened the bonds between British and Continental union leaders. It is true that the Russians were no less eager to help, but while proffering offers for aid, they accused the British trade-union leaders of having betrayed the working class, and charged such left wingers as Purcell, Hicks, and Swales with having "surrendered" to the right during the strike. Although meetings of the Anglo-Russian Committee continued to be held for some time, a breach between London and Moscow was apparent, and continued Russian "ill-instructed and presumptuous criticism"—in the words of the British Trade Union Congress in 1926—made the final death of the committee unavoidable. Its end came at the Trade Union Congress in 1927, which decided to break off all relations with the All-Russian Council of Trade Unions. At the Congress of the I.F.T.U. in 1927, the Continental delegates decided once and for all to end British flirting with Moscow. The British regarded the conflict somewhat as a nationalist affair, with

[4] For this and the following two paragraphs, see Lewis L. Lorwin, *Labor and Internationalism*. New York, Macmillan, 1929, pp. 324–38.

the Continentals under German leadership turning against British influence in the I.F.T.U. After they had staged a sensational walk-out from the congress, the British turned around and agreed to a settlement. The two hostile secretaries, Oudegeest and Brown, resigned; and Citrine, a right winger, the secretary of the British Trade Union Congress, became president succeeding Purcell. Thus ended Communist efforts to permeate the European trade-union movement.

PART III

Labor in the Great Depression

Chapter 7

"DOCTOR OR HEIR"

1.

"ARE *we sitting at the sickbed of capitalism, not only as doctors who want to cure the patient, but as prospective heirs who cannot wait for the end and would like to hasten it by administering poison? We are condemned, I think, to be doctors who seriously wish to cure, and yet we have to maintain the feeling that we are heirs who wish to receive the entire legacy of the capitalist system today rather than tomorrow. This double role, doctor and heir, is a damned difficult task.*"

These often quoted words were spoken by Fritz Tarnow, a German trade-union leader, at the German Social Democratic party congress of 1931. They reveal the basic problem of Socialist reformism—its inability to build a bridge between its everyday activity and its ultimate goal of socialism.

For a revolutionary no such problem existed. His position was simply that "whoever forwards the process of recovery of the capitalist system must understand that he does not render any service to the working class," as a speaker at the same congress put it. This attitude implied readiness to take advantage of the economic crisis, "to mobilize and concentrate all forces to achieve the most rapid death of the sick body of capitalism," and to seize power by revolutionary means so as to establish a Socialist order of society. For this task, however, none of the labor parties, Socialist or Communist, were prepared. Neither their organization nor their leadership was equipped for a revolutionary uprising and the establishment of a new social order.

The moderate approach was no less sterile. The Reformists'

duty would have been to use the economic crisis for a gradual transformation of the capitalist society. This was the moment for constructive Socialist action demonstrating that Socialist methods were equal to the crisis, while capitalist methods were utterly failing. Without such a demonstration, moderate socialism could not claim to have a constructive policy.

It was true that the crisis weakened the trade unions. When millions of workers were unemployed, those fortunate enough to have jobs were not prepared to risk them lightheartedly. Mass unemployment constituted a heavy drain on trade-union funds. The trade-union leaders could hardly be induced to wage large-scale battles.

The political force of labor was less exposed to the weakening influence of the crisis. While labor's economic weapons were rendered impracticable, new avenues were opened for political action. Millions of former adherents of middle-class parties began to doubt the wisdom of their party leaders and were prepared to support new methods at wide variance from traditional ways of handling social and economic problems. Confidence in capitalism was shaken. A labor party offering a way out of the crisis—no matter whether or not it was compatible with capitalist institutions—could have recruited millions of new supporters.

Events, however, soon demonstrated that the Reformists had no constructive policy. In most European countries, Reformist Socialism was a bulwark of laissez faire economic policy, with which it combined trade-union demands in obvious contradiction to its laissez faire policy. Reformist policy was thus a queer mixture of laissez faire orthodoxy and anti-laissez faire pressure-group attitudes.

This strange state of affairs was due to the failure of Reformist Socialism to develop a policy for a gradual transition from capitalism to socialism. No such policy was needed as long as the movement believed in its ability to seize power by revolutionary means and to build a full-fledged socialism out of the revolutionary chaos. The abandonment of the revolutionary creed involved working out an alternative strategy. However, as long as the movement was small and far from political power, the need for such a program did not seem very urgent.

Almost overnight, however, the First World War had made labor, in a great many countries, the strongest political force. It has been shown how, in this situation, German labor immediately after the war relied upon the personnel and to a large extent the policies of the former imperial regime to fill the hole in labor's political equipment. By 1929 labor was still lacking not only a constructive program but even insight into the need for such a policy. Without much hesitation the party leaders took refuge in the intellectual equipment of progressive middle-class groups. Their policy was that of laissez faire.

To an American reader it must seem strange that progressive groups, even of the middle class, should follow the inspiration of Adam Smith and David Ricardo. In the United States this is the theory of the most conservative politicians. The struggle against feudalism and mercantilism, however, gave laissez faire in Europe the halo of a revolutionary movement. The old-time English "Radicals" of the Manchester type and the Continental Liberals had been labor's allies in freeing humanity from the fetters of feudalism and the control of an absolute king. Moreover, their successors, the younger Liberals, had adopted social insurance and extended government services for the poor in addition to their basic laissez faire creed.

As has been pointed out before, Marxist tradition was by no means hostile to laissez faire. The Marxist theory, devised to separate socialism from middle-class progressivism, turned against its author. In all essentials, it said, capitalism could not be reformed. It had to be destroyed to enable the working class to advance economically and socially. This idea was to give revolutionary impetus to the Socialist movement in its drive for political power. But, since a revolutionary struggle now was considered impossible, the conclusion drawn from the Marxist thesis very frequently was that capitalism had to be run according to capitalist rules. In this view, laissez faire was the embodiment of the laws of capitalist economy.

Social services in combination with free trade, the gold standard, and resistance to government interference with a depression once it had started were the main tenets of laissez faire which most Socialists took over unquestioningly. Some went so far as to resent the fact that concern for trade-union interests compelled the labor parties to combine laissez faire with such highly contradictory policies as the maintenance of wage rates and unemployment benefits at their pre-depression level. Apart from these concessions, however, most labor leaders strictly adhered to the rules of laissez faire.

While many workers felt that the crisis of the early thirties required new methods for its solution, the Reformists, eager to follow the traditional course, were forced to pretend that the crisis was by no means different from previous depressions. So they stressed all the points in which this crisis was essentially akin to all those since the early nineteenth century.

Fritz Naphtali, one of the leading experts of German Social Democracy, wrote late in 1930: "My impression is . . . that earlier crises showed in varying degrees phenomena which were similar, even in their quantitative effects, to those we are witnessing at present." [1] A year later, in 1931, the trade-union leader Tarnow admitted that "the present crisis is undoubtedly more extensive and deeper in its effects than all earlier crises." Yet, even then, most labor leaders believed that the crisis would soon be overcome by the automatic recovery forces of the capitalist institutions.

Interference with these forces would do more harm than good. The crisis was regarded as a necessary corrective for past economic mistakes. Until the depression had purified the economic structure from the consequences of such mistakes, the leaders considered it harmful to end the depression. Interference with the "natural" course of the depression would lead to permanent waste of productive resources.

This conception was clearly expressed in Naphtali's words:

I don't believe that we can do very much, nor anything very decisive, from the point of view of economic policy, to overcome the crisis until

[1] Fritz Naphtali, *Wirtschaftskrise und Arbeitslosigkeit*. Berlin, 1930, p. 24.

it has run its course. When prosperity has developed so far, so disproportionately, and so unchecked as is now normally allowed under capitalist conditions—and as has occurred in recent years on a world scale—then it is hardly possible to stop the crisis during its actual progress. For then, the crisis with all its destruction of the value of capital, with its changes and shifts of purchasing power, is a means of correction which must necessarily be accepted. Afterwards, on the basis of large-scale capital destruction, a better proportion will emerge between production and consumers' purchasing power, which is the condition for a new upswing. I believe, therefore, that we must stick to this tenet: if we tend toward a policy of controlling the business cycle in its various forms, corrective measures must not be taken at the time of the crisis but during the period of prosperity.

Since the Reformists viewed the crisis as a necessary liquidation of past mistakes, deflation was unavoidable. True, expansionist policies might alleviate the crisis, and the introduction of additional purchasing power might shorten the deflationary period—but this would be achieved only at the price of preventing necessary liquidation and thus preparing new crises.

As a result of this theory, the Reformists favored price reductions which would increase real wages. Consumption would be stimulated and demand outgrow the output, after having absorbed stocks on hand. Production would increase to meet growing demand, and thus a new phase of prosperity begin. If not hampered by interference, deflation would finally lead to new economic expansion on a sounder basis.

To prevent disturbing interferences with recovery the Reformists advocated balanced budgets. As Naphtali said: "It was always Social Democracy which demanded: 'First of all, the public household must be put in order.' Unless Reich, states, and municipalities have established order in their finances, we cannot have any reasonable and successful economic or social policy."

Currency manipulations were anathema. This was partly due to laissez faire principles, but also, in Germany, to the terrible experience of post-war inflation. Labor leaders who remembered the dreadful times when wages were unable to keep up in the race with rising prices and when trade-union funds vanished overnight, owing to fantastic price increases, made a solemn vow to prevent the recurrence of such a catastrophe. "No tampering with the currency" was therefore the almost unanimous slogan of the left.

This theory implied passivity during a crisis in order to permit the natural forces of recovery to come into play, but the trade-union leaders could ill afford to follow such a comfortable philosophy. Their members were threatened by wage reductions, and the jobless by cuts in unemployment benefits. Under the pressure of the trade unionists, the Socialist leaders merged the trade-union demands with their laissez faire policy.

The result of this amalgam could be seen in a joint program which the Labor and Socialist International and the International Federation of Trade Unions worked out early in 1931.[2] Their program represented the well-considered policy of reformism.

The statement began with a brief analysis of the causes of the crisis, which was explained as a "disproportion between productive capacity and consumption." What was needed, the laborites argued, was an increase in consumption and the "most important task of the labor movement at the present time . . . is to oppose wage reductions with all its energy and in all countries." This general declaration was implemented with a list of well-known trade-union demands, such as the forty-hour week, workers' holidays, and unemployment insurance.

How crisis-stricken employers should fulfill these demands, was not explained. Five years later, Léon Blum, premier of France, argued that an increase in wages, although it caused an increase in production costs, could be borne by the employers since production would rise as a consequence of expanding consumers' purchasing power. Increased production would result in reduced production costs per unit of output, and thus make up for the rise of wage costs.

In other words, labor believed that the cost of social reforms could be compensated, in the long run, by a better use of existing industrial plants. Wherever put to a practical test, this theory proved a failure; it failed to consider the "short run," vital for many employers. Assuming that labor's theory of the cause of the

[2] This document is reprinted in *Fourth Congress of the Labour and Socialist International, Vienna, 25th July to 1st August 1931*. Labour and Socialist International, Zürich. London, Labour Party, Publications Department, I, 34 ff.

crisis was correct, and that an increase in consumers' purchasing power was necessary, the question arose whether this increase was to be effected at the expense of the employers or by introducing additional purchasing power through government action, by mobilizing idle capital funds. This was the decisive issue, and by asking that the burden be put on the employers' shoulders, labor chose the wrong answer. This was inevitable as long as labor thought exclusively in the terms of the worker-employer struggle, rather than in terms of governmental policies.

The program of the two Internationals advocated a second method of recovery. It "pointed out with emphasis that the disproportion between productive capacity and consumption . . . can be modified, not by the reduction of state expenditure in times of economic crisis, but by the greatest possible expenditure for productive public works." This very important idea, however, lacked elaboration in two vital directions. A program of public works in times of crisis depends upon a fiscal and monetary policy related to the task of expanding purchasing power. Large-scale public expenditure is obviously impossible in times of crisis as long as a balanced budget is considered vital. Moreover, public works financed out of taxation cause, as a rule, merely a shift in purchasing power without creating additional demand for goods. In this case additional spending at one point means reduced spending at another, owing to increased taxation. To combat unemployment public works have to be financed by borrowing, thus tapping idle capital funds. German and British labor considered it a paramount task to balance the budget, or at least to effect the greatest possible reduction of budget deficits. They feared that a government which depended upon the capital market would come under the domination of the banks controlling access to that market—the greater the need for credit, the better the opportunity for the banks to blackmail the government. Labor knew that high finance first of all would demand a reduction in unemployment benefits, which labor was determined to refuse. In addition, many labor leaders believed that unbalanced budgets would lead straight to monetary inflation, which they considered the greatest catastrophe that could befall the working class.

On this point, the program was categorical. It opposed inflation as well as deflation, but as far as the latter was concerned, the opposition was directed against wage reductions rather than against price cuts. "If during the years immediately following the war," the program said, "the inflation in many countries impoverished the working class, at a later time a deflationist policy in certain countries provoked serious economic convulsions."

The program made no distinction between inflation and devaluation. By implication labor thus rejected any departure not only from the gold standard, but also from the gold parity of the currencies. By adopting this position, and by also rejecting deficit-spending, labor blocked every approach to an expansionist economic policy.

In all essentials, labor's policy during the crisis coincided with that of orthodox laissez faire liberalism. Balancing the budget, defense of the gold parity of the currency, non-interference with the "natural course" of the depression were common salient points of labor and laissez faire business-cycle policy. In most countries labor resisted efforts toward increased tariff protection as vehemently as did the orthodox Liberals. The labor movement carried the banner of economic liberalism which the Liberal parties, practically wiped out in most European countries, had abandoned.

2.

The main opposition inside the labor movement to laissez faire practice came from the trade unions. As we have seen, the influence of the trade unions forced the labor parties to add the standard trade-union demands to their otherwise standard laissez faire policy. In spite of theoretical efforts to merge the two aspects of labor's crisis policy into a logical unit, the inner contradiction between the laissez faire and the trade-union elements could hardly be concealed. How could money wages be maintained—which, owing to the price fall, meant increased real wages—while the depression continued and deepened, without ruining many businesses and thus increasing unemployment? How could unemployment benefits be protected against cuts while the budget was being balanced? Thus the two doctrines of many labor leaders were bound to clash during the depression.

In Germany Fritz Tarnow, supported by a well-known statistician, W. Woytinsky,[3] and by an agricultural economist, Baade, suggested abandoning passive acceptance of deflation and advocated measures to raise the price level. The implication was, of course, devaluation or abandonment of the gold standard. This proved an insuperable obstacle for the success of the so-called W-T-B plan (after the initials of the authors' names). In Britain Keynes for a long time was almost alone in criticizing the monetary policy of the country, and Snowden's financial orthodoxy was hardly disputed until the summer of 1931, when that policy became untenable. Mosley's financial plans were half-way measures; their connection with semi-dictatorial ideas prevented serious discussion by the movement. Not until the summer of 1931 was there a clear-cut divergence of views. When MacDonald and Snowden broke away from the party, the split corresponded more or less accurately to the division between the laissez faire theoreticians and the trade unionists.

The decisive handicap of the trade-unionist opponents of laissez faire within labor was their lack of a well-rounded plan. Limited in their outlook by pressure-group thinking, they could offer no alternative to the laissez faire system.

Moreover, laissez faire was strengthened by internationalism. It was argued that if isolated countries acted individually, sometimes in direct opposition to efforts in other nations to meet the world crisis, these actions would strengthen political nationalism. The joint program of the Labor and Socialist International and of the International Federation of Trade Unions thus asked for international credits, the resumption of international trade, and international public works to be financed by international credits. At the height of the German banking crisis in the summer of 1931, an International Socialist Congress urgently asked for international credits to Germany to prevent the complete breakdown of its economic life. "The economic collapse of Germany," the congress

[3] W. Woytinsky, *Internationale Hebung der Preise als Ausweg aus der Krise.* Leipzig, Buske, 1931.

declared, "must be prevented by generous international credit action." This was considered so essential that the world was described as being faced with the dilemma of international aid to Germany or catastrophe: "No choice remains to the world but this: either immediate and generous international action to save economic life, democracy and peace, or catastrophe and civil war."

This was a fairly accurate forecast and one corresponding to the internationalist creed of labor. But international coöperation had broken down during the crisis, and labor was not sufficiently strong to overcome the powerful inert drag of political resistance to international action. This failure enhanced laissez faire passivity within labor's ranks and greatly contributed to the defeat of labor and the rise of nationalist fascism.

3.

If Socialist action against the crisis was sterile, the Communist attack upon its problems was even more so. Meeting in the summer of 1928, the Sixth World Congress of the Communist International adopted a new program embodying, on the whole, the radical policy which World Communism followed during what the program called "a partial stabilization of capitalist relations," which "can be only a partial, transient, and decaying stabilization."

The program also contained a reference, ominous in the light of later developments, to the "fascist role" which Social Democracy was alleged to play often "in periods when the situation is critical for capitalism." This did not seem to have any deeper meaning at the time since, as we shall see, similar allusions had been made in the past without any consequences for Communist party strategy. The program went on to state that "throughout the entire prerevolutionary period a most important basic part of the tactics of the Communist parties is the tactic of the United Front, as a means toward a most successful struggle against capital, towards the class mobilization of the masses, and the exposure and isolation of the Reformist leaders."

A year later, however, the term "social-fascism" became the main slogan of Communist propaganda, marking the transition from the Second to the Third Period of Communist strategy. After the years from 1917 to 1922–23, which were devoted to direct revolutionary struggle, and the second period of "temporary stabilization," the Comintern proclaimed that a new period had begun, one characterized by the assertion that Social Democracy had become an ally of fascism.

The term "social-fascist" to designate alleged Socialist support of fascism was invented by Zinoviev, the president of the Comintern, as early as 1924, just a year after the German crisis of 1923. Anxious to explain why this last opportunity for a Communist victory had passed, he accused the Social Democrats of being fascists. "Ten years ago we had opportunists," Zinoviev wrote in a pamphlet, *Lessons of the German Events,* "but could we say that they were Fascist Social-Democrats? No. It would have been absurd to say it then. Now, however, they are fascists. . . . The international Social Democracy has now become a wing of fascism." Shortly afterwards Stalin took the cue in stating: "Fascism is a fighting organization of the bourgeoisie dependent upon the active support of Social Democracy. Objectively, Social Democracy is the moderate wing of fascism." [4]

These, however, were but expressions of a passing temper, and they did not prevent the Comintern from embarking upon its policy of a United Front with the very same Social Democrats whom Zinoviev and Stalin had branded as fascists. But four years later, the Comintern adopted the slogan "social-fascism" officially and used it for several years. It became the dominant theme of Communist policy after the Comintern declared that the "provisional stability" of capitalism had come to an end.

The most official definition of the term "social-fascism" was given in a statement of the Executive Committee of the Comintern in July, 1929: "In countries where there are strong Social Democratic parties, fascism assumes the particular form of social fascism, which to an ever-increasing extent serves the bourgeoisie as an instrument for paralyzing the activity of the masses in the struggle against the regime of fascist dictatorship. By means of this monstrous system of political and economic oppression, the bour-

[4] *International Press Correspondence.* Vol. 4, Oct. 9, 1924.

geoisie, aided and abetted by international Social Democracy, has been attempting to crush the revolutionary class movement of the proletariat for many years." Even the Socialist left wingers were not excluded from this sweeping condemnation. On the contrary, the Communist parties were asked to pay "special attention to an energetic struggle against the 'left wing' of Social Democracy, which retards the process of disintegration of Social Democracy by creating the illusion that it—the left wing—represents an opposition to the policy of the leading Social Democratic bodies, whereas, as a matter of fact, it whole-heartedly supports the policy of social-fascism."

It was hard to explain at the time, why the Social Democrats, in the very recent past potential partners for United Front alliances, suddenly had become fascists themselves and thus part of that force against which the United Front was supposedly directed. There was no change in the character of Social Democracy between 1927 and 1929, for instance. What had been altered was the policy of the Soviet Union, which was embarking upon the First Five Year Plan. This implied a drastic turn toward the left on the part of the Soviet government and of the Communist party of the Soviet Union, a revision of what was left of the concessions made to the peasantry during the New Economic Policy, and a sharpening of the terror. Stalin began his offensive against the right wingers in the Comintern, and Bukharin, one of their leaders and in 1928 president of the Comintern, was forced to resign from his post. The sudden turn of the Comintern in 1929 toward more extremist policies and slogans was apparently a reflection of the change toward the left in Soviet Russia's domestic policy. It was also, as will be remembered, part of the bargain by which Stalin "appeased" the Radicals in the Comintern.

The world crisis, beginning late in 1929, came to the rescue of Communist theory and belatedly presented it with a justification of what had already happened. The economic breakdown, although it did not explain the preceding Communist turn toward extremist policies, gave it apparent reasonableness. The violent Communist attacks upon Social Democracy and trade-union leaders now corresponded to the temper of desperate unemployed.

Communist parties in several countries, especially in Germany, succeeded in winning new recruits among the jobless workers. But the absurd extremism of the Communists, their renewed efforts to split the unions, wrought havoc with Communist influence among the employed workers. If here and there the Communists made inroads into the ranks of middle-class parties, owing to widespread bankruptcy among lower middle-class groups and peasants, such gains were very small. As a whole, Communist influence increased somewhat with unemployment—except for Britain, where the Communist party remained weak, although the Labour party was an easy target for Communist propaganda during the lifetime of the second Labour government.

Communist policy during the Third Period expressed Radical supremacy over Leninism. Defeated within the Communist International when that organization under Lenin's leadership adopted the more moderate policies of the Second Period, the Radicals were in opposition to Comintern leadership throughout the Second Period. The turn toward the extremist slogans and revolutionary inactivity of the Third Period enabled the Radicals to stage their come-back. The combination of the extremist slogans with Communist inability to carry out threats and promises corresponded to pre-war Radical ways of thinking and talking, and to Radical inactivity. Under the Third Period policies, the Comintern put its seal belatedly upon pre-war Radicalism.

In their practical policies the Communists were even more orthodox than most Socialists. Whenever Communists stooped to discuss concrete measures to overcome the crisis, they supported extreme laissez faire conceptions. If it was a matter of balancing the budget or reducing a budget deficit, the Communists would not question the purpose itself, but would instead concentrate upon their slogan "Tax the Rich!" When monetary manipulations were suggested, the Communists, clinging to stubborn orthodoxy, would describe any departure from the gold standard as a capitalist swindle to exploit the poor. Although they defended themselves against "charges" of being free traders, Communists held that tariffs were merely designed to enrich the propertied classes at the expense of the poor. As partners of the French Popular Front, the

Communists did their best to delay Blum's policy of recovery by attacking any deviation from orthodox laissez faire practice. The main Communist contribution to the everyday struggle of the working class was thus a strengthening of laissez faire, together with an almost ridiculous outbidding of Socialist demands in favor of workers and unemployed.

In their innermost hearts the Communists were full of contempt for efforts to overcome the crisis "within the framework of capitalism," since only a proletarian revolution could achieve new prosperity. If such a revolution should not intervene in time, capitalism would fall into a permanent crisis, accompanied by "nothing but the gradual decay and eventual ruin of human society," according to John Strachey.[5] Eugen Varga,[6] another leading Communist theoretician, wrote at a late stage of the crisis,

> In recent years the economic prerequisites for the revolutionary collapse of capitalism have developed by leaps and bounds. . . . The same causes that entail the particular nature of the present depression also determine the future course of capitalist economy. The general crisis of capitalism, the end of temporary stabilization, and the ensuing aggravation of imperialist and class contradictions, as well as the general instability of all relations, will produce another and still greater deformation of the industrial cycle. Except for a few countries, perhaps, the present depression will drag on for many years, with brief booms and sharp relapses, without passing into a period of prosperity, and finally it will be succeeded by a new deeper and more devastating economic crisis. . . . Such would be the outlook if the outbreak of a world war and outbreak of a proletarian revolution were delayed for many years to come. This, however, is highly improbable.

True Radicals, the Communists did nothing to prepare a proletarian uprising. Throughout the whole Third Period, the Comintern made not a single serious effort to use the economic crisis for a revolt.

Their extremism, in addition, prevented them from establishing contact with the Social Democratic masses. Since the Socialist leaders were now considered fascists, no United Front was possible

[5] John Strachey, *The Nature of Capitalist Crisis.* New York, Covici Friede, 1935, p. 387.

[6] Eugen Varga, *The Great Crisis and Its Political Consequences; Economics and Politics. 1928–1934.* New York, International Publishers, 1935, pp. 79–80.

with them. Skillfully masquerading as a labor party, the Socialists prevented sincerely revolutionary workers from joining the Communist ranks, the Communists claimed; without Social Democracy, the fascist bourgeoisie could not permanently hold down the working class. The Social Democrats, not the fascists, were the main enemy of the Communists.

In actual practice, this philosophy led to an alliance, precarious and involuntary, but nevertheless often effective, between Communists and Nazis. In the spring of 1931 the Communists joined the Nazis in a plebiscite against the Socialist-led Prussian government. Nazis and Communists together led a large strike of the streetcar employees in Berlin against the wishes of the trade-union leadership, late in 1932, at a time when only the Nazis could profit from unrest. This Nazi-Communist relationship of the Third Period was a repetition on a larger scale of short-lived Communist-Nationalist coöperation in Germany in 1923, and similar to that inaugurated again in 1939. Undoubtedly, the Communists in 1931 believed that they would be the final victors, once Nazism had destroyed German democracy. But it was Hitlerism, not Communism, that emerged victorious out of the overthrow of the German Republic.

The following chapters describe Socialist and Communist attitudes and actions with regard to the great depression. The British, German, and French examples of unsuccessful efforts to cope with the consequences of the crisis and the successful Swedish example will, it is hoped, demonstrate the correctness of the preceding analysis.

Chapter 8

BRITISH LABOR BLUNDERS THROUGH

I.

THE election platform of the British Labour party is "the most fantastic and impracticable program ever put before the electorate. . . . It is Bolshevism run mad."

It was no Tory who pronounced this verdict, but Philip Snowden in a speech broadcast to the British public on October 17, 1931, less than two months after he and Ramsay MacDonald had broken up the second British Labour government and formed the first "National" cabinet. After having helped to build the political representation of the British working class, Snowden now devoted all his energy and his acrimonious wit to the task of destroying the Labour party. He did not succeed entirely, but although the party survived the desperate struggle of October, 1931, it was terribly weakened. From the 287 seats which the Labour party had held in the House of Commons as a result of the 1929 election, its representation now sank to a mere handful of 52 seats. This defeat was due not alone to the fact that MacDonald and Snowden broke with the party and took the lead in the fight against it. Far more important, the second Labour government had patently failed to solve the economic crisis, a failure directly attributable to the policies of Snowden, though afterwards he tried to pin the responsibility on his former colleagues.

The formation of British Labour's second government in June, 1929, coincided with the peak of world-wide post-war prosperity. Alone of all major powers, England seemed unable to share in the growth of the world's wealth. Under the Conservative government of Stanley Baldwin unemployment had continued to be high, never falling below the million mark. While the United States developed the greatest boom in history, England remained a country of industrial depression even though backwashes of America's prosperity were felt in a small degree.

To give England its share of the world's economic advances, labor pledged itself to a policy of monetary expansion which was to supersede the deflationary policy followed by Britain with little interruption since the early twenties.

This was the background for the victory of the Labour party at the general elections of 1929, the greatest election victory it ever obtained. Yet even with 287 seats out of a total of 615, the party still depended upon the support of at least some of the Liberal members, many of whom had borrowed copiously of the Labour party's slogans during the election campaign.

To understand Labour's policy during its second government, it is necessary to be aware of the evolution that had led the party into power and made MacDonald the undisputed master of the movement.

2.

In 1918, British Labour had adopted a Socialist program for the first time. After the cataclysm of the war, formerly conservative union leaders had come to accept Sidney Webb's program "Labour and the New Social Order." [1] In this statement Webb announced the final collapse of capitalist civilization and the advent of a new social system based upon the democratic control of industry. This new system was described "as a thing that would emerge gradually out of capitalism, by a series of piecemeal changes."

In 1918, this program expressed no more than a hope. The Labour party was still weak, the third party in size after the Conservative and Liberal, and the "patriotic rage" at the end of the war had weakened whatever influence the small labor group in

[1] A study of the Webbs by G. D. H. Cole in *Persons and Periods*. London, Macmillan, 1938. Cf. particularly pp. 116–37.

Parliament might have exerted in normal times. The main weapon of the movement was thus the industrial organization of labor, for trade-union membership had considerably grown at the end of the war. Several of the unions were under a leftist leadership. The workers were discontented because they felt deceived by Prime Minister Lloyd George. During the war labor had abandoned its trade-union rights to strengthen the fighting forces; he had promised to restore these rights after the armistice, but the workers claimed that he failed to keep this promise.

Thus, in 1920 when Britain began to embark upon a deflationist policy to restore the depreciated currency to its pre-war parity with the dollar and a general attack upon wages developed, the unions were in the forefront of the struggle. The conflict centered in the coal mines, England's main war casualty.

The miners were "at war" practically from the very day the World War ended. Under the threat of strike, the government appointed the Sankey Commission early in 1919. In an interim report presented soon afterwards the commission recommended a reduction of hours to seven, wage increases of two shillings (about fifty cents), and restriction of the price of coal. More important for future developments than these recommendations was Sir John Sankey's statement that "even upon the evidence already given, the present system of ownership and working in the coal industry stands condemned, and some other system must be substituted for it, either nationalization or a measure of unification by national purchase." The commission was also "prepared to report now that it is in the interest of the country that the colliery workers shall in the future have an effective voice in the direction of the mines." Subsequently, at the request of the miners, the government declared in a written statement by Bonar Law, that it was "prepared to carry out in the spirit and in the letter the recommendations of Sir John Sankey's report."

In exchange for this solemn promise, the miners abandoned their strike preparations; but just as soon as this threat was removed, Lloyd George announced in the House of Commons that Justice Sankey's recommendation of public ownership could not be accepted by the government. This the workers regarded as another breach of a pledge and it had a long-lasting effect—being a remote cause of the general strike in 1926.

A struggle was inevitable under the circumstances. The miners felt prepared for one, since shortly before the war three big unions, the miners, the railway men, and the transport workers, had concluded an agreement for common action. When, early in 1921, the miners were again threatened by a general wage cut, the railway men and transport workers promised their support to stave off what they realized was the prologue to an all-round offensive against wages. The miners, however, not only fought to defend their wages, but raised additional demands for a national pool of coal-mine earnings to equalize conditions among the different mining districts, and for a national agreement. In the opinion of old-fashioned union leaders, imbued with the pressure-group ideology, these latter demands were political, rather than economic. Many railway and transport workers' leaders were hesitant to commit themselves to strike action for what they regarded as political objectives. Their lack of enthusiasm for the proposed strike was accentuated by the fact that they had had no voice in the establishment of these demands. To complete the confusion, conflicts broke out among the miners themselves; many violently opposed the apparent willingness of the miners' secretary, Frank Hodges, to compromise on the profit-pool issue. The railway and transport union leaders interpreted his attitude as relieving them from their promise of coöperation. On Friday, April 15, 1921, J. H. Thomas, the railway men's leader, called off the sympathetic strike which had been arranged for that day. The transport workers joined the railway men in their refusal to cease work. The "Triple Alliance" broke down completely. Alone, the miners were easily defeated. "Black Friday," as the day of the collapse of the Triple Alliance came to be known, ushered in a period of economic retreat for British labor. Wage cuts and trade-union defeats rapidly ensued.

On the political front it was a different story: the labor movement made swift headway. In the general election of November, 1922, that resulted from the breakdown of the Lloyd George coalition, the Labour party gained 67 seats, returning 142 members strong to the House of Commons. As the second party in size—the

Liberals were relegated to third rank—the Labour party became the official opposition. By a narrow majority the Parliamentary Labour party elected MacDonald its leader. His opponent, J. R. Clynes, became deputy leader. MacDonald was supported by the left wing of the party, and the divisions of the war years when MacDonald headed the pacifist opponents of the pro-war party leaders were forgotten.

The Labour party, although the official opposition and thus, according to British tradition, the "alternative government," hardly expected to be called upon soon to form a government in view of the huge parliamentary majority of Stanley Baldwin's Conservative party. In November, 1923, however, Baldwin suddenly decided to appeal to the country for a mandate to introduce a protective tariff as a remedy for unemployment. The Labour party again increased its representation from 142 to 191 seats at the general elections, while the Conservatives lost heavily. Together with the Liberals, Labour now held a majority in the House of Commons, but no single party was able to form an independent majority. When the Liberals decided to vote against the Conservatives, Mr. Baldwin was forced to resign.

For the first time in its history, the British Labour party was called upon to form a government. Less than four years before Winston Churchill had denied, in utter contempt, that labor was "fit to govern." By now Ramsay MacDonald was again the leading figure in British labor, and the Labour party represented nearly all sections of the working class which stood for independent political action. The opposition on the left of labor was impotent. The British Communist party was a small faction, with no influence upon the body of the organized British workers. The Communist party had been formed out of the remnants of the Shop Stewards movement, an unofficial trade-union group, which originated in the Clyde metal industries during the war. Under the influence of American "industrial unionism" and of the idea of "One Big Union," the Shop Stewards opposed the narrow craft structure of the existing engineering unions, but their movement petered out within a few months after the end of the war, most of its leaders joining the newly formed Communist party of Great Britain. Another group from which the Communists recruited members was the British Socialist party, one of the several Socialist propaganda societies within the British Labour party.

The most important Socialist body within the Labour party was the Independent Labour party (I.L.P.), to which MacDonald and Snowden, the leaders of the Labour party, belonged. Until the end of the war the I.L.P. was no more than a propaganda agency to spread Socialist ideas among the members of the larger organization. Since the Labour party itself was composed exclusively of organizations and refused to accept individual membership until the end of the war, the various affiliated societies offered the only possible means of entrance into the movement to those ineligible for trade-union membership. After the war the Labour party adopted a new constitution which enabled individual members to join local labor parties, thereby causing the Socialist societies to lose part of their reason for existence. Under these new conditions, the I.L.P. began to develop into an organized faction within the Labour party, promoting not only general Socialist ideas but also definite tactical concepts.

When in January, 1924, the first Labour government was formed, the I.L.P. argued that a parliamentary defeat over an issue of great social significance would be better than to govern for a long time while sacrificing the Labour party's Socialist aims. Such a defeat would offer a splendid opportunity to bring basic Socialist issues before the electorate, the I.L.P. stated, through an election which would, for the first time, be fought over the issue of "Capitalism versus Socialism." In this situation, the I.L.P. said, the Labour party platform would become known to everyone in England, and a propaganda campaign under such conditions might succeed where normal party work had failed in the past. In short, the I.L.P. believed that the parliamentary "accident" which had put the Labour party in office should be used to prepare for another Labour government, based upon a Socialist majority in the House of Commons, rather than to carry out only those proposals which the Liberals would tolerate.

Ramsay MacDonald and a huge majority of the party leadership rejected such a policy. Wishing to prove that labor was as capable of governing as were those classes which so far had a monopoly in the government, they wanted not propaganda but action. Since the government depended upon Liberal support, MacDonald's plan was to realize a number of progressive measures which the Liberals were prepared to accept. Labor's policy should be based, MacDonald believed, upon gradual progress by education. Labor's success in government would be its best means of education; moreover MacDonald was convinced that neither the working class, nor conditions in general, were ripe for the attainment of a Socialist order. In a speech at Dundee in September, 1924, MacDonald revealed his basic belief that socialism was a far-away dream. Even were he to be prime minister for fifty years, MacDonald said, "the pledge I have given you from my heart would still be unfulfilled . . . not because I fainted or failed, but because the corn was still green.[2] Other party leaders feared that a bold Socialist policy might lead to an alliance between Conservatives and Liberals which would keep the Labour party out of office for an indefinite period.

MacDonald's tactics inevitably produced modest results. As a matter of fact, in view of its brief lifetime and its difficulties in controlling the House of Commons, the first Labour government achieved all that it possibly could do from the point of view of Ramsay MacDonald and his followers. But to those who expected more than modest social reforms, the first Labour government in Britain was a bitter disappointment. Labour behaved like nothing more than a moderate working-class wing of British Liberalism.

Whatever the judgment about the accomplishments of the British Labour government, there can be no doubt that its end was disappointing. In October, 1924, the government started proceedings against J. R. Campbell, editor of the Communist *Workers Weekly*. Suddenly the case was dropped. Since at the time trade negotiations were under way with the Soviet government, the opposition parties succeeded in creating the suspicion that some connection existed between these negotiations and the suspension of the suit against Campbell. Liberals and Conservatives jointly voted

[2] London *Times*, Sept. 10, 1924.

against the government, which they accused of having interfered with justice; although this was not a major defeat, MacDonald dissolved the House.

This by itself was unfortunate enough, from the Labour party's point of view, for the issue over which the election was bound to be fought offered little opportunity for expounding the Socialist program before the country. Ramsay MacDonald increasingly resented the Liberal party's hold on the government and used the first pretext to arrange for general elections. He entertained the not unjustified hope that the Liberals would be the main losers and Labour become the heir to the Liberal party. Very likely, also, the prime minister foresaw defeat over his plan for government guarantee of a British loan to Russia and merely anticipated the unavoidable dissolution.

In the course of the election campaign an incident gave tremendous impetus to the Conservative onslaught. On October 10, the British Secret Service submitted to the Foreign Office a secret letter allegedly written by Zinoviev (the president of the Communist International) giving instructions on anti-militarist propaganda to the British Communists. There is hardly any doubt today that the so-called "Red Letter" was a forgery more or less deliberately accepted by a leading official of the Foreign Office, but at that time public opinion considered the letter genuine. The publication of the "Zinoviev letter," which somehow found its way from the government offices to the conservative *Daily Mail* five days before the polling date, caused great excitement, and MacDonald added fuel to the fire. Torn, apparently, between conflicting loyalties to his party and to the officials of his department, he remained "mysterious and equivocal."

The Bolshevik scare created by the "Red Letter" sent hundreds of thousands of frightened people to the polling booths who might otherwise not have voted, and they voted against Labour; still, the party increased its vote by a million, though it lost 42 seats. MacDonald's hopes came true, for the Liberals were almost wiped out, losing 119 out of their 158 seats. The middle-class vote concentrated upon the Conservatives, who returned a huge majority over the Labour and Liberal Parties combined. From now on, however, Labour was definitely established as the normal alternative to Conservative rule, and the right honorable ex-cabinet ministers of the first Labour regime sat on the front benches opposite the government leaders.

Disappointed by the results of political action, labor turned its principal attention once again toward the trade-union movement. Industrial action was taken up as the weapon to express labor's increased power and prestige. As in the past, the coal industry was the focal point of the conflict, and after their partial eclipse the leftist union leaders came once more to the fore. Under their direction, British labor carried through its first general strike in modern history.

3.

At midnight on May 3, 1926, three million British workers struck.

Conservative Prime Minister Baldwin branded the strike a revolutionary undertaking. "Constitutional Government is being attacked," he wrote in the *British Gazette* of May 6, the government newspaper printed by strikebreakers. "The General Strike is a challenge to Parliament and is the road to anarchy and ruin." For the strike leaders and the workers themselves, however, the demonstration was only an industrial weapon lacking in political objective. It was a matter of giving the miners "a square deal," of settling an old industrial dispute, and of supporting the miners' demands. Nothing was further from the mind of the strike leaders and the great mass of organized workers than the idea of revolution. Apart from the three or four thousand members of the Communist party and those affiliated with its various subsidiary organizations, no one among the strikers raised any political demands during the strike. But Conservative die-hards who controlled the government—among them Winston Churchill—regarded the general strike as a decisive struggle between middle-class democracy and the forces of revolution.

The government used every means in its power to break the strike and to stave off "the threatening victory of revolutionary forces." The strike leaders for their part carefully avoided any action that might have given basis to the government's accusation of "unconstitutional conduct." One side was fighting with its gloves off, the other, the workers, respected law and order. Under such conditions the defeat of the strike was inevitable from the outset.

As one looks back upon the strike, it must be admitted that even if both sides had considered the struggle as merely an industrial dispute, the miners' cause was doomed. The coal industry was hardly able to fulfill the workers' demands which the ardent new miners' secretary, Arthur H. Cook, summarized in an effective slogan: "Not a penny off the pay, not a minute on the day!" A reduction in wages seemed inevitable as early as 1925, when profits throughout the industry fell sharply, but it failed to materialize because the unions were in a militant mood and the employers felt unprepared for any decisive action. The General Council of the Trade Union Congress, the newly created central body of the trade-union movement, made the miners' struggle its own, and the all important transport unions prepared plans for a general refusal to handle coal in the event of a stoppage in the mines. When the employers remained adamant, instructions were actually issued to stop transporting coal on July 31, 1925. Confronted with this threat, the government intervened by announcing that it would pay a subsidy to the mineowners to enable them to continue existing wages until May 1, 1926. A royal commission under Sir Herbert Samuel was set up to investigate the economic condition of the industry.

This was a trade-union victory, but it was temporary. Government subsidies could not be a lasting solution. Between the industry's inability to maintain wages and the miners' refusal to accept a wage cut or an increase in hours of work, deadlock seemed inevitable. The crux of the problem was Britain's monetary policy. As long as it remained what it was the issue was circumscribed between the owners' losses and the miners' refusal to bear the burden of their industry's crisis.

Not that the monetary policy was the only cause of the trouble in the coal industry. Readjustments were made necessary by other factors as well, such as the backwardness of the mining industry, technological changes, and the advance of competitors on the Continent. These problems would have existed whatever Britain's monetary policy might have been, but the main trouble was the overvalued currency. When Britain returned to the gold standard in 1925, at the pre-war exchange rate between pound sterling and dollar, British export prices were above the world market level. In other words either the currency had to be devalued or export prices be reduced to enable Britain to resume her export trade. A devaluation was rejected, and a general price reduction involving a reduction of wages was thus inevitable. The real enemy of the workers was not the employers, who under the circumstances had no alternative but to cut wages. The real foe was the government's monetary policy, but the most labor expected from the government was a subsidy for the miners. The coal problem was essentially a political problem and could not be solved by pressure-group methods.

The labor movement, unfortunately, did not realize this fact. Labor leaders had protested against undue haste in returning to the pre-war gold parity, but never against the concept of such a return. In 1925, when Winston Churchill was chancellor of the exchequer, Philip Snowden stated in the House of Commons that "a return to the gold standard *with undue precipitancy* may aggravate the existing grave condition of employment and trade depreciation," but against the objective of the government's policy no voice was raised in the ranks of labor. The return to the prewar gold parity was part of the general desire to return to the prewar conditions which were identified with normalcy rather than to build a new English economic structure adjusted to the post-war world. Even labor followed this trend.

This lack of a constructive spirit was one of the main causes of Labour's defeat in 1926. It was to be instrumental in the catastrophe of 1931.

4.

"The miners are elated at what they regard as a great victory," reported the New York *Times* on August 1, 1925. The entire trade-union movement, that had backed the miners, this time without reservation, felt that the struggle in the coal industry was the key to the entire industrial situation. The success of the strike threat and the progress of the Labour party at a series of by-elections increased the British workers' self-confidence. Miners' Secretary Cook proudly asserted that the movement had "already beaten, not only the employers, but the strongest Government in modern times." [3]

Undoubtedly labor had defeated the government, but it had merely won a single battle. All labor had obtained was a nine-months truce which the workers used to far less advantage than their opponents. The government prepared a scheme for road transport and food distribution in case of a general strike; a private "Organization for the Maintenance of Supplies" was set up to aid the government; and a small fascist organization sprang into existence, led by army officers and patronized by the home secretary, Sir William Joynson-Hicks. The Trade Union Congress, for its part, neglected to make any elaborate preparations for the impending struggle. Many unions refused to surrender permanently their autonomous rights to a central authority which would lead a general movement. Surprisingly enough, the miners were foremost in delaying preparations.

Sir Herbert Samuel was known as an opponent of the nationalization of the coal industry, yet the facts obliged the Royal Coal Commission to stress the need for a reorganization of the industry. On the other hand, the commission recommended a "temporary sacrifice by the men in the industry" in the form of a wage cut. No increase was to be made in the hours of work and the national agreement was to be maintained.

This report satisfied neither side. The owners demanded district agreements, and the workers refused a wage cut. Prime Minister Baldwin declared the government was willing to accept the report, provided mine owners and workers did the same. Frank Hodges, former British miners' secretary, and later filling a similar post for the International Federation of Miners' Unions, welcomed the report, but among the miners his voice was a cry in the wilderness.

[3] Crook, *The General Strike*. Chapel Hill, University of North Carolina Press, 1931, p. 368.

The Communists in control of the so-called Minority Movement in the unions branded the report an effort to split labor and to induce the Reformists to give up the fight. Although Miners' Secretary Cook was closely associated with the Minority Movement, its influence on trade-union leadership was not very great. As a matter of fact, the leaders of the Trade Union Congress thought that a compromise might be possible on the basis of the report, and the Prime Minister actually encouraged the resumption of negotiations. He suggested that negotiations be carried on in the presence of third parties, a proposal which the owners rejected. Instead of publicly criticizing the mineowners for their refusal to negotiate, Baldwin more and more openly took their side against the workers, whom he asked to accept the principle of a wage cut as a preliminary to opening negotiations. It was obvious that the Conservatives desired a showdown.

Against their wishes the right-wing trade-union leaders were thus forced into consenting to issuance of the call for a general strike for May 3. J. H. Thomas and his right-wing friends were apparently more fearful of a victorious strike than of a serious "negotiated" defeat.

In the interim until May 3, the General Council continued its desperate efforts to start negotiations. Success in these endeavors seemed in sight when an unauthorized strike broke out on the ultra-Conservative London *Daily Mail,* the printers refusing to set up a leading article describing all who supported the miners as revolutionaries. Without inquiring whether the General Council was responsible for the strike or had even endorsed it, Baldwin used this pretext to break off negotiations unless the general strike scheduled for the night of May 3 was unconditionally abandoned.

No alternative was left to the disappointed union leaders than to enforce their threat to call out the workers. Even the Communists were surprised that a general strike was to be called. As late as April 30, the Communists demanded merely an embargo on coal and a stoppage of the "lying capitalist press."

5.

On Tuesday, May 4, 1926, London woke up to find its economic life crippled, its traffic paralyzed, and its supplies threatened. Although labeled a general strike, the walk-out was far from being universal. The General Council had called out only the "first line" of the labor forces, the railwaymen and transport workers, plus the printers, builders, and iron and steel workers—these last so that the transport men would not complain of having always to bear the brunt of the battle alone. The main purpose was to prevent transportation and a few key industries from functioning and to stop the newspapers, which were almost unanimous in their hostility to the workers. Owing to the intricate structure of many craft unions and to the lack of preparations, mistakes were unavoidable in the management of the strike. Men were called out needlessly, and the stopping of the press, giving substance to government accusations that the workers were threatening constitutional rights, was regarded later by most people as a bad error. Moreover, the official paper of the General Council, the *British Worker,* had difficulties in reaching the union members out in the country, while the government effectively used radio broadcasting and succeeded in bringing out its own paper, the *British Gazette,* dedicated exclusively to a campaign against the strikers.

The response to the strike call was excellent, and the completeness of the stoppage came as a surprise both to the government and to the strike leaders. In spite of preliminary confusion, the unions soon improvised an effective machinery of coördination. There were few defections, and although their number increased toward the end of the "Nine Days," they had little significance. The failure of the strike was due to its lack of clear-cut objective, rather than to lack of enthusiasm on the part of the workers. The strike leaders defended themselves continuously against the standing government attack that "they were threatening the basis of ordered government, and going nearer to proclaiming civil war than we have been for centuries past." [4] Nothing was further from the minds

[4] Baldwin in the House of Commons, May 3.

of the strike leaders than revolutionary plans, but nevertheless many middle-class people were frightened into believing the government accusations and the charge that the unions were actually running the country wherever their power reached..

Since the strike leaders had no wish to overthrow the government, the only chance of success for the strike was a weakening on the part of the government. But how could the government compromise on an issue as fundamental as the Constitution? After having spread the idea that the government was struggling to avert the danger of "some Soviet of trade unions" [5] being set up, the government leaders, unless threatened by revolution, could hardly be expected to meet the prospective members of the "British Soviet Government" half-way. Without a compromise, the strike could be won only by deliberately doing the very thing the government falsely accused the strikers of plotting, namely, using revolutionary methods. As long as the strike lasted, the possibility existed that the strikers might realize the dilemma with which they were confronted, and prefer revolution to capitulation. The strike leaders, however, would never have agreed to revolutionary methods, and they called off the strike, hopeless from their point of view, as soon as it became clear that no compromise could be expected. J. H. Thomas hinted at the revolutionary potentiality of the general strike when he said in the House of Commons on May 13, the day after the official end of the strike: "What I dreaded about this strike more than anything else was this: If by any chance it should have got out of the hands of those who would be able to exercise some control, every sane man knows what would have happened. I thank God it never did."

The government was determined to score a complete victory. During the walkout thousands of special constables were armed, and the emergency service for the transport of food supplies was organized. For the rest, the government waited patiently for the strike leaders to realize the inner contradiction between their real aims and what Sir John Simon called "the perfectly obvious consequences of what they deliberately do." [6]

Relations between the leading men of the General Council and

[5] Winston Churchill in the House of Commons, May 3.

[6] Sir John Simon, Three speeches on the general strike, Crook, *op. cit.*, p. 401.

the miners soon became strained. The council was anxious to escape by some compromise from its dilemma of either capitulating or heading for revolutionary action. The miners clung to their old formula of rejecting any concession. Sir Herbert Samuel, the chairman of the Royal Coal Commission, finally enabled the General Council to find a way out. He suggested a compromise on terms better than those embodied in the original report of his commission, but still involving large sacrifices for the miners. The General Council believed—or pretended to believe—that Sir Herbert was speaking on behalf of the government, or at least with its consent, although Samuel had made it clear that he was acting without official status.

The miners rejected the proposal, unwisely, since by now it should have been clear to them that the General Council had decided to end the strike at almost any price. Without special authorization from their rank and file, the miners' leaders stated, they could not depart from their original attitude.

On May 11 the General Council abandoned the general strike, nine days after it started. To follow the miners "in a policy of mere negation," a General Council report said afterwards, would have caused "the splendid response of the sympathetic strike to evaporate by a process of attrition, which would have brought the unions to a position of bankruptcy, would have undermined the morale of their membership. . . . The Council was satisfied that, however long they continued the strike, they would still be in the same position as far as the attitude of the Miners' Executive was concerned, and consequently the Council was not justified in permitting the unions to continue the sacrifice for another day."

In the country the sudden and unexpected order to resume work caused confusion, bewilderment, and, in some cases, despair. The General Council asserted that the Samuel Memorandum had served as a basis for the settlement, but the government refused to consider itself bound by that document. There was an almost general resumption of the strike when the workers found that their leaders had failed to obtain guarantees; this resulted in the refusal of some companies to rehire a number of strikers, and individual settlements had to be worked out to end a series of new strikes. When everything was over, it was realized that the general strike had ended in failure and that, contrary to the first announcements of the General Council, the miners had not agreed to ending the strike. Once again they were left to themselves.

The mining strike actually dragged on for more than six months. Although it was clear that the strike was futile, the miners continued in dogged determination until by November they were starved into submission. They were forced to accept terms far worse than those of the Samuel Memorandum, or even of the original Samuel Report. The general strike and the miners' strike thus ended in utter defeat.

6.

"The General Strike is a weapon that cannot be wielded for industrial purposes. It is clumsy and ineffectual. It has no goal which when reached can be regarded as victory. If fought to a finish as a strike, it would ruin trade unionism, and the Government in the meantime would create a revolution; if fought to a finish only as a means to an end, the men responsible for decisions will be charged with betrayal." [7] Thus wrote James Ramsay MacDonald after the strike.

Following the defeat, the right-wing leaders gained full control of the entire labor movement. MacDonald and Henderson led the Labour party; J. H. Thomas, Walter Citrine, and their friends, the trade unions. Ernest Bevin of the Transport Workers was perhaps the outstanding exception. Although by no means a left winger in 1926, he was open-minded, maintaining contact with Socialist intellectuals whom the right wingers considered anathema. C. T. Cramp, a railway men's leader, drew the lesson from the defeat that never again would British labor engage upon such a venture. Although the rank and file's first reaction to their leaders' capitulation was unrestrained criticism, during which the Communists made inroads into Labour party ranks, the leaders themselves were determined to reject extreme policies forever after.

[7] *Socialist Review,* June, 1926.

Walter Citrine (later Sir Walter) who was elected secretary general of the Trade Union Congress in 1925, defined the new trade-union policy by stating that the unions were "concerned with the prosperity of industry," and demanded to have a voice as to the way industry is carried on so that "it [the trade-union movement] can influence the new developments that are taking place." He contrasted this policy of active coöperation with deliberate striving to bring about a revolutionary situation on one hand, and passive "standing aside," on the other.[8] Citrine, one of the coming men of the movement, well expressed the majority's point of view. They refused to follow the Communists' revolutionary slogans or to accept the Radicals' pseudo-revolutionary passivity. But Citrine's policy was not real reformism, for in his view it was a matter of the unions "influencing" decisions and not of realizing them themselves. Thus the unions felt and acted precisely as a pressure group.

Government vengeance for the strike was severe. The Trade Dispute and Trade Unions Bill of 1927 declared sympathetic strikes to be illegal, along with other strikes "designed or calculated to coerce the Government either directly or by inflicting hardship upon the community." The bill also restricted picketing, excluded government officials from unions connected with non-government employees, and severely reduced union contributions to the Labour party.

The right-wing victory within the movement found its expression in anti-Communist measures. The Labour party had rejected demands of the Communist party for affiliation with Labour and, subsequently, the unions had been asked not to send as delegates to Labour party conferences known supporters of parties ineligible for affiliation with Labour. Within the trade-union movement, as differentiated from the political party, Communist influences had still persisted. After 1926, however, most unions joined in the party's anti-Communist drive, warning British labor against taking part in Communist inspired United Front organizations.

Much of this was part of a necessary process to develop the Labour party from a loose federation of individual and autonomous organi-

[8] Annual Report to the T.U.C. for 1928.

zations into a well-disciplined party, with at least a basic common denominator of outlook. Since this process occurred under right-wing leaders, it was inevitably directed against the leftists.

The defeat of the general strike thus enhanced MacDonald's and Snowden's hold over the movement. They were in complete control by 1929, when Labour for the second time took over the government.

7.

A slight upward swing in business conditions, coinciding with the Labour government's entrance to office, permitted the enactment of a few measures of social reform. While still low, the national income was rising, thereby making available larger funds for social policies without an undue reduction in business profits. But this heyday was not to last for long. By the fall of 1929 the world crisis set in, and outside influences, instead of alleviating the particular British post-war depression, now accentuated it.

From the outset the government was impaired by the fact that any expansionist economic policy was bound to endanger the stability of the currency in terms of gold. The same monetary problem that had led to the defeat of the general strike now threatened the Labour government. For, as a consequence of the overvaluation of the currency, the Bank of England was continuously threatened by a loss of gold. Even before 1929 this situation was becoming steadily worse as prices fell on the world markets. Any expansionist measures would have increased the passive balance of foreign trade by increasing imports and reducing exports. Such a strain would have been more than the currency could withstand. Thus, maintenance of the gold parity of the pound sterling implied the repudiation of the Labour party election platform, which contained promise of measures leading to business expansion. Under the conditions created by the world crisis, the defense of the gold parity indeed involved a deflationary policy totally excluding any large-scale scheme of public works.

When prices abroad began to fall, British industries found it increasingly difficult to compete with foreign industries abroad and even at home. Under free trade the price fall on the world markets was bound to depress British price levels and, consequently, British wages.

Thus, the government was permanently between what it considered the devil of "tampering with the currency" and the deep sea of deflation. Since the cabinet steadfastly refused to envisage abandoning the gold standard or a change in the gold parity of the pound, employers strove for cuts in wages and a reduction in taxation as their only means of competing in the world markets. Trade unions, on the contrary, regarded defense of the existing level of money wages as their main task, while some elements within the Labour party clamorously demanded increased public spending. But as long as wage rates and prices were maintained at high levels, cheaper foreign goods were bound to pour into the country, to force British goods out of their markets, and steadily to make more unfavorable the balance of trade. Yet Snowden, as chancellor of the exchequer, and the cabinet rejected any suggestion of introducing measures to protect at least the home markets.

Blocked both by its decision to protect the currency at almost any price and by the resistance of the working-class organizations to wholesale wage cuts, the government had little room for action. MacDonald and Snowden, pressed by their own supporters to carry out the election promise of far-reaching social reforms, while the business community urgently demanded reduction in taxation and consequent retrenchment in social policies, followed the line of least resistance and did nothing that mattered. The Labour government drifted aimlessly along until it was overpowered by the events of 1931.

8.

When James Ramsay MacDonald formed his second government, he entrusted the leader of the Railway Men's Union, J. H. Thomas, with the task of drafting the policy for the struggle against unemployment. Thomas was appointed lord privy seal, a title without departmental charge, and was to have the assistance of the first commissioner of works, George Lansbury, and of Sir Oswald Mosley, chancellor of the Duchy of Lancaster, another title without administrative responsibility. However, apart from certain small-scale proposals—drops in the bucket compared with the tremendous and growing size of the problem—this committee was unable to make any headway.

Much was done, on the other hand, to extend unemployment benefits to every unemployed person in the United Kingdom. This revision of the law unfortunately coincided with a rapid deterioration of the labor market. By 1930 the insurance fund was nearly one hundred million pounds in debt and was still borrowing. During a depression of unusual intensity and length such a combination of almost complete paralysis in the realm of economic policy and honest desire to alleviate the suffering of the unemployed was obviously destined to end in disaster.[9]

With the exception of the small group in James Maxton's Independent Labour Party (I.L.P.), the bulk of the Labour party patiently waited for the government's decisions with regard to unemployment policy. At the Labour party conference in October, 1929, four months after the cabinet had been formed, J. H. Thomas met with no serious criticism despite his failure to present any message of encouragement. The only sound remedy for unemployment, he said, was to be found in greater export trade, but how this could be substantially increased he failed to tell. As a matter of fact, the beginning world crisis not only prevented Britain from recovering foreign markets lost after the war but actually reduced British exports, particularly in manufactured goods.

By 1930, however, when conditions still showed no signs of improvement, the party began to grow restive. The conflict between the I.L.P. and MacDonald came to a head, and the Prime Minister resigned from the party in which he had been a member since 1894.

[9] "It [the Labour party] made the mistake in office of seeking to survive by accepting a Liberal tradition which was already obsolete. Under Mr. MacDonald's leadership, it sought merely to extend the boundaries of Social reform. When it made the treatment of the unemployed, instead of the reconstruction of industrial organisation, the pivot of its domestic policy, it was in grave danger of assuming that a mere policy of cash concessions to the underdog would suffice to win popularity for it. The election taught it how erroneous were its assumptions." Harold J. Laski, *The Crisis and the Constitution: 1931 and After*. Day to Day Pamphlets No. 9. London, the Hogarth Press, 1932, p. 42.

Soon afterwards Sir Oswald Mosley resigned from the government in protest against its lack of enterprise in the struggle against unemployment. Sir Oswald, together with Lansbury and Johnston, had drawn up a memorandum which suggested raising a huge loan for public works. Sound as this proposal was in itself, it was unacceptable unless a decision in favor of devaluation or exchange control was taken at the same time. The rejection of his proposal led directly to Sir Oswald's break with the Labour government.

As a consequence of this crisis in the government, J. H. Thomas also resigned as lord privy seal and took another cabinet post, while the prime minister himself replaced Thomas as the chief director of unemployment policy. The chancellorship of the Duchy of Lancaster, which Mosley's resignation had left vacant, was entrusted to Major Clement Richard Attlee, who was later to become leader of the party. But even the most drastic changes in personnel could effect no solution of the unemployment problem as long as the government's basic policies, particularly its monetary policies, remained the same. Discontent continually growing within the Labour party furnished Sir Oswald Mosley for a time with strong support in his criticism of the government, but when he began to add to his economic proposals suggestions in favor of a quasi-dictatorial "super cabinet," the government could safely ignore him. The bulk of the party refused to follow Sir Oswald's rapid conversion to fascist philosophy. When he broke away from the Labour party in February, 1931, he was followed by only five other Labour members of Parliament, all of whom were immediately disavowed by their constituencies.

The party did not become reconciled to the government's handling of the unemployment situation. On the contrary, dissension grew when early in 1931 the chancellor of the exchequer announced impending economy measures and declared that if the budget was to be balanced, schemes involving heavy expenditure must be deferred until prosperity returned. Yet at the end of July, 1931, a committee chosen to make economy proposals forecast a deficit of £120,000,000 for the next budget year. Unemployment passed 2,300,000. The situation was becoming intolerable when the financial crisis broke.

9.

The crisis forced the government to stop its evasion of the main issue. Snowden had to choose almost immediately between devaluation of the pound or radical deflationary measures. This choice was in effect put before the Labour government by the conditions said to have been made as a preliminary to the American banks' granting a loan to Britain. The deficit, it was said, must be reduced if Britain were to receive financial assistance. Whether the American bankers specifically asked for a reduction in unemployment benefits has never been made fully clear. MacDonald and Snowden denied it, while the Labour party accused the American bankers of having interfered with Britain's internal affairs. Whatever the bankers' demands may have been, no serious reduction of the budget deficit was possible without a cut in the main item responsible for the deficit, the subsidies to the unemployment insurance fund. Any effort to maintain the gold parity of the pound depended upon foreign loans, since capital flight was by now added to the many worries of the Bank of England. Under these conditions sharp economy measures, which would necessarily affect unemployment benefits, were inevitable unless the alternative of devaluation was accepted.

James Ramsay MacDonald, Philip Snowden, and J. H. Thomas may claim the merit of having been the first members of the government to acknowledge that the time had come for a final choice. The rest of the government "had very little idea of what was happening" and continued to avoid a decision. Presumably the influence of the trade unions and loyalty to what they considered the immediate interests of the working class, rather than a different conception of British financial policy, prevented the majority of the cabinet from following MacDonald's and Snowden's lead.

It very soon became clear not only that the prime minister and the chancellor of the exchequer, by preferring economy measures to the inevitable devaluation, made the wrong choice from the point of view of the working class, but also that MacDonald was influenced by a long-cherished idea of replacing the government of his own party by a "National" emergency cabinet. Propaganda for such a solution had started several months before the critical days in August, 1931. Only a non-party government, it was claimed, could make and carry out the decisions considered necessary by MacDonald, namely, sharp economy measures and perhaps also the introduction of a protective tariff. The financial crisis offered the prime minister an opportunity for carrying out his dream of a "National" coalition led by himself.

In addition, MacDonald had come to disdain most of his colleagues in the government, or at least to feel vastly superior to them. "The Prime Minister was not in the mood to find time or energy for that friendly social intercourse with the members of his own party or even with his ministerial colleagues, which goes so far to avert friction and produce the 'team spirit,' " one of his colleagues in the cabinet, Sidney Webb (Lord Passfield), wrote in March, 1932. "More and more he tended to spend his scanty leisure in less disagreeable society," [10] which actually was *the* "society" of London.

Thus objective and subjective factors united in bringing about the Labour party's catastrophe of 1931.

10.

The events leading to the breakup of the Labour government started with the crash of the Austrian Credit-Anstalt in May, 1931. From Vienna the financial crisis spread to Germany and thence, by way of the financial connections between German and English banks, to London. The report of the May Commission appointed to suggest economy measures, which was published at the end of July, painted a gloomy picture of the state of public finances and helped speed the situation to a head. The commission recommended the instant elimination of £96,000,000 of expenditure, two thirds of it at the expense of the unemployment insurance fund and some of the remainder by a reduction in public pay rolls. The flow of capital away from England, already well under way, increased to

[10] Sidney Webb, *What Happened in 1931: a Record.* Fabian Tract, No. 237, London, Fabian Society, 1932.

a torrent after publication of the report. The Bank of England was forced to borrow from New York and Paris, but this first loan was exhausted within a few weeks. Another loan was considered necessary, but this time the American bankers allegedly laid down the conditions previously referred to. In any case, the proposal to cut down the rate of unemployment benefits was made in the cabinet and described as unavoidable if foreign credits were to be made available.

The Labour cabinet, though unanimously in favor both of balancing the budget and of instituting economies, refused to accept this particular economy suggestion.[11] The members who followed Arthur Henderson's leadership first considered a revenue tariff and later favored additional taxation and economies, each to cover half of the deficit. This met opposition from Liberals and Conservatives, who insisted upon a far greater share of economies. At a later stage they asked specifically for a reduction of at least 10 percent in unemployment benefit payments. The trade-union leaders, on the other hand, rejected any such cut—for that matter, any cut in social services—and declared that nationalization of the Bank of England would solve the currency problem. MacDonald, Snowden, and J. H. Thomas accepted the conditions of the opposition, at least a part of which had to be won over if the program were to be carried through Parliament. Arthur Henderson and the majority of cabinet members refused to submit and were prepared instead to see the government resign and the Conservatives under Baldwin take over.

What they did not expect, however, was the formation of a "National" government under MacDonald's leadership and his subsequent separation from the Labour party. Suddenly they found themselves opposed by the two men who more than any others represented the Labour party before the British public.

While still a member of the Labour government, MacDonald had secretly negotiated with Conservative and Liberal leaders to prepare the way for the "National" government. Instead of advising the king to ask Baldwin to form a new government, as he should

[11] "The balancing of the budget itself was, apart from satisfying the conditions of the international bankers, a simple matter upon which there was no disagreement in the Labour Cabinet." Laski, *The Crisis and the Constitution,* p. 21.

have done according to constitutional practice, MacDonald presented to the king a plan for a cabinet in which Conservatives, Liberals, and Labour would be represented. Each of the parties was to engage in limited commitments for definite purposes, of which the chief was to maintain the gold standard. MacDonald believed that no party government could successfully fulfill this task. Obviously, he expected to be followed by the bulk of labor, and he may even have assumed that any break within the Labour party would be temporary, since the "National" government was intended to be only an emergency solution.

Only fourteen Labour members of Parliament followed MacDonald, however, and the party expelled them. Of the cabinet members Snowden, J. H. Thomas, and Lord Justice Sankey found places in the new government.

The following weeks soon destroyed MacDonald's illusion that his separation from Labour would be temporary. Parliament was dissolved and the ensuing general election created deep bitterness between Labour and its former leaders. The party fought under the double handicap of its failure in government and of the opposition of MacDonald and Snowden. Although the National government, formed to defend the gold parity of the currency, had failed in its task, causing England to leave the gold standard in September, the general public held the Labour party responsible for the crisis which had led to the devaluation. At the same time, Philip Snowden, roused to fury by the party's unwillingness to follow, started a series of sharp attacks upon his former colleagues. The man "with the sweetest smile and the bitterest tongue in the House of Commons," [12] as he was once described, directed his stinging sarcasm against the Labour party. "A sick man into whom the iron had entered to a degree that seemed pathological," Snowden had no word of protest when government propaganda spoke of a "Socialist threat to the savings of the poor," referring to the by no means new practice of lending postal deposits to the Unemployment Insurance Fund. As Labour chancellor of the exchequer, Snowden himself had been responsible for this practice.

[12] Arthur W. MacMahon, "The British General Election of 1931," *American Political Science Review*. XXVI. (April 1932).

In a broadcast on October 17, 1931, during the height of the election campaign, Snowden tried to justify his latest action by violent attacks upon the Labour party. "I joined the National Government," he said, "to carry out the financial policy I pressed on my late colleagues in the Labour government. They knew this policy was necessary. But when it came to the point of having to face up to it, they hadn't the courage to face the unpopularity and opposition which necessary measures of economy would naturally meet within certain quarters." The issue of the election was, according to Snowden, "whether we shall hand over the destinies of the nation to men whose conduct in a grave emergency has shown them to be unfitted to be trusted with responsibility." Then he employed the epithet "Bolshevism run mad." The National government was but a "temporary expedient" and he concluded by stating that he was "still serving the best interests of the working classes and safeguarding their future progress."

Altogether, the anti-Labour campaign was based upon the assertion that in case a Labour government should be returned, the citizens' "savings would be swept away in the general collapse of financial confidence, their employment lost, or at best their wages drastically curtailed with the breakdown of industry, even their houses snatched from them by a predatory government ready to adopt any method of confiscation in order to save itself from disaster." [13]

This campaign could not have been as effective as it proved to be without recognition by many voters that Labour had failed to solve the crisis, and without the internal confusion over policy which the party showed so clearly during the election campaign.

Not only had Labour followed a line which increased rather than alleviated the crisis, but even after the breakdown of the government the party was unable to understand what had happened. Labour propagandists were inclined to look upon the financial crisis as an isolated phenomenon rather than as the outcome of a mistaken economic and financial policy pursued by various governments since the end of the war. The Labour people blamed the bankers of England, America, and France, whom they accused of

[13] From G. D. H. Cole, *A Short History of the British Working Class Movement,* p. xvi. By permission of The Macmillan Company, publishers.

having conspired against labor and unemployment insurance. But although American bankers may perhaps have been inclined to stave off the "danger" of America's following Britain's lead and introducing the "dole" in the United States, few British Labour people asked themselves how the bankers could so easily achieve their ends against a Labour government. Also, Labour directed bitter attacks against its former leaders, MacDonald, Snowden, and Thomas, whom the party openly branded as traitors, yet the Labour party still failed to point out an alternative policy.

The basic reason for this bankruptcy of ideas lay in the fact that under the leadership of MacDonald and Snowden the British labor movement had become the heir to the peculiar British brand of Radical liberalism. Free trade was the cornerstone in the ideological edifice of a British Radical, and it was characteristic that Philip Snowden, after having followed MacDonald into the National government, broke with his colleague over the issue of protectionism.[14] He had accepted the break with his party, but refused to submit to protectionist demands. In addition he bitterly opposed every effort tending toward government control of foreign trade, such as the Independent Labour party suggested.

Free trade was holy gospel to a British Radical for several reasons, not the least of these being the belief that protection would foster war and that removal of all trade barriers would guarantee peace. An international monetary standard, they felt was the necessary means to facilitate world trade, which in turn would serve pacifist ends. Unfortunately, the gold standard was often identified with the existing gold parity of the pound, although devaluation could of course have been combined with a return to the gold standard at a lower parity. Earlier devaluation even might have saved the gold standard, but long delaying of the inevitable induced many Britishers to throw overboard both the gold parity and the gold standard.

[14] Even after Snowden's departure, free trade tradition was very powerful in the party. While the (Labourite) *Daily Herald* asserted that "Labour has never been a rigidly doctrinaire Free Trade body of opinion," actual electoral propaganda was carried on by posters such as these: "Workmen, beware! The Tories want to cut your wages by food taxes. Vote Labour and defend your wages!" Or, referring to the crisis in Detroit, "a city of death," a dodger read: "What happens in tariff-ridden America . . ." Cf. Arthur W. MacMahon, *op. cit.*, pp. 333 ff.

Philip Snowden and, following him, the Labour party, believed in the necessity of balancing the budget. As the world's great financial center, "Britain could not afford to have an unbalanced budget. An unbalanced budget is regarded as a sign of impending national bankruptcy," Snowden wrote as late as 1934.[15] A consequence of this theory was that reduction of public expenses became necessary in exactly those times of crisis when private spending was reduced to a minimum, thus increasing unemployment.

Prisoner to its belief in free trade, the defense of the gold parity, and the need for a balanced budget, the second Labour government was bound to fail in a period of severe economic crisis. In spite of its professed Socialist philosophy, the Labour party in fact followed the most orthodox principles of economic laissez faire. Austen Chamberlain, the Conservative leader, once referred to Snowden as "a Socialist, grafted on to the narrowest type of mid-Victorian economic pedant."

The economy measures which the National government later carried out were the logical consequence of Snowden's laissez faire principles. The trade unions were bound to reject the economy program in the interest of their members, but few union leaders realized that by opposing the National government's policy the Labour party was actually repudiating the consequences of the very same principles which it enthusiastically accepted. As long as it remained true to these principles, the Labour party was unable to propose an alternative program.

II.

After 1931 the Labour party was powerless, with its mere 52 seats in the House of Commons, although its popular vote of 6,600,000 votes still represented 30.6 percent of the total. Under the British electoral system, a loss of 1,700,000 votes and a reduction of Labour's proportion in the total poll from 36.9 to 30.6 percent cut the Parliamentary Labour party from 287 members to 52. The Independent Labour party, now completely separated from the main

[15] Philip Snowden, Viscount Snowden, *An Autobiography*. London, Nicholson & Watson, 1934.

organization, returned five members under James Maxton's leadership.

No less consequential than the loss in numbers, but altogether wholesome for the movement, was the defeat of almost the entire party directorate. After MacDonald's break with Labour, Arthur Henderson was elected leader. Foreign secretary in the second Labour government against MacDonald's wishes, Henderson had been the outstanding success of the government. In the conflict with the prime minister, "Uncle Arthur" was the leader of the revolting cabinet members. Not being reëlected to the House, Henderson could not lead the party in Parliament, and when he later won a by-election, his work as president of the World Disarmament Conference kept him in Geneva. When he resigned as parliamentary leader, George Lansbury was elected his successor. A religious Socialist and convinced pacifist, Lansbury came into conflict with the party in 1935, when Labour strongly advocated sanctions against Italy's aggression in Africa. Though universally respected and perhaps the most beloved Labour man in England, Lansbury was forced to resign.

The choice of his successor was almost automatic since it was restricted, according to custom, to former government members—of whom only two, Attlee and Sir Stafford Cripps, in addition to Lansbury, were in the House. Sir Stafford at the time was opposed to collective security, and as the party was committed to this policy, Major Clement Richard Attlee, former postmaster general, was thus the only candidate left.

Not even Attlee's best friends can claim that he has that powerful and inspiring personality that goes into the making of a leader. But Attlee has grown considerably in stature since his election; his intellectual ability and steadiness command general respect. At the outbreak of the war in 1939 Attlee was seriously ill and the deputy leader, Arthur Greenwood, acted in Attlee's place as head of His Majesty's most loyal opposition. Like many other younger labor leaders, Greenwood is an intellectual, a former teacher of economics, and highly reputed as chief of the research division at the party's headquarters.

Herbert Morrison, though not the official leader, is the most outstanding man of the party. His greatest handicap is a divergence of views from some of the trade-union leaders, dating back to the time when as transport minister he rejected workers' representation on the board of the nationalized London Transport System.

Trade-union opposition was one of the reasons why Herbert Morrison was not elected parliamentary leader when he returned to the House in 1935 after a four years' absence. The left also preferred Attlee, as Morrison is regarded as a moderate right winger. Everyone, however, agrees that the former messenger boy is a tremendously successful organizer, who led the London Labour party to the conquest of the London County Council and thereby to the administration of the empire's capital. As minister of transport, he was no less efficient. In any crisis, Morrison is the man toward whom labor instinctively turns. Although little trained in international affairs, he has more understanding of the Continental labor movements than any other British leader and he realized the significance of international resistance to fascism long before most of his colleagues. Still in his early fifties, Herbert Morrison is a rival of Ernest Bevin in influence within the movement.

Chapter 9

GERMAN LABOR'S "TOLERATION" POLICY

I.

"TODAY *you refuse to accept this compromise because it imposes certain sacrifices upon you. But the time will come when you will have to tolerate much worse demands from the government.*" This was the warning of Rudolf Hilferding, former minister of finance and one of the leading members of the Socialists in the German Reichstag. These words were spoken at a meeting in March, 1930, when the group decided to reject a government proposal for an increase of the workers' contribution to unemployment insurance.

Hilferding's warning was in vain. The Social Democratic members of the German Reichstag refused to change their attitude. The Socialist vote immediately caused the resignation of the Social Democratic chancellor, Hermann Müller, and of his three Socialist colleagues in the Reich government.

Hilferding was the intellectual leader of German Social Democracy after the war. An Austrian by birth, he came to Germany long before the war to teach economics at the Workers University in Berlin. He became editor of the Socialist newspaper in Berlin, the *Vorwärts.* Though a doctor by profession, he wrote a book, *Finanzkapital,* which was the outstanding post-Marxian economic tract written along Marxist lines. In the post-war years he came to play a leading role in the Independent party, and was appointed editor in chief of its Berlin daily, *Freiheit.* He was a bitter critic of the moderate Majority Socialists; when in control, they took their revenge by delaying his naturalization in Germany and thereby prevented his attaining public office for some time.

Hilferding was the leader of the Independent's right wing, which opposed submission to the twenty-one conditions of the Communist International. When Zinoviev, the Comintern's president, appeared in person at the Independent Congress in Halle in 1920 and made a long speech designed to persuade the party to join the Communist International, Rudolf Hilferding was chosen to speak in behalf of the anti-Communist faction. Zinoviev spoke for many hours, ending his speech shortly before the lunch recess. At lunch the leaders of the anti-Communist Independents met and asked Hilferding to answer the famous president of the Comintern for them. Hilferding, though an experienced debater, always encountered certain difficulties when speaking, and was inclined to stutter, particularly at the beginning of a speech. On this occasion he was even more severely taxed, since he had little time to prepare his address. Nevertheless, his reply to Zinoviev was one of the greatest documents of post-war socialism. He pointed out that Marx had based his hopes for a Socialist revolution on the most highly developed capitalist countries, not on backward countries such as Russia. The one-party dictatorship in Russia and the violent terror were, in his opinion, the necessary result of the lack of a powerful industrial working class. Western labor, with its different background, could not follow the example of Russia but had to develop its own path to power and socialism.

Zinoviev won the day, however, and the split of the Independent party destroyed Hilferding's hopes for a revolutionary labor movement in Germany independent of Moscow. This disappointment changed Hilferding completely. When the right-wing Independents joined the Majority Socialists to form the Social Democratic party, he became an ardent Reformist, in fact, the leading theoretician of Reformist thought in Central Europe. As minister of finance in 1923, he prepared the way for the stabilization of the mark, though Schacht succeeded in appropriating the credit for himself. Hilferding's position within the Social Democratic party, however, remained very influential. The Socialist left had no theoretical leader who could successfully have opposed Hilferding's justification of the Majority's Reformist policy.

An expert in economics, Hilferding had become so strongly impressed by the intricate mechanism of a highly developed capitalist economy that he considered almost any interference with it to be dangerous; he came close to being a Manchester Liberal. Playing the same role as did Snowden in England, he rejected the many schemes advanced during the crisis to hasten the return of prosperity, convinced that such efforts would at best only prepare the way for even worse economic collapse. Hilferding's prestige was so great that it led the party to support Hermann Müller in spite of the Social Democratic chancellor's failure to adopt any measures to combat the crisis except for hopeless efforts to maintain unemployment benefits. These endeavors proved increasingly difficult, for the middle-class parties pressed the chancellor to slash unemployment benefits. Hilferding favored accepting what he considered the inevitable cut in order to avoid a crisis which would force the Social Democrats out of the government into powerless opposition. His pleading, however, was of no avail. The leftist groups within the Social Democratic party joined with the trade unions in opposing the compromise which had been devised in painful negotiations among the various government parties. Almost unanimously the Socialist parliamentary group decided to vote against the proposal if it were submitted to the Reichstag.

Immediately afterward the cabinet met under Müller's chairmanship and resigned; through their action the last German government in which the Social-Democratic party was represented and at the same time the last strictly parliamentary government ceased to exist.

Brüning succeeded Müller as chancellor. Six months later, on September 14, 1930, the Nazis won the first in a series of election victories, obtaining 107 seats and gaining the second largest representation in the Reichstag. As Hilferding had predicted, the Social Democrats were forced to tolerate, in fact to acquiesce to, increasingly severe deflationary measures from the government. For in spite of the heavy sacrifices imposed on the working class, the Social

Democrats had no alternative but to support the chancellor or help a Nazi government into power. Labor's influence upon the fate of the German Republic was rapidly declining.

2.

Yet, Müller's chancellorship had begun under what seemed at the time excellent auspices. After the stabilization of the Reichsmark in 1923–24, Germany had entered upon a period of rapid economic development, improved living conditions, and political stability that lasted until 1928, when Müller became chancellor.

While the nationalist and fascist groups rapidly dwindled in this atmosphere of normalcy, labor had broken down so completely during the inflation period that several years were needed before its recovery was complete. The middle class was thus firmly in control. A sign of this trend toward the right was the election after the death of President Ebert in 1925 of Paul von Hindenburg, former commander in chief of the Imperial Army, as his successor. The Social Democrats, after having run the Socialist Prussian premier, Otto Braun, in the first election, which ended in a stalemate, united with the other Weimar parties in voting for the conservative Center leader, Wilhelm Marx; but Hindenburg's tremendous popularity and the support of the Nationalist parties carried the day. The Communists obtained two million votes for their leader Thaelmann, and the Nazi candidate, General Ludendorff, polled less than 300,000 votes. While the extreme parties on the right and on the left were thus reduced to the status of factions, the Conservatives succeeded in winning the presidency of the Reich. Conservatives hostile to the Republic and the military clique now controlled the position of the chief executive of the Republic.

Middle-class parties dominated the Reich, but the Socialists were the leading party in Prussia. As this was the largest single "state" in Germany, the Prussian government was a great power in German politics. As a consequence, the Socialists were continuously halfway between opposition and coöperation. Their struggle against the Reich Cabinet was softened by the fact that the parties represented in the Reich cabinet were Socialist allies in the Prussian government.

Under the circumstances Socialist policy was bound to be moderate, but during the years of economic advance this policy obviously met with the approval of most workers. In May, 1924, when recovery had hardly begun, the Socialists polled six million votes, compared with four million Communist votes. At the general elections of May, 1928, the Social Democratic party polled nine million votes and gained 22 seats—which made a total of 153, while the Communists obtained little more than three million votes. It was the greatest Socialist victory since 1918; the majority in the Reichstag was shifted toward the left. Gustav Stresemann, the almost permanent foreign minister of the Reich, rejoiced over the Socialist advance. Although he was the leader of the right-wing People's party, his foreign policy, favoring a reconciliation with France, found little support among his own group and even less among the Nationalists, which together formed the bulk of the government majority in the Reichstag. On the other hand, the Socialists stood whole-heartedly for his policy. The election, by giving Stresemann a sizable bloc of Socialist votes, enabled him to end his complete reliance on the Nationalists within the government majority, and thus to obtain far more homogeneous support for the government's foreign policy.

This new majority extended from the Socialists on the left to the People's party on the right, and combined representatives of labor with spokesmen of big business. In domestic problems cooperation between these parties was not as easy to obtain as in foreign affairs. The government continuously was forced to devise compromises between employers and workers, but the economic prosperity prevailing at the time made mutual concessions possible without hurting anybody's vital interests. Unemployment was at a low ebb in 1928, with wages and profits rising together. Germany seemed to have overcome the consequences of both war and inflation in a surprisingly short time. Her industrial production, increasing more rapidly even than that of the United States, passed the pre-war level in 1928, although after the war she occupied a smaller territory. While England's industry declined in some branches and stagnated in others, Germany again took Europe's industrial lead. The blood stream feeding this amazing expansion consisted of foreign capital, which entered Germany by billions of marks after the currency stabilization in 1923.

Close observers, it is true, were doubtful whether lasting prosperity could be built upon the basis of foreign credits, particularly since the main source was the United States, whose capital exports tended to be unstable. As a matter of fact, the year 1928 witnessed the first slackening of American capital exports, owing mainly to the powerful attraction of the American stock-exchange boom. In addition, the process of rationalization of industry, which had given impetus to industrial expansion during the preceding years, began to slacken. The brisk trade of 1927 fell off markedly early in 1928, and by the end of that year a slump in several industrial branches heralded the coming crisis. But wage increases still continued, and for the time being the influx of foreign capital, although reduced, helped to bolster failing concerns. The great social conflicts which were to develop as the depression progressed were still in the future when the new cabinet took office.

3.

There were enough comparatively petty political conflicts between the government parties to keep Chancellor Müller and Herr Stresemann busy even during the first rosy months of the new government's existence, but they were all over-shadowed by the dispute over the armored cruiser [1] within the Social Democratic party itself.

Thus, the honeymoon of the new government majority was marred by internal dissension. Foreign policy alone offered a rallying point, particularly in view of current or impending international negotiations for the evacuation of the Rhineland—still occupied by Allied troops according to the Peace Treaty—and for a new settlement of the reparations problem. While these negotiations were carried on, the economic situation grew worse; the gov-

[1] See Chapter IV, p. 39.

ernment was faced with a life-and-death struggle against the rising tide of the extreme right and the radicalized extreme left.

With the year 1929 the tragic war on two fronts which the German Republic was to wage to its bitter end entered its first phase. In May, 1929, the prohibition by the Socialist police president of Berlin of the traditional May Day celebration caused a Communist outbreak in one of the working-class districts of the capital; this resulted in many deaths and in the dissolution of the Communist Red-Front League. The Communist party had won twenty-four seats at the general election in May, 1928, polling about 10 percent of the total vote. A Communist threat existed only in the imagination of anti-democratic propagandists, but recurrent Communist outbreaks gave this propaganda some semblance of truth, at least in the eyes of many middle-class people.

Of far greater significance was the alliance, concluded in 1929, between Geheimrat Hugenberg's German National People's party and Adolf Hitler's National Socialists. Alfred Hugenberg, one of the most influential leaders of the right wing in German politics because of his control of newspapers and moving-picture production, led his Nationalist party into open conflict with the democratic constitution. By combining with the Nazis, he gained the younger party's enthusiasm and dynamics, in return for the respectability and publicity which the German Nationalists could grant to Hitler's small and violent movement. The first joint action of the alliance, which was called the Harzburg Front because of its first joint meeting place, concerned foreign policy. The Harzburg Front forced the government to hold a plebiscite, according to the constitution, over a Hugenberg-Nazi proposal that the government be instructed to protest officially against Article 231 of the Versailles Treaty, which made Germany responsible for the great war; to reject the new reparations settlement; and to abandon the policy of reparation and reconciliation with the former enemy powers. Ministers and officials who favored a policy of European coöperation, the League of Nations, and the international conferences in general were to be put on trial for high treason. Fewer than six million voters expressed themselves in favor of this proposal, which was thus rejected. But the main battles were still to come. The real battleground was internal politics; foreign policy served mainly as an instrument to arouse the masses, suffering under unemployment and bankruptcy, to nationalism and hatred of the democratic regime.

4.

When the crisis broke, the German government was faced by a double problem, the two parts of which were closely connected. The German balance of foreign payments became passive, since foreign money left the country. Meanwhile increasing unemployment and the loss of public income due to reduced private incomes upset the precarious balance of the budget. The first problem was not considered too serious in the beginning, although it later became the determining factor in economic policy. But balancing the budget was from the outset the main source of worry.

The crucial question was how to meet the increasing requirements of the unemployment insurance agency, which constituted a heavy drain on the budget since the normal insurance resources soon gave out under the strain of lasting mass unemployment. In different terms, the struggle within the government concerned the share of the financial burden of the crisis to be borne by the various classes of the population. As the national income decreased, each of the government parties endeavored to place the greatest possible portion of the loss upon the shoulders of supporters of other parties.

In the unending series of intra-governmental conflicts the Social Democrats were the losers from the outset. Mass unemployment vitiated the fighting spirit of the working class, or rather of those workers who were fortunate enough to be still employed. While the unemployed, abandoning any hope of finding new jobs in the near future, were radicalized and attracted toward the Communists and the Nazis, the employed workers were afraid of losing their jobs and unwilling to engage in activities they considered a risk to their employment. They were prepared to lose their lives rather than their jobs. The rising tide of Nazism, mainly directed as it was against the "Marxists," strengthened the reactionary parties within the government. Socialist influence dwindled, while simultaneously big business was encouraged in its resistance to labor demands by both the crisis and the growth of Nazism.

In addition, the death of Foreign Minister Gustav Stresemann deprived the German People's party of the leader who had favored coöperation with the Social Democrats and strengthened the reactionary tendencies within this big business group. Under these conditions, the worries of 1929, small as they were compared with what the future was to bring, were sufficiently large to lead to this government's first great crisis and to a severe defeat for the Socialists.

The reduction in taxation yield during the second half of 1929 placed before the Social Democratic minister of finance, Rudolf Hilferding, a difficult economic and political problem. For a time the lack of funds was so critical that the government had to borrow money to pay officials' salaries. While the minister of finance was frantically trying to obtain a loan from the German banks, the president of the Reichsbank, Dr. Hjalmar Schacht, presented the government with an ultimatum specifying certain conditions to be fulfilled by the Reich before the Reichsbank could coöperate in raising funds for the cabinet. Dr. Schacht's ultimatum was heaven-sent support for the reactionary campaign already under way to force the Socialists out of the government.

Hjalmar Schacht entered politics as a member of the Democratic party, a left-wing middle-class group which coöperated with the Socialists in the government. He was appointed president of the Reichsbank in 1923 over the protest of the right and of the bank itself. Reich President Friedrich Ebert, a Social Democrat, came out in favor of Schacht and succeeded in forcing through his election. The bank president, however, soon followed the general evolution of the German republic toward the right. By 1929 he had reached the point of coöperating with the reactionary wing of the German People's party against the Social Democrats, and a few months later he was to resign in order to join forces with the Hugenberg led coalition of Nazis and Pan-Germanists.

A few days after his ultimatum Dr. Schacht and the German People's party obtained Hilferding's resignation, and the position of minister of finance passed into the hands of a representative of the German People's party. The reconstructed Hermann Müller cabinet carried on for a few more months, but no one doubted that the right wing of the government was working hard to break up the entire coalition and to force the Social Democrats out of those positions they still held. The only reason the Socialist defeat was not complete at the time of Hilferding's resignation was the belief that with international negotiations in progress for the revision of the reparations settlement, Socialist participation in the Reich government would help in getting better conditions for Germany than a right-wing nationalist government might obtain. From the moment of the conclusion of these negotiations the Müller cabinet was doomed. The pretext for the breakup of the coalition was easily found in the permanent problem of the unemployment insurance agency. The Socialists were forced to resign at the end of March, 1930, causing the leadership of the German Republic to pass from the Social Democrats to the Catholic Center party. Labor's influence upon the fate of the republic decreased, and soon the working class was to be but a passive spectator while Nazism embarked upon its rise to power.

5.

The two wings of the German political labor movement, Social Democrats and Communists, held different views as to the policy to be followed in the crisis. Both their policies ended in failure. For the Communists the crisis of 1929 was first and foremost an opportunity for exposing the Social Democrats. The official Comintern approval in 1929 of the appellation "Social-Fascists," invented as early as 1924 to brand the Social Democratic labor movement, meant that the struggle against the right-wing labor party became the main task of the Communists. Unlike the Socialists, the Communists had the great advantage of being an opposition party which, therefore, could not be held responsible for the misery of the masses. But this advantage was more than outweighed by the ultraradicalism of the Communists, which ran counter to the thinking of the politically educated mass of the workers. By concentrating their attacks upon the Social Democrats and the trade-union leaders; by putting forward obviously absurd demands which no government, not even a Communist one, could fulfill; and by competing with the Nazis in nationalist slogans, the Communists separated themselves from the masses, particularly from the employed workers. They did succeed in winning new recruits among the unemployed. The Communists' votes at the elections of September, 1930, rose to 4,600,000 as compared with 3,300,000 in 1928. But this increase was slight compared with the avalanche for the Nazis, which boosted their vote from 800,000 in May, 1928, to 6,500,000 in September, 1930.

Heirs to Socialist pre-war radicalism, the Communists were convinced that this crisis would put an end to capitalism, although they hardly prepared for a decisive struggle to bring about a new social order. Holding to this viewpoint, the Communists regarded the Hitler movement as merely a passing phenomenon. After the election of September 14, 1930, which resulted in making the National Socialist (Nazi) party the second in size in the Reichstag, the official Communist newspaper, *Rote Fahne,* announced that the "high point" of the Nazi wave in Germany had been reached. "What comes after this," the paper said, "can only be decline and fall." Even much later, when a Nazi victory seemed certain to almost everybody, the Communists persisted in proclaiming that their victory was bound to follow on the heels of the inevitable breakdown of the Nazi dictatorship. "We are the victors of the coming day," the Communist leader, Remmele, shouted in the Reichstag, "and the question is no longer one of who shall vanquish whom. This question is already answered. The question now reads only: at what moment shall we overthrow the bourgeoisie?" The Nazis, according to Communist prophecies, would soon start inflation, which would in turn let loose the proletarian revolution. "After Hitler, our turn," the Communists sincerely believed. As a matter of fact, it was not until 1934 that Moscow admitted that Nazism had come to stay for some time.

Since the Hitler movement in 1929 represented a foe worthy of not more than secondary Communist attention, the main force of Communist propaganda could continue to be directed against the Social Democrats. During the lifetime of the Müller government the Communists strove hard to create difficulties for it, and the government in turn did its best to offer the Communists ample cause for criticism. The riots, on May 1, 1929, were one case in point. After the resignation of the Müller cabinet the Communists directed their attacks upon the remaining positions in Germany and in Prussia still held by the Social Democrats. Thus, they were led into an alliance with the Nazis, as for example in 1931, when the Communist party called upon its members to support a Nazi referendum against the Socialist led Prussian government.

There was only one point in which the German Communists seem to have taken the Nazis seriously: the more effective the Nazi propaganda became, the more faithfully did the Communists adopt the Nazis' nationalist slogans. The election platform of the Communists bore the title "For National and Social Liberation." Nationalist adventurers who desired the Soviet Union's support for a war against the West joined the Communist party and became its leading spokesmen. Since the Social Democrats stood for reconciliation with France, a policy Moscow always suspected of being a first step toward a united front against Russia, foreign policy became another battleground between Socialists and Communists. Again Communists and Nazis were in concord, at least as far as anti-French feeling was concerned.

The inevitable result of the Communist policy was that the gulf between the two German labor parties widened, and joint defense against the common enemy became practically impossible. It may be that the extreme policy of the Communist party during the crisis had its advantages as far as gaining support at the expense of the Social Democrats was concerned. But labor as a whole suffered badly.

The Social Democratic policy during the crisis was bound to be basically different from that of the Communists, if only because at first the Social Democrats were in office; and later, after the resignation of the Hermann Müller government, because they prevented the downfall of the Brüning government by what was called a policy of tolerance. The Socialists could not embark upon a purely propagandistic policy. Neither could they compete with the patently nonsensical demands put forward by either Communists or Nazis. On the other hand, the Socialists had the immense advantage of being a government party and speaking with the authority of a responsible organization whose past made it impossible for any decent opponent to accuse it of sanctioning irresponsible adventures. Despite these favorable conditions the Social Democratic failure was as conspicuous as the Communists'.

The Social Democrats did not expect a crisis of unusual intensity or duration, but even as late as 1931, when the economic blizzard struck with full force, they persisted in a policy which did little to alleviate the crisis itself but was mainly directed toward mitigating the immediate suffering of the working class. Many Socialists and trade-union leaders clung to the orthodox doctrine that state intervention in the crisis could bring immediate relief only at the price of making the crisis more lasting and preparing another slump, even more severe in nature. Social Democrats and trade unionists, therefore, made no effort to change the deflationist economic policy of the government, but opposed it only so far as it threatened wages and unemployment benefits. It is true that they stressed the economic significance of maintaining consumers' purchasing power by keeping wage rates and unemployment allowances stable; but this was primarily a "rationalization" of their concern with the immediate consequences of the crisis for their supporters. The Social Democrats had no economic policy but only a "relief" policy. They fought for keeping the unemployment insurance agency solvent and, consequently, for a balanced budget that would enable the government to provide for the needs of the unemployment fund. But they did not attack the roots of unemployment. They rejected deflation, but they also protested against any inflationist measures, among which they counted devaluation. "Neither inflation nor deflation," an official statement of policy declared. Any manipulation of the currency was formally rejected.

The memories of the terrific German inflation from 1919 to 1923 were still fresh in the public mind. Any "tampering" with the currency would be considered by the German public as the beginning of new inflation, the Socialists and trade unionists thought, and since the Germans had had their experience with monetary inflation, it would be impossible to stop at any given point. At the first sign of a decline in value of the mark, the population would rush to buy whatever it could in order to get rid of all its money holdings. Prices would soar at break-neck pace, and no power, certainly not a weak government such as Brüning's, could prevent the inflation once started from going to its farthest limit. Regulated inflation would be impossible, and devaluation would lead straight into an inflation that would engulf the Republic and throw the Nazis into power.

Thus, though they opposed Brüning's wage cuts, the German Social Democrats were unable to offer any practical alternative. Any policy of economic expansion would necessarily have been jeopardized by the passive balance of international payments. Only devaluation or perhaps a strict exchange control might have checked the outflow of gold in the wake of economic expansion. In spite of efforts on the part of some groups in the trade-union movement to induce labor to come out for devaluation and a policy of raising the price level, the majority of the Social Democratic party and of the trade-union leadership maintained their purely negative attitude. "Neither inflation nor deflation" meant that in a country in the midst of a terrific upheaval where everything was threatened, including the constitution and all life's social values, one thing was to be kept stable at any price: the gold value of the currency.

The Social Democrats and the trade unions protested against the wage cuts, but their protest was bound to be ineffective since their policy was dictated primarily by the fear of a political crisis which might lead to formation of a government with Nazi participation. This, the labor groups correctly estimated, would give the Nazis access to the power wielded by a government and would be the greatest danger to what remained of democratic liberties. A government crisis, therefore, was to be averted at all costs. The Socialists were convinced that the crisis would pass very soon and that if they could keep Brüning in power until prosperity returned, the Nazis would quickly lose their artificially inflated support among the electorate. As soon as the danger of a Fascist dictatorship was removed, the Social Democrats could reorganize their ranks and regain their former strength. The party leaders felt that even at the risk of a temporary loss in popularity the best policy should be to "tolerate" Brüning.

Thus, Socialist opposition to Brüning's deflationist policy, with its cuts in wages and unemployment benefits, always stopped short of provoking a government crisis. Socialist members of the Reichstag made opposition speeches, but the Socialist group carefully abstained from voting with Nazis and Communists against the government and from trying to force its resignation. By coming to the support of financial orthodoxy at a time when only new and bold policies had a chance of success, German labor lost its political independence and became the ineffectual tail on Brüning's majority.

Chapter 10

THE FAILURE OF THE FRENCH NEW DEAL

1.

SINCE the catastrophic fall of France a great deal has been said and written about the responsibility of the Popular Front for the defeat. The social reforms hurriedly enacted in the summer of 1936 have been accused of having delayed French military preparations. The almost revolutionary forms of the class struggle under the Blum regime set one class against another, it is claimed, and decisively weakened national morale. The infiltration of Communists into leading trade-union positions, favored by the Popular Front, is alleged to have undermined the will to resist of the French working class. To a certain extent, this was the thesis of the tribunal at Riom before which Léon Blum and Daladier were to be judged as leaders of the Popular Front alleged to have failed to prepare France for the war. In the democratic countries, too, similar criticisms have been uttered.

The first question that has to be answered is whether 1936, the year of the Rhineland occupation by Nazi troops and of the Spanish War, permitted extensive social reform in a country such as France, directly threatened by Hitler's rising military power. French working-class pressure for such reform, at a time when all national energies should have been devoted to preparations for the inevitable war, seems another example of that labor pressure-group spirit which disregards vital national interests.[1]

[1] The foreign policy of the Popular Front is discussed below, in Chapters XVIII, XIX, and XX.

Such a narrow outlook on the part of the French Socialists, the leading group of the Popular Front, may seem particularly surprising. In line with the general French dislike for organization, the Socialist party, though the largest in the country, had little more than 200,000 dues-paying members at its zenith, and this membership consisted, almost exclusively, of men vitally interested in politics. The large body of the French working class voted for Socialist or Communist candidates at the elections, but few workers actually joined the labor parties. The party membership consisted primarily of intellectuals who were, so to speak, the general staff of larger popular movements. Unlike Britain or Germany, relations between the unions and the Socialist movement were not too intimate. The British Labour party consisted of the trade unions and a small though increasing number of individual members, with the unions controlling the party financially and frequently politically. Almost all outstanding leaders of the German unions held front rank in the Social Democratic party. In France, however, the unions kept aloof from the political movement. At first, before 1914, anti-parliamentary syndicalist tendencies successfully opposed a close association of unions and party. After 1920 the unions thought they could avoid being torn apart by the Socialist Communist rift only by keeping out of politics—and even then a Communist trade-union center broke away from the rest. Léon Jouhaux, by far the most outstanding French trade-union leader, maneuvered skillfully to keep unions and Socialist party at the right distance —close enough to enjoy Socialist support in parliament, and not so close as to hurt the feelings of traditional syndicalists and Communist sympathizers. In a certain sense it might therefore be said that as a consequence of the average French worker's reluctance to join a political party, the French Socialists and Communists followed the Leninist principle of organization. It might have been expected that such a party organization would be particularly unfavorable to the growth of pressure-group spirit, and that French Socialists and Communists would, in a period of national crisis, know how to integrate group interests into those of the nation as a whole.

To understand why the French Popular Front proceeded as it

did, it is necessary to trace briefly the events leading to the victory of the Popular Front in 1936.

2.

For many years before 1936, Blum had striven to avoid governmental responsibility for himself and for his party. He had preferred the split which led to the formation of the Neo-Socialist party under Marcel Déat and Pierre Renaudel rather than to compromise the future of the Socialist movement by what he considered premature government experience. In unending discussions which, to quote an American writer, had "the fascination of theological disputes for French Socialists," [2] he explained his attitude. His thinking was dictated partly by fear of the Communists, partly by lack of cohesion within the Socialist movement itself.

At the time of the Socialist-Communist split in 1920, the Communists were considerably stronger than Blum's organization. The framework of the original Socialist movement and the famous newspaper *L'Humanité* went with the Communists, since they had a majority of the delegates at the decisive party congress. Only slowly and gradually did Blum and Party Secretary Faure succeed in rebuilding the Socialist movement; they were aided by the continuous conflicts among the Communists themselves, which enabled the Socialists to grow at the expense of the extreme left. Nevertheless, the Communists remained a strong mass party. At the general elections of 1928, they polled 1,100,000 votes, compared with 1,700,000 for the Socialists. If Communist representation in the Chamber was small, it was due to the French law which favored electoral alliances and to the Communist tactic of rejecting such alliances. The Communists regarded all other parties, even the Socialists, as organizations of the capitalist bourgeoisie. In view of the Communist strength at the polls, Blum feared that an alliance with non-labor groups on the basis of a compromise temporarily disappointing to the masses would give new impetus to Communist propaganda.

Moreover, orthodox radicalism of the pre-war type was power-

[2] From Charles W. Pipkin, *Social Politics and Modern Democracies.* New York, 1931. Vol. II, p. 298. By permission of The Macmillan Company, publishers.

fully entrenched in the Socialist movement. The reformists who had been led by the great Jean Jaures, assassinated in 1914, were badly defeated within the Socialist movement at the end of the war. They controlled the movement in 1914 and were associated with the government during the war, but by the end of the war, under the impression of the Russian revolution, the internationalists succeeded in winning over a majority of the party to their point of view. The leading internationalists, such as Jean Longuet and Paul Faure, were radicals of much the same type as their German colleagues. So strong was the radical majority that not even the breakaway of the Communists enabled the reformists to stage a come-back. The relative weakness of the Socialist movement, which prevented it from obtaining impressive practical results, and the strong conservative influence among the non-labor groups, which would probably have made sterile any Socialist middle-class coöperation had the Socialists accepted reformist proposals in favor of such coöperation, kept radicalism in the saddle.

The question of whether to participate with Herriot's party in forming a government led to long-drawn-out conflicts within the Socialist movement. In these factional conflicts Blum stood in the center of the party. The left wing, led by Paul Faure, Alexandre Bracke, and Jean Zyromski, supported Blum against the right wingers, whose main spokesman was Pierre Renaudel. Renaudel's lieutenant was Marcel Déat, the main advocate of French collaboration with Nazi Germany after the defeat of 1940 and the "Crown Prince" of the Socialist party in the early thirties. Professor at France's intellectual training center for the elite, the École normale supérieure, the brilliant Déat was predestined in spite of his youth to take over the party leadership after Blum. But Déat was impatient. He wanted to be a member of a French government, while Blum rejected a policy of alliances with middle-class parties, which alone would have enabled the Socialists to enter a government. In order to coöperate with conservatives, Blum felt, the Socialists would be forced to make heavy sacrifices; the Communists would not have neglected to take advantage of any so-called "Socialist betrayal." Déat, however, argued that for many years to come the Socialists by themselves could not hope to win a majority in the Chamber. Without a coalition, therefore, they would be in no position to carry out even minor sections of their reform program. In Déat's view, Blum's policy condemned the party to eternal opposition and, accordingly, to sterility.

Whenever offers for coöperation were made to the Socialists by other political groups, the issue menaced the continued unity of the party. Blum was supported by all those Socialists who felt more at ease in the role of an opposition without the responsibility for constructive action. They used radical shibboleths, such as that of the irreconcilable opposition between Socialists and middle-class parties, which they said prevented any fruitful coöperation; actually most of these radicals simply preferred pressure-group policy to responsibility. On Déat's side stood men who felt that the movement had to make a contribution to French social progress then and there, but also many job seekers for whom the party was merely a steppingstone in their personal careers.

During several years of bitter argument Blum succeeded in defeating Déat and his friends. When the "Crown Prince" realized that Blum's position was impregnable, he broke with the Socialist party to form his own group, the Neo-Socialists. In the bitterness of this conflict Déat did not shrink from exploiting anti-Semitic prejudices against Blum. Thus began the intellectual somersault that caused Déat to become the most ardent champion of appeasement right through to the outbreak of the war and later to support Laval in his efforts to bring France into the war on Germany's side.

Déat's uncontrolled outbursts of hatred against the party leaders were primarily due to the vanquished's feeling of frustration. Hardly had Déat left the Socialist movement and succeeded in becoming minister of the air forces when the victorious Popular Front forced him out of the Cabinet to make place for a government headed by Léon Blum. Had Déat remained in the Socialist party, there is little doubt that he would have obtained one of the most important offices in Blum's cabinet. Déat's break with Blum thus defeated its own purpose. His mood was not at all improved by the fact that the very man whom he had accused of political sterility now produced a whole series of reforms. The wave of mass enthusiasm for these accomplishments of Blum's government forced even Déat to praise, when actually he was eager to criticize.

3.

Out of the struggle with Renaudel and Déat, the Radical wing of the Socialist movement emerged with additional strength. It was with a certain amount of reluctance that, giving way to the wave of mass pressure, Paul Faure accepted the formation of the Popular Front and of the Popular Front government led by Léon Blum. In his innermost heart Paul Faure, who rejected both Communist revolutionarism and constructive constitutional action, felt at ease only when his party was in opposition to the government. Even while a member of the Blum government, Paul Faure continued to think and act as a radical. He favored the measures of social reform which the government enacted, but he was little concerned with the more basic economic changes necessary to make these reforms possible and lasting. Foreign affairs and particularly a foreign policy that might have involved sacrifices on the part of the working class seemed to him a mere diversion from what he considered "the real work" of the party.

As general secretary of the Socialist party and minister of state in the government, Faure was an influential man. Still, without the particular economic and social evolution which preceded the advent of the Blum government, Faure's pressure-group thinking would have had little chance of being as powerful a factor as it was in shaping the attitudes of the working class itself.

Of all industrialized nations of Europe, France was the most backward in social reform and the most conservative in economic policy. In a country of predominantly small-scale business and with large industry restricted to a few regions, the trade-union movement never obtained an importance similar to that of the British or German unions. The high development of social insurance in England and Central Europe had no adequate counterpart in France, where the family continued to play the role which a government-organized system of social security held elsewhere. Moreover, the thrifty French worker tended to accumulate small savings which tided him over a period of stress.

Under such conditions, France, in spite of her politically progressive ideas, tended to be highly conservative economically and socially. After the sad experience of currency inflation which ended in 1928 in the devaluation of the franc and its stabilization, currency manipulation was regarded as anathema. When the great depression and the currency manipulations of so many countries forced down world-market prices, the French government, supported by public opinion, steadfastly refused to follow the example of British and American devaluation. Again, as in the case of Britain and Germany, defense of the gold parity of the currency meant pressure upon prices and wages and therefore intensified depression and larger unemployment.

As a consequence of the experience with post-war inflation, French public opinion had come to regard unbalanced budgets as inevitably leading to inflation. Actually, once the depression had set in, no budget was really in balance, but every government felt it its duty to make at least an effort to reëstablish an apparent equilibrium between revenue and expenditure. During the last two or three years before the advent of the Popular Front government, the budget had been "balanced" about a dozen times. Each time actual revenue fell behind the expected figure with the result that new cuts of expenditure had to be arranged to reëstablish the balance. Each time this was followed by a reduction of the national income, causing government revenues again to fall behind estimates.

This policy of "accountancy," as Blum branded it, reached its climax in Premier Pierre Laval's "decrees of misery," which reduced the already very low salaries of the civil service. The working class was bitterly opposed to the policy of deflation, and the victory of the Popular Front at the general elections of 1936 gave the signal for mass movements to undo the unbearable sacrifices imposed upon the workers under the preceding governments.

The full attention of the French workers was thus focused upon their own standard of living, and the wave of mass strikes that swept over the country during the summer of 1936 was an irresistible elementary force.

It is quite possible that a large-scale increase in the standard of living of the working class was beyond what the country could afford at the low level of production existing in 1936. Blum expected, however, that higher wages would cause production to be increased so that the wage increases would become economically defensible. In this hope he was disappointed, as will be shown later, and it was his failure to increase production, rather than the wage increases themselves, which undermined the economic and military strength of the nation. Blum's decisive weakness was not so much in the field of reform, as in that of recovery.

It is true, on the other hand, that, given this failure to engineer recovery, social reforms tended to divert energies which, in the national interest, should have been devoted to strengthening the country against its foes outside. But the strength of the popular revolt and its disregard for the critical international situation of the country were due not only to the radical orthodoxy and the pressure-group thinking of the French working class, but also to the sins of the governments that preceded the Blum administration. It was the delay in the enactment of necessary social reforms that caused the Blum government to rush through such reforms without careful analysis of what the country could afford to do under the existing circumstances. For years French employers had refused to deal with unions, while collective bargaining had become a matter of course in England and, for several years, in Germany. Now, with the victory of the Popular Front, collective bargaining was imposed upon the French employers, with the result that both sides, suspecting sinister intentions in every move of the opponent, stood ready like mobilized armies to attack each other at the first opportune moment. Obviously, this state of affairs was not favorable to national unity and opened wide the doors for fifth columnists.

In other words, the social reforms enacted by the Blum government were inevitable, because after the victory of the Popular Front the pressure of the working class enhanced by the preceding years of deflation broke like a torrent through the dam. Blum's failure lies in his inability to make the unavoidable reforms economically possible by increased production. And it was the sudden wave of reforms thrown upon recalcitrant employers, who so far had refused to the French workers what was commonly accepted in most industrially advanced countries of Europe, which contributed so largely to national disunity in the face of Hitlerism. France had delayed necessary social reforms for so long that when the workers felt strong enough to impose them, they did so regardless of the economic and international situation of the country. In 1936 France paid the price for its social backwardness.

The Popular Front and its opponents were of approximately equal strength. French social evolution during the latter half of the thirties had very clearly reached the stage of a balance of class forces. Neither side was political minded enough to be able to solve the social issues in a way favorable to national unity. France was in a state of hardly concealed civil war, and Hitler was not slow in taking advantage of his enemy's internal weakness.

Much of what has been said about France must sound familiar to American ears. Like France, the United States has been passing through great social changes in the last decade, and no perfect adjustment seems yet to have been reached in employer-labor relationships. Social reforms have been enacted that would have appeared fantastic or communistic to many before 1933. The labor unions have expanded in a measure comparable only to the growth of labor organizations under the Popular Front regime in France. No doubt that all this has created in the United States problems not entirely dissimilar from those of France, and a careful study of the French experience might help in solving American problems. Yet it seems that, in the last resort, national cohesion is considerably stronger in the United States than it was in France. Mutual fear on the part of labor and employers, though not completely absent, is less acute and therefore less apt to open breaches in the national front through which the enemy might advance into the heart of the country.

4.

Léon Blum, the new premier, held office for the first time. He was a strange combination of refined intellectual and labor leader. Not a "career" man in the French Socialist movement, he had been a member of the party since 1905, though little concerned with politics until the war broke out. In his youth he had been active in the pro-Dreyfus movement, but after it was over he returned to his literary "ivory tower." Yet when he reëntered active politics during the war, he started near the top of the ladder, for so great was his intellectual prestige that Marcel Sembat, socialist minister of public works, made Blum his "chef de cabinet," a function similar to that of a parliamentary private secretary in England.

Elected to the Chamber of Deputies for the first time in 1919, Blum immediately became the leading spokesman of his party. Even Poincaré—safe, thanks to his huge parliamentary majority—came to respect and to fear the spokesman of the small but brave Socialist opposition. In later years, many "premiers" anxiously looked toward Blum's seat in the Chamber, where often enough the fate of a cabinet was being decided. Indeed Blum had the reputation of having overthrown more governments than any other deputy.

As will be remembered, Léon Blum endeavored to avoid allowing the Socialist party to enter into a coalition government as long as the party was not strong enough to claim the lead in such a coalition. He was convinced that the Socialist party was too weak, after the Communist-Socialist split in 1920, to risk taking major responsibilities. On the other hand, Blum was anxious to prevent reactionary governments from coming into power. He was therefore always willing to support governments of Herriot's Radical party against the rightists when the Radicals pursued progressive policies.[3] In actual fact, the Radical governments usually started out with progressive programs and finished with reactionary and deflationist measures. Blum then was merciless. Through his efforts one Radical cabinet after another was defeated after the elections of 1932 had given the left a majority in the Chamber of Deputies. At the risk of endangering the parliamentary system, he voted against Radical governments whenever, under the pressure of their own right wing, they introduced deflationary measures. All he demanded, Blum liked to say, was that the Radicals remain loyal to their own election program, which repudiated deflation. This

[3] The reader must be cautioned to distinguish between the "Parti Radical et Radical-Socialiste," often abbreviated to "Radicals," and those whom the present author calls Radicals. The first is the name of a party founded by Camille Pelletan and led during the period under review by Édouard Herriot, Édouard Daladier, Camille Chautemps, Joseph Caillaux, and others. It was a progressive middle-class party which had little to do with socialism. The Socialist "Radicals" were a current in modern socialism.

policy often caused Blum to be criticized as a typical Socialist radical who forced his party into sterile inactivity to prevent it from being compromised by action.

When Blum became premier, it was under precisely those conditions which he had always considered the best. The Socialists led the government majority and—further advantage—the Communists were a part of the government majority, although they did refuse to be represented in the Cabinet. Thus, the Socialists held the initiative within the Popular Front, and at the same time the danger that the Communists would attack the Socialists for whatever action the government took was considerably lessened, though by no means entirely averted.

Léon Blum's attitude to the Communists was a peculiar mixture of sympathy and hatred. He sincerely believed that the reëstablishment of a unified labor movement was indispensable for the advance of socialism. In 1920, at the time of the Communist-Socialist split, he opposed the Communists, not because of their revolutionary ideas but because of their concept of revolution. He himself believed that a dictatorial period—which he labeled "vacation of legality"—would be necessary to establish the foundations for a Socialist society, but he accused the Communists of having falsified the Socialist theory. In his view, the Communists wrongly identified the revolution with the conquest of power by the working class, while he regarded the transformation of the social order as the really revolutionary event. The Communist accent on the conquest of power, he thought, was at the bottom of Socialist-Communist divergencies and explained the adventurous character of Communist policy. Yet Blum always refused to enter into any coalitions directed against the Communists in order not to disturb whatever chances existed for a final reconciliation between the two labor parties. In September, 1939, he called upon the Communists to repudiate the Soviet-German Pact in order to avoid the dissolution of the French Communist party. He did not wish to create the impression that the Socialist party was in alliance with the middle-class state against another labor party.

Many, even among Blum's best friends, feared that as leader of the government in a critical hour he would prove to be no man of action. But the *littérateur* was *un homme de poigne,* a man of fist, as the French say. He knew how to act and to act powerfully. During the sit-down strikes the refined and good-mannered premier coerced the employers into accepting collective labor contracts which French employers until then had considered an unbearable restriction of their property rights. His handling of crowds was masterly. He used to say that he was responsible not only to the Chamber of Deputies but also to the masses themselves. After having read his Ministerial Declaration before the Chamber of Deputies, he appeared before a large meeting of the Parisian workers and asked that they give him the same expression of confidence as the Chamber had voted him. He never missed an opportunity to explain his policy to the workers. When non-intervention in Spain created discontent among the workers of Paris, Blum called a large meeting to discuss frankly the divergent opinions and explain his own point of view. It is unlikely that he succeeded in convincing the crowd, but few believed he followed his policy for reasons which the workers could not approve. Even the Communists did not accuse him then of betrayal.

Blum's greatest drawback was his "humanitarian" sentiment. Psychologically he was incapable of understanding an anti-humanitarian phenomenon like the Nazi movement. He could never be entirely convinced that force and the threat of force were the only arguments which the Nazis could understand. So overwhelming was Blum's humanitarian sense that it prevented him from following, in foreign affairs, the policy which his intelligence told him was the only way to save peace. He knew that he had to take risks, but whenever the risk of war seemed imminent he was unable to continue a gamble whose stake was millions of human lives.

Some critics have accused Blum of cowardice. But his courage was proven beyond doubt when he opposed Poincaré during the occupation of the Ruhr, and later when he carried the banner of anti-fascism during the events following the fateful day of February 6, 1934. Fascist hatred against Blum found its crowning expression when on February 13, 1936, Royalists and fascists attacked and wounded the Socialist leader. Never before had Léon Blum been so close to the heart of the French worker; the attempted assassination confirmed more than anything else his leadership of the Popular Front.

Again before Marshal Pétain's tribunal Blum has demonstrated his moral and physical courage. Not in this field is the explanation of Blum's failures, but rather in the grandeur and the limitations of the nineteenth century whose spiritual child he was. It was his belief in the force of moral and humanitarian values that disarmed him when he faced an enemy such as fascism, which stood outside the pale of accepted morality.

5.

Of the five main organizations which formed the Popular Front only three were represented in Léon Blum's government: Socialists, Radicals, and the "Socialist Union," an intermediary group between the two large leftist parties. The Communists, as will be remembered, refused to accept Blum's invitation, preferring instead to establish themselves as a "ministry of the masses" outside and above the Cabinet. However, they announced that they would support the government loyally. The trade-union center also refused to be represented in the government, partly because the unions traditionally rejected association with parliamentary politics, partly also because the powerful Communist element within the unions resisted.

A congress of the Socialist party, held at the end of May, 1936, authorized Blum to form a government. Blum explained how he conceived his task:

> We did not have a majority at the last elections. Not only did the Socialist party not obtain a majority, but the proletarian parties did not obtain it either. There is no Socialist majority, there is no proletarian majority; there is a majority of the Popular Front whose rallying point is the program of the Popular Front. . . . The consequence is that we shall act within the framework of the present order, the same order whose contradictions and vices we have shown during our election campaign. This is the object of our experiment. The real problem which this experiment will raise is whether it is possible . . . to obtain within the framework of this order sufficient relief for the misery of those who suffer . . . and to prepare in men and things the inevitable transition to that order which remains our objective.

Alluding to a definition which he had used many times in the past, Blum recalled that there was a basic difference between what he called "the conquest of power" and "the exercise of power"—the first being a revolutionary, the second a constitutional act. The Socialist party could "exercise power" only within the limits of the existing constitution and laws, and this solely through coöperation with other parties.

Some newspapers had referred to Blum as a Kerensky, preparing the way for a French Lenin. "I hope," Blum said, "that the government which the Socialist party will form will not be a Kerensky government. If it is, believe me, in the France of today it will be no Lenin who will succeed us."

On June 4 the new cabinet took office. Léon Blum was premier; the Socialist party secretary, Paul Faure, minister without portfolio; the Socialist Roger Salengro, minister of the interior; the leader of the Radicals, Édouard Daladier, was minister of national defense; another Radical, Yvon Delbos, minister for foreign affairs; the Socialist Vincent Auriol, minister of finance; and another Socialist, Spinasse, was minister of national economy. For the first time three women, among them Mme Joliot-Curie, were members of a government. A new era in the organization of the government, which was grouped under seven main headings uniting various departments, and certainly a new era in ministerial personnel had begun in France.

A few days before the party congress, the first sit-down strike had broken out at the Usines Nieuport in Issy-les-Moulineaux, where eight hundred workers occupied the airplane factory. By the time the new government took office the stay-in strikes had become a mass movement, extending throughout the whole Paris area and even beyond. It was the greatest labor upheaval in the history of France and the more remarkable in that it was spontaneous to a very large extent. None of the labor organizations, not even the trade-union federation, Confédération Générale du Travail (C.G.T.), could claim full control of the movement, although new millions of members streamed into the unions. From about one million members which the newly united C.G.T. counted before the summer of 1936, its ranks increased to approximately five million.[4] As was

[4] About the merger of the two trade-union centers, compare p. 268.

the case in the rapid increase in trade-union membership in the United States in the thirties, the sudden expansion of the French movement gave the Communists great opportunities to occupy strategic positions in the labor organizations. The old union bureaucracy was unable to cope with the sudden influx of members. Leaders and sub-leaders were urgently needed to direct new trade-union groups, and the Communists sent their trained men by the hundreds and thousands to do their duty in the labor movement and, at the same time, to expand Communist influence over the unions.

In his speech before the Chamber on June 6, 1936, the premier admitted that the stay-in strikes were "not in agreement with the rules and principles of French civil law," but he added that no one so far had asked the government to use force against the strikers. If he were asked, he said, and if the use of force against the strikers were "what you expect from the government, I must tell you that you will wait in vain."

Instead the government submitted three bills to the Chamber, concerning the forty-hour working week, collective contracts, and holidays with pay, and asked that these bills be discussed and voted upon rapidly. In addition, the government started negotiations between the C.G.T. and the largest employer organizations and helped to effect the famous "Matignon Agreement," providing for collective labor contracts, freedom of organization, the election of workers' delegates, and wage increases ranging from 7 to 15 percent. A law defining the procedure for establishing collective agreements was passed, and the government was empowered to act as a mediator between unions and employers. Since collective-bargaining agreements had scarcely existed in France before 1936—except for a brief spell in 1919 and 1920, before the split of the trade-union movement—the Matignon Agreement marked a "new era in industrial relations." As Léon Jouhaux wrote, "The working class has won the greatest victory in its history."

Two-weeks vacations with pay and a legal basis for collective contracts were voted by Parliament with practically no opposition. The forty-hour week law, providing for an increase in wages and salaries to make up for the reduction in hours, encountered opposition in the Senate, but under the pressure of the mass strikes even this bulwark of conservatism gave way. The first industry to which this law was applied was coal mining. Realization of the tremendous adjustment necessary caused the government to delay application until late in September.

"Neither devaluation nor deflation" was the slogan of the Popular Front. Blum and Auriol had attacked former Premier Pierre Laval's deflationary measures with the argument that budget equilibrium could not be achieved by measures detrimental to the economic life of the country. What was essential was to bring back a period of prosperity, which automatically would balance the budget; tax returns would increase and expenditure for relief could be reduced. Devaluation of the franc, on the other hand, was strongly opposed by many Radicals and particularly by the Communists, who branded it as state-organized robbery of the poor. Blum and Auriol therefore rejected both deflation and devaluation. Once prosperity was reëstablished, they thought, capital would return from its hiding places in the country and abroad and thereby would cause the international balance of payments to shift in favor of France so that the franc would be saved. Auriol arranged for restoration of a considerable part of the budget cuts made under the Laval regime. A public works plan with a total expenditure of eighteen billion francs was adopted, but very little of it was carried out for lack of means. Auriol was afraid of increasing the government's debt with the Banque de France too greatly, and a public loan, the Auriol "baby bonds," to be subscribed by the general public, brought a mere four billion francs. What available funds there were, went into the armaments budget, particularly after Germany extended the duration of its military service in August, 1936.

Capital flight, rather than the hoped-for return of capital, upset Auriol's monetary policy. The general staff considered a gold reserve of fifty billion francs the indispensable war chest minimum, and during September the actual gold reserve fell below this limit. On September 25 devaluation had to be decided. To make the decision appear more in line with previous government statements, a three-power agreement on monetary coöperation was concluded with England and the United States which enabled the government to present French devaluation as part of an agreement providing for a new "alignment" of the franc. The Communists protested, though not too violently, and some fascists tried unsuccessfully to make political capital out of the government's broken promises, but the bulk of the country accepted without much criticism, or even approved, devaluation as a necessary surgical operation. Blum provided for a "social counterpart" which was to consist of a sliding scale for wages so as to compensate the workers for the expected increase in the cost of living, but the Senate rejected this, authorizing the government instead to arbitrate in labor disputes caused by increased living costs. Auriol decreed that all profits from gold holdings should be taxed away, but, since this prevented the much desired return of flight capital, this tax had to be abandoned in December.

By then the government was already on the defensive, and the conservative forces, represented mainly by the Senate, started their come-back. In October stay-in strikers had been forced off factory premises for the first time. Prosperity failed to materialize, and the lower middle class began to resent the recurrent strike movements which it held responsible for the continued crisis. The labor offensive had been based upon the general sympathy of the lower middle classes—represented by the Radical party—with the demands of labor, and upon the acknowledged need for resisting fascism. In the opinion of most lower-middle-class people, labor had obtained what it deserved and further labor unrest was unjustified, although the workers very often were striking only to force the employer to carry out what he had previously agreed to. A fascist danger no longer existed. Thus the alliance between the lower middle classes and the labor parties began to break.

At the end of February, 1937, Blum was forced to announce a "pause" to consolidate the results so far achieved. The program of the Popular Front was not abandoned, he said, but its application was to be delayed for some time. The mere announcement was of little avail. Gold continued to flow out, and the right, encouraged by the government's retreat, attacked with even more vigor. Blum made a further retreat early in March, pledging himself not to increase ordinary budget expenditure and to reduce the extraordinary budget by six billion francs. This meant a large cut in public works.

The right seemed satisfied for the moment, capital flight stopped, and a new defense loan was subscribed to the amount of eight and a half billion francs. Then a local riot between Communists and Croix-de-Feu fascists in the Paris suburb of Clichy on March 16 started a new series of social and political conflicts. Political strikes were organized, the Communists spoke bitterly of the government's alleged surrender to the reactionaries, and the C.G.T. was in a bad mood, particularly since the government had rejected trade-union demands for large public works. Finally, by the beginning of June, the franc was again in danger. Blum demanded plenary powers to defeat what he considered a bankers' conspiracy against the government. The Senate refused, and Blum resigned on June 20.

6.

What has sometimes been called "l'expérience Léon Blum" extended for little more than four months, from June to September, 1936. As in President Roosevelt's American program, with which Blum liked to compare his own experiment, reform and recovery measures were intertwined into a whole in the French "Little New Deal." The months from October to February, 1937, were a waiting period; they were followed by the formal announcement of the "pause"—which actually was a retreat into deflationary measures, characterized by new efforts to reduce expenditure and to balance the budget. The basic idea of the reform and recovery period was the popular theory that increased wages, adding to consumers' purchasing power, would end the depression.

Blum claimed in a speech before the Senate on June 16 (four days before he resigned) that he could pursue a policy similar to the New Deal under better conditions than President Roosevelt. "Because of the banking situation he [Roosevelt] was faced by an almost complete moratorium of the banks, and the entire liquid capital of America consisted of bank deposits. We are in the presence of a phenomenon which did not exist in America, namely of huge internal hoarding." Recovery in the United States, at least in the early stages, was caused, Blum claimed, by an increase of consumption, which was in turn a consequence of devaluation. Blum endeavored to obtain the same result not by devaluating the franc, but by increasing consumers' purchasing power through wage increases, shorter hours of work, and public works.

The total result of Blum's economic policy, however, was a rise of only 3 percent in the index of industrial production.[5] Blum never succeeded in bringing about a real increase in the purchasing power of the masses. All he obtained was an increase in their money incomes which was almost entirely offset by increased costs of living and the reduction of the number of working hours. Léon Blum's recovery policy amounted to little more than a "share the work" program.

Only those workers who were employed for less than 48 hours a week in 1936 enjoyed a rise in real earnings, and since there were a great many of them, total industrial working-class income increased not inconsiderably. This increase in consumers' purchasing power was, however, canceled by the fall of the real incomes of the people with fixed incomes, such as the state officials, pensioners, and so forth, who suffered badly under the rise in prices. Total consumption thus remained stationary and investments continued at a low ebb, for big business was obviously not too eager to invest capital under what many feared might any day become a full-fledged communistic regime.

Since wage increases thus added little to the total of available purchasing power, everything depended upon public spending. The increased deficit, it is true, indicated increased borrowing, but considering the increase in prices and living costs, the real deficit and, therefore, deficit spending rose by very little. In addition, the increasingly passive balance of foreign trade exerted a deflationist pressure which offset part of the rise in public expenditure.

No substantial increase in public spending was possible without a solution of the currency problem. French public opinion was accustomed to regard budget deficits as a prelude to inflation, de-

[5] See M. Kalecki, "The Lesson of the Blum Experiment." *Economic Journal*. Vol. XLVIII (1938).

spite the fact that even in times of currency stability France had had probably more deficit budgets in the last fifty years than any other country. But in the past these deficits had usually been well concealed; this time they were frankly admitted. When the right-wing parties, dwelling upon the dangers of unbalanced budgets, started their campaign against the Blum government, they easily convinced the public that the stability of the currency ought to be defended at all costs. Public deficit spending was impossible without either devaluation or exchange restrictions, or possibly both. Since Blum refused at first to devalue, devalued too little when events forced him to do so, and rejected any control of foreign exchange, large scale deficit spending was impossible.

Blum's reference to Roosevelt's New Deal was justified by the similarity of some of the methods used, but the French premier failed to realize that the more permanent elements in American recovery were linked with deficit spending—not with the N.R.A. or with the immediate consequences of devaluation. Blum and Auriol, however, remained loyal to the primitive purchasing-power theory and were confident that wage increases could achieve prosperity.

Blum was a less orthodox liberal than the leaders of British or German labor, although nowhere was orthodox liberalism stronger than in France, but he was restrained in many ways from carrying out his own ideas. He was handicapped first of all by his allies. Daladier's Radicals rejected exchange control; the Communists, many Socialists, and a considerable number of the Radicals were hostile to devaluation. Communist policy never went beyond the slogan "tax the rich," which was of little use from the point of view of recovery. The Radicals, loyal allies of labor in the political struggle against fascism, felt uneasy when the budget deficit increased; they defended laissez faire ideas against the trade unions' demand for exchange control. Blum himself showed much distrust of economic "planning"; he was afraid that some of the planning projects were essentially fascist in character. Although he set out to create a new era, his policy contained too many orthodox and too many contradictory elements to be successful. If the Socialists had resolutely embarked upon a policy of economic expansion, they might have been able to overcome both Radical and Communist resistance, particularly during the first period of the Blum government when neither Chamber nor Senate dared to provoke the striking workers. But the Socialists lacked any such program: consequently, laissez faire tradition regained strength and prevented the French Left from achieving its objective.

7.

With the resignation of the first Blum cabinet, the Popular Front was defeated. Nevertheless, Blum strove stubbornly to keep the leftist alliance alive. He succeeded to the extent that the subsequent cabinet, led by a member of Daladier's party, Camille Chautemps, was still officially known as a Popular Front government. The discovery of armed fascist conspiracies against the Republic, the unearthing of secret arms and munitions dumps belonging to a foreign-financed underground organization, "Csar" (Secret Committee for Revolutionary Action), cemented the Popular Front for a while longer. As soon as economic and financial problems came to the fore, however, the three leftist parties started to disagree. True, the Socialists showed a surprising readiness to compromise. They voted for a resolution definitely excluding any control of foreign exchange, although most Socialists had by now come to believe that only exchange restrictions could save the social reforms. Yet Chautemps and his minister of finance, Georges Bonnet, were out to win the conservatives in order to save the franc, which was once again imperiled in spite of a second devaluation in June. The price to be paid for conservative support was the formal smashing of the Popular Front.

Thus, in January, 1938, Chautemps himself forced the Communists into opposition by openly stating that he did not wish their support. The Socialists, loyal to their allies, thereupon resigned from the cabinet. Chautemps, having accomplished his objective, formed a homogeneous Radical cabinet without Communist or Socialist representation. Blum, meanwhile, put forward for the first time the idea of a "national" government, which would include all sincerely republican elements under leftist leadership, to cope with the increasingly threatening international situation. The serious state of affairs in Europe was indicated in March when German troops marched into Austria and achieved the dreaded *Anschluss* without the French government's even considering resistance. Chautemps had resigned a few days before when the Socialists refused to support plenary powers for the government. Many thought that Chautemps had sought his own defeat, having had some inkling of what Germany was planning and preferring to run away rather than to face the crisis. The third "Popular Front" government was out of office.

A new Blum government was formed, superficially almost identical with the first, but actually a mere shadow of the past. Blum by now had abandoned much of his former resistance to planning. Rearmament claimed so large a share of the country's resources that the liberal system, Blum thought, would lead to bankruptcy. His new plan was based upon two main elements: first, a veiled form of exchange control to prevent further capital losses by the flight of gold abroad; second, increased production through credit expansion and a "readjustment" of the forty-hour week. To maintain a balance in the sacrifices of the various classes and to help finance rearmament, a small capital levy was suggested. Altogether this was a first step toward economic planning for rearmament.

Such a plan might have been successful when Blum became premier for the first time in June, 1936. At that time no one, not even the conservative Senate, could have successfully resisted his demands, and everyone had the feeling that new economic and financial methods must be tried out. By March, 1938, Blum's plan was an anachronism, doomed to failure not because the plan was bad in itself, but because it no longer corresponded to the relationship of social forces in the country. The Conservatives had won the upper hand. Joseph Caillaux, the Senate's financial expert, was out to defeat Blum as swiftly as possible. The conversion of the left to ideas adapted to the new conditions of post-war or rather pre-war Europe, had come too late. France was now hopelessly committed to economic and financial methods completely outdated by the highly organized economy of Nazi Germany.

The fact that the new government's advent to power was accompanied by a renewal of sit-down strikes contributed to sealing the cabinet's doom. It has never been fully explained why, after a prolonged lull in the strike movement, strikes began again when Blum took office and petered out as mysteriously when Blum resigned. It is possible that they were organized by the extreme left of the Socialist party, led by Marceau Pivert, who believed in driving the movement ahead toward an armed revolt. But Pivert's influence with the workers was hardly great enough to cause the huge strike movement in March, 1938. The Communist leaders claimed to have no responsibility for the movement, although its center was the Paris engineering industry which the Communists controlled. It is possible that the workers expected a repetition of the original strike wave under a Socialist premier and thought that this opportunity of obtaining compensations for the increased living costs should not be missed.

The sit-down strikes, which had strengthened the government two years before, now were the last nail in the government's coffin. No one any longer feared the strikers. The Senate refused to grant Blum plenary powers to carry out his economic plan, and Blum resigned on April 8, three weeks after he had formed his government.

Édouard Daladier, Blum's minister of national defense, was the predestined successor. By having loyally supported Blum and the Popular Front, he enjoyed the confidence of the leftists, but he had also convinced the right that he was no longer the "killer" who had ordered the police to fire upon the facist rioters in February, 1934. The composition of his cabinet indeed confirmed the confidence of the right. The Socialists, who had become angered by the Radical Senators, refused to enter the cabinet. Daladier invited some center and right-wing deputies to join the government. Although the Socialists were not hostile to Daladier until the general strike in November, 1938, the cabinet from the outset clearly had nothing to do with the Popular Front. From now on, the left wing of the Conservatives led France. The coalition between labor and the progressive middle-class groups was superseded by the traditional alliance of Conservatives and lower-middle-class parties which ruled France until the war.

Chapter 11
SWEDISH LABOR'S SUCCESS

1.

THE world crisis had reached its climax when the Swedish Labor government was formed late in 1932. Having witnessed the failure of the orthodox economic policies of British and German labor, Swedish Social Democracy was resolved to follow a different course. The bugbear of the gold standard, largely responsible for the defeat of British and German labor, had been removed from Swedish politics since September, 1931, when the Swedish currency had gone off gold in the wake of the pound sterling. By the beginning of 1933 the first halting signs of revival began to appear. Conditions were thus more favorable in Sweden than they had been in Britain and Germany, and Swedish labor made the best possible use of its opportunities. Where its conservative predecessors in the Swedish government had failed to meet the crisis, the labor government achieved remarkable successes. Allowing even for a large measure of good luck which the Swedish Socialists themselves admit, the conquest of unemployment, the expansion of social services, and the rise in the standard of living were impressive achievements.

Before the advent of the labor government, power had been in the hands of a right-wing coalition whose policy was based upon the theory that "thrift and reduction of expenditures" were necessary to economic recovery. Public works were undertaken, it is true, but only as relief works for unemployed; expenditures for such purposes were kept at the lowest possible level, and the government urged all authorities to postpone or reduce capital investments. Inflation was considered the main danger by the government, particularly after the country had gone off gold. Sweden paid a heavy price for this policy. In 1932 one out of four workers was unemployed.

In conjunction with the trade unions, the Social Democratic party fought this course. Unlike their confreres in other countries, who accepted deflation, but opposed its application to wages and unemployment benefits, the Swedish labor leaders offered an alternative. They suggested an expansion of public investment to compensate for the reduction of private spending during the depression. Under this plan, circulating purchasing power would be kept as stable as possible. In the elections of 1932 the party carried its program to success. With this initial victory Swedish labor began its astonishing series of achievements unparalleled in the international labor movement.

Most of the development of Swedish labor had been unobserved by the rest of European socialism. During the First World War, neutral Sweden had played an important role in the efforts to reestablish the pre-war International, but after the war Swedish developments had been neglected. The language barrier contributed greatly to the failure of European labor to follow the progress of the movement in Northern Europe. It was only after 1932, when the world's attention was drawn to the little country that had conquered unemployment, that European labor as a whole became attentive to the achievements of the Swedish party.

To their surprise, European labor leaders discovered that Swedish Social Democracy had developed a long line of brilliant and creative leaders. Per Albin Hansson, the prime minister, was perhaps the most popular man in the country; everyone referred to him simply as "Per Albin." He was the great friend of every worker in Sweden. Rickard Sandler, who translated Marx's works into Swedish, was foreign minister and—until the failure of sanctions against Italy—an ardent protagonist of active democratic foreign policy. Gustaf Moeller, the all-powerful secretary of the party, was a brilliant minister of social affairs during the period of the struggle against unemployment. Ernest Wigforss, minister of finance, was supported by some of the outstanding leaders of the Swedish school of economic science, one of the most famous in the world. Gunnar

Myrdahl and Erik Lindahl, two of the leaders of the Swedish school, were intimately associated with the preparation of the economic policy of the government. Oesten Unden, head of the University of Uppsala, was minister without portfolio. Arthur Engberg, ardent admirer of Latin and French civilizations, directed the Ministry of Education. Together, these men formed a brilliant team, unexcelled in the European labor movement.

2.

In March, 1933, shortly after the labor government had come into power, Sweden counted 187,000 unemployed. Compared with other countries of similar population, this was perhaps not many. But for Sweden, this figure represented the trough of the severest depression in history. The new government placed before the Riksdag (Parliament) proposals for a new economic policy based upon a fresh conception of the struggle against the crisis.

According to these recommendations, the government would not allow the crisis to evolve along the lines of so-called natural laws. Nor would Swedish labor approve of the measures taken by the preceding government to reduce public expenditures. That deflationary policy had aggravated the depression. If continued, it would reduce the standard of living for a long time, and destroy some of the most cherished social reforms. But it was not enough, the Swedish labor leaders said, merely to oppose the social consequences of deflation, without advocating an alternative economic policy. Since the depression had found its expression in reduced private spending and a corresponding decrease in circulating purchasing power, the government was to make up for the slack in private business by increasing public spending. This would stimulate consumption and production in general.

Accordingly, the Swedish labor leaders advocated extensive public works, not merely relief works, but huge emergency investments. They felt that this program should not be financed by increased taxation, for this method would mainly shift, not create, purchasing power. The correct method of financing, as they saw it, consisted in the government's borrowing money. The budget was to be deliberately underbalanced, the deficit being the source of the additional purchasing power created by the government. National budgets are usually unbalanced during a depression, but most ministers of finance skillfully manipulate the figures so as to hide at least part of the deficit. The Swedish labor finance minister, Wigforss, went to the other extreme by expressly pointing out in a statement accompanying the budget estimates in January, 1933, that the apparent balancing of the ordinary budget was fictitious, and by drawing attention to the planned borrowing of 160,000,000 kronor to finance public works. "The budget is based on the assumption," he said, "that the international situation will undergo no appreciable change and that in Sweden there will be no spontaneous tendency towards recovery, except to the extent that the policy of the state will help to bring it about. . . . In seeking to achieve this objective, the state's financial policy must obviously play an important part."

The theoretical foundation for this proposal was given by Professor Gunnar Myrdahl, who exposed the fallacy of the popular view that a sound financial policy requires a balance each year between total government income and expenses. Acceptance of the orthodox theory had forced state finances merely to reflect business fluctuations, while preventing government from influencing the business situation through appropriate fiscal measures. In depression years the state was supposed to cut its expenditures, increasing thereby the decline of purchasing power; while during the boom the state would expand its investments, at the risk of adding further impetus to the boom. Any government finds it difficult to reduce expenditures during a depression, since relief for the unemployed becomes an urgent necessity. But financial orthodoxy frowns at this "extravagance" of the authorities and endeavors to obtain at least a few cuts in spending and additional taxation. If, however, the assumption is abandoned that the budget must be balanced on a yearly basis, the government obtains a certain latitude for applying measures to maintain purchasing power at a stable level; it can increase expenditures during the depression and reduce them in times of prosperity. If the budget is to be balanced, not on the basis of one year but of a whole business cycle, then increased revenues in years of prosperity can be used to repay the debts incurred during the depression. This second part of the new fiscal policy, the repayment of the depression loans was, of course, an indispensable part of the policy.

A further condition of the success of this expansionist policy was that the currency be free, not tied to gold or any international standard which would prevent the adoption of necessary economic measures. Sweden had left the gold standard in 1931, but its currency was linked to the British pound sterling. However, since economic expansion proceeded in Britain at the same time and with similar swiftness as in Sweden, this arrangement did not hamper Swedish reflation. Had a discrepancy developed between the maintenance of the exchange rate and reflation, the government would have sacrificed exchange stability to the main aim of economic expansion. The Swedes engineered a rise in wholesale prices and determined the limits of that rise in consideration of the cost of living rather than of the external value of the currency.

3.

Such a departure from well-established practice was bound to meet serious resistance. Within the labor movement itself "one could observe a certain hesitancy," as Finance Minister Wigforss put it ". . . to accept the consequences of its [the government's] demands for public works, credit expansion, and increased purchasing power with regard to a general increase in the price level. This may be explained chiefly by the fact that the Labor party for a long time represented the interest of consumers against the demand of different producers' groups for price-raising measures." Although this hesitancy disappeared very soon, it was characteristic of the struggle between the traditional pressure-group forces and those of creative reformism within the labor movement.

The problem arose in an acute form when the government was looking for a parliamentary majority to support its program of reflation. Labor was reluctant at first to accept the peasants' demands for an increase in agricultural prices. For the Social Democratic party represented the consumers' unwillingness to give up the benefits of low prices for foodstuffs. Without the peasants' support the government could hardly find a majority in favor of reflation. Eventually, though, labor came to realize that the lessened purchasing power of the agricultural classes would hamper the progress of reflation, and the two groups came to an understanding in support of the government's economic program. The agreement thus reached extended the benefits of reflation to both industry and agriculture.

Another danger for the government program appeared when the banks expressed their dislike for the new-fangled ideas of labor by tightening the capital market. Interest rates, which had been steadily falling before the Labor government came into power, began to rise in November, 1932, and continued to do so until April, 1933. For a large-scale borrowing program, this was a signal of extreme danger. Not only would the public debt service be increased, with a consequent necessity to reduce deficit spending, but higher interest rates, by exerting deflationary pressure upon private business, would run counter to the very purpose of deficit spending. Confronted with unrelenting energy in the pursuance of the government's policy, however, the banks very soon abandoned their opposition and the interest rates declined.

The results of the labor government's policy were gratifying. Recovery started in the second half of 1933, production increased, and unemployment diminished. From an average of 164,000 in 1933, the unemployment figure decreased to 115,000 in 1934, and continued to fall until by 1937 total unemployment amounted to 18,000. In 1938, Sweden was a country without unemployed. The Swedish labor government had conquered the crisis. Discussions of how to prevent an excessive boom now superseded the former anxious query of how unemployment could be reduced.

Prices increased in accordance with the government's wishes. Between 1932 and 1936 wholesale prices rose by about 20 percent, while the cost of living increased by only 2 to 3 percent. Toward the end of 1936, to be sure, wholesale prices began to rise more sharply, owing to the boom on the world market; this was responsible for the turn in public discussion from measures to foster expansion to steps that might prevent a speculative boom. Before the danger really materialized, the boom broke and wholesale prices turned downward.

The favorable economic evolution permitted the government to repay even more quickly than was originally intended the money borrowed in 1933 and 1934 for the unemployment program. Thus, the basic principle of the new fiscal policy that budgets have to be balanced within a complete business cycle was fulfilled. Beyond repaying the crisis debts, the labor government was able to make large increases in the social services, among which achievements housing improvements ranked first. Real wages were higher than ever before by 1935, and continued to rise. Although agricultural prices increased on a modest scale, the cost of living remained almost stationary, while wage rates increased. A fiscal policy to achieve a more even distribution of the national income combined with the greatest prosperity in Swedish history to lift the country's standard of living to record heights.

The country quickly realized the advantages of labor's policy. At the general elections of 1936 the Social Democratic vote increased by 300,000, from 41.7 to 45.9 percent of the total. The number of Socialist seats increased from 104 to 112, out of a total of 230. Together with six members of a separate Left Socialist party, and five Communist members of the Riksdag, the Social Democrats held a comfortable majority over all middle-class parties combined. Nevertheless, the party leaders decided to continue coöperation with the Peasant party as in the preceding four years. They preferred such an alliance to a Socialist-Communist combination, which would have forced the government to resort to extreme Socialist measures in an international situation which the Socialist leaders considered distinctly unfavorable. The Social Democratic party succeeded in mobilizing large numbers of formerly indifferent groups in the population. It took the international crisis of the Second World War to weaken the proud structure of Swedish Social Democracy.

4.

There was little agreement in Sweden itself on the question of how far recovery was due to government measures and how far to good fortune, particularly the rapid increase in Swedish exports resulting from the post-1933 armaments race. The opposition claimed that the emergency projects had little to do with the upswing, which started before any appreciable number of new public works were under construction. Since the effects of the emergency projects did not materialize until 1934, the rise of exports in 1933, rather than government policy, was described as the main cause of the amelioration of the economic situation.

Government supporters countered with the assertion that the rise of exports exerted little influence upon unemployment. The most decisive diminution of unemployment began in the spring of 1934, when the emergency works program started to operate, though its full effects were realized some time afterwards. Admittedly, public works were started too late, since the labor government had first to work out the necessary plans, which the preceding government, rejecting large-scale public works, had refused to do. But, while the effects of work creation came late, they were still of tremendous influence. The revival was due far more to increased demand from the home market than to sales on foreign markets, as was shown by comparing the greater advances of industries working for internal consumption with the smaller progress of export industries.

However the respective merits of good fortune and government policy be evaluated, the fact cannot be denied that the Swedish labor government developed a new conception of the role of the state in a crisis, and that its policy contributed toward the country's rapid recovery. The development of this new conception, breaking sharply with tradition and opposed to orthodox laissez faire policies, was the great merit of Swedish labor. It acknowledged the fact that the maintenance of social reforms is impossible during a depression by merely opposing attacks upon them from reactionary quarters. It demonstrated that a successful social policy depends upon an equally successful economic policy. Swedish labor recognized that in a crisis, narrow trade unionism is bound to fail. Events themselves forced labor to broaden its view beyond those of the traditional trade unionists. Swedish Social Democracy thus became one of the pioneers in constructive Socialist reformism, sharing this role, as we shall see, to a certain extent with the Viennese Social Democrats.

PART IV

The Rise of Fascism

Chapter 12

THE EMERGENCE OF FASCISM: ITALY

1.

AT the International Socialist Congress of 1928 Otto Bauer's report on the world political situation held the limelight. In a comparatively brief speech, the Austrian leader reviewed the prospects for the international working-class movement. He dealt with Central and Western Europe, where new Socialist victories seemed imminent; with the Russian workers who were, he felt, no longer separated from their Socialist comrades elsewhere by any decisive issue, after the Communist admission of a "temporary capitalist stabilization"; with the workers in America, Asia, and the British dominions overseas, whose support, he claimed, would turn the Socialist International into a world-wide force of decisive significance. Bauer embraced the whole world—with a grave exception: a word rarely mentioned in his speech was the word "Fascism." And the manifesto adopted by the Congress did not go beyond a conventional protest against Italian Fascism.

Even the far-sighted Otto Bauer failed to see the international significance of Mussolini's victory in Italy. Fascism, most Socialists felt, was a phenomenon peculiar to Italy, and the Fascist leader strengthened this impression by his well-known and often reiterated remark that "Fascism is no article for exportation." Even when the world economic crisis made Mussolini change his mind and Fascism became a major Italian export item, many Socialists and progressives in general took refuge in Francis Delaisi's theory that a serious Fascist threat was restricted to the "countries of the four-legged horse," while democracy was the natural form of life in the countries of "mechanical horsepower." It required the advance of Hitlerism in Germany, Europe's foremost industrial nation, to convince labor that it was menaced everywhere by its deadliest enemy, Fascism.

This neglect of the Italian experience is hard to justify. Italian Fascism contained many elements that recurred elsewhere, of which a sound knowledge might have assisted in the organization of effective anti-Fascism. As long as Fascism was considered a purely Italian development, foreign Socialists were inclined to regard the Black Shirts in much the same way as curious spectators look at strange animals in a zoölogical garden: as interesting specimens, but hardly beasts that might affect one's own life. To study them might satisfy human curiosity, but would bring little practical knowledge.

Yet any careful observation of the events that led to the Fascist victory in Italy would have brought to light a series of vital facts for labor elsewhere. Such a study would have shown that Fascism rose as an anti-capitalist force and that it gained in strength during a period of economic decline, such as the post-war crisis. The record would have made clear that the situation which nurtured Fascism was characterized by a progressive disintegration of the nation due primarily to the stagnating equilibrium between the two main antagonists on the Italian social scene, the working class and the middle class. Social conflicts in such a situation tended to reach no conclusive decisions; the struggles became, therefore, a permanent feature of national life. This continuous unrest was fertile soil for the rise of Fascism, because the unending social conflicts enhanced the desire of the general public for a more stabilized social situation, regardless of its nature.

Penetrating study of post-war Italy thus would have made it clear that Fascism became victorious after both labor and middle class had proven incapable of overcoming the stalemate in the social and political struggles of the country.

2.

"This war is also the greatest political and social revolution in history, greater even than the French revolution," said the Italian premier, Orlando, in the Chamber of Deputies a few days after the 1918 armistice. The tremendous advance of the Italian Socialists and their revolutionary temper seemed to confirm his opinion. With two million Socialist votes out of a total of five and a half million votes at the general election of November, 1919, and a general shift of the popular vote towards the left, the political balance of forces pointed in the direction of basic social changes. The leading group among the Socialists, the so-called "Maximalists"—typical pre-war radicals—openly stated that the workers' next step would be the "creation of a Socialist Republic and the establishment of a proletarian dictatorship." Serrati, the Maximalist leader, held the support of a majority in the party, while moderates like Turati, Treves, and Modigliani were forced into the background. With the revolutionary tension mounting among the workers in the city and the peasants kept in semi-feudal servitude in Sicily and southern Italy, the Maximalists seemed chosen by fate to carry out a social revolution in the country.

Typical radicals, the Maximalists did nothing to prepare themselves and the workers for their task. They failed to establish contact with the peasants. When, in 1919 and 1920, the peasants in Sicily and some parts of Southern Italy took over the uncultivated land of absentee landowners and distributed it among themselves, the Socialists remained aloof, instead of coördinating this movement with that of the industrial workers who were concentrated in the North. The Maximalists made radical speeches in the cities, correctly pointing out that Italy was on the verge of a revolution; but instead of taking the lead, the Maximalists discussed with the reformists and the Communists the best methods of achieving Socialist objectives. Unable to reach agreement among themselves, the Socialists remained passive. Almost any action would have been better than to leave the workers and peasants wasting their energies in dispersed efforts, without leadership from the party. Even a revolutionary defeat or a disappointing government experience under reformist leadership would have been better for labor and democracy, since the stalemate between the middle classes and labor would have been overcome in either case.

As it was, the working class was strong enough to destroy the weak structure of Italian capitalism and to force the Italian middle class to submission under a totalitarian dictatorship, but was too deeply involved in verbal radicalism and too lacking in creative thought to establish its own rule. The revolutionary temper of the masses, continual threats of labor leaders, and the uncoördinated actions of workers and peasants paved the way not for socialism but for a dictatorship over both the middle classes and labor.

The Maximalists claimed the leadership in the coming Italian revolution. The election manifesto of the party in 1919 ended with the words: "All power of the organized proletariat to the [Workers'] Councils! Whoever does not work, shall not eat!" Yet, as a matter of fact, all revolutionary or unconstitutional actions undertaken by workers between 1918 and 1920 were spontaneous, not due to any influence exerted by the Socialist Party.

Maximalist speeches, full of threats, when read against the background of the Russian Revolution, sent "shudders through all traditionally-minded men." [1] Continuous unrest, strikes, factory occupations, expropriation of land—all this convinced the middle class that a revolution was impending and that the democratic middle-class state was powerless to stave off the danger. Public opinion became more and more convinced that a strong man was needed to establish law and order.

The decisive incident was the occupation of the factories in August, 1920. A wage conflict in the metal industry led to passive resistance by the workers, which some employers in turn answered with a lock-out. The workers organized a stay-in strike, involving about 500,000 workers. While occupying the factories, the workers endeavored to keep the machinery going, at the same time preparing arms to resist the evacuation of the factories and minting coins. All this created the impression that the workers intended to stay where they were. There was little violence and the workers so effectively kept strict discipline under the leadership of their councils, that the public authorities refrained from interfering with the workers.

So far the movement was limited to metal factories. But the workers in other branches of the industry urged their leaders to fol-

[1] Carl T. Schmidt, *The Corporate State in Action,* p. 27.

low the example of the metal workers, whose Socialist, Catholic, Anarchist, and Republican trade unions together had taken over the means of production. "The whole country waited tensely for the next move of the strikers, of the millions of other organized workers, and of their leaders. Had the Socialist chiefs been ready to seize political power at this moment, they might well have been successful. No one seemed to stand in their way. But the leadership of the party was not prepared for such a decision. On the contrary, it was divided and uncertain. . . . No—it was argued—Italy was not yet ready for a new social order." [2]

With this fateful decision, the Socialists reaffirmed their pressure-group policy; they did so at the moment when Italy, in its state of social dissolution, most needed an integrating force. According to the plans of the Socialist leaders, the factory occupation was to remain an incident in a trade-union conflict. A narrow majority of the trade-union representatives rejected Maximalist suggestions to use the factory occupation as the starting point for a revolutionary movement in the entire country. Without a struggle the Maximalists accepted the trade-union decision and threw away their greatest opportunity for ascent to governing power. Negotiations began with employers' representatives, who agreed "in principle" to the trade-union demand for workers' control in industry, and the workers left the factories. In appearance it was a trade-union victory, but the workers were bitterly disappointed and marked the day as one of defeat. The employers, on the other hand, felt that they had narrowly escaped a revolution, without the government's making the slightest effort to resist. Although the working class now was in retreat, big business, having faced so closely the danger of revolution, was anxious to prevent the recurrence of a similar crisis. With the unsuccessful occupation of the factories began the decline of the Italian labor movement and the emergence of Fascism.

Another and the last opportunity for the Socialists to act as the leaders in a political and social reconstruction of Italy opened in the fall of 1921, when an effort was made to form a Socialist-Liberal coalition government to save the country from the threatening civil war. The right-wing Socialists advocated such a coalition and they

[2] *Ibid.*, p. 32.

found the warmest support among the non-urban Socialists who were anxious to obtain government protection against Fascist lawlessness. Had this proposal been accepted, the crisis, which had not been solved in a revolutionary way—owing to Maximalist lack of decision—could possibly have been solved by a compromise between middle classes and labor; these then jointly could have defeated Fascism. But the same Maximalists who, a year before, meekly accepted the reformist anti-revolutionary decision, now rejected the reformist coalition plans. The crisis therefore had to be solved against labor.

When, early in 1922, the Fascist offensive against the cities began and civil war spread over Italy, government and big business sided with the Fascists. One after another the city strongholds of the Socialists fell into the hands of the Fascist "Squadristi," the Storm Troopers. Bologna, Novara, Genoa, Livorno, finally Milan and Naples, were occupied by Black Shirts. The workers tried to resist, and proletarian self-defense organizations, like the "Arditi del Popolo," were formed. Characteristically, many Maximalist theoreticians considered it an illusion to believe that the workers could defeat the Fascists as long as the latter were under the protection of the government. Later experience has shown that the Maximalists were right in considering that a Fascist-government alliance is almost always superior to any force the working class can organize for its own defense. The obvious conclusion, one would think, would be to prevent such an alliance by forming a government willing and able to resist Fascist violence. Yet, the very same Maximalists who rejected proletarian self-defense organizations refused to use the only alternative method left to Italian labor to prevent a Fascist victory with government support.

The workers were without allies in their struggle against the rapidly growing Fascist movement and its supporters among the military and the police. Working-class resistance remained spontaneous, lacking centralized direction, dispersed in hundreds of small riots, while the Fascists proceeded according to plan and under centralized command. The general strikes with which the workers often replied to Fascist occupations of cities were in many cases more damaging to the workers' cause than to the Fascists. Public opinion was tired of continuous strikes, and every new walk-out increased public sympathy for the Fascists, who asserted that they would soon end unrest once and for all.

Thus the Italian general strike of August 31, 1922, failed despite almost 100 percent support from workers throughout the country. After the strike was over, the Right-Wing Socialist paper *Giustizia* wrote: "We are today in so painful, so catastrophic a situation because the various solutions have been *tried too late*."

The way was now open for the Fascists. Mussolini became premier with the support of the king, large parts of the army and bureaucracy, and economically ruling classes. To complete the victory and establish a totalitarian dictatorship, the Fascists needed final encouragement. For, in spite of the support of the powers that be and of large masses of former adherents of middle-class parties, the Fascist regime during the first two years after the "March on Rome" was far from being totalitarian. There was no centralized control, for the Fascist state, so highly centralized at the time of the conquest, now broke up into thousands of semi-independent local dictatorships. Fascist economic policy was reëstablishing full economic control by big business, and was inspired by the most old-fashioned laissez faire ideas.[3] As late as 1924 the Fascist party entered the election campaign as part of a governmental bloc rather than as a totalitarian ruler.

At these elections the government was in a minority in all industrial centers in spite of the Fascist reign of terror which the Socialist deputy Giacomo Matteotti denounced in his last speech before the Chamber. Socialists and Communists together polled more than one million votes, with the Maximalists losing their numerical superiority among the labor parties to the right-wing reformists. In cities and countryside combined the opposition parties were almost as strong as the government. Thus, even a year after the Fascist military victory, the stalemate in Italian politics was not completely overcome. Mussolini himself realized that Italy was living under an old-fashioned dictatorship of a type similar to Czarism. At the

[3] "The Fascist leaders lost little time in rewarding the propertied men whose money had helped them to victory. Those elements in their program that had been borrowed from the Socialists were now forgotten. Indeed, they actually moved in the direction of laissez faire at this time." Carl T. Schmidt, *op. cit.*, p. 51.

end of June, 1924, he said, "I want Parliament to function. . . . It is not my intention to govern by executive decrees."

However, the stalemate could not continue for very long. The assassination of Giacomo Matteotti on June 10, 1924 and the subsequent action of the opposition parties, were the factors that caused Italy finally to adopt the new pattern of totalitarian dictatorship.

In answer to Matteotti's assassination on orders from Mussolini, the Parliamentary opposition, the so-called "Aventin," left the Chamber of Deputies. This action was typical of the weakness of Italian anti-Fascism. The country was in the throes of a moral crisis. Mussolini's responsibility for the death of his opponent, his hypocritical condolences to the widow, shocked not only the anti-Fascists, but also many supporters of the regime. Those who had believed in Mussolini's anti-capitalistic slogans were disappointed over Fascist subservience to big business. A wave of disgust and shame swept over the country. By withdrawing from Parliament the Aventin gave expression to this attitude. Some government groups, such as the ex-service men and some former Liberals who had joined the Fascist party after 1922, seceded from the government majority as a result of Aventin's withdrawal. The "reconciliation" between Fascism and the "traditional institutions" which had brought Mussolini into power was threatened.

Dangerous as the situation was for Mussolini, mere protest was not sufficient to effect his defeat. The Communists suggested the formation of a counter-Parliament. This might have led to organized resistance against the regime in case Mussolini had dared to use force against the rival authority. But the opposition parties rejected the Communist proposal, hoping instead that the regime would disintegrate by itself. They had not yet learned to think in terms of power. Fear that the Communists might lead a mass movement outside Parliament may have been an additional cause for the rejection of their proposal.

The Aventins' withdrawal from the Chamber of Deputies thus was only an expression of a moral protest. The opposition failed to take effective measures to challenge Mussolini's power. Mussolini, who first hesitated, expecting the worst, soon regained his former vigor and passed to a counterattack. His totalitarian dictatorship grew out of the defense of his regime against the Aventin. A new wave of terror prepared the ground for this new evolution; trade unions, political parties, and cultural organizations were either disbanded or placed under Fascist control. Parliament was transformed into a Fascist party meeting, local autonomy was abolished, the last remnants of the opposition press were destroyed. By 1926, the façade of parliamentary government was openly abandoned and totalitarianism was fully established.

Chapter 13

A FASCIST DEFEAT: AUSTRIA

1.

MUSSOLINI'S victory was due, in the last analysis, to a permanent stalemate in Italian politics. Organized labor and the middle class held each other in check to such an extent that neither could develop and pursue a constructive policy. The deadlock prevented Italian democracy from functioning, and since neither of the two hostile social groups gave way, fascism took advantage of their paralysis to establish its rule over both of them. Had either of these groups succeeded in defeating the other, or had fruitful coöperation been established between parts of them at least, the stalemate might have been broken. Any method which could have given life and freedom of action to democracy might have averted fascism.

Similar situations created like problems elsewhere. In Austria a stalemate threatened for many years between the rising force of Social Democracy and the united front of the middle class. By clever parliamentary tactics the Austrian middle class succeeded for a while in using its narrow parliamentary majority with great effectiveness. Acting in the interest of democracy, Austrian labor abstained from exploiting its political resources to the extent of paralyzing parliamentary government. But tension increased between the two hostile groups and the fascist forces did not fail to take advantage of this situation.

Austria might thus have witnessed a repetition of the Italian experience but for a last-minute compromise between labor and a group of democratic middle-class leaders. Fascist and reactionary movements had existed in the country since the birth of the republic, but for almost a decade they remained without mass support.

The rise of Austrian fascism to a serious political force was closely connected with the incidents of July, 1927, which brought to the open the bitter hostility between the two blocs of the right and of the left in the country. The stalemate which, owing to prudent Socialist tactics, had so far not paralyzed the regime now became manifest.

2.

On July 15, 1927, a street riot in Vienna developed into firing between police and workers. When night fell, ninety bodies lay on the pavement. And out of this bloody struggle eventually emerged the great onslaught of Austrian fascism.

With a Socialist-ruled capital city and a violently anti-Socialist federal government, Austria lived in a state of perpetual stalemate and tension. Despite the Socialists' flexible tactics, a clash between the clerical and anti-Socialist countryside and the Labor party, powerfully entrenched in Vienna, had become almost inevitable. The street riots of July 15, 1927, were the climax of a long evolution.

During the revolutionary post-war period, Austrian labor had taken advantage of the favorable international situation to wrest concessions from the middle-class parties.

As long as the Hungarian Soviet Republic existed, its mere existence brought pressure to bear upon the Austrian middle-class parties. Fearing that the Bolshevist revolution might spread, Austria's conservative politicians did not dare to resist the democratic demands of the Socialists. Parliament expropriated the Habsburg family, democratized the administration, reorganized education on a progressive basis that was held up as a model for Europe, and enacted far-reaching social reforms. When, with reactionary victories in Hungary and Bavaria, the international situation turned against the working class, middle-class resistance to Socialist demands increased; at the same time, owing to the progressive reorganization of economic life, the masses lost their revolutionary temper. Then labor's influence upon the government of the Republic declined.

Just as after the war the Austrian working class did not advance as far on the revolutionary path as its German brethren and never did seriously attempt to establish a proletarian dictatorship, now the reaction in Austria was far less powerful than in Germany. In addition, the Austrian Communists lost most of their popular support; the working class was thus united in the Social-Democratic party. This enabled Austrian labor better to resist the reactionary onslaught than did the split German labor movement.

As soon as it became clear that the Austro-German *Anschluss* could not be achieved because of the resistance of the Allied powers, the Social-Democratic foreign minister, Otto Bauer, resigned. The coalition government continued, but the Socialists no longer had the controlling influence. Within the leadership of the Christian Social party, the middle-class representatives superseded the peasants, who so far had shown eagerness to coöperate with the industrial working class. The middle-class leaders were unwilling to submit to Socialist predominance, and among the peasants much ill-will against the Socialist cities was aroused by requisitions to provide food. A stalemate began to develop within the government, with Socialists and middle-class parties holding each other in check. Whenever the international situation was favorable for a while to the workers, the Socialists were able to overcome this stalemate and to obtain certain political or social advantages for the working class. The defense laws were enacted under such trends, and the army was reorganized, according to the conditions of the Peace Treaty but at the same time with the army's proletarian and republican character maintained. Apart from such extraordinary situations, however, the government was less and less able to function.

Under these conditions it was inevitable that many workers became dissatisfied with the results of Socialist participation in the government. Russia's military successes and a highly effective international working-class action to prevent Allied aid from reaching Poland during its war against the Soviet Union strengthened the revolutionary temper of the Socialist movement. Many Socialists advocated resigning from the government rather than continuing to compromise with the middle-class parties. Had the Socialist leaders refused to heed these voices, their party might have been split much as the German Independent Social Democratic party was split by the Communists at about the same time. By taking fully into account the changing mood of the workers and resigning from the government rather than alienating a considerable part of the working class, the Austrian Socialist leaders succeeded in preventing a split within the ranks of their party.

The best barometer for measuring the temper of the workers was the still existing Workers' and Soldiers' Councils. From the outset the Communist members had opposed Socialist-middle-class coöperation, but after the Communist defeats in the spring of 1919, this opposition could be safely neglected by the Socialist leaders. Now, however, Communist criticism of Socialist "coalition policy" found support among an organized Social-Democratic "New Left," which proudly considered itself the heir of the wartime internationalist leftists. The Socialist ministers hastened to complete some important reforms already in progress, and then resigned in June, 1920.

At the subsequent general elections, held in October of the same year, the Social Democrats lost 200,000 votes and the Christian Socials increased their poll by about 150,000. The Communists received only a few thousand votes. Although the elections clearly showed the decline in Socialist influence, Austrian labor remained far more powerful than the German workers' organization. The unity of the labor movement within the Austrian Social Democratic party was practically complete. To preserve this, the Socialist leaders had abandoned government participation and they continued to do so until fascism destroyed the party.

3.

With the Socialists' withdrawal from the Austrian government, the revolution came to an end. From that moment on, the struggle against counter-revolutionary dangers continued almost without interruption. For many years this danger was far less threatening and imminent than in Germany, but it could never be neglected. Reactionary victories in neighboring Hungary and Bavaria, and later the Fascist triumph in Italy, turned Austrian democracy into an island within a hostile sea. All reactionary movements in Austria felt encouraged by the example of labor's defeat in the countries bordering on the little republic. The Austrian Socialists, on the other hand, felt pride in stressing the difference between the fate of their own party and that of the Hungarian, Bavarian and Italian movements, due primarily, they were convinced, to the Austrian Socialists' better leadership and organization. The specific Austrian Socialists' pride in their party, often referred to as "party patriotism," originated in this period.

The great opponent of Social Democracy was the Christian Social chancellor, Father Ignaz Seipel, who succeeded in winning the support of all middle-class groups for a crusade against Austrian labor. The middle-class coalition and labor faced each other like hostile armies. A battle could have been avoided only if either side had backed down to the extent of accepting some form of coöperation on the other's terms. This the Austrian middle-class leaders refused to do, because consecutive labor defeats in the neighboring countries encouraged their belief that the same result could be obtained by a strong anti-labor policy in Austria. The labor organizations, on the other hand, were confident of their power to resist reactionary onslaughts. The street riots in Vienna were the result of this stalemate.

Ten days before the bloody July Friday, a trial had opened involving several members of a small fascist organization. They had laid a trap against a Social Democratic procession in Schattendorf, a small village in Burgenland in eastern Austria, and had shot and killed a Socialist war invalid and a little boy. On July 14 a jury acquitted the accused. The decision was another in the long series of what the workers regarded as miscarriages of justice. They pointed out that many political murders in which the victims were members of the left, had gone unpunished. After having borne patiently for years official disregard of the deaths of their colleagues, the workers now lost their patience. The Socialist party leadership, misjudging the seriousness of the working-class protest, decided to let things take their course without interference from the organization. It might be useful, they thought, to let the government and the public see a spontaneous working-class demonstration, one which could not be minimized—as in the past—as having been staged through the use of the party machinery. Besides, if the party had controlled the demonstration, the Socialist leaders would have been compelled to indicate its aim. Against what could the protest be directed? The murderers had been acquitted by a jury and the jury system was a democratic institution against which Social Democrats could not protest. For the first time since 1918, the party thus neglected to give direction and control to a working-class demonstration.

On the morning of July 15, tens of thousands of workers gathered on the world-famous Ringstrasse to protest against the jury's verdict.

The police, no longer accustomed to dealing with spontaneous workers' demonstrations, sent out mounted officers. These charged across the street—blocking the way for thousands of roused workers who filled the Ringstrasse—and rode in upon the crowd. More and more workers arrived in processions, alarmed by the action of electrical workers who had pulled the power switches. To hold off the mounted men, low barriers were swiftly constructed out of benches and wood was gathered from half-built houses near by. Shots were fired. The angry crowd, goaded by the city rabble whom the spectacle had attracted, stormed the Law Courts and set fire to them.

Now the Social Democratic party intervened. Small detachments of the Republican Defense Corps, a party steward troop, were sent to shield the workers against the police, but also to prevent excesses by the crowd. Unarmed, these groups were too weak. The crowd prevented fire brigades from entering the Law Courts. Finally, the Socialist mayor, Karl Seitz, appeared on the scene in the hope of ending senseless violence. He climbed on one of the fire engines to lead it close to the building. The crowd barred the way, and the engine was able to advance only at a snail's pace. It nevertheless succeeded in reaching a spot just a few yards from the entrance. At that moment the police, by now armed with rifles, started to shoot. Volley after volley swept the streets. Maddened by the resistance and the violence of the crowd and feeling themselves in danger, the officers of the law ran amok.

The workers gathered in front of the Socialist party headquarters, asking for arms to defend themselves against the police. The party had stores of arms, but these were destined to defend democracy against fascists or monarchists, not for a civil war between the workers and the police. Besides, if in this civil war the workers defeated the anti-Socialist government under Father Ignaz Seipel, could a Socialist revolutionary government maintain itself in little Austria, surrounded as it was by hostile counter-revolutionary or Fascist countries? Obviously, Italian Fascism and the Hungarian counter-revolution would not tolerate a proletarian dictatorship in Austria, and the conservative German government of the day would hardly come to Socialist Austria's rescue. In the opinion of the Socialist leaders, a revolutionary struggle thus was out of the question. They refused to arm the workers. Instead, a one-day general strike was called, to be followed by a three days' transport strike. In this way, the party hoped to regain control over the masses, giving the passionate feelings of indignation the form of an organized protest.

A strike bulletin issued by the Social Democratic party the day after the bloody Friday, reported on the progress of the strike and warned the workers against the arguments of the Communists:

> The orders of the Party Executive and the Trades Union Council have done their work. Rail traffic has been stopped since midnight in all Austria. The postal, telephone, and telegraph strike has been carried on throughout Austria. The protest strike of the working class has been carried out with strength and dignity. The Republican Defense Corps is in readiness in all Austria. We ask you, comrades, to preserve full discipline and not to permit yourselves to be diverted from our orders under any kind of provocation.
>
> Do not allow yourselves to be misled by the Communists!
>
> The Communists are agitating for the instant arming of the working class. We must declare against this. The arming of the working class at the present moment would mean immediate civil war, as a result of the armed struggle between the working class and the military formations of the state. Civil war would mean (1) fresh horrible sacrifice of life; (2) the most terrible economic catastrophe, famine, and increase of unemployment; (3) the ruin of the working class in the agricultural districts, and the great strengthening of armed Fascism in those districts; (4) the gravest danger for the existence of the Republic.
>
> We do not want to experience what the working class of Italy and Hungary has endured. We desire, therefore, to make all efforts to avoid civil war. We beg all comrades to resist all Communist provocateurs and to hold firmly to the orders of the party and of the trade unions.

Although the Socialist leaders were much disturbed by Communist propaganda, the Austrian Communist party was far too weak and had too little prestige among the workers to influence events. The strike thus passed with only minor troubles. Far greater was the danger to the Socialists from the fascist groups. In the countryside the events of July 15, and the subsequent communications strike gave powerful impetus to armed fascist organizations, which threatened to march on Vienna and made forceful attempts to break the strike. As it was, the walk-out was brought to an end just in time to avert the worst for the working class.

After July 15, 1927, the fascist danger began to take shape in Austria. The Heimwehren, a private army consisting mostly of the sons of well-to-do peasants and led by officers of the Imperial Army, aristocrats, and German Free Corps leaders, steadily expanded. It gained the support of the government, of big business (which was eager to destroy the trade unions), and of the Catholic Church (which was bent on weakening the Socialists). July 15, 1927, was the first act in a drama that lasted until late in 1930.

4.

The post-war Labor and Socialist International considered Austrian Social Democracy as the model of a Socialist party. In proportion to the size of the population, the Austrian Socialist party was the strongest in the world, both as to the number of dues-paying members and electoral votes. A few weeks before the bloody Friday, on April 24, 1927, the party polled 42 percent of the total vote at a general election. In Vienna the Socialists were in control, with a two-thirds majority. The party organization was the most efficient Europe had ever seen. "The miracle of Vienna" was the way German newspapers dubbed this Socialist organization—high praise indeed coming from Germans, themselves masters in organization. The Socialists had almost completely succeeded in building a world of their own within capitalist Austria. Once one had joined the party, there was no need for him to come into contact with the middle-class world outside of his business hours. He could live in houses built and controlled by Socialist municipalities; buy whatever he needed in Socialist coöperatives; spend his recreation hours in Socialist cultural organizations; and finally be buried by a Socialist led coöperative burial group.

Vienna was the main stronghold of the party. Of the capital's less than two million inhabitants, 500,000 were dues-paying party members. In its administration Vienna was

> probably the most successful municipality in the world. By means of an ingenious if Draconian taxation system they (the Viennese Socialists) financed paternalistic reforms of unparalleled quantity and quality; they built health clinics, baths, gymnasia, sanatoria, schools, kindergartens, and the imposing sunshine dwellings which, in decency and cleanliness if not luxury, housed sixty thousand families—Socialist families. They eliminated slums; they cut down drastically the tuberculosis rate; they took money from the rich, who could spare it, and used it for the benefit of the worthy poor. The achievements of the Vienna Socialists were the most exhilarating social monuments of the post-war period in any European country.[1]

Outside the urban areas, however, the Christian Social party was in control, and with the aid of other small middle-class parties it ran the federal government against the Socialists. By holding all middle-class parties in line against the Socialists, Father Ignaz Seipel managed to keep the Socialists out of government, although they were gaining in strength from one election to the next. The workers felt that Seipel somehow prevented them from enjoying the well-deserved fruits of their election victories, cheated them out of power. Verdicts such as that of Schattendorf, coming after many other similar cases, were considered as having been instigated by the government. The workers felt too powerful to brook such provocation indefinitely.

Was it true, however, that the working-class party was as strong as its members believed it to be? Army and police, the workers thought, could not be used by the middle-class government against labor since soldiers and policemen had been organized in trade unions since 1918, and many of them also belonged to the Social Democratic party. The government realized this situation and carefully refrained from using the executive forces against labor, until a slow and gradual change could be effected. During seven years

[1] From *Inside Europe,* p. 280. Copyright, 1933, 1934, 1935, 1936, 1937, 1938, 1940 by John Gunther. Published by Harper & Brothers.

of uninterrupted anti-Socialist government, known Socialists were dropped from the army and police; to fill their places came "reliable" youth from the countryside, recommended by village priests and Christian Social organizations. By 1927, the middle-class government had forged its new weapon. July 15 proved that the workers erred in considering the police and army of that day as the same one that had emerged from the revolution of 1918.

The Social Democrats thus suffered a heavy defeat. But if previously the workers had overrated their power, now the fascists and reactionaries gave way to the illusion that suddenly the moment had come for the complete destruction of Social Democracy. The Heimwehren, encouraged by Father Seipel, began a campaign for the establishment of a fascist dictatorship in Austria. Instead of stabilization, Bloody Friday ushered in a period of heightened political tension that lasted for more than three years.

5.

At first it seemed as if the tragedy of 1927 was merely an episode, without after-effects. The early part of 1928 brought economic improvement—a reduction of unemployment and a furthering of internal peace. Social Democracy obtained several election successes, and on the anniversary of Bloody Friday in 1928, the Socialist newspaper *Arbeiter-Zeitung* proudly asserted that the party was stronger than ever before.

Under the surface things looked otherwise. The political stalemate between government and labor continued. The Heimwehren, meanwhile, were organizing and arming. By the fall of 1928, they were ready for a great offensive that was to culminate in 1930. This was not a political struggle in which arguments counted, but propaganda backed by force. Both sides, Heimwehren and Social Democrats, endeavored to intimidate each other by displays of strength. Military parades of the private armies of the right and the left followed each other around Austria. The government encouraged the Heimwehren to carry their demonstrations into "Red" districts; the left regarded these parties as deliberate provocation which had to be answered by counter-demonstrations held at the same time and at the same place. Thus, on a Sunday, a hundred thousand armed men of hostile political camps would concentrate in the same city, separated from each other by a small police force or a group from the regular army, and the population would wait anxiously for news whether the dreaded civil war had actually begun. Repeatedly the Social Democrats suggested negotiations for what they called "internal disarmament" in the hope of relieving the constant tension, but on each occasion Chancellor Seipel, thinking that victory over the "Reds" was in sight and that acceptance of the Socialist proposals might endanger his triumph, never once deigned to give an answer.

The Socialist leader, Otto Bauer, fully realized the dangers of the prolonged political stalemate. In 1926, the Social Democrats adopted a new program, which considered government coalitions a solution, though only for emergencies and special situations, and restricted the use of violence to proletarian defense against unconstitutional violence used by middle-class parties or middle-class governments.

This so-called Linz program of the Austrian Socialists was hailed at the time by many leftist Socialists as an alternative to reformist capitulation to middle-class parties and to the Communist urge to violent adventures. But in the particular situation existing in Austria, the program probably did more harm than good, for the reactionaries skillfully exploited the veiled threat of violence contained in the statement.

Many began to look for a strong man to combat what was called "weak parliamentary government" and "political horse-trading." After Bloody Friday, new men appeared on the political scene. Prince Ernst Rüdiger von Starhemberg, who had taken part in Nazi activities in Germany, used his large inherited fortune to arm a private corps which was an integral part of the Heimwehren. He was surrounded by officers of the Imperial Army, such as Major Fey; by adventurers like Herr Pabst, famous German organizer of counter-revolutionary movements who had left Germany after its stabilization had thrown him out of his job; and by business men such as Herr Mandl, a big munitions producer and Mussolini's handy man in Austria.

At the moment when civil war seemed inevitable, an effort was made to overcome the deadlock by compromise. The permanency of the danger of a civil war led influential middle-class groups under the leadership of the Viennese police chief, Schober, to seek a compromise. The tension was a threat to economic life, and a civil war would have caused an economic catastrophe, not only for labor but for every section of the population. The compromise, arranged through a change in the Constitution, which increased the government's authority at the expense of Parliament, satisfied neither the Heimwehren nor the Socialists, but at least it could be presented to a hopeful public as a way out of the stalemate and a method to preserve stability against disturbers of peace on the left and on the right.

The tension seemed to lessen when the Heimwehren discovered that, far from paving their way to power, the compromise was a battle lost for fascism. As a consequence of the compromise, some middle-class groups supported the Socialists' resistance to renewed fascist unrest. The Heimwehren had to strike fast if they were not to lose all.

At the last possible moment, therefore, an alliance was concluded between the Seipel wing of the Christian Social party and Starhemberg and his lieutenants. They wanted to force the issue, against both the Socialists and those middle-class groups which for the first time in many years now refused to follow Seipel's direction. In the fall of 1930, when the Nazis obtained their first great election victory in Germany and Father Seipel innocently hoped that a Nazi government would be formed in the neighbor republic, he arranged for a Christian Social-Heimwehren Cabinet in Austria.

This government was without parliamentary majority, since some middle-class groups rejected Seipel's pro-Fascist course. Parliament was dissolved, and in November, 1930, new elections were called to produce a parliament suitable for a fascist government. In the meantime, Chancellor Vaugoin and Vice-Chancellor Starhemberg used all their power to weaken the left and to place "reliable" men in charge of all key economic or political positions in the country. One of the men who during these days bathed in the limelight of public action for the first time was a young secretary of the Chamber of Agriculture in Lower Austria, Dr. Engelbert Dollfuss. In the administrative shuffle he was appointed president of the federal railroads.

The Heimwehren soon realized that the elections would result in a defeat for the pro-fascist government; accordingly they urged their Christian Social allies to prepare for a coup d'état, to postpone the elections indefinitely, and to govern dictatorially. The Christian Socials refused, partly because they knew that many of their middle-class supporters opposed a policy that would have led inevitably to armed Socialist resistance and to a civil war.

Fear of the labor movement thus forced the government to go ahead with the elections. The fascists were defeated, as they themselves had foreseen. The government remained a minority in parliament, with the Social Democrats defending their position and the anti-fascist middle-class groups obtaining nineteen seats, enough to prevent a pro-fascist majority. Out of a total of one hundred and sixty-five seats the Heimwehren obtained only eight seats—as compared with seventy-two Socialist seats—and the Christian Socials lost so heavily that the Social Democrats became the strongest party in Parliament.

A new middle-class government was formed, this time under democratic leadership and with the Heimwehren excluded.

Austrian fascism was defeated—at least for the moment. It lost because the political stalemate to which fascism owed its existence was eliminated by a labor-middle class compromise imposed upon both, labor and middle class, by the threat of civil war.

Chapter 14

HITLER WINS

1.

THE Austrian struggle was important, but the truly decisive battle over the fate of European labor was fought in the pre-eminently industrial country of the Old World, Germany. No defeat was more fateful for labor than the Nazis' destruction of the German working-class organizations. No less consequential was the fact that after constant guerilla warfare and colossal preparations for a final "win-or-lose" battle between labor and Nazism, the German working class capitulated without resistance.

On the night of the Reichstag fire in February, 1933, I left by train for Berlin. My instructions were to get to Berlin by whatever means of transportation I could obtain. No one thought that trains would continue to run after the first wave of Nazi terror engulfed Prussia. I was amply provided with foreign currency, since it was considered possible that the expected outbreak of the civil war in Germany would cause the Germans to refuse German money. When I climbed into my berth in the sleeping car at the German-Swiss frontier, I was all set to be rudely awakened sometime during the night by a conductor informing me that the long-anticipated general strike had been called by the labor organizations against the Hitler government. To my consternation I found when I arose in the morning that we were approaching Berlin precisely on schedule. On the train a few people were whispering excitedly. In Berlin itself many houses were decorated with swastikas. Apart from this, the German capital looked normal. Nowhere could I see preparations for a last-minute stand for the defense of the democratic Republic, and my conversations with those of the labor leaders who were still at large and in Berlin—many had fled to a temporary refuge in Bavaria—were to confirm my impression; German labor was about to submit rather quietly to its Nazi enemy.

How can this flight from the political battlefield be explained? Why did both Socialists and Communists retreat rather than make a last desperate effort to stave off the Nazi victory? To understand the utter hopelessness of the Socialists and the fantastic illusions of the Communists that led both wings of German labor into capitulation, one must go back at least to 1930, the year of the first great Nazi success at the polls.

When, on September 14, 1930, the Nazis in a gigantic upsurge obtained six million votes and became the second party in size in Germany, the shock paralyzed not only labor, but all democratic forces. The Socialists felt that the main democratic task consisted in keeping the Nazis out of the government. If the Nazis should attain governmental authority, their dynamism, strengthened by control of the state machinery, would prove irresistible. To prevent the Nazis from entering the government and to keep parliamentary democracy somehow intact, the Socialist leaders believed it necessary to support all anti-Nazi middle-class parties, even when their policies held little appeal for the working class. Hence Socialist "tolerance" with regard to the Brüning government in spite of its policy of wholesale wage reductions. The Socialist strategy was based upon the idea of a retreat behind the protecting walls of conservative middle-class democracy.

Such a strategy was not apt to create or even to maintain fighting spirit among the workers, since the policy of "tolerance" forced the Socialists into a series of consecutive retreats. Each new sacrifice of working-class positions increased the discouragement of labor. Few—under the circumstances, surprisingly few—Socialists abandoned their party, and the Socialist vote decreased very little between 1930 and 1933. But this was the stubbornness of a rock rather than the aggressive courage of a fighting army. Without the ability to engage in offensive operations, German Social Democracy, like any other force engaged in warfare, was bound to be defeated. The decisive test came on July 20, 1932.

On that day, Chancellor von Papen, openly violating the Constitution, ousted the Socialist led government in Prussia. The Social Democratic premier, Otto Braun, and the Social Democratic minister of the interior, Karl Severing, were deposed. The last great bulwark of the democratic Republic was falling. At a hurriedly called meeting, the Socialist Party Executive and the leaders of the trade unions deliberated on the answer to be given to the chancellor's coup. It was a fateful decision which the Social Democrats were to take.

Since May 30, 1932, when President von Hindenburg had dismissed Chancellor Brüning, the Prussian government constituted the stronghold of the anti-Nazi forces. Under Socialist leadership and with the support of anti-Nazi middle-class parties, the Prussian cabinet controlled the police of the largest of the German "states." With the Prussian police as a cornerstone, the Social Democrats had established their own defense system. A self-defense organization, the "Reichsbanner Schwarz-Rot-Gold"—so named after the colors of the Republican flag—had been set up; this consisted mostly of Socialists and trade unionists and was under the joint control of Social Democrats, Catholic Center party men and members of the Democratic party. Their strategic concept was that in case of a Nazi rebellion the Reichsbanner should coöperate with the Prussian police in suppressing the Nazi Storm Troopers. The Reichsbanner had few arms and they lost many men in the unending series of small clashes with the Nazis that characterized the period between 1929 and 1933, commonly called the "little civil war." In the case of a large-scale Nazi rebellion it was expected, however, that the Prussian police would give the Reichsbanner men the necessary armament.

Socialist strategy was thus based upon the coöperation of the powerful Prussian police, well armed and carefully trained, in resisting the Nazis. Under the Socialist minister of the interior in Prussia, Karl Severing, the personnel and officers of the police had been thoroughly "cleaned" of men suspected of Nazi sympathies, and—though used more frequently against the Communists than against the Nazis—the police force was on the whole a reliable anti-Nazi weapon.

The coup of July 20, 1932, placed this weapon in danger of being destroyed. Left to Papen and his henchmen, the police would soon be "reorganized" along an anti-democratic line. If the Prussian police troops were to be saved as backbone of the anti-Fascist struggle, Papen's coup should have been the signal for armed resistance. However, one powerful factor on the German scene loomed large and threatening and it paralyzed whatever desire to fight might have existed among the Socialist leaders: the Reichswehr. In Socialist speculations, the Nazis had been the one and only enemy, with the Reichswehr neutral and resting on the sidelines. This forecast of the army's attitude was doubtful under the most favorable circumstances. In July, 1932, with Hindenburg president and Papen chancellor, it was more than likely that the army, whatever the issue, would have entered the battle against labor; on July 20, it was patently a case of Prussia versus the Reich, regardless of how flimsy the constitutional basis of Papen's coup. No doubt existed in the Socialist leaders' minds that open resistance on the part of the Prussian Cabinet would have found Reichswehr and Nazis solidly arrayed against the democratic forces. Such a battle, the Socialists knew, could only result in a crushing labor defeat.

Some of the Socialist leaders, particularly the trade unionists, might have recalled the death blow which a general strike gave to the Kapp *Putsch* way back in 1920. A general stoppage of work, combined with the passive resistance of large parts of the government bureaucracy, had nipped that other reactionary coup in the bud. Could that achievement now be repeated? The Socialist leaders felt that in the midst of mass unemployment a general strike might soon degenerate into a violent struggle between strikers and unemployed eager to fill the jobs left vacant by the strike. Within a few hours after the beginning of the strike, it might be transformed into a full-fledged civil war in which labor was bound to be defeated by joint Nazi-Reichswehr action.

Hermann Goering, Hitler's first lieutenant, once said: "Never stop firing. I would rather shoot too far or too close, but I would not give up without shooting." But Goering is an adventurer with little sense of responsibility, to whom violence per se holds a strong appeal. The Socialist leaders were of a different type. They were parliamentarians, trained organizers, men with a high sense of responsibility, to whom the idea of leading their followers into a battle with little hope of success was utterly abhorrent. But why did the Socialist workers themselves not take up arms spontaneously, without waiting for orders from their leadership? Because a democratic mass organization does not foster independent group action. A party whose organizational structure and life were directed toward winning elections rather than organizing violent uprisings is not apt to change overnight into an army bent on fighting with guns in its hands.

Should not a sense of honor have forced the Socialist leaders into staging a desperate, though hopeless, last-minute struggle? There is no doubt that many Socialists would have answered with a categorical "yes"—but it is one thing to die and another to order other people to die for a hopeless cause. The Austrian Socialist leaders were capable of doing it in 1934—perhaps because they were accustomed to thinking in long-term periods and realized that a last-minute struggle, though defeated, would matter a great deal for the later reconstruction of the movement. The German laborites, bewildered by events and hoping desperately for some final miracle—such as the proclamation of martial law and the establishment of a military dictatorship—failed to see that the present was definitely lost and that only the future mattered.

Thus no other alternative seemed open to the Socialist leaders than to accept—under protest—the ouster of the Prussian cabinet. Realizing the implications of this capitulation, Otto Wels, president of the Social Democratic party, took refuge in an analogy of a rather flimsy character. In November, 1930, the Austrian Socialists had been confronted with the deliberate provocations of the Catholic-Fascist cabinet of Vaugoin and Starhemberg; but following the advice of their leaders, the Austrian workers, though better armed than the Germans, had refrained from using their arms against the government, and staked their future and that of Austrian democracy upon the issue of forthcoming general elections. Violence would have given the government a pretext to postpone—perhaps forever—the elections from which the fascist forces emerged as so insignificant a minority that the cabinet was forced to resign. Now, in July,

1932, elections were pending in Germany. Wouldn't it be best, Wels asked, if the German workers too would trust in the ballot to defeat fascism?

Unfortunately for German democracy, there was a conspicuous difference between the results of the German and the Austrian elections. In Austria they demonstrated the weakness of popular support for fascism, in Germany the strength of the Nazis.

2.

The Socialist policy of "tolerance" with regard to Chancellor Brüning was designed exclusively to maintain contact with anti-Nazi middle-class groups. As long as this policy dominated the Socialist course, no sincere Socialist effort to reach an understanding with the Communists was possible. Anti-Communism was part of the price which the Socialists had to pay for collaboration with the middle class, but even had the Socialists seriously considered joint action with the other labor party, the Communist attitude would have made any such approach impossible.

True, at regular intervals the Communists suggested proposals for a "United Front" against fascism, but it was difficult to take such offers seriously. Since 1928–29, as will be remembered, Communist policy had been in its "Third period," in which the struggle against the "Social Fascists," as the Communists termed the Social Democrats, was its focus. "Our main blow," the German Communist paper *Rote Fahne* announced in November, 1931, "is directed at Social Democracy," which it held to be merely the left wing of the fascist forces. The "United Front" offers were openly proclaimed efforts to separate the Socialist workers from their "treacherous" leaders. Destruction of the Socialist movement was the main objective.

The spirit in which united front proposals were made could be seen from a discussion in *Pravda,* the Russian Communist newspaper: "The Weimar Republic is bankrupt. The revolutionary proletariat is not for a moment supporting the Weimar bankrupts; it is mobilizing its forces against the Weimar Republic, against

Hitler's Third Kingdom, and the Social Democratic 'Second Republic,' for the Soviet Republic." [1]

It was not until February, 1933, when Hitler was already chancellor, that the Communists accepted, though in a noncommittal way, a Socialist invitation to discuss joint resistance to the Nazis. The first meeting was arranged for the very same evening that the Reichstag went up in flames. Obviously, the meeting could not be held. Socialists and Communists were thus destined to meet for the first time in exile, after a capitulation that disheartened the workers in all countries.

[1] The *Pravda* article is reprinted in *International Press Correspondence,* July 26, 1932, No. 33, p. 675, "The Situation in Germany," by V. Knorin.

Chapter 15

THE CANNON OF FEBRUARY

I.

NOWHERE were the consequences of the German catastrophe more immediately felt than in Austria. A few days before the German elections of March 5, 1933, which confirmed Hitler's dictatorship, a railroad strike over an insignificant issue ended in complete success for the workers. A few days later, Chancellor Dollfuss, taking advantage of an incident in the Austrian Parliament, prevented a meeting of Parliament and established his dictatorship without encountering more than verbal resistance on the part of labor. The only explanation for this sudden change in the political climate of Austria was the Nazi triumph in Germany. The capitulation of German labor discouraged the Austrian workers and strengthened tremendously the anti-democratic forces in Austria.

At the last Austrian general elections held in November, 1930, it will be recalled, the Social Democrats under the brilliant leadership of Otto Bauer had defeated two fascist opponents. The Clerical-Fascist Heimwehren, headed by Prince Starhemberg who enjoyed Italy's support, received 8 out of 165 seats. The day before the elections Prince Starhemberg had dreamed about the dictatorship of his Heimwehren; the results clearly proved that his was the smallest of all parties represented in Parliament. The Nazis were even weaker than their Catholic competitors; not a single Nazi entered the Austrian Parliament. The Communists had no more luck than the Nazis. Holding 72 seats, the Social Democrats were the strongest party in the country, but despite their number they were an opposition to the government majority formed by the Christian Socials, the Heimwehren, and a Nationalist Peasants party, the "Landbund."

With Hitler's progress in Germany, the Nazi wave in Austria rose rapidly. Provincial elections during 1932 gave the Nazis 16 percent of the vote in Vienna, 18 percent in Lower Austria, 22 percent in Salzburg. Most of these advances were at the expense of the Christian Socials. The Government had a majority of exactly one vote in Parliament over the combination of the two opposition parties, Social Democrats and Pan-Germans, and the Nazi advance further weakened the Government. The Christian Social chancellor, Dr. Dollfuss, a devout Catholic, was driven into despair—but despair gave him audacity. While everyone expected him to come to terms with the Nazis or with the Socialists who offered him help against the Nazis, Dollfuss believed he had discovered a third way out. He took on both opponents at the same time, struggling against the old and the new, the Socialists as well as the rising Nazi danger.

Such a policy could not be carried through with a one-vote majority in Parliament. So on March 4, 1933, the chancellor succeeded in getting rid of parliamentary democracy altogether. After the general strike of the railway men, the House had voted on a resolution asking the Government to refrain from punishing those who had taken part in the strike. A Socialist member made a mistake when voting, and later asked the Socialist president of the House to rectify his vote. The president did so, but the Dollfuss majority protested. The president thereupon resigned. Under the standing rules, the president could not take part in the vote. Since the government majority was so narrow, government victories were sometimes won only because a Socialist—namely, the president of the House—took no part in the vote. Karl Renner, the president, had been exposed to criticism for some time for keeping the government in power simply by retaining his parliamentary office. He used the opportunity offered by the majority's protest against his decision to rectify the mistake in voting and resigned. The Socialist opposition now had a voting majority in Parliament, but they could not use it as the two vice-presidents followed Renner's example and resigned as well. Seizing upon this situation, Dollfuss declared that only a president could convene the House, and that since there was no longer a president, Parliament could not meet.

From that time on, Chancellor Dollfuss governed by emergency decrees in a dictatorial manner. The main force of his attack was directed against the Socialists. The chancellor apparently hoped for some arrangement with the Nazis which would sacrifice what little was left of Austrian democracy but preserve the country's independence and the dominant influence of the Catholic Church. Step by step the Socialists were pushed back. True, the Nazi party was outlawed on June 19, 1933, but Nazi atrocities continued undisturbed, openly supported by radio broadcasts and leaflet air-raids from Germany.

The Socialist defense corps was dissolved; Socialist-governed Vienna was arbitrarily deprived of a considerable part of its income; Socialist workers were ordered, under the threat of losing their jobs, to join Dollfuss' new party, the "Patriotic Front," which was to supersede all parties and to bring about "national unity." Obviously, the final onslaught was being prepared against the Socialist bulwark, the city administration of Vienna with its Socialist two-thirds majority. In the meantime Dollfuss officially announced his plan to abolish parliamentary democracy forever, and to rebuild Austria as a Christian, corporate and federal state, according to the principles of the papal encyclical, "Quadragesimo Anno." Austria was to be the first country in the world ruled according to the Pope's ideas.

The Social Democrats were eager to avoid an open conflict with Dollfuss. True, they had learned the lesson from Germany that resistance had to begin at the first sign of departure from democratic practice, and that delay only encouraged the anti-democratic forces and demoralized the left. But there was a decisive difference between Germany and Austria. Austrian workers were threatened by two Fascist enemies at the same time, by Dollfuss and the Heimwehren on one front, by the Nazis on the other. An open conflict between the workers and Dollfuss, the Socialists feared, might end in victory for the Nazis. They held little hope of defending Austria against Hitler unless some sort of coöperation could be arrived at between all elements opposed to Nazism—in effect between the government and the Socialist workers. Delay and temporizing seemed the best solution for the Socialist leaders, since it offered at least some hope for an agreement with Dollfuss. The Social Democrats waited and watched while the government's attack upon the positions of the left progressed. When the last desperate stand was made, in February, 1934, the moral and material strength of the left had already been broken down by the long siege.

Dollfuss—and later Schuschnigg—were praised by the world as anti-Nazi heroes, sometimes to their own distaste. Dollfuss was primarily an enemy of the "godless" Social Democrats. He had lost his respect for the Austrian Social Democrats when Hitler destroyed the German Social Democratic party without resistance. So far these opponents had prevented decisive victories of the particular brand of Catholic policy which Dollfuss represented, but, after March, 1933, the chancellor foresaw new possibilities. Something had to be done about the Nazis, Dollfuss also thought, because they were unwilling to permit his Catholic Fascism to reap where the pagan Nazis had sown. Until his death Dollfuss remained convinced that some sort of arrangement could be concluded with exponents of the Nazi type of authoritarian thinking. Several times, indeed, Dollfuss and Prince Starhemberg actually entered into secret negotiations with Hitler. It was not Dollfuss' democratic principles that prevented him from coming to terms with Nazidom, but Berlin's insistence upon a full-fledged capitulation and Dollfuss' and Starhemberg's mutual jealousy. Schuschnigg, who had his full share in Dollfuss' early efforts both to crush the left and to negotiate with Berlin, may have learned from Dollfuss' failure. When he was chancellor, however, it was too late; the international situation had definitely turned against Austria. A whit less reactionary, perhaps, than Dollfuss, Schuschnigg was seriously handicapped in his anti-Nazi policy by his German Nationalist feelings. He simply could not bear the idea of Austrian soldiers fighting the German Army.

The events of 1933 offered Dollfuss a threat, but also an opportunity—a threat to what he held most sacred, the authority of the Catholic Church in Austria, which the Nazis refused to recognize; an opportunity to crush the Social-Democratic party. In his state of mind, he was not amenable to any compromise with the Socialists, who nevertheless continued to hope for an anti-Nazi united front.

Clinging to this straw, the Socialist leaders refused to face the realities of the situation until it was too late. The decisive mistake, according to Otto Bauer, was made by him and his colleagues as early as March 15, 1933. One of the two parliamentary vice-presidents who had resigned summoned a Parliament meeting for that day. Chancellor Dollfuss announced that he would prevent such a meeting, by armed force if necessary. At first the Social Democrats acted as if they would take up the struggle forced upon them on this occasion; they would carry through the meeting at all costs, they announced. March 15 thus seemed destined to be the decisive day in the brief history of Austrian democracy. Both sides issued defiant statements. Yet all ended in what the Austrians call a *Pallawatsch,* a typical Austrian mess. Parliament met half an hour earlier than had been announced, with the vice-president closing the meeting immediately after opening it. Police, sent to prevent Parliament from convening, arrived too late. Both sides claimed victory. Two main facts stood out: Parliament continued to be in recess—forever—and the workers, after having waited the whole day for a call to armed resistance, were losing their fighting spirit and faith in their party. In the long run, Dollfuss proved to have been the victor and democracy the loser on March 15.

Dollfuss realized that he had won the first great battle against Social Democracy. On April 11 he went to Rome to consult Mussolini. He offered Austria and received in exchange Mussolini's protection. From now on Austria was an Italian protectorate, with Dollfuss serving as Mussolini's viceroy. Backed by Mussolini, Dollfuss was in a position to proceed with his efforts to destroy the Social-Democratic party. Mussolini fully supported Dollfuss in this venture as the Austrian trade unions had been responsible for the so-called Hirtenberg affair. In January, 1933, the Socialist *Arbeiter-Zeitung* in Vienna revealed that an Italian arms transport destined for Hungary had arrived under a false declaration at Herr Mandl's armaments' factory in Hirtenberg, Austria. As Hungary was forbidden under the Peace Treaty to import arms from abroad, the Socialist revelation led to a painful incident and a diplomatic defeat for Mussolini. To rearm his ally Hungary, he realized, he first had to destroy the Austrian Social Democrats.

Upon his return from Italy, Dollfuss issued new decrees against the Socialists; or rather, decrees officially declared to be directed against the Nazi terrorists were used primarily against the Social Democrats.

By September, 1933, the Socialists regarded a complete showdown with Dollfuss as inevitable. The party called upon the workers to resist in case certain basic Socialist positions were attacked—if the party or the trade unions should be dissolved, if the Socialists should be forced out of the Viennese city administration, or if a fascist constitution should be imposed. Dollfuss, however, was too clever a strategist to act as openly as the Socialist leaders expected. He continued to undermine the leftist positions by small-scale measures. None of these taken individually was considered by the Socialist leaders important enough to warrant armed resistance, but finally these attacks destroyed the last remnants of Socialist influence in Austria, and the continuous retreat of the left hopelessly discouraged the working class.

2.

It is very unlikely that Dollfuss had a clear-cut plan prepared in his mind when he set out to destroy Austrian democracy. He was essentially pragmatic in his thinking, finding his way from day to day amid the throes and difficulties that confronted him, little understanding the historical significance of his actions. One of his main driving forces was his fear of Otto Bauer. A master in parliamentary debate, Otto Bauer some time before 1933 had directed his sarcasm against Dollfuss in a meeting of Parliament. When in 1933 someone suggested in Dollfuss' presence that Parliament ought to be reconvened to achieve a rapprochement between the chancellor and the Social Democrats, Dollfuss burst out, "I sit again in a Parliament with Otto Bauer? Never, never!"

Still, Dollfuss needed final encouragement to complete the destruction of democracy in Austria. It came when French democracy seemed on the verge of a breakdown, leaving the strongest Continental power apparently paralyzed in its international action by the threat of civil war. February 6, 1934, the day when blood was shed in the streets of Paris and fascism made its first assault upon French democracy, heralded the downfall of what remained of Austria's freedom.

Dollfuss depended upon Italy's military aid against Germany, but he continued to maintain certain links with France, partly because of Austria's need for financial support, which Italy could not give, and partly because no one in Central Europe could believe at the time that France would completely withdraw from the Austrian compact in favor of Italy. In exchange for a French credit Dollfuss had promised the French government that the main institutions of Austrian democracy would never be destroyed. Only under this condition had the French Socialists been willing to vote for the credit, and their support was necessary to keep the French leftist majority together after the elections of 1932. The events of February 6 ended the French government to which Dollfuss had pledged his word and destroyed the remnant of hope that France would not completely abandon its Austrian bastion. The French Gardes Mobiles, firing upon the crowd on the Place de la Concorde, sealed the doom of the Austrian Republic. As a result of the February 6 incident, Foreign Minister Paul-Boncour, to whom Dollfuss had given his promise, resigned along with Premier Daladier. When the civil war in Austria began, on February 12, 1934, France was in the grip of a general strike, called to stave off the fascist danger.

The most outspokenly fascist wing of Dollfuss' supporters was the Heimwehren, under Prince Starhemberg and Major Fey. For years their members had been drilled and prepared for the civil war with the Socialist workers. Part of the Heimwehren had joined the Nazis, and Dollfuss could not regard the remainder as a particularly trustworthy support. Against the left, however, they could be relied upon to do their best, although in actual fighting their value proved less than anticipated.

On January 30, 1934, the Heimwehren in Tyrol marched into Innsbruck, the provincial capital, and submitted to the provincial government a series of demands of a clearly fascist nature, among them a call for the dissolution of the Social Democratic party. Shortly afterward this action was repeated by the Heimwehren in

Upper Austria, who occupied Linz. Then came all other provinces, one after the other, with the exception of Vienna. On February 9, Dollfuss declared, "We shall probably begin very soon to realize our plans." Two days later Vice-Chancellor Fey declared that Dollfuss now was won for the plans of the Heimwehren. "Tomorrow," he said, "we are going to start cleaning up Austria; we shall make a complete job of it."

Tomorrow was February 12. Early in the morning police searched for arms in the Socialist headquarters in Linz. Workers in the house resisted, and firing began. Three hours later, the Viennese electrical workers struck—the pre-arranged signal for a general strike. Then firing began in Vienna. The civil war had come.

It lasted four days. All possible bad fortune seemed to be in store for the workers. A small minority of the Socialist workers, mainly members of the Republican Defense Corps, took up arms—as far as arms were available. Some of the largest secret depots could not be found; the few men who knew of them had been arrested. No official call to a general strike could be sent out since it had been forgotten to make arrangements with the electrical workers for the use of the Socialist printing presses. The mass of the workers sympathized with the fighting members of the Republican Defense Corps, but they did not strike. Discouraged, demoralized, they worked, while close by small Socialist groups were overwhelmed by cannon and machine guns. When the outcome of the struggle was clear, Otto Bauer and Julius Deutsch, the leaders of the revolt, fled to Czechoslovakia, and by February 16 the fighting was over. Eleven men, among them Deputy Koloman Wallisch, were hanged. One member of the Republican Defense Corps, who had been severely wounded in the fighting, was brought to the gallows on a stretcher.[1] The decrees which Dollfuss had professedly directed against the Nazis without until then daring to apply them, now worked against the Socialists who had fought for the democratic constitution.

The way was open for a Catholic-Fascist regime, born out of the despair of the most strongly anti-Nazi sections of the Austrian population. From now on, Austria's independence was to hang

[1] See G. E. R. Gedye, *Betrayal in Central Europe,* New York, Harper, 1939, p. 109.

upon a regime whose popular backing was limited to a small percentage of the citizenry. The downfall of Austrian Social Democracy proved a fatal blow to this independence.

3.

After 1934, the Austrian labor movement was driven underground. For a brief period, the Communists seemed able to take advantage of working-class bitterness and despair for democracy, but soon the so-called "Revolutionary Socialists" succeeded in uniting the many dispersed Socialist groups that had sprung up in the early days of "illegal" work. The "Revolutionary Socialists," commonly called "R.S.," built up a network of underground trade unions, and when Hitler presented Schuschnigg with an ultimatum on February 12, 1938—four years to the day after the beginning of the fighting in Vienna—the "R.S." were again a powerful factor in Austrian politics.

One of the conditions which Schuschnigg had to accept under the terms of Hitler's Berchtesgaden ultimatum was an amnesty of all Nazis in Austrian prisons or concentration camps. Schuschnigg fulfilled his part of the contract but went beyond it by releasing almost all imprisoned Socialists and Communists, members of the leftist underground organizations. A few days later, in a great speech in answer to Hitler's Reichstag address, Schuschnigg described Austria as a "Christian, German, Federal State" omitting the Dollfuss formula "Authoritarian and Corporative," the two words most hated by the left. He added some attacks upon "International Communism," a phrase which was resented by the workers, including those outside the Communist ranks, for they knew well that every antilabor action in Germany and Austria had been disguised as mere "anti-Communism." Nevertheless, they realized that a change in the system which had oppressed them until now was under way.

Schuschnigg seemed to have recognized the catastrophic mistake which Dollfuss had committed in driving the Austrian Social Democrats underground and into bitter hostility toward the new system which governed Austria. It was a "deathbed repentance," as G. E. R. Gedye, the New York *Times* correspondent called it, and like most deathbed repentances it came too late. Not until March 4, three weeks—valuable weeks—after Berchtesgaden, did Schuschnigg receive for the first time the representatives of the Viennese workers—the real representatives, not his own figureheads, nominated and imposed by his dictatorship upon the defeated workers.

On February 20, after a Reichstag speech by Hitler, in which he failed to give the promised guarantee of Austria's independence, work was stopped in a number of large factories in Vienna. The Shop Stewards, mostly former Social Democrats, met in conference. Deputations chosen by these conferences laid a resolution before the official fascist-dominated trade-union center, which was sponsored by the government to fight Socialist influence upon the workers. It pointed out that the workers wished to defend Austrian independence, but that they would be able to use their fighting strength to the utmost only if they were given back their liberties. The government trade-union leaders distorted this resolution in publishing it. Instead of the demand for liberty they inserted a proclamation of loyalty to Schuschnigg and to a "corporative" Austria, and submitted this text as a workers' petition to be signed in the factories. Having ruled the workers for four years by petty tricks, the fascist trade-union leaders still clung to their old practices—even though the enemy was fast approaching. As a result the workers refused to sign the doctored petition, and the episode led only to further estrangement between the government and the working class. The underground "Revolutionary Socialists," the "illegal" heirs to the former Social-Democratic party, distributed leaflets which described the full seriousness of the situation but concluded:

We do not say that Austria is lost—we only say that it can be no longer saved by the patriotic-authoritarian methods. We do not say that the Nazis are bound to be victorious—we only say that Schuschnigg's policy cannot prevent this victory. We do not say that the preservation of Austrian independence is impossible—we only say that it is impossible on an authoritarian basis.

On March 4, Schuschnigg was willing to receive the men who led the underground struggle of the workers against both the Clerico-Fascists—as the Socialists called the Dollfuss system—and the Nazis. Schuschnigg knew at this moment that Mussolini had abandoned him to his fate. The Clerico-Fascist Heimwehren, formerly Mussolini's agents in Austria and later a part of the government's Storm Troopers, hardly existed any more, the bulk of their supporters having gone over to the Nazis. The chancellor was frantically looking for new allies. The spokesmen of the workers, who were even then wanted by Schuschnigg's police, declared the workers' willingness to fight against the Nazis in the same spirit that the Austrian workers had fought against Dollfuss and his minister of justice, Kurt von Schuschnigg, four years before. But they added "that only free men will fight, not slaves. Give us something worth fighting for." They set forth their demands, which included "freedom to profess Socialist ideas"—a liberty such as had been given to the Nazis for their "Weltanschauung"; self-administration of the trade unions instead of administration by government-appointed functionaries; and authorization to publish a trade-union paper.

Schuschnigg accepted these demands in principle and appointed a committee to continue negotiations in behalf of the government. He asked the workers to bear in mind that it would be a grave mistake to do anything that might give the Nazis a pretext for accusing him of "conspiring with the Bolsheviks."

On March 7, the illegal, anti-fascist trade-union leaders met openly for the first time since February, 1934. They discussed the matter of agreeing to their delegates' recommendation to support Schuschnigg, and drew up their final demands. The Communists favored supporting Schuschnigg unconditionally, but many Revolutionary Socialists doubted that the workers could forget so easily the events of February, 1934; the hanging of Wallisch, Weissel, and other Socialists; the concentration camps; and the imprisonment of hundreds of Socialists for having read a copy of the illegal Socialist paper *Arbeiter-Zeitung*. It was necessary for the government to show that it had definitely changed its policy toward the workers, that it would give them at least the same rights that the Nazis had been granted under German pressure. The Revolutionary Socialists held a large majority at the meeting and the demands of the delegates who had seen Schuschnigg were endorsed.

Accordingly the negotiations with Schuschnigg's committee were begun.

The discussions proved surprisingly laborious, as Schuschnigg's negotiators obstinately resisted the workers' demands, despite the chancellor's general acceptance. Time was pressing and the underground workers' organizations were paralyzed in their efforts to mobilize the working class against the Nazi threat. When Schuschnigg announced a plebiscite on Austria's independence, to be held on March 13, the negotiations were still far from completion, and the labor leaders had not yet been given any means, other than their own underground channels, to communicate with their supporters.

Nevertheless, the Revolutionary Socialists decided to vote for Schuschnigg. "The Austrian worker," said a leaflet which still had to be distributed by underground means although it supported the government, "cannot answer 'No' to Schuschnigg's question on Sunday, because this would aid Hitlerism. Sunday is not the day to repay Austrian fascism and the authoritarian regime for all the crimes committed against the workers since February, 1934, by voting against Schuschnigg. Sunday is the day for showing our bitter hostility to Hitler's fascism. On that day, therefore, the whole working class must vote 'Yes'!"

This decision was adopted and printed late at night on March 11. On the following afternoon the workers' negotiators were to see Schuschnigg for final arrangements, and Karl Hans Sailer, one of the leaders of the Revolutionary Socialists, was to broadcast in the evening. Instead, the radio brought Schuschnigg's farewell to Austria—and the final catastrophe. The efforts to organize Austrian resistance had been half-hearted and had come too late. When the Nazi troops invaded Austria, they met with no resistance.

Chapter 16

NEW LABOR TACTICS: NEO-SOCIALISM AND LABOR PLANS

1.

THE rise of National Socialism and its victory in Germany came as a terrific blow to the European labor movement. Age-old traditions and routines were rudely shattered and, for the first time in many years, new ideas were advanced within the labor movement.

Earliest of these new concepts was the so-called Neo-Socialist philosophy, expressed mainly by two French Socialists, Adrien Marquet, major and deputy of Bordeaux and a second-rank leader of the French Socialist party, and Marcel Déat, the "crown prince" of the party.

The philosophy of the Neo-Socialists was expounded in rather cautious terms by Marquet at the International Socialist Conference in 1933, called to discuss the lessons of the German catastrophe:

Socialism has been stagnating or has even been in retreat in some countries. We have believed that when we had the true doctrine we had at the same time the power to attract. But since the war, we have been living in a world where the true doctrine does not have power of attraction any more. Today, attraction is exercised by action and will power. When faced by the barbaric intentions of our opponents, have our leaders always had the will power and the aggressiveness necessary for resistance?

At the present moment, when disorder and crisis are troubling humanity, to speak of order is to speak a truly revolutionary language. If we as Socialists do not speak of the matters indicated by concepts such as will, action, and order, if we do not demonstrate to the masses that a democracy which is inspired by socialism when in power can prove capable of dominating capitalism itself, I am afraid that in our country and in countries near us, we may suffer the fate of the countries where the Socialists have been exiled.

Shortly before, at a French Socialist Party Conference, the Neo-Socialists had for the first time come out more openly in favor of new party slogans. According to Déat and Marquet, the main lesson to be drawn from the debacle of German Social Democracy was condensed in three new slogans: "Order, Authority, Nation." Internationalism, the Neo-Socialists said, was obviously a romantic Utopian ideal since German Social Democracy had been destroyed by Hitler. "Order" and "Authority" were to express the will power necessary for decisive action.

Otto Bauer referred to the latter slogans in his report to the International Socialist Conference, saying:

The French Party Conference produced an idea which I regard as really essential. The idea was given expression there in a sharp form and in a form which gave rise to many fears, that democracy can only maintain itself at the present time if it reveals a great deal of strength and activity. . . . There is no doubt that the suffering masses—and here I refer not only to the workers, but to the petty bourgeoisie, peasants, and intellectuals—these suffering masses are very dissatisfied today when they see the daily play of parliamentarism, the intrigues in the corridors, and the game of majorities and coalitions. All this sufficed for them and satisfied them in times when conditions were quiet. Today, when things are not going well for them, when they are desperate, it seems to them that Parliament lacks sufficient energy, sufficient capacity to master the problems of this unsettled world. There is no doubt whatever that this impression has driven them to make capitulations to the slavery of leadership, to the idea that the people are incapable of governing themselves and that they need a master to free them from their distress. . . .

Paul Henry Spaak, then leader of the extreme left wing of the Belgian Labor party, later an outstanding Socialist right-wing leader, Belgian prime minister and foreign minister, expressed the anti-democratic conclusions which some Socialists drew from the criticism of parliamentary democracy during the crisis. He said during the discussions of the International Socialist Conference:

"In our eyes, the old methods and ways have now become insufficient and ineffective. In our opinion the question is not at all whether one is for or against democracy, but the question is whether democracy as it exists today is an effective method against fascism." Spaak concluded "with a single sentence which expresses the will and the thoughts of the left wing and of youth: 'It is not sufficient to be in the right, we want to win!' "

The Neo-Socialists realized that the victory of fascism was but a symptom of a crisis caused by the intellectual decline of the labor movement. According to Marx's doctrine, the economic and social evolution would lead to a final struggle in which, on the international scene, the great mass of the exploited would be united in fighting a small group of exploiters. The rise of fascism did not correspond, the Neo-Socialists claimed, to Marx's predictions. The Socialist movement was confronted not by a small group of monopolistic industrialists, but by a mass movement professing to defend the public weal against the private interests of big business, using Socialist slogans similar to those of the Socialist movement itself, and claiming even the name "Socialist." The Neo-Socialists consequently felt that the traditional methods of Socialist struggle were patently useless in this new historical phase. "One has the feeling," Marcel Déat said at the Socialist Party Conference in July, 1933, "that some element of socialism has been falsified, that some part of its spirit, of its program has been stolen by its [Fascist] adversary." Confronted and confused by so unexpected an enemy as fascism, the Socialist movement was unable to resist.

Since their own traditional weapons were of no avail against an opponent which used similar propaganda instruments with the greater vigor of a youthful movement, the Socialists were confronted with the dilemma of either remaining helpless or being compelled to use strange weapons. Some of them fought the Nazis in the name of the existing order of things, thereby unconsciously becoming spokesmen of conservative ideas. Others—such as the Neo-Socialists—began to borrow some of the fascist slogans, stressing the need for a strong authoritarian government, in opposition to the traditional Socialist allegiance to democracy and personal liberty. They favored national as opposed to international action. They tried to repeat what fascism appeared to have done successfully to socialism: to steal its thunder by taking over and assimilating some particularly impressive ideas of the opposition.

Listening to Adrien Marquet's speech at the French Socialist Party Conference in 1933, Léon Blum burst out in words which became famous: "Je suis épouvanté (I am appalled)." He accused the Neo-Socialists of having adopted fascist ideas that they might better combat fascism.

In answer to the Neo-Socialist drive for greater activity, even at the price of sacrificing essential Socialist ideals, Blum overstressed the need for caution, which in the line he took meant passivity. He spoke of "periods of transition," "intermediary forms of society," during which the Socialist movement should abstain from assuming the responsibilty of power in order not to compromise the Socialist ideal and force of attraction. Fascism, he said, might be one of these necessary forms of transition from capitalism to socialism. This expression of what the Neo-Socialists attacked as "sterile immobility" strengthened the Neo-Socialist appeal to the more active elements in the movement. These did not fail to take advantage of resolutions adopted by the Socialist Youth ending with the words, surprising in the mouths of Socialists and young men, "Long live traditional socialism!"

The Neo-Socialist movement was a mixture of two elements, an activist youth group and the dissatisfied right-wing Reformists, who revolted against Blum's "extremism." The two groups that formed the Neo-Socialist party after its break with Blum's Socialist party had little in common; this inner weakness was the cause of the downfall of Neo-Socialism.

Marcel Déat and Marquet found support at first among the Socialist right-wing deputies under Pierre Renaudel, who revolted against Blum's refusal to enter into a coalition government with Herriot's Radical party. The new Chamber elected in 1932, like its predecessor in 1924, had a leftist majority, but Radicals and Socialists were unable to agree on a common government program. One cabinet after another was overthrown by the Socialists, who refused to support the Radical party's financial policy. Blum stressed the fact that although all Socialist proposals corresponded to the election platform of the Radical party, they were nevertheless rejected by the Radicals themselves. Paul Faure, secretary of the Socialist party, accused the Radical party leaders of treating their election program "as so many scraps of paper once they are seated on the Government bench." As one cabinet followed another into dissolution, the right-wing Socialists grew restive, and the continuous massacre of governments began to irritate public opinion. Some thirty Socialist deputies led by Renaudel broke away from the party to support Radical governments. They gained Déat's faction, although from the outset disagreements existed between the two groups.

The Fascist revolt of February 6, 1934, ended the leftist majority in the Chamber and with it the particular situation which had caused the Renaudel split. Renaudel died soon afterwards, and most of his followers returned to the Socialist party.

Déat's activists were overwhelmed by the sudden impetus which the French left received as a consequence of the fascist threat and the Communist Popular Front policy. With the Socialists in the center of all this activity, Blum no longer advocated passive waiting. Déat was defeated by a Popular Front candidate, and the remnants of the Neo-Socialist group in the Chamber sought refuge with other leftist groups. Few followed Déat in the later stages of his political career. Rejected by the left, he turned to a passionate defense of "appeasement" which culminated in an article in the summer of 1939, entitled "Mourir pour Dantzig? (To die for Danzig?)." After the war broke out, Déat was arrested under the suspicion of having been a Nazi agent in France, an accusation that was completely proved by his ardent pro-Laval campaign after the French defeat.

2.

Some of the Neo-Socialist ideas corresponded to conceptions expressed in the "Labor Plan" movement which the Belgian Socialist leader Hendrik de Man inaugurated in 1934.

De Man had an unusually varied political career. It began on the extreme left of the Belgian Socialist movement, long before the

First World War. During the war De Man served in the Belgian Army. Later he traveled in the United States, particularly the West. He returned to work as a professor in Germany, where he witnessed Hitler's ascent to power. During that period he published a sensational book in which he, the former orthodox Marxist, sharply criticized the Marxist doctrine. In 1933, he went back to Belgium and prepared his "Labor Plan" for the movement, which rewarded him by electing him vice-president of the Belgian Labor party. A brilliant speaker in both Belgian languages, Flemish and French, De Man carried on a campaign for his "Labor Plan" that was unique in Belgium's political history. He was greeted as the savior of the oppressed, and old women kissed his hands to express their gratitude and admiration. Yet there was a streak of instability in him which contributed largely to the failure of his plan.

The main ideas of his Plan were based to a large extent upon his experiences in Germany and in the United States. De Man considered that the great depression of 1929 had been the beginning of a period of capitalist decadence. Within the framework of existing capitalist institutions even simple reforms could no longer be achieved. "The existing social order," he wrote, "becomes every day more unbearable. It can no longer be bettered. It does not merit anything but overthrow." In a period of capitalist decline and shrinking national income, De Man held, it was impossible to achieve reforms; even those reforms attained in many years of social progress were threatened. The mere defense of present achievements necessitated offensive action. It could no longer be directed toward reforms of the distribution of national income among the different classes. Reformism itself must become revolutionary, in the sense of changing the essentials of the existing order, if reforms were to be achieved. The traditional forms of the class struggle, in which each group strove to obtain a larger part of an increasing national income, were doomed, since the national income itself was decreasing. What mattered now was to increase the national income; this could be achieved only by a change in the structure of society.

Since reformism under these circumstances was bound to be revolutionary, De Man believed that the traditional division of the

Socialist program into immediate and final objectives had become meaningless. The final objective had never been anything but a vague symbol for reformist socialism. Its proposals had undergone a threefold process of watering down. Immediate programs, established well in advance of electoral battles, were superseded by campaign platforms, and governmental programs in turn were extracted from those election platforms.

Instead of this division into three or four conflicting—or at least different—sets of demands, De Man advocated the adoption of a single program, a Plan. It was to be at the same time a set of immediate proposals and a final objective, for the overthrow of the existing order had become, in De Man's view, an immediate necessity. He maintained that the principal points of this Plan ought to be the socialization of banks and of key industries of monopolistic character and the expropriation of big holdings of landed property wherever they still existed. The Plan should set out in all detail the measures necessary for implementing these demands in a form that would make it possible to realize them immediately; it should even contain the sequence in which the different points would have to be taken up.

The result would be that a socialized part of the economic structure would exist next to another sector still under private capitalist control. By a state monopoly in foreign trade the government could also gain some measure of control over the private sector.

Such a Plan, De Man pointed out, could become the common objective not only of the industrial working class educated in a Socialist spirit, but equally of large sections of the middle class to whom the Plan would offer protection against monopolistic oppression, free development within the private sector of the economic structure, and, owing to the general recovery, credits and expansion. Thus, the Plan would prevent the middle class from becoming the instrument of fascism to smash democracy and the labor movement.

De Man regarded the policy embodied in his Plan as opposed to reformism, as well as to "insurrectionary" socialism. The Plan was revolutionary, he said, because it aimed at fundamental changes, but it could be carried out by constitutional methods, rather than by revolts which would be disastrous under Western European conditions.

Essentially, the Plan was a crisis program based upon the fact that almost all social groups, apart from big business and high finance, were hit by the depression and were violently opposed to a deflationist policy. De Man's political strategy counted upon the revolt of the lower middle classes to form an alliance between them and the industrial workers, instead of turning against the workers under fascist leadership.

In a manner similar to that of the French Neo-Socialists, De Man was trying to "steal for socialism the thunder which will otherwise be appropriated by fascist demagogues," as a commentary put it. His Plan was a mode of socialism reduced to the size that might fit the middle classes. His planning within the framework of a nation under the control of a powerful government was the counterpart to the Neo-Socialists' slogan "Order, Authority, Nation."

Since the Plan visualized a situation then common to most European countries, held in the grip of a general depression and threatened by deflationary policies, many Socialist parties in Western and Northern Europe were inspired by De Man's ideas. The Belgian Labor party was the first to adopt a Labor Plan at its congress on Christmas, 1933. The Plan succeeded in forming a bridge between the right wing leadership and the leftist opposition under Spaak, who was at the point of splitting the party. Under the slogan, "The Plan, the whole Plan, nothing but the Plan," a powerful propaganda campaign was set in gear during 1934.

De Man believed that his Plan was destined to supersede reformism. But the party so far had not been reformist in any constructive sense. Actually De Man's main achievement was to help defeat the traditional pressure group of the party, and to transform it into a truly reformist party determined to realize a constructive program. In the same way, but with different methods from those of the Swedish Labor party, De Man pointed out that under the circumstances a reform policy had to be based upon appropriate economic ideas. His Plan was intended to achieve certain reforms, not merely because they were abstract ideals but primarily because they were recognized as necessary measures to meet the crisis. Socialist reforms were immediate tasks in the emergency. Finally, De Man succeeded in working out his Plan so that it corresponded to a political strategy in the Socialist struggle for power under Belgian conditions.

3.

None the less, his Plan failed, owing to three main causes; first, to accidental factors like the breakdown of the Belgian Workers' Bank, which ruined the movement financially; second, to the fact that in spite of the promises held out in his Plan, De Man offered a concrete political, but not a well-defined economic, program for recovery; third, to De Man's failure to understand the importance and the problems of Socialist foreign policy.

The political situation in Belgium was particularly favorable at first for De Man's action. The strongest middle-class party, the Catholic, had a large working-class following. If the Belgian Labor party had succeeded in driving a wedge between the Catholic workers and their reactionary leadership, it would have made possible a workers' government formed by Socialist and Catholic workers to carry out the Plan. By abandoning some Socialist ideas and concentrating upon those about which Socialist and Catholic workers could agree, De Man prepared the way for a complete reversal in Belgian politics in favor of a Socialist led "Plan Government."

The economic policy of the Belgian middle-class governments gave added impetus to the Plan movement. Repeated efforts were made to reduce wages and prices so as to enable Belgian industries to compete with the exports of other nations, especially those of Britain. While maintaining the gold parity of the belga, the middle-class governments had entered into a race between their deflationary policy and the rapid devaluation of the pound sterling. Both the working class and the lower middle class revolted against deflation. De Man's plan was regarded as an alternative to the misery and unemployment created by the contest between devaluation in England and deflation in Belgium.

Meetings swept the country. For some time the success of the Plan campaign was akin to the enthusiasm aroused by Nazi propaganda in Germany during the last years of the Republic. The Plan offered an immediate objective attainable in a short time, not in a distant future like the Socialist "final objective." The Plan government would end deflation, give jobs to the unemployed, and further economic expansion. Almost religious ardor animated the Plan propagandists, and the mass meetings attracted unheard of crowds. Yet, when almost in view of the goal, the campaign ended in failure and disappointment.

In 1934, the Belgian Workers' Bank, to which the workers' organizations had entrusted their funds, broke down, freezing at least for some time the funds reserved for the Plan campaign. Shortly afterwards a new, though slight, depreciation of the pound sterling rendered further defense of the belga impossible. The government, unable to continue its declared deflationary policy, resigned. De Man and the Socialist left-wing leader, Spaak, jointly advocated the Labor party's entry into a coalition government to devaluate the currency and embark upon a program of large public works to combat unemployment. Thus, the Belgian Labor party assumed government responsibility before the political objective of the Plan campaign, the splitting of the Catholic party, was attained. The Van Zeeland government was formed, with the three major parties of the country—Catholic, Labor, and Liberal—represented. De Man himself became minister for the struggle against unemployment.

For some time the party endeavored to convince its supporters that the Van Zeeland government was a Plan government. Public opinion, however, soon realized that the new policy, though progressive and anti-deflationary, was far from corresponding to the original Plan suggestions. In spite of the slogan, "The Plan, the whole Plan, nothing but the Plan," the Socialists supported and had representation in a government which realized only a small part of the measures contained in their new program. The Plan had become what De Man had opposed so bitterly: a program out of which certain parts were extracted to form a government program of immediate action. The traditional gulf between "immediate program" and "final objective" reappeared. What had been announced as a new departure in Socialist action ended by being merely a new edition of time-honored Socialist coalition policy.

Still, the economic policy of the Van Zeeland-De Man government was fairly successful in reducing unemployment. Though little was done along the lines of the Plan, the combined efforts of devaluation and public spending were felt in a considerable decrease in unemployment. Yet, fascism, whose growth De Man's new policy had been devised to prevent, made rapid headway. For a time the government's devaluation and price policies hit the lower middle classes severely. A Catholic fascist movement, similar to the Heimwehr movement in Austria, emerged under the leadership of Léon Degrelle. A young adventurer whose good looks and ability for public speaking were his major assets, Degrelle founded the Rexist party and made large inroads into the Catholic party. The Rexists obtained twenty-one seats in the Chamber at the first general election in which they participated. During the same period fascist tendencies became accentuated among the Flemish Nationalists, and the government coalition found itself suddenly in a difficult defensive position. Only Degrelle's impatience and his premature claim for full power prevented a major political crisis.

De Man's ideas exerted considerable influence upon labor outside Belgium. The French trade unions, the Danish, Dutch, and Swiss Socialist parties, drew up plans of labor which frequently had little in common with De Man's essential idea except the name "Plan." International conferences for Socialist planning were organized. Eventually its failure in Belgium and the emergence of the successful Popular Front movement forced the Plan idea into the background. Problems of foreign policy began to dominate European labor politics. De Man came out strongly in favor of appeasement. As a former front soldier, he advocated trusting the other front soldier, Adolf Hitler, thereby alienating some of his supporters. As minister of finance in a later Belgian Government, De Man was not conspicuously successful and was forced to resign. Spaak superseded De Man in the leadership of the Belgian Labor party.

Yet in the critical moment during the confusion which followed the German catastrophe, the Plan suggestions had the great merit of giving new inspiration and new self-confidence to the Socialist movement. Although unsuccessful, the Plan was a major contribution to the advance of the Socialist movement from pressure group to political party.

PART V

Fascism on the International Scene

Chapter 17
SOCIALIST FOREIGN POLICY AND FASCISM

1.

WITH Hitler's successful consecutive violations of the Peace Treaty (culminating in the military occupation of the Rhineland in March, 1936, with no international resistance to his coup), fascism ceased to be primarily a domestic problem. The international solidarity of fascist powers, later extended to include Japan, became the dominant factor of international relations. Fascism now was definitely an export item. Everywhere fascist organizations sprang up, financially and morally supported by the Axis powers. This was true particularly for Southeastern Europe, where a tempest of dictatorial tendencies destroyed what little there was of democratic institutions, until Czechoslovakia alone was left, a democratic island in a sea of dictatorship. With the outbreak of the Spanish War resistance to fascism became openly and patently an international problem.

The crucial moment in the sequence of events leading to fascist international aggression was March 7, 1936, when German troops marched into the Rhineland. None of the subsequent German offensive moves in Central and Eastern Europe would have been possible without the separation of Western from Central Europe by a line of German fortifications in the Rhineland. Austria, Czechoslovakia, Lithuania, and Poland were threatened, and France's system of alliances was shattered by this strong move of Germany. It was the last moment, perhaps, to nip Adolf Hitler's plans of conquest in the bud without danger of a new world conflagration, for Germany's army was still far from being equal to the French military machine. That moment passed with no action being taken.

British and French labor combined forces to prevent their governments from effectively opposing the new violation of a treaty on the part of the Nazi government. One group within the French government was in favor of resisting Hitler's move according to the terms of the Rhineland pact, which authorized the French to consider the German march into the Rhineland as an "unprovoked act of aggression." "The first inclination of the French government," according to the *Survey of International Affairs,* "appears to have been to order partial mobilization." No such plan was carried through, much to the relief of the British government. The French government declined to act, partly because it doubted that French finances would stand the strain of mobilization, partly because the British were reluctant to support the French, partly also because the Socialists staunchly opposed any measure that might involve the risk of war. As, apparently, no one knew what the German answer to any effective action might be, nothing at all was done.

Paul Faure, Secretary General of the French Socialist party, wrote in his column in the party newspaper *Le Populaire* on March 8:

> Those who have favored a revision of French positions, which had slight theoretical solidity and were actually rotten, have been branded in the past as bad Frenchmen.
>
> They [Faure's political opponents] have covered themselves with a policy of prestige.
>
> The results are these: Little is left of the text and the spirit of the treaties, and of the policy of prestige. . . .
>
> One possible consequence which we refuse to face is that war might be the outcome of the diplomatic conflict started by the *coup de théatre* of Berlin.
>
> Hitler proposes a general discussion of the situation. The answer must come from Geneva, where three great powers, France, England, and Russia, can save the peace of the world.

Thus Paul Faure rejected military action or even the threat of military action. While Premier Sarraut replied with a categorical

"No" to Hitler's suggestions for diplomatic negotiations as long as no reparation had been made for Germany's repudiation of its obligations, Paul Faure seemed eager to enter into a parley with the German dictator. In order to make his and the Socialist party's attitude doubly clear, Faure led a Socialist deputation to the premier, protesting against Sarraut's radio broadcast of March 8, which Faure thought was couched in threatening terms.

British labor fully agreed with the French Socialists in rejecting any serious countermove to the Rhineland occupation. The British government was ready to grasp Herr Hitler's apparently outstretched hand and almost enthusiastically willing to replace the treaty which Germany had violated by still another treaty with the German dictator. Though expressing opposition to the government, British labor was in full agreement with its policy on this question.

Major Attlee, the leader of the Labour party, said during the debate in the House of Commons on March 10 that

> He did not propose to say anything about what had occurred over the week end, except that the Opposition had always stood for the rule of law and for carrying out the obligations of treaties (Cheers) and they were not indifferent to the action of the rulers who claimed the right to disregard any treaty they pleased. They realized—and they would have these rulers realize—the difficulty which people of good-will all over the world found in taking at their face value promises which followed immediately on acts of repudiation (Cheers).
>
> But it was part of the Opposition's case today that there was a widespread disregard of treaties; treaties were not immutable; they must be changed from time to time with the consent of the signatories. The world could not be held down by any system of treaties. We were not living in a static world, and it was the task of statesmanship to deal with big questions as they arose. . . .

Hugh Dalton, former undersecretary of state for foreign affairs in the second Labour government, supported his leader:

> . . . whatever they thought of the Hitler regime, however much they might distrust the man and reprobate the repudiation of a treaty freely entered into, it was indisputable that they must talk to this man frankly. The Opposition welcomed the government's intention to join in frank discussions, and he trusted that they might persuade the French Gov-

ernment to join, without too much legalistic difficulty, in such discussions. . . .

Thus French and British Socialists joined in advocating acceptance of Hitler's *fait accompli.*

2.

The reaction to the Rhineland occupation was by no means an isolated case of passive acceptance by the Socialists of treaty violation by Nazi Germany. Ever since Hitler's advent to power British and French Socialists had resisted their governments' rare and weak moves to prevent the rebirth of an aggressive military power in Central Europe. A few examples are worth noting.

During the discussion of the army budget in the French Chamber of Deputies on June 15, 1934, Léon Blum opposed an increase in French armament expenditure which had been proposed by the government. His speech was reported as follows:

> The Socialist leader recognizes that German rearmament is throwing "a new and disquieting act" into the debate without, however, his wishing to say that "for a regime such as Hitler's, rearming corresponds to a fixed desire to make war. Rearmament may be related to other purposes."

The report adds that these remarks were accompanied by "mouvements divers," the standard phrase used to describe cheers intermingled with protests. Blum then went on to develop his theory that pressure of a nonmilitary character should be applied to Germany, pressure based not upon the military clauses of the peace treaty but upon a new international disarmament agreement.

A year later the French government demanded the extension of military service to two years, to compensate for the decrease in the birth rate during the war. This measure too, was opposed by Blum in the name of the Socialist party; he described the government's plan as an effort to build French militarism:

> This is in fact what is attempted, with the help of a danger which in any eventuality is not imminent; to which we could have answered and could still answer, I am convinced, by other methods.

Blum, a newspaper report stated, was of the opinion that this government plan was intended to make possible the achievement of strategic offensives of a Napoleonic character of which the government was perhaps not aware. He was convinced that all French workers would rally to answer aggression by Germany.

The Socialist leader declared that in view of Germany's numerical superiority France could not find its security in new armaments, in which France would always be surpassed. The Socialists believed that France's real protection consisted in *la levée en masse* (the rising of the people) in organized defense, in the possibility of reprisals, and, above all, in progressive disarmament, mutual assistance, and arbitration.

His friends and he himself, Léon Blum said, were the most determined foes of the Hitler regime, just as they had always been enemies of German rearmament; but they had always maintained that if the Geneva Conference were unsuccessful, Germany would declare itself free from its obligations. In their opinion the only chance of peace lay in imposing upon Germany if necessary a system of disarmament, of supervision, and of assistance. (The report here recorded laughter on many benches.)

During the same debate, Maurice Thorez, speaking for the Communists, also opposed the government project.

Édouard Herriot, the respected leader of the Radical party, answered Blum:

> A great change has occurred since the period when great hopes were born, hopes which it is permitted to think will some day be born again. . . . We have known a period when here and there active, if not powerful, democratic parties existed. Where are they today? Ask yourself whether we are not responsible for the democratic interests in certain countries where democracy was destroyed. We defend the democratic idea at the same time as national security. . . .

The British Labour party was even more outspoken in its criticism of government efforts either to strengthen British armed forces or to oppose German war preparations. For some time the Labour party newspaper, the *Daily Herald,* was extensively quoted by German newspapers, anxious to prove that important sections of British public opinion understood and even approved the measures taken by the German government. Of course, the British Labour party was bitterly hostile to Hitler, and the *Daily Herald* condemned Nazi cruelties in violent terms. In foreign policy, however, many spokesmen for labor, in particular the *Daily Herald,* considered it their main duty to concentrate criticism upon the British government's alleged unfriendliness toward Germany and British subservience to French militarism. So unrealistic was British labor's foreign policy at this time that even Continental Socialists could not refrain from publicly expressing their misgivings.

It was at this time that one British newspaperman asked a colleague whether he thought the pro-Nazi foreign policy of the *Daily Herald* might be explained by some of Goebbels's money finding its way into the labor paper. "It is even worse than that," was the answer, "they do it for nothing."

While France extended the term of military service to two years, the British government, though still anxious to negotiate with Hitler, published a "Statement Relating to Defense," which openly denounced Germany as a possible aggressor and suggested certain measures of rearmament considered necessary to cope with the increasing threats to peace. The British Labour party declared war upon the White Paper, and the leading article in the *Daily Herald* on March 6, 1935, commented characteristically:

> The immediate effect of Mr. MacDonald's White Paper has been to complicate the diplomatic situation, to make the coming conversations more difficult and the chances of their success more remote.
>
> The clumsiness at such a moment is grotesque.
>
> There are many phrases in the document which, though surely not intended, were quite certain to arouse German resentment, which were described in the London conservative press as "stern words" and a "warning" to Germany.
>
> She is roundly accused of "treaty breaking," of "aggravating" the situation, of tending to "produce a situation where peace may be in peril."

3.

Until about 1936 the Socialist parties in Western Europe showed little interest in the implications of Hitler's victory in international politics. Their main concern was directed toward the lessons for their own philosophy and tactics to be drawn from the defeat of German labor. The interest in certain aspects of the conflict between Socialists and the so-called "Neo-Socialists" in France, the "Labor Plan" movement spreading from Belgium to several European countries, and passionate discussions regarding the Socialist-Communist United Front were all expressions of Socialist efforts to adapt themselves to the victory of fascism in the most industrialized country of Europe. Very little was done, however, to extend this process of adaptation to a revision of Socialist foreign policy. Hitler's victory shook many traditions in European labor movement, but few considered Hitler's threat to European peace serious and urgent.

An international conference of the Labor and Socialist International, held in Paris in the summer of 1933, dealt almost exclusively with tactical questions. The official announcement contained only one item on the agenda, "The tactics and strategy of the labor movement during the period of the fascist offensive." In the light of the new German experience the majority of the speakers discussed the old problem of the "way to power" and democracy versus proletarian dictatorship. The struggle between Blum and his "Neo-Socialist" opponents led by Pierre Renaudel, Adrien Marquet, and Marcel Déat within the Socialist party aroused the most interest among the delegates. They listened impatiently to Paul Henri Spaak, the young Belgian delegate, spitefully attacking democracy as "the ideal of an older generation," little realizing that within less than two years' time he would join the ranks of the despised reformists and become minister of the king of the Belgians. Very few delegates asked whether the traditional foreign policy based upon disarmament and arbitration could be continued after Hitler's advent to power.

As a matter of fact, the long resolution adopted in the end by the conference seemed to indicate that the Socialists saw very little change in the international situation as a result of the events in Germany. The essential sentence in the resolution was rather ambiguous. It declared that the conference "recognizes for Germany, as well as for all other countries, the claim to equality of rights and duties," but it opposed "any rearmament of the military structure, which holds the German people in subjection." Since it could hardly be expected that France would do now what she had refused to do since 1919, namely, disarm to the same extent as Germany had been forced to do under the Peace Treaty, it remained a mystery how German "equality of rights" could be established without German rearmament.

Besides this, the resolution contained a reference to the policy of collective security; it called "upon all free peoples to unite against the war danger constituted by the German and Italian Fascist regimes." Apparently no one foresaw that the Western governments might not be eager to make war upon German fascism, for the conference solemnly warned the working class against being misled by the idea of using war as a means of "emancipating enslaved peoples." Even such a war, the conference proclaimed, would end as an imperialist war, and would in all probability create "still more terrible forces of despotism." Another resolution, adopted jointly by the Labor and Socialist International and the International Federation of Trade Unions, sounded a different note. It proclaimed the "imperative duty of the governments to show no accommodating spirit in regard to violations of international agreements." The sentence ended rather surprisingly, however, with an appeal to the same governments "to refrain from associating themselves with any weakness in the task of disarmament."

This was in 1933. At the time it was still quite possible for European Socialists to demand international disarmament and resistance by the democratic governments to fascist war threats, without being guilty of any inconsistency in their program. The military superiority of France and Great Britain was still indubitable. Some measure of French and British disarmament would not have weakened those countries dangerously in the face of the Third Reich and of Fascist Italy, though it would have given the victorious countries a better moral basis for resisting German rearmament. The ambiguous reference to the German claim for "equality" occasioned much discussion after the Conference. It became increasingly clear during the course of this debate that Otto Bauer, who had been responsible for the main ideas of the resolution and had acted as *rapporteur,* was influenced by two considerations. The

Austrian Socialists at the time were engaged in a struggle on two fronts, against the Catholic Fascism of Dollfuss and the Heimwehren and against the rising tide of Nazism. To be associated with an international organization which refused to Germans the same right to national defense which the organization accorded as a matter of course to British and French would have endangered the Austrian Socialist position against the Nazis. In addition, Otto Bauer was, and had been for many years, strongly opposed to the system of professional armies which the Peace Treaties had imposed upon the defeated countries. The German Reichswehr was a state within the state and contributed greatly to the rise of Nazism. After having begun as a force of the democratic left, the little Austrian Army had slowly but irresistibly been transformed by the uninterrupted series of anti-Socialist coalition governments into an instrument of reaction. Bauer believed that a popular army corresponding perhaps in its structure to the Swiss militia, representing all political shades existing among the population, would be less likely to be used for internal politics. Therefore he favored giving Germany "equality" by changing the military clauses of the Peace Treaties so as to introduce general conscription for short-term service in Germany and Austria, and by disbanding at the same time the existing professional armies. The German claim for equality could be fulfilled, Otto Bauer believed, without strengthening the "military structure which holds the German people in subjection"—that is the professional army led by reactionary officers and dominated by an anti-labor bias.

Whether such a policy, which might have been very useful from a democratic point of view some years before, was still practical in 1933 seems doubtful now. Nevertheless it was perfectly logical, and probably the only policy which Bauer's party, faced as it was by the internal situation in Austria, could adopt in its struggle against Nazism.

In actual practice and without this explanatory background the statement of the international Socialist conference permitted the Western European Socialists to continue their weak policy with regard to Nazi Germany. Continuation of the traditional struggle against the alleged militarist plans of the French and British governments seemed more important at the time to the Socialist parties in these countries than swift resistance to Nazi war preparations.

4.

In the years which followed, Socialist pacifism continued to outweigh those forces within the labor movement which urged resistance to fascism on the international scene. Resolutions passed by international conferences did not reflect fully the predominant role which pacifism played within such leading Socialist parties as those in Britain and France. For some years an open cleavage existed between the policy of collective security laid down by the Labor and Socialist International and the continued pacifist policy of the parties that were members of the International.

The delegates sent to international meetings were usually those Socialists who were known, within their parties, as internationalist minded. Often they were opposed to the pacifist policy of their own parties. Their vote, therefore, did not represent the policy of their parties. Delegates from Socialist parties in so-called neutral countries voted for strongly worded anti-Fascist resolutions because they believed that such resolutions did not apply to their own countries, but only to the great powers. It was all right for the Socialists in Britain and France to urge a determined stand against fascist aggression upon their governments, but no one, these delegates thought, could expect their small countries to act.

As early as November, 1933, the Bureau of the Labor and Socialist International (L.S.I.) adopted slogans calling for action "Against any rearmament of Germany! Against any concessions to German nationalism and militarism! Against any separate negotiations with the Hitler government!" At the same time the International presented the theory which linked this policy with a general peace program by declaring that "a policy which would allow such privileges to Germany today would give the impression that Germany was being rewarded for its withdrawal from the League of Nations." This open step in Hitler's preparation for aggression had been taken in October, 1933. The resolution continued by stating that concessions to Germany "could only lead to a reinforcement of German nationalism and militarism and, consequently, to new demands based upon increased military power."

This was the line which the International consistently held during the following years. Allusions to the need of international disarmament receded as German rearmament progressed. Nevertheless, the foreign policy of the two politically decisive branches of the International, the British and the French, continued to be torn by conflicting emotions—pacifism, shame for the iniquities of the Peace Treaty, and the acknowledged need for resistance to Nazi Germany.

The British Labour party combined these contradictory policies without, apparently, being aware of the contradiction. The party conference in Hastings in October, 1933, adopted a resolution which pledged the party "to take no part in war and to resist it with the whole force of the labor movement." It even considered a general strike as a weapon in this struggle. On the other hand, the party maintained its traditional approval of the League of Nations and collective security without discussing at all whether support of the League might not under certain conditions imply taking part in a war.

A similar contradiction was apparent between a resolution branding German fascism as inhuman and a "permanent source of danger to freedom and peace" and the tendency to explain German rearmament by Britain's alleged refusal to disarm. The Rt. Hon. J. R. Clynes came out openly in support of Hitler's justification of German rearmament:

> We are paying very bitterly for the pledges which many nations in the world have broken since the Treaty of Versailles, for at the time when that Treaty was framed those nations pledged themselves to imitate in due time the conditions which as victors they had imposed upon the vanquished. They made Germany disarm and they pledged themselves to follow that example. They have utterly failed to keep their word, and it is no wonder that Germany, seeing how their promises have been violated, is demanding rearmament for herself.

Both attitudes, the protest against Hitler's inhumanity and the defense of Hitler's armament policy, continued to exist side by side within the party, both in the House of Commons and in the *Daily Herald*. The defense of Germany's rearmament was of great service to Hitler during the most dangerous preparatory stages of his rearmament program and far outweighed labor's general attitude of anti-fascism in significance. Labor's protest against the persecutions of Socialists, trade unionists, and Jews in Germany changed the conditions in Germany very little if at all. But the Labour party's and the *Daily Herald's* favorable treatment of Germany's case against the Western Powers, particularly France, was a powerful deterrent to what little desire existed in Downing Street to resist Hitlerism in its early stages.

By 1934, however, the party leadership began cautiously to feel its way toward a new policy. The contradiction between uncompromising opposition to any war and loyal support for the League was becoming too obvious to be ignored. In its report to the Annual Conference in Southport, October, 1934, the Party Executive stated:

> While the movement would strenuously resist any attempt on the part of the government to involve the country in a patently aggressive action against another nation, in view of the recent events on the Continent it was felt that there might be occasions when the movement would assist any defensive action taken to preserve the nation and its democratic institutions.

Still, the party was far from seriously facing the specific problems of sanctions and of mutual assistance which would have given meaning to its League of Nations policy. To demand an international police force was a poor substitute for a real understanding of Britain's role in Hitler's Europe. In addition, there was still no consistency between the party's opposition to the Nazi rule in Germany and its policy toward German demands. The opinion prevailed that it was best to accept German *faits accomplis* since acceptance "saved" the peace. The strong pacifism of the electorate promised support to a party that would adopt a purely pacifist attitude. Besides, much of the traditional anti-French feeling survived among British progressives, and there was a widespread tendency to acknowledge that Hitler's actions were justified by former French stubbornness and vindictiveness.

The Southport Conference of the Labour party in 1934 made a further step forward by distinguishing between "aggressive wars" and "a war undertaken in defense of the collective peace system." "Labor policy," the resolution on "War and Peace" continued, "recognizes . . . the duty unflinchingly to support our government in all risks and consequences of fulfilling its duty to take part in collective action against a peace-breaker." This new policy, strongly backed by Ernest Bevin, the powerful leader of the big Transport Workers' Union, faced a double opposition. The extreme pacifist wing, led by George Lansbury, Lord Ponsonby, and Wilfred Wellock, rejected support of war under any circumstances. On the other hand, the "Socialist League," a left-wing group led by Sir Stafford Cripps, brilliant debater and outstanding lawyer, and William Mellor, argued that war was inherent in capitalism and that no confidence could be placed in a capitalist-governed League of Nations. Both wings of the opposition were numerically weak, and the policy embodied in the resolution submitted by the Executive was adopted by a large majority.

Still the movement had to face a double test. So far the party regarded collective security primarily as a means to prevent a war. Would British labor dare to pursue its policy if it threatened to involve Britain in a war? And would the party do so even if the British government should oppose Britain's entry into a war? The Southport resolution merely pledged labor's support to the government under certain conditions; it did not declare the party's intention to oppose the government if it proved reluctant to carry out its League obligations. British Labour, though slowly abandoning its former naïve pacifism, had not yet developed an independent foreign policy based upon its anti-fascist and anti-aggression philosophy.

Early in 1935, when the Italian threat to Ethiopia began to materialize, the Labor and Socialist International declared that it would be "intolerable if the League of Nations . . . did not enforce against Italy, the aggressor, the provisions of its Covenant." The British Trade Union Congress, held in September, 1935, endorsed this policy, and British and French delegates to a joint meeting of the L.S.I. and the International Federation of Trade Unions held in Geneva in September, 1935, supported the International's demand that sanctions should be applied against Italy. Thus British Labour followed a definite pro-League policy, and the labor movement took an active part in the famous "Peace Ballot" conducted by the British League of Nations Union. In this ballot more than ten million British citizens declared their support for sanctions to stop an aggressor, while about seven million were in favor of using military measures, if necessary. The new policy of the Labour party thus corresponded to the shift in the point of view of a considerable part of British public opinion.

Within the party, however, the acid test of reality provoked sharp conflicts which came to a head at the party conference in Brighton in October, 1935. Dr. Hugh Dalton spoke for the Party Executive:

> The policy they stood for, was one of pooled security. . . . Economic and financial sanctions rigidly applied might be enough to prevent war and, if war broke out, might be sufficient to re-establish peace. . . . The question for us is: Shall we throw the full weight of this movement into the maintenance of peace—unbroken if we can—and if peace is broken, not through our action, break the aggressor with a minimum of human suffering and delay? . . .

Sir Stafford Cripps had resigned from the party executive shortly before the conference as a protest against the party's support of sanctions against Italy. He said that:

> Economic sanctions meant the highly probable use of military sanctions, and military sanctions and war were the same thing. They would commit the workers to the capitalist military machine. He could not trust them not to misuse their military power in the future as they had always done in the past. Had they a workers' government in this country as they had in Russia, the whole situation would be completely different. If the workers were in control of foreign policy and the military machine, they could prevent the misuse of war.

George Lansbury led the pacifist opposition. Although the leader of the party, he opposed its foreign policy:

> I want everyone to understand that it is bitter and difficult for me to stand here today and publicly repudiate a big fundamental piece of policy. If I were in any doubt about that policy, I would not take the line I am taking, but I ask the Conference to believe me when I say that I have never been more convinced that I am right and that the movement

is making a terrible mistake, than I am today. I agree with those of my friends who think that it is quite intolerable that you should have a man speaking as leader who disagrees fundamentally on an issue of this kind. . . .

Never in any circumstance have I believed that by force we could obtain Socialism. I have taken up my attitude because of One whose life I revere and who put it on record that those who take the sword shall perish by the sword.

As always the conference listened with great admiration to Lansbury's profession of creed, but adopted the resolution submitted by the Executive; more than two million votes were cast for the Party Executive, against a hundred thousand votes which represented the combined pacifist and leftist oppositions.

Cripps's attitude would have led the party into complete inactivity in the field of international affairs. He himself stated at the conference in Brighton that since he feared support for the government more than anything else nothing could be done, although he would have liked to see Italy checked. "It is unfortunate, tragic, but inescapably true that the British workers cannot at this moment be effective in the international political field." Cripps clearly felt the need for an independent foreign policy of the party, but he sacrificed the contents of this policy—the relentless struggle against aggression—to the party's duty of opposing the government under any conditions.

The campaign for effective sanctions against Italy, carried on under the leadership of the newly elected party leader, Major Clement Richard Attlee, exposed the party to much abuse. A strong section of the Conservative party branded the Labour party as an organization of warmongers and for some time—practically until 1939—the traditional position of the two parties seemed reversed, Labour stressing the need for a more courageous foreign policy while Conservatives preached peace, conciliation, and concessions. But if the party's stand with regard to Italy was now consistent with its pro-League of Nations policy, its attitude towards Nazi Germany still remained contradictory. Since Hitler had not yet committed any open acts of aggression but was merely preparing them, the British public and most labor leaders did not feel that the time had come to resist. There was hardly any real opposition to the

Anglo-German Naval Treaty of 1935, although German violations of the disarmament clauses of the Peace Treaty were thereby sanctioned. When Germany marched into the Rhineland in March, 1936, the Labour party was still far from understanding the significance of the German move and welcomed the proposed international negotiations suggested by Hitler.

The decisive step toward an anti-fascist foreign policy, which would obviously have been one divorced from that of the British government, was still to be taken when the Spanish Civil War broke out and completed the evolution of British labor's foreign policy.

5.

Foreign affairs and the Third Reich's threat to peace played a surprisingly small role in the discussion within the French labor movement after Hitler's advent to power. In the passionate debates which shook the French Socialist party and finally led to an open split, international affairs and the dangers to France from Hitler Germany were hardly mentioned. It required the Spanish Civil War to awaken the French working class to a realization, however incomplete, of the external dangers confronting the French Republic.

Two currents determined French Socialist thought with regard to war and militarism during the period preceding the first World War. Jean Jaurès and his followers favored *la levée en masse,* an army of the people on the Swiss model, with general conscription, short term service, and a minimum of permanent cadres. Such an army would be essentially democratic in domestic affairs and would mobilize all popular energies in a struggle against an external enemy for a war of defense. It could not be used, however, for aggressive military action. Pierre Renaudel carried Jaurès' tradition into the post-war era.

This theory met strong resistance within the movement. Édouard Vaillant advocated a general strike as a means to prevent the outbreak of a war. At the International Congress in Stuttgart, 1907, Vaillant was defeated, and Jaurès' policy of support for a defensive war determined French Socialist policy in 1914. But pacifism made such rapid progress among the French workers during and after the war that for many workers Socialist internationalism became equivalent to pacifism. It was the tradition of Vaillant and the war-born pacifism of the French workers which gave Paul Faure's policy of appeasement the halo of French Socialist doctrine. Jaurès' *levée en masse* was reflected, after 1933, in French working-class resistance to the extension of the length of the military service in answer to German rearmament.

Léon Blum himself never expected before 1933 that Hitler would succeed in winning power. According to Blum's theory, Hitler was no more than a tool of German big business and reaction, being used to reduce German labor's influence. Blum expected that Hitler would be dropped by his masters as soon as this task was complete. When Hitler assumed full control in Germany and the working class withdrew from the battlefield without open resistance, Blum considered for some time whether he ought not to resign from the leadership of his party. After having battled for many years for a reconciliation with Germany and having affirmed that a new Germany, ready for peaceful coöperation, had been born after the war, he doubted whether he could still represent the French Socialists before his country now that another German regime had become even more threatening than imperial Germany. However, Blum still enjoyed the confidence of his party, and in the subsequent conflict with the "Neo-Socialist" faction, he was the undisputed leader of the majority of the party.

During 1933 the issue of fascism was mainly a humanitarian question for the Socialists in France, who were receiving thousands of refugees from Germany. Early in 1934 French fascism appeared on the scene and for a time absorbed the attention of the French labor movement. The United Front between Socialists and Communists, and later the Popular Front, were in the beginning almost exclusively concerned with the defense of the democratic regime against its internal enemies. The policy of collective security had been officially adopted by the Socialist party, as it had by practically all French parties. Most Frenchmen understood this policy to be solely an obligation for other countries to aid France against German aggression. Few fully realized that there might be a similar role to be played by France. Even the network of alliances covering the entire Continent led few people to consider that French obligations to her Allies might involve France in a war. France was still so superior to Germany, from a military point of view, that German aggression against an ally of France seemed out of the question.

Léon Blum's foreign policy in these years was based upon two main points. First, France should never deal alone with Germany but should always face Berlin in Britain's company. French cooperation with Britain, he reasoned, would give the democracies a tremendous superiority in strength and exclude any danger of armed conflict. This, however, was only a method to prevent war; what was needed even more was a constructive policy. This was the second part of Blum's program. Since both the German and the Italian dictatorships claimed to be peaceful, eager to disarm, provided only the rest of the world would follow their example, Blum suggested that the democracies should "force them to live up to their bombastic promises. Let us compel them to organize peace with us; let us make them disarm; let them prove that they really intend to disarm." The democracies should draft a disarmament treaty according to fair standards, provide for their own and the dictatorships' disarmament, and present the treaty to the dictators. If they were willing to collaborate in drafting the treaty, so much the better. If not, a fair treaty drawn without the dictatorships would prove an irresistible weapon.

Late in 1934 Blum developed this theory in the Chamber of Deputies during a discussion on supplementary military credits. Referring to a debate between two right-wing deputies on the question of whether Hitler's peace assertions were made in good or bad faith, he said:

> This discussion does not matter. There is only one sign, one touchstone, today of the good faith of Germany and Hitler, and that is to participate in the general disarmament convention and to return to Geneva. If Germany refuses, we have always admitted, we have always declared, and we continue to hope that an equitable convention, even concluded without her, would be inevitably imposed on her by the force of unanimity and of the world community.

There was something mystical in Blum's belief in the irresistible moral force of what he called world unanimity against the dictatorships. But there was also another more practical element in his policy; the recognition that the Peace Treaty alone could no longer constitute a sufficiently strong basis for action against German rearmament, and that only some measure of French disarmament could justify, before the world, pressure on Germany to force her to abandon illegal rearmament. Such a policy was both logical and safe in 1934, when France was still far stronger than Germany. To maintain this policy while German rearmament progressed in feverish haste was a different proposition. But Blum was the principal author of a resolution adopted by the Bureau of the Labor and Socialist International in May, 1935, which demanded that a disarmament convention "should be drafted with the coöperation of Germany, if she decides to return to Geneva. It should be submitted to her for signature even if she persists in her present isolation." Basically, Léon Blum followed this idea of disarmament with or against Germany even in later years, and the Labor and Socialist International advocated Blum's policy as late as March, 1936, even after the occupation of the Rhineland by German troops. "Hitler now seeks to conceal his aggressive intentions under professions of good will," an international resolution read. "Hitler claims to be a peacemaker. He can prove the sincerity of his proposals only if he is prepared to join with other nations in limiting armaments by international agreement and submitting them to international inspection and supervision."

It was in full agreement with this policy that the party protested against the idea entertained by several members of the French government of mobilizing against the occupation of the Rhineland. Blum and his party agreed in excluding warlike measures from their arsenal of political weapons. Reason might have shown them that resistance with every means, even military, might be the only logical conclusion of their own acceptance of the principle of collective security. German rearmament and the fortification of the Rhineland would prevent France from effectively aiding Germany's neighbors in Central Europe, and would thus paralyze collective security. Yet the French Socialists refused to accept the specific demands of a general policy which they loudly acclaimed.

The Ethiopian crisis proved that most Frenchmen shared the Socialists' reluctance to approve the implications of a program which they all professed to follow. The right-wing parties violently opposed sanctions against Italy and started a rabid campaign against the "British warmongers," who, it was claimed, were using the League of Nations in general and France in particular for British imperialistic interests. The French left, at least a large part of the left, was by no means eager to apply effective sanctions against Italy. The Socialists accepted economic sanctions. Even Paul Faure, later the leading spokesman of the pro-Munich wing in the Socialist party, attacked Premier Laval's hesitations. "By declaring in advance one's intention to oppose sanctions," Faure wrote on September 4, 1935, "one only encourages aggression. Laval, with his 'mediation' and 'conciliation' is not rendering a service to the League. If Britain, France, and the Soviet Union were in agreement, they could soon enforce peace." As soon, however, as the problem of military sanctions appeared on the horizon, the Socialists too became hesitant, and with the exception of the Communists, who kept silent, the rest of the left voiced their pacifist faith. Thus, when the British navy was sent into the Mediterranean, Blum wrote an article entitled "England's Mistake" in which he accused the British Admiralty of "playing into the hands of the pro-Mussolini press by suggesting that sanctions are inevitably military. I notice in the last two days," Blum added, "that French opinion is in a state of great bewilderment." The leadership of the Popular Front as a whole was no less ambiguous. In a resolution it favored "observing the whole Covenant" of the League, but it added that the Popular Front, "which is passionately attached to peace, rejects with horror the idea of a conflict with Italy or any other country, and is uncompromisingly opposed to any application of armed force."

After hostilities between Italy and Ethiopia broke out, Blum wrote: "A defensive war is just as atrocious as a war of aggression; but it is still better than if the world made a cowardly surrender to wars of aggression." Rationally Blum was convinced of the necessity of applying sanctions, but he was far from welcoming action which involved the prospect of France at war against Mussolini. Even the Communists lacked fervor in their campaign for closing the Suez Canal. Naïvely, without any conscious selfishness, the French were convinced that after all the primary purpose of the

League was to support France against German aggression. That the roles might be changed and that France should support the League against what many considered a potential ally in France's struggle against Germany, was beyond the powers of imagination of many Frenchmen. The Hoare-Laval Plan to hand Ethiopia over to Italy, which aroused a tremendous wave of protest in Britain and forced Sir Samuel Hoare out of the Cabinet, had no similar consequences in France. Apart from Pierre Cot and Édouard Herriot, few Radicals joined the Socialist and Communist protests, though even then the Socialists did not advocate military sanctions. When the Radicals withdrew from the Cabinet, shortly afterwards, their act was due less to Laval's dubious attitude toward the League of Nations than to the country's revolt against the government's deflationary economic policy.

When Laval resigned, the Franco-Soviet Pact was signed but not yet ratified. Laval himself had signed the pact when he still maintained friendly relations with the left and wished to please the pro-Russian Radicals and Communists. When he moved toward the right, he delayed ratification. He hoped to arrive at an understanding with Germany, which the pact with the Soviet Union might have prevented. Furthermore, French public opinion, which had at first welcomed the alliance, was later divided on the question. Most Conservatives believed in an Italian alliance as an alternative to coöperation with the Soviets. Laval himself now sided with the right in opposing the pact which he himself had concluded. Yet, the feeling prevailed among the right that it would be better to ratify not so much in order to have the Soviet Union as an ally, but rather to prevent it from coming to an understanding with Germany. When Laval's successor, Pierre Etienne Flandin, submitted the pact to the Chamber, ratification was voted by an imposing majority.

The Radicals, led by Herriot and Pierre Cot, supported the ratification of the Soviet Pact and so, of course, did the Communists. The Socialists, however, were rather lukewarm. Spinasse, the future minister of economic affairs in the first Popular Front government, who was official spokesman of the Socialists in the Chamber debate on ratification, said:

The whole value of such pacts depends on the orientation one is prepared to give them. They are beneficial in so far as they bring us nearer the aim we have set ourselves and in so far as they may help us to take up again the interrupted task of general disarmament and to draw up a convention which the European nations can propose or oppose to Nazi Germany, and in so far as they create a situation more favorable to the examination of the real problems of peace—such as the economic problems.

If the Socialists voted for ratification it was due much more to the need of keeping the Popular Front intact than to enthusiasm for a Russian alliance. Many Socialists disliked Russia more intensely than some of the Radicals did, since Socialists suffered more from Communist competition than the Radicals; moreover many Socialists continued to hope for a final peaceful arrangement with Germany, and the understanding with Russia was believed to exclude definitely a rapprochement with the alleged archenemy of Bolshevism.

And so on March 7, 1936, when Germany tore up the Treaty of Locarno and thereby paved the way for the tragedies of 1938 and 1939, the French right was jubilant for not having allowed the British to lead them into a quarrel with Italy, while the Socialists protested against Premier Sarraut's warning that France would not allow Strasbourg to be exposed to German guns. Few French leaders seriously considered resistance. Fewer realized that France's failure to act would lead, in a surprisingly short time, to a breakdown of the French system of Continental alliances and to a tremendous and irreparable loss of prestige. They did not foresee that less than two years afterwards Hitler at Berchtesgaden would say sneeringly to Schuschnigg, faced by a German ultimatum: "Are you counting on France and England? When I occupied the Rhineland in March, 1936, they didn't budge. Do you imagine they are going to budge for you?"

Party strife and class struggle around the problems of foreign policy went on in France, with the Socialists torn between intellectual understanding of what Nazism meant and humanitarian inability to accept the risk of war. Thus the scene was set for the French breakdown in the Spanish War.

6.

After the failure of the League in the Ethiopian War and France's paralysis during the occupation of the Rhineland in March, 1936, the small European countries hurried to withdraw from the battlefield, and most Socialist parties abandoned the policy of collective security in practice though they clung to it in theory.

The Dutch Social Democrats were perhaps the only exception in this mad rush toward illusionary isolation. They had favored, until 1934, complete disarmament of their own country, if possible as part of an international agreement, but if necessary as an isolated measure. In 1934 the party began to recognize that this policy could no longer be upheld, and two years later it was formally dropped in favor of a strong national defense and active coöperation in measures of collective security.

In the Scandinavian countries, governed by Socialist led cabinets, the revolt against the League system followed the breakdown of sanctions against Italy. The Scandinavian governments insisted upon a change in the League's Covenant to free them from taking part in international actions against aggressors. In September, 1938, they were to declare officially that in their opinion the sanctions clauses were no longer binding. Sweden decided upon rearmament to defend its neutrality in case of war. The Danish Social Democrats considered military efforts to defend their little country utterly hopeless; rearmament proceeded on a modest scale. Coöperation among the Scandinavian nations, so complete in other respects, never went so far as to guarantee mutual assistance against aggression.

Since the First World War the Swiss Social Democrats had rejected the principle of national defense under a capitalist regime. Now they adopted a new program which recognized the need for military force to guarantee the country's time-honored neutrality.

In Belgium the remilitarization of the Rhineland and the numerical increase of the Flemish element of the population combined to bring about a change in the traditional pro-French and pro-League policy of the country. When France accepted without resistance the fact that German troops occupied the Franco-German and Belgo-German frontier zones, Belgium felt threatened and became doubtful of the value of French support. The Flemish movement always opposed close relations with France, since such collaboration would naturally strengthen the French-speaking Walloons against the Flemish. Many conservative Walloons who had steadfastly supported the alliance with France were frightened by the French Popular Front, considering it the first step toward a revolution which might spread to Belgium if the old relationship with France were maintained.

The Belgian Labor party, which had ardently believed in collective security and close coöperation with France and Britain, was no longer unanimous. A new generation was coming into its own and with it came leaders like Hendrik de Man and Paul Henri Spaak who were less ardent internationalists than the older leaders like Emile Vandervelde and Louis de Brouckère. De Man declared his confidence in Hitler's desire for peace—one ex-service man trusting the other—and Spaak professed a "national" socialism as opposed to the "out-dated and impractical" philosophy of internationalism. The Belgian party was split over the issue of foreign policy, and the deciding factor was finally the trade unions. Opposition to the new neutrality policy (which the king openly supported) would have endangered the existing government coalition of Socialists, Liberals, and Catholics. Since the middle-class parties favored neutrality, a Socialist stand for collective security would have brought only internal dissension. The trade unions, wishing to retain representation in the government, therefore threw their weight on the side of De Man and Spaak. Thus, Belgium embarked upon a policy which was labeled "independent," but which in fact amounted to a unilaterally declared neutrality under the leadership of the Socialist foreign minister, Spaak. This was the beginning of the road that led to Belgium's helplessness in the face of Nazi aggression and to the disaster of spring, 1940.

Czech and Polish Socialists saw little reason to change their foreign policy after Hitler's advent to power. They had always supported national defense and collective security. The reëmerging

German power which immediately threatened their own countries only strengthened their stand for military preparedness and international coöperation against aggression.

What really counted as an expression of Socialist policy in world affairs, however, were not the statements of the small parties or those of the Labor and Socialist International, but the actions of British and French labor. It is true that the British Labour party soon after 1936 advocated a strong policy of collective security. But the French Socialists' attitude continued to be ambiguous, and during the decisive years when Germany was preparing for future aggression, the Socialist forces in Europe advocated a kind of pacifism which unwillingly, but effectively, aided Nazi policy.

Chapter 18

THE POPULAR FRONT

I.

"AFTER Hitler—our turn" was the German Communists' guiding slogan late in 1932, and even after March, 1933, the Communist International maintained that no change of any significance had occurred in Germany. In Communist eyes Social Democrats continued to be Social-Fascists and supporters of the Nazis, although thousands of Socialists were being sent to Nazi concentration camps. The Communists felt that their party had not been defeated; indeed, they foresaw their victory as imminent. Fritz Heckert, a member of the Central Committee of the Communist party wrote: "The talk of the alleged defeat and political death of the German Communist party is the Philistine chattering of stupid and ignorant people." [1] The Central Committee of the Communist International stated: "The establishing of an open fascist dictatorship, by destroying all the democratic illusions among the masses and liberating them from the influence of social democracy, accelerates the rate of Germany's development towards proletarian revolution." [2] And elsewhere the Communists declared: "The complete elimination of the Social-Fascists from the state apparatus, the brutal suppression even of social democratic organizations and press organs alters nothing of the fact that at present as in the past it [Social-Democracy] constitutes the main support of the dictatorship of capital."

That these were more than phrases intended only to maintain the fighting spirit of the Communist workers was shown in a speech

[1] Fritz Heckert, "What Is Happening in Germany?" *International Press Correspondence,* English edition. Vol. 13, No. 18 (April 21, 1933), p. 393.

[2] *International Press Correspondence,* English edition. Vol. 13, No. 17 (April 13, 1932), p. 378.

of Piatnitsky before the Presidium of the Executive Committee of the Comintern in July, 1934. Piatnitsky declared: "We stated that the fascists would not retain power (in the resolution of the Presidium of April 1, 1933, immediately after their advent to power). The resolution of the Presidium has been corroborated; the crisis in the fascist camp is beginning." [3]

In line with this theory the Communist underground movement in Germany was working on a "short-term" basis. Since the breakdown of Hitler's dictatorship was expected in the near future—Fritz Heckert "demonstrated" that Hitler's dictatorship was much weaker than Mussolini's—the Communists carried on their propaganda without much concern for their members' safety or lives. They suffered frightful losses through arrests. When the expected revolution did not materialize, the party was forced, after having wasted thousands of heroic workers' lives, to adopt more cautious methods. Sheer lack of numbers was the decisive reason for this change.

On the international scene, too, Communist tactics at first remained unchanged, in spite of the events in Germany. On February 6, 1934, French Communists took part in demonstrations arranged and led by Fascists against the Daladier government. The understanding with Germany, which dated back to the time of the Rapallo Conference in 1922, was maintained in Moscow as well as in Berlin, although Hugenberg, official German delegate to the World Economic Conference in London, bluntly expounded Germany's intention to "colonize" the Ukraine. Moscow was not afraid of Hitler, who it was held, was a mere pawn of German big business and of the Reichswehr, with which Moscow had been on the most intimate terms for many years.

2.

Yet Hugenberg's announcement had created a stir in Moscow. Karl Radek, for many years the leading Communist exponent of a Russo-German understanding against the West, came out in May, 1933, with an article entitled "The Revision of the Versailles

[3] *The Communist International,* Vol. XI, No. 16 (August 20, 1934), p. 645.

Treaty," [4] which brought the first hint of an impending change in the Comintern's policy.

> The path of revision of the robbers' peace at Versailles is the path to the new World War [Ràdek wrote]. All the attempts of the interested parties to represent the matter as though it were a question of peaceful transformation of the old treaties cannot deceive us. The diplomatic fuss with regard to the revision of the Versailles Treaty is only one of the forms for the preparation of the war. The word "revision" is only another name for the new World War. . . .
>
> This program for the revision of the Versailles Treaty by means of the creation of a still worse form of the Brest Treaty [At Brest, Imperial Germany imposed a peace treaty upon Soviet Russia which deprived it of the Ukraine and large parts of southwestern Russia] is the foreign policy of German Fascism.

But a decisive change in Russia's policy, and consequently in that of the Comintern, came only after the events of June 30, 1934, had convinced Moscow that the Nazi dictator had complete control over all factions of his party, and that the Nazi rule had come to stay.

Russia's foreign policy so far had been based upon an understanding with Germany. It protected Russia against isolation and rendered impossible the resumption of foreign counterrevolutionary interventions in the Soviet Union. In exchange, Russia supported Germany against France and Britain. From the Russian point of view, the only danger was a Franco-German understanding, which Moscow feared might finally lead to a united front directed against the Soviet Union. As noted before, Moscow always looked with suspicion at the efforts of the German Social Democrats and of Stresemann to bring about a reconciliation between France and Germany. Now that Hitler apparently had to be taken seriously, Moscow began to fear a different type of isolation—a situation in which Germany might attack the Soviet Union while Western Europe would stand by as neutral or even support in some measure the German venture. Every advance of the Nazi party at the expense of the Reichswehr, Moscow's old friend, increased Russia's concern.

Under these conditions, Russia had to look for new allies to pre-

[4] *International Press Correspondence,* Vol. XIII, No. 22 (May 19, 1933), p. 475.

vent being isolated. Since Germany was fast developing into the most dangerous foe of Russia and France, it was natural that Stalin looked towards France for aid—"Our enemy's enemy is our friend."

The internal evolution in France favored such a change in Russian foreign policy. After the fascist assault of February 6, 1934, in which Communists took part by unconsciously supporting the fascists' tactics, a wave of popular democratic enthusiasm compelled the Communists into united action with the Socialists and the trade unions. Events forced the French Communists to abandon the "Social-Fascist" credo whether they wished to or not, even before Moscow officially adopted its new course.

Out of these two elements, the need for new allies to replace the lost support of Germany and the spontaneous United Front in France, a new Communist tactic was formed. It was formally endorsed by the presidium of the Executive Committee of the Communist International in July, 1934. Speaking before that body, V. Knorin said:

> The situation in Germany has altered. But even now it is correct to call Wels [German Social Democratic leader] a Social-Fascist, and it is true that the Fascists and Social Democracy led by Wels were twins. But the illegal Social Democratic groups which are now carrying on work in Germany are not Social-Fascists and do not constitute the social support of the bourgeoisie. They are on the way towards Communism, and must be won for the Communist party.[5]

Symbol of the new course was Gregorij Dimitroff, the hero of the Reichstag fire trial. His influence in the Comintern came to supersede that of Molotoff, Manuilski, Kuusinen, Bela Kun, and Karl Radek, who had been its principal leaders since the eviction of Bukharin. A member of the Bulgarian Communist party, he was involved in the bitter internal quarrels that had shaken that once strong organization since the semi-fascist coup of 1923 overthrew the Stamboliiski regime. For several years he had been living abroad on orders of the extreme leftist leadership of his party, who wished to have him out of the way. His brilliant and courageous defense in the trial in Leipzig had made him famous the world over.

[5] Reprinted in the *Communist International,* Vol. XI, No. 16 (August 20, 1934), p. 638.

His stand against Goering and the extreme left in his own party made him the proper symbol of the change toward moderate policies in the service of an anti-Nazi campaign which Moscow was preparing.

The Seventh World Congress of the Comintern, held in 1935, made Gregorij Dimitroff secretary general of the Communist International. But he had led the Comintern some months before this date and directed the actual change from the Third Period to the Popular Front policy inaugurated in 1934.

Germany and to a lesser degree Japan now were the archenemies of the Soviet Union. Consequently, Russia concluded in 1934 what amounted practically to an alliance with France and Czechoslovakia, endeavored to come to a similar agreement with Rumania, entered the League of Nations, and made friendly overtures to England and the United States. In Asia, Russia supported Chiang Kai-shek, the man who had slaughtered the Chinese Communists. Collective security, resistance to aggression as symbolized by Nazi Germany and militarist Japan, defense of democracy—these were the new slogans replacing the former support of the struggle against the "imperialist robbers' treaty" of Versailles. A democratic united front against Germany became the major objective of Russia's new foreign policy, instead of the former coöperation with Germany against the West. A year and a half of Hitler's rule transformed the entire traditional pattern of Soviet Russia's foreign policy.

A whole series of changes in Russia's domestic policy accompanied and completed the turn of the diplomatic tables. A new constitution was to prove that Russia rightfully belonged among the democratic states. There was a certain relaxation in the struggle against the Church. In 1932 and 1933 Trotsky's supporters who favored coöperation with the Socialists had been presented as traitors in the service of Social-Fascism; now, the few Communists who dared to oppose the reconciliation with the Socialists were labeled Trotskyites.

In the Comintern the new party line wrought havoc not only with the tactics of the Third Period, but also with principles that had been considered part of the holy Leninist gospel. Official Communist doctrine so far had rejected "national defense under a capitalist regime." Communists had been pledged to vote against any military credits and to follow a policy of revolutionary defeatism in case of war. This had been the strategy of Lenin during the First World War. After 1934 the Communists became ardent protagonists of national defense in order to strengthen all countries which might oppose Hitler in case of war. Communist speakers developed a quasi-Jacobin patriotism that could hardly be distinguished from a clumsily concealed petty-bourgeois nationalism. While the Jacobins had based their patriotism upon the progress of a revolution, the Communist neo-Jacobins abandoned the revolutionary part of the program, retaining only patriotic appeals to the revolutionary past of France and Czechoslovakia. Communist newspapers which formerly had made fun of the army now published enthusiastic reports on army maneuvers and ardent descriptions of the workers' part in the defense of their country against fascist aggression. Until 1934 the Communists had stressed the point that there was little difference between fascism and bourgeois democracy. Now this difference became vital, and the Communist parties came to be the champions in the defense of democratic liberties.

The slogan of Social-Fascism was dropped. Instead the Communists offered their coöperation to the same Socialist leaders whom previously they had branded as archenemies of the working class. It was not only the Socialists who became potential allies of the Communists, but middle-class democrats; at a later stage, practically everyone who might possibly be induced to oppose Nazi Germany was courted by the Communist leaders. Catholics, the Pope, Austrian monarchists, even "sincere" Italian Fascists were objects of Communist united front offers. "National reconciliation" in the face of Hitler Germany's threats superseded the old slogan of the class struggle which not even the First World War had been able to stop.

To create sympathy for the Soviet Union in Western Europe, leading intellectuals, artists, and writers were invited to Moscow and feted. A new set of organizations sprang up to win mass support for the new Communist foreign policy and the united front attitudes of the various Communist parties. André Gide's statements in favor of the Soviet Union were hailed as a great victory. While Stalin in Russia praised "the Communists outside the Communist Party"—something unheard of and unthinkable before 1934—the few remaining Communist trade unions outside Russia were dissolved and merged with the Socialist led unions. For a while the French Communists even pretended to consider seriously the fusion of their party with the French Socialist party.

Within a short time the Communists, hitherto the extreme left of the Labor movement, veered completely around to the extreme right.

The country upon which Communist attention was focused and where the new policy was inaugurated was France. The French Communist party now held the place of honor in the Comintern which had been lost by the German Communists, whose defeat was now officially admitted.

3.

On January 8, 1934, French police discovered a body in a villa in Chamonix. It was the corpse of Monsieur Alexandre Stavisky, whom the newspapers accused of having engineered a sensational financial scandal at Bayonne, France; a bullet had pierced his brain. Stavisky had had such influential friends among the police and judiciary and in Parliament that a trial in which he was involved had been postponed nineteen times. The extreme right-wing press, with the Royalist *Action Française* in the lead, accused the left, especially Daladier's Radical party, of having been Stavisky's friends and protectors.

The Chamber election in 1932 had given the leftists a majority, but, as has been pointed out, the two leading leftist parties, the Radicals and Socialists, could not agree upon a joint financial and economic program. No less than five governments came and went between the elections in May, 1932, and September, 1933. The Chautemps Government, in office at the time the Stavisky scandal broke out, did not fare better than its predecessors. Monsieur Raynaldy, minister of justice, involved in another shady affair, resigned and the government followed his example on January 25,

1934. Édouard Daladier, the new prime minister, was to bear the brunt of the Stavisky scandal.

As Stavisky's finger seemed to point from the grave to one after another among the high dignitaries of the regime, a feverish atmosphere existed in the country. Ministers, deputies, high-ranking judges and officials were accused of having been Stavisky's accomplices. The fascists were quick to exploit this unhappy situation. On February 6, 1934, while the Chamber was discussing a motion of confidence in the Daladier Government, which had just presented itself before Parliament, fascist rioters interspersed with Communists almost succeeded in storming the Chamber. Twenty rioters and one policeman were killed. Daladier, branded by the right and also by the Communists as *le fusilleur* (the killer), capitulated and resigned. Fascism seemed triumphant. A democratically elected government had been forced by violence to resign. Colonel de la Rocque, leader of the "Croix de Feu," the most promising of the many fascist organizations that had sprung up, announced that "the first objective had been attained." Daladier was succeeded by Doumergue, a former president of France and candidate of the right-wing parties.

The Socialists were the first to realize the significance of the event; the Radical party was simply stunned, and the Communists continued to shout "murderer" at Daladier. On February 7 the Trade Union Federation (C.G.T.), together with the Socialists and a few smaller groups of the left, called a twenty-four-hour general strike for February 12. Three days later, the Communist trade unions (C.G.T.U.) announced that they would join in the strike. During these three days the Communists had begun to understand that the French workers regarded the February 6 incident as a fascist venture, and that the Communist leaders were in danger of being deserted by their own members. After having called first for a separate Communist strike on February 9, the Communists gave in to the continuous and irresistible pressure of the workers and followed the lead given by the C.G.T. and the Socialists. No organization of the left could have dared to oppose working-class pressure for unity of action. What was usually considered the weakness of the French labor movement, the lack of well-disciplined mass organizations, now became a source of strength. Party loyalties had prevented the establishment of a united front in Germany. In France the workers outside the organizations were now acting. They imposed their will upon the leaders of the comparatively weak working-class organizations.

As a demonstration the general strike was a complete success. It was as near to a one hundred percent strike as general strikes can possibly be, and it followed closely the plans of its organizers. Hundreds of thousands of Socialists and Communists demonstrated, separately convoked but actually joining forces in Paris. Thus was born the "Common Front" of Socialists and Communists. To establish it definitely, lengthy negotiations were carried on by the two parties. On August 27 a Pact for United Action was solemnly signed.

The Socialist party accepted the pact by an overwhelming majority. The dissident minority was led by Frossard, a founder of the French Communist party, who had resigned from it when the Comintern began to interfere with the internal affairs of the French Communists and later joined the Socialist party. He feared that by coöperating with the Communists the Socialist party would "isolate itself from democracy." The Communists, in accepting the pact, recognized the strength of popular pressure; they were forced to acknowledge that mutual criticism should be banned during the period of common action. At the time of the earlier united front maneuver such criticism had been the main objective of the Communists' united-front proposals.

On an international scale coöperation between Socialists and Communists was far more difficult to establish. In February, 1933, the Labor and Socialist International had made overtures to the Communist International "with a view to the conclusion of an agreement for united defense against fascism." Pending such an international agreement, the L.S.I. "recommended to its affiliated parties that they conclude no local pacts." The Communists at that time refused to accept the "Social-Fascist" invitation, preferring to continue their time-honored practice of seeking united-front agreements with Socialist workers which would be directed against Socialist leaders.

By 1934 both the Comintern and the Labor and Socialist International had changed their positions. The British Labour party, the Dutch and the Scandinavian Social Democrats refused to enter into any negotiations with Communists; Moscow, on the other hand, now was ready for an agreement with the L.S.I. When Emile Vandervelde and Friedrich Adler, president and secretary of the L.S.I., met Marcel Cachin and Maurice Thorez, the delegates of the Comintern, at Brussels on October 15, 1934, to discuss support for the Spanish miners then fighting in Asturia, the Socialist representatives could make no commitments. A meeting of the Executive of the L.S.I. proved unable to agree upon a definite answer to be given to the Communists. With the greatest difficulty a compromise was reached, over the protest of Léon Blum, the Spanish Socialists as represented by Del Vayo, the Austrians, and some other groups. Since a "Common Front" had been established in France, the International bowed before the accomplished fact. International negotiations, looking toward a similar end, were impossible because of the resistance of the British, the Dutch and the Scandinavians. The L.S.I., however, did reverse its former stand to the extent of declaring its affiliated parties "free to act in this matter in accordance with its [that is, the Socialist party within the International] complete autonomy." The way was thus open for joint Socialist-Communist action in any country where the Socialists were willing. But this action represented a distinct weakening of the centralized control exerted by the Socialist International. On a vital question the Socialist parties publicized their internal dissensions in contrast with the well-disciplined Comintern.

The Common Front in France was by no means hailed with undivided enthusiasm by the leaders of the two labor parties. At the beginning, between February and July, 1934, the Socialists were the active force, while the Communists hesitated. The Communist party had given way to mass pressure in February, but since Moscow had not yet ratified the new course, the Communist leaders resisted so far as their rank and file permitted. The Communist publications, in particular the theoretical magazine of the party, *Cahiers du bolshévisme,* continued to vituperate against the Socialist leaders. In July, after the presidium of the Comintern had endorsed the new course, the French Communists began to be wholeheartedly in favor of the Common Front. But by then the Socialists were considerably cooler. Not only the right wing under its new leader, the former Communist Frossard, but also Blum were skeptical. Still, Blum acknowledged that the workers would destroy any working-class organization that might resist the new trend.

"The masses of the people would not have understood," Blum wrote on February 25, 1935, in his newspaper, *Le Populaire,* "and they would have come to dislike us. There was also a danger that our party would have split. . . . This united action has been and may still be an object of apprehension, but it was none the less necessary, or, if one prefers, inevitable."

The distrust among the Socialists was the more understandable because of the rapidity of the Communist conversion. Still, for the time being, there was little in the Communist activities that could have been justly criticized as a violation of the pact. On the contrary, discussions about the fusion of the two parties were started, although both sides operated in a way which could best be described as maneuvering for positions. "Organic unity" (unity by complete fusion) became a slogan almost as often and as enthusiastically shouted by demonstrating masses as "unity of action" before August, 1934.

The two trade-union centers, the C.G.T. and the Communist led C.G.T.U., were actually merged. Léon Jouhaux, the C.G.T. leader, remained at the head of the unified organization.

Tentative efforts were made to extend the leftist alliance to other groups, particularly the Radical party. In this respect the Communists took the lead, with the Socialists tending to hold back. Blum was not convinced that a left-wing majority in the existing Chamber of Deputies would be solid, especially when confronted with the grave financial situation of the country. Viewing the general elections to be held in 1936, he favored coöperation out of which might come a Chamber with a definite leftist majority capable of working in harmony. A preliminary election victory of the left at the communal elections in May, 1935, furthered the plan to include the Radicals in the leftist union and to extend the Common Front into a Popular Front.

Symbol and climax of this victory was the election of Professor Paul Rivet in the Saint Victor quarter of the formerly arch-reactionary Quartier Latin, the students' district of Paris. The seat had been held by Monsieur Lebecq, one of the leaders of the February 6 *Putsch*. In the first ballot four candidates of four different leftist parties together polled a total of 42 votes more than the reactionary. They all withdrew in favor of a new candidate, Professor Rivet, a Socialist with a high scientific reputation, who became the standard bearer of the united left. Increasing his majority to 150 votes, Rivet defeated the reactionary Lebecq. The Quartier Latin election was paralleled by other considerable advances of the Socialists and Communists outside Paris.

This victory strengthened those Radicals who opposed further coöperation with right-wing and center parties. Daladier, in the background since his inglorious exit in February, 1934, came forward in favor of the Popular Front and was supported by the so-called "Young Turks," the young leftist elements in his party who were led by Pierre Cot and Jean Zay. They succeeded in persuading the party to take part in a joint Socialist-Communist demonstration arranged for July 14, 1935, Bastille Day. This demonstration, the biggest Paris had ever witnessed, marked the birth of the Front Populaire. Yet there was still some distance to go before a real understanding beyond mere sentimental enthusiasm was reached. In foreign policy, the most vital problem for the Communists, the parties were far from being in agreement. The Communists were the most ardent supporters of collective security and of the Franco-Soviet Pact, but were not overanxious to demand sanctions against Italy, which was just about to embark on its war against Ethiopia. The Socialists were in favor of collective security, as practically every Frenchman claimed to be at that time, but doubtful about the merits of a pact with Russia, and even less urgent than the Communists in their demands for sanctions against Italy. In the Radical party, less exposed to Communist competition than the Socialists, sentiment for the pact with Russia was more heartily expressed, but sanctions against Italy were almost universally rejected. Under these conditions the left could not obtain Laval's defeat over the issue of his resistance to sanctions. When the Radicals finally were induced to revolt against Laval's deflationist policy, the Cabinet soon resigned. The simultaneous election of Daladier as president of the Radical party was a symbol of the victory of the Popular Front among the Radicals.

In spite of Laval's resignation in January, 1936, the Front Populaire did not yet consider that the time had come to claim succession. Blum wanted to wait until the general elections, due the following May. The newly elected leftist deputies, who owed their seats to the combined vote of the left, would, he assumed, be more eager to maintain Popular Front coöperation than their predecessors in the present Chamber. The Radical leader, Albert Sarraut, was therefore asked to form a stop-gap government.

It was during the Sarraut regime that Germany occupied the Rhineland. France hardly realized the full significance of that event. Except in the border provinces, the subsequent election campaign was fought over the Popular Front domestic program, the defense of democracy against the fascist leagues, and the restoration of purchasing power as a means to overcome the economic crisis. The most popular slogans were those directed against the "Two Hundred Families," allegedly the secret rulers of France; against the "marchands de canon," the armament manufacturers; and in favor of the abolition of wage cuts carried out under Laval's emergency decrees. There was a chapter on the "defense of peace" in the program, which contained the traditional formulas of collective security, automatic sanctions, peaceful change, and the extension of international agreements after the model of the Franco-Soviet Pact. Foreign policy, however, played a subordinate role in the election campaign, and very few of the leftist leaders, not to speak of the masses themselves, realized the full implications of their own program.

The Communists did more than the other parties of the Popular Front to create at least a state of mind favorable to a strong foreign policy. In May, 1935, when Laval visited Moscow to sign the Franco-Soviet Pact, Stalin openly approved rearmament. French Communists and Socialists at that time opposed Laval's plan to extend military service to two years. After Stalin's statement the Communists immediately stopped their campaign, although the Socialists carried on. This was one of the many reasons for discord in the Common Front. The Communists faithfully followed Stalin's dictum during the election campaign; their slogan was *Pour une France libre, forte et heureuse!* (For a free, strong, and happy France!) Revolutionary topics were banished. The Communists were suddenly transformed into mild progressives and patriots eager to trace the origin of their ideas back to the French Revolution of 1789. A sign of this sudden transition was the adoption of the *Marseillaise* and the Tricolor as party symbols.

Labor's new unity paid dividends in the elections on May 3, 1936. The Popular Front won a decisive victory, obtaining a clear majority in the Chamber of Deputies. The Socialists, with 146 Deputies—a gain of 45—were the leading group within the Front Populaire. The Communists increased their number from 10 to 72, while the Radicals lost 42 of their former 158 seats. Blum was the premier designate of the next government. He entered office formally on June 4, at a time when France was passing through its greatest social crisis.

4.

On May 15, shortly before Blum assumed office, he developed the basic lines of his foreign policy. "We wish to coöperate with all nations of the world, whatever may be their internal policy in eliminating the causes of conflict which might some day lead to war," Blum said. "We wish to work with all nations and for all nations, provided they sincerely desire to work with us in building up peace. Let it not be supposed for a moment that we Socialists may ever dream of adopting an aggressive attitude or of avenging our persecuted comrades or of destroying this or that regime. We do not believe, as our ancestors of 1792 and 1848 did, that war can have a liberating and revolutionary virtue. We reject war absolutely."

The fear of being suspected of wishing war for the cause of antifascism or to avenge anti-Semitism was to be a dominant factor in Blum's foreign policy.

Another main current running through all the foreign affairs actions of Blum and his foreign minister, Yvon Delbos, was the desire for closest possible coöperation with England. Never before had Franco-British friendship been as close as under Léon Blum, who became a popular hero in London. As long as England and France worked hand in hand, Blum thought, there would be no war in Europe. Peace depended, in his opinion, upon whether the Nazis met with failure in their frantic efforts to drive a wedge between the two western democracies. In practice, Franco-British coöperation came close to subordination of the French Popular Front government to the Conservative rulers of Britain. Thus started the fateful course which made France act for some time as if it were a British colony.

The main advantage which Blum gained from his dependence on British leadership was his ability to shift the burden for the failure of the sanctions experiment on to London. In this way he succeeded in partially appeasing those among his supporters who favored a strong policy of collective action against Italian aggression, since obviously no one could expect France to be more League-minded in this case than the British. Shortly before taking office Blum still had hope for some compromise that would save the League's face. "We shall make every effort," he wrote, "to save what still remains to be saved of international law in the Ethiopian affair." But when on June 16 the British cabinet dropped sanctions without further ado, France gladly followed suit. The French right, and many leftists too, hoped that this step would be followed by a complete reconciliation with Italy and the resumption by Mussolini of the "Guard on the Brenner" to defend Austria's independence. What really happened was just the opposite. As soon as sanctions were lifted, Mussolini felt free to coöperate unreservedly with Hitler.

The Austro-German Pact of July 11, 1936, seriously jeopardizing Austria's defense against Germany, was the first result of the Italo-German understanding. The abolition of the democratic Constitution by the Danzig Nazi Senate guaranteed by the League of Nations was the second result; it followed a week later. The French answer was a visit by Blum and Delbos to London and an effort to cement Anglo-French relations more firmly. The Allies still hoped for an understanding with Germany, a new Locarno to replace the old Treaty which Hitler had just torn up. They went so far as seriously to consider in case of success "the widening of the area of discussion" with Germany—which meant the conclusion of security pacts for eastern Europe.

Hitler's reply was shattering. He declared that he would never negotiate with the Russians. Within a few weeks France discovered that Germany had gone beyond merely refusing diplomatic negotiations. Hitler was moving quickly. The Civil War in Spain was fast developing into a German-Italian interventionist war.

On June 23 Yvon Delbos said in the Chamber that Herr Hitler had often proclaimed his wish to be friendly with France. "We have no intention," Léon Blum's foreign minister continued, "of doubting the words of a man who during four years knew the horrors of the trenches."

Now Hitler realized that he had nothing to fear from the French Popular Front government. The Spanish War and Austria proved him to be right in this assumption. The democracies were still under the spell of pacifist illusions. With the war in Spain, democratic pacifism supported by large labor groups, reached its climax.

Chapter 19

WAR IN SPAIN

1.

WHEN General Franco's troops revolted in Morocco and Spain in July, 1936, the Spanish government was in a state of almost complete paralysis. The alliance of the leftist parties which, four months before, had won its great victory, was decisively weakened by Anarchist defection and the internal struggles of the Socialists. Immediately after the elections the Anarchists, whose votes had decisively contributed to the victory of the government parties, had withdrawn into their traditional refusal to take part in parliamentary politics. Within the Socialist party, the largest government group, factional disputes had reached a climax. The short history of the Spanish Republic, filled with intense party conflicts, had sown the seeds for the paralysis of the Republican government and for the Civil War.

In April, 1931, King Alfonso of Spain had been forced to go into exile as a consequence of a Republican victory at communal elections. His abdication was the final result of a pact signed on August 17, 1930, in San Sebastian among the Socialists, Republicans—including their conservative wing—and left Catalan groups. The agreement contained a plan for revolutionary action against the king and it was strengthened by the promise of the Socialist led trade unions, the U.G.T., to call a general strike whenever the joint committee so desired. At the municipal elections in April the coalition parties put forward joint candidates, who were successful in practically all the cities, although sentiment in the countryside remained monarchical. Faced with this defeat, the monarchy broke down without even offering resistance. In a wave of Republican enthusiasm the democratic regime was established.

At the time of the election victory the Communists were still considering the struggle against the "Social Fascists" as their main task, and so they remained outside of and hostile to the democratic movement. At a national conference the Communists decided "to fight with the utmost energy the attempts of the right and left wing Social-Fascists who, with the support of important sections of the Anarchist movement (Pestana), attempted to form a united front with the Liberal and Republican bourgeoisie." Their threat, however, meant very little, since the Spanish Communist party was numerically insignificant. Besides, a series of internal crises was shaking the party, group after group being excluded because of "Trotskyism," with which term the Communists then branded any demand for a united front with the Socialists.

Three years after its formation the Republic was in mortal danger. Catholic-Fascist groups under Gil Robles, similar in their views to those which constituted the Dollfuss dictatorship in Austria, had been received into the government majority. After the Austrian experience, the Spanish workers had decided to resist fascism before it could fully develop. Gil Robles had been allied with the Monarchists during the elections of 1933, and his later acceptance of the Republic was suspect to most Republicans. He opposed the land reform, the social reforms in favor of the industrial working class, and local autonomy and advocated a program closely akin to the Catholic Fascism of the Austrian type.

On October 5, 1934, a general strike was called against the fascist threat. Catalonia, under a leftist government, proclaimed its independence. The Socialists were the leaders of the uprising and the Communists joined them in the struggle, the Comintern having adopted its new policy a short time before. But the Communist support was more than offset by the aloofness of the numerically far more important Anarchists, whose passivity helped bring about the swift defeat of the movement in Catalonia.

The other center of the revolt was Asturia, where the miners succeeded in overpowering the authorities. Isolated through the defeat of the Catalans and the failure of Madrid to rise, the Asturian miners were doomed. Government airplanes and warships shelled Oviedo, the Asturian capital, and after a prolonged and heroic struggle, the miners were crushed. It was during this fighting that Dolores Ibarrurri, called La Pasionaria, assumed front rank in the Spanish Communist party.

In spite of the Asturian defeat, the Popular Front idea made rapid headway. The savage repression which followed only served to cement the coöperation between Socalists and middle-class Republicans. The Communists joined this entente, and the Anarchists were forced by their rank and file to give at least undercover assistance. The news of the atrocities committed by the government after the defeat of the rebels morally strengthened the left. A pamphlet, written by Fernando de los Rios, later Spanish Ambassador to Washington, which dealt with the suffering of the prisoners taken during the fighting, was circulated clandestinely in thousands of copies. Another report by the former Republican minister Gordon Ordas closed with the words: "If the Republic must rely on crimes in order to live, it is better for it to disappear at once than to sully itself to such an extent."

Thus, the government victory in the Civil War boomeranged into a source of weakness for it. It was fast losing ground in the country, a fact which became increasingly clear in November, 1935, when the chairman of the Socialist party, Largo Caballero, was acquitted of the charge of having incited the workers to armed rebellion.

Under the leadership of the opportunist Lerroux—a renegade of the Republican anti-monarchical conspiracy committee—and the Catholic reactionary Gil Robles, the government set out to destroy every vestige of progress that had been made by the Republic. It was a simple case of a return to an inglorious past without any sincere effort to build something new. Resentment grew among the masses. The hatred created by the cruel repression after the Asturian revolt added fuel to the fire.

After the middle of 1934 the Socialist party had moved toward the left; the Asturian revolt was partly a result and partly a cause of this evolution. Previously the Spanish Socialist party had represented a particularly timid form of reformism, and Largo Caballero was one of the main spokesmen of this policy. Under the dictatorship of Primo de Rivera, Caballero established a sort of truce between the dictator and the trade unions. As minister in the first Republican government he showed nothing of his later aggressiveness. His conversion to more extreme ideas was apparently caused by disappointment over the ultimate destruction, under the Lerroux government, of everything the Republic had achieved, but probably also by the events in Germany and Austria. In Germany, Caballero thought, fascism had been victorious because the workers offered no armed resistance; in Austria the fascists had been victorious because the workers took up arms when fascism already possessed all key positions. Caballero resolved that Spanish labor would fight the very first symptoms of fascist advance. To prepare the workers for this task became his main idea.

Although the center of the Socialist party under Indalecio Prieto and the right wing headed by Julian Besteiro resisted, the Socialist party followed Caballero's lead toward the left. Its foremost task was to win the elections due in 1936. To this end, the Socialists concluded an alliance with the leftist Republican parties. The small Communist party and a Communist opposition group, the "Workers Party of Marxian Unity" (P.O.U.M.), also joined the Popular Front. What was to be decisive for the election victory of February 16, 1936, was the fact that the Anarchists, who so far had abstained from taking part in elections for reasons of principle, now decided to vote for the Frente Popular. Thousands of Anarchists were political prisoners, and the victory of the Popular Front was the only hope for their liberation. The Anarchist leaders had to give way to the pressure of their supporters, and the large Anarchist vote in favor of the left greatly contributed to its victory.

The left was again in office, a victory symbolized by the election of Manuel Azaña as president of the Republic. This was no longer the mildly progressive left which had taken power in 1931, nor even a Popular Front of the same type as the French. Although the Socialists refused to enter the cabinet which Casares Quiroga formed, the new Spanish government was far more militant than the Socialist led French Popular Front government. On the other hand, the Spanish government had far less authority, since the backbone of the Popular Front, the powerful Socialist party, remained outside the cabinet. Caballero preferred to wait for an opportunity for the party to act more decisively than merely to govern according to parliamentary rules. The masses, both peasants and industrial workers, were no longer satisfied with such modest reforms as 1931 had brought them. They insisted upon radical changes, especially upon real agrarian reform.

With 98 members in the Cortes parliament, the Socialist party was the strongest group of the Popular Front; it was closely followed by President Azaña's Left Republicans, who held 81 seats. The Communists had 16 seats and continued to be of little significance. Within the Socialist party the left under Largo Caballero was in control. *Claridad,* Caballero's newspaper in Madrid, competing with the official party paper, *El Socialista,* thus described the new Socialist policy:

> We shall be on the side of the government in order to help it carry out with all necessary determination the joint program, even if this program does not satisfy us entirely. We will, however, not give the government our unreserved confidence, as we did from 1931 to 1933. The lesson was too hard and we will not renounce our right to criticize in order to maintain the vigilance of the working class, which is now marching forward to the final goal of our class, and at the slightest sign of weakening to set the working class itself against its present allies.

In practice this meant Socialist inactivity combined with thinly veiled threats of an impending Socialist revolution. For the cabinet the Socialist attitude was fatal. Only a premier of extraordinary ability and energy could have prevented the government's failure; in spite of his great reputation Casares Quiroga had neither of these qualities. True, he tried to purge the army of counter-revolutionary officers. General Franco, who as early as February had announced an impending coup d'état against the new government, was sent as commander to the Canary Islands. The premier apparently thought that this and similar measures were sufficient to nip in the bud the threatened revolt of the army. At least that is what he proclaimed, announcing that no acute danger existed. On July 17 and 18, however, the generals rose.

Quiroga's cabinet was immediately swept away by those who came to the rescue of the Republic and the Popular Front. The new premier, Martinez Barrio, who refused to arm the trade unions, followed Quiroga into the abyss. Giral, the third premier on the same day—July 19—armed the workers as well as he could. Quickly they defeated the revolting army in Madrid, Barcelona, and six out of the seven largest cities in the country—altogether in half of Spain. The working class, represented mainly by Socialists and Anarchists, was thus practically pushed into control by these events, although their party leaders still refused to take office. The rising of the generals forced the Socialists to do what in their newly acquired radicalism they had refused to do—namely, to act.

The Civil War was on. It was soon to develop into a dress rehearsal for the Second World War.

2.

The revolt of the army left the government practically without executive force. The troops who fought against the army in Madrid and Catalonia were mostly armed workers belonging either to the U.G.T. of the Socialists or to the Anarchist trade unions (C.N.T.). Actual power thus was in the hands of the working class wherever Franco was defeated, but the middle-class Government continued to carry on.

After a few weeks, President Azaña began to organize a new army. The right-wing Socialists supported this move; so did the Communists. It was clear that a real military force had to be organized, since an untrained workers' militia was no match for Franco's troops. The decisive political problem was whether the new army was to be formed out of the militias, or independently of them; the answer to this question would decide the relationship of forces inside the government. If the new organization were a workers' army, officered by technicians who enjoyed the workers' confidence, power in the Republic would remain in the hands of the working class. But if Azaña were able to create a new army under his own supreme command and appoint officers of his own choice, the militia groups were bound to lose most of their influence and power would return to the constitutional middle-class government. In this form the issue arose as to whether the new Spain should be a middle-class or a workers' republic.

Prieto, Caballero's rival in the leadership of the Socialist party, was convinced that Spanish labor had not yet reached the stage where it could claim full power. He therefore supported the government's plan to create a new army. The Communists agreed with him, though for different reasons. To strengthen its anti-Nazi foreign policy the Soviet government was anxious to see the new formula of the Popular Front succeed everywhere, particularly in France. It was necessary to convince potential allies among the progressive middle-class groups that the Communists now sincerely supported middle-class democracy outside the Soviet Union. On July 22, a few days after the outbreak of the Civil War, the Communist London *Daily Worker* wrote: "In Spain Socialists and Communists fought shoulder to shoulder in armed battle to defend their trade unions and political organizations, to guard the Spanish Republic and to defend democratic liberties so that they could advance toward a Spanish Soviet Republic." But a few days afterwards, on August 6, one of the Spanish Communist leaders, Jesus Hernandez, repudiated any revolutionary intentions. He wrote in the Communist *Mundo Obrero:* "It is absolutely false that the present workers' movement has for its object the establishment of a proletarian dictatorship after the war has terminated. It cannot be said that we have a social motive for our participation in the war. We Communists are the first to repudiate this supposition. We are motivated exclusively by a desire to defend the democratic Republic." [1] And the Paris *Humanité* published the following official statement: "The Central Committee of the Communist party in Spain requests us to inform the public in reply to the fantastic and tendentious reports published by certain newspapers that the Spanish people are not striving for the establishment of the dictatorship of the proletariat but know only one aim: the defense of the Republican order while respecting property." [2]

Caballero opposed the creation of a new army independent of the militia. On August 20 *Claridad* declared: "To think of another type of army to be substituted for those who are actually fighting and who in certain ways control their own revolutionary action is to think in counter-revolutionary terms." The article went on to quote Lenin

[1] Morrow, *Revolution and Counter-Revolution in Spain,* p. 33. [2] *Ibid.*

against the Spanish Communists and concluded that the Socialists had to "take care that the masses and the leadership of the armed forces, which should be, above all, the people in arms, should not escape from our hands." [3] This was consistent with Caballero's stand for a dictatorship of the proletariat, which had been expressed in the new program adopted by the Caballero controlled Socialist organizations of Madrid in April, 1936. Such a dictatorship, the program said, should be exerted by the Socialist party alone, since it represented the overwhelming majority of the non-Anarchist working class.

A sort of coalition thus existed among Prieto, the right-wing Socialists, and the Communists against a proletarian revolution; while the Caballero wing of the Socialist party and the Communist opposition P.O.U.M.—formed under Trotskyite influence, concentrated in Catalonia, and led by Andres Nin and Joaquin Maurin—wanted to transform the war into a proletarian revolution. Next to the P.O.U.M., the Communist party was the smallest of these groups, but thanks to Russia's influence, it was soon to play a decisive part.

Six mysterious airplanes flew over Algeria on July 30, 1936. One of them crashed, another made a forced landing on French soil. French officers quickly discovered that both were military planes manned by Italian officers who had been mobilized for service in Spain three days before the outbreak of the Civil War. The Fascist "International" was at work. Where was the international solidarity of the left?

The case for the French Popular Front government to support the Spanish Loyalists was overwhelming. According to international law, French citizens and the French government "were fully entitled to supply war materials to the government at Madrid, who, in the eyes of the law, were a legitimate government contending with an unlawful rebellion." [4] The French government parties were bound to sympathize with Madrid, since in both countries ideologically similar governments were in power. French rightist patriots ought to have desired the victory of Madrid, for a Franco triumph with the

[3] *Ibid.*, p. 37.

[4] Arnold Toynbee and V. M. Boulter, *Survey of International Affairs*, 1937. Vol. II. "The International Repercussions of the War in Spain" (1936–37). Oxford University Press, 1938. (Royal Institute of International Affairs.)

support of Italy and Germany implied a serious threat to French security.

From the outset, however, the Spanish Civil War split France into three factions bitterly opposing each other; a pro-Franco group, the extreme left backing the Loyalists, and a large pacifist and therefore, in practice, neutral group. The right-wing parties, neglecting France's national interest, associated Franco's struggle against the Spanish Popular Front with their own opposition to Blum's government. As a result the "Nationalist" groups on the right were opposed almost to a man to any help for the Madrid government, even at the risk of a foothold beyond the Pyrenees being gained by Germany and Italy under the cover of a Franco victory. The French Communists and a part of the Socialist party under Jean Zyromski favored immediate support for the Loyalists by large-scale arms and munitions transports. *Des avions pour l'Espagne!* ("Airplanes for Spain!") became the main slogan of the most active elements within the Popular Front. But the left was not unanimous on this policy. Most Radicals opposed active help to Spain for fear of international complications and of a dangerous increase in France's internal tension. Pacifist tendencies were particularly strong among the Socialists, and weakened their official position of favoring support for the Spanish Republic. The Paris Federation of the Socialist party, under the control of Marceau Pivert and his half-pacifist, half-Trotskyite supporters, combined by some miracle a demand for complete disarmament of France with a campaign for French support of Spain.

It was clear from the outset where Franco's sympathies lay in international affairs. Nevertheless, domestic political considerations weighed more heavily with the French right wingers than the patent national interests of their country, and a few days after the outbreak of the Civil War, the French rightist press began to attack the government for supplying the Spanish "Reds" with arms. Reports about Italian and German support for Franco were played down or suppressed.

British pressure supported the French Conservatives and determined the official policy of the Popular Front government. Speaking of the Spanish War in July, 1936, Sir Samuel Hoare treated the Madrid government and the rebels equally as "rival factions" between whom Britain by implication had to be neutral. The British ambassador in Paris, it was reported, informed Blum that Britain would not come to France's support if by aiding the Spanish Loyalists France should come into conflict with Germany or Italy. Right-wing pressure grew extremely formidable. Some right-wing papers openly appealed to Hitler to prevent France from aiding the Spanish government. They published information about alleged French arms transports to Spain, thus giving Hitler moral justification for his intervention. The Radicals and many Socialists were reluctant to accept the risk of acting in the Spanish situation, especially since Britain threatened to remain neutral in a conflict between France and the fascist powers. On July 25 the French cabinet decided not to export any war matériel to Spain, and a week later the government appealed to Italy and Great Britain for "the rapid adoption and rigid observance of an agreed arrangement for nonintervention in Spain." In the meantime France abandoned of her own accord her indisputable right, under international law, to sell arms to the Spanish government.

This was a fateful decision. By bowing to the admittedly heavy pressure of the noninterventionists, Léon Blum definitely subordinated French foreign policy to that of Britain. Having to choose whether Britain or the Soviet Union should have top rank among France's allies, Blum threw in his lot with a Britain representing nonintervention, rather than with a Russia which was soon to announce openly her support of the Loyalists. It was not a free choice on Blum's part, for only by following the British lead could he hope to keep his government majority together. French foreign policy became merely an extension on the international scene of domestic quarrels. A French satirical weekly now could justifiably call Yvon Delbos the "British Undersecretary of State for French Affairs." Paris's dependence upon London became almost slavish. The pressure of the French right and the internal weakness of the French left in foreign policy soon shifted the leadership of the European democracies to those English ultra-Conservatives represented by Neville Chamberlain. Blum's decision led directly to Munich.

The nonintervention policy opened for the first time a gulf between the Popular Front government and a part, at least, of its supporters. While Blum did manage to send some arms and airplanes to Spain—thereby giving the rightest press opportunities to accuse the government of breaking its nonintervention promise—what he could do under the policy's limitations was not enough for the Communists and for Zyromski and his leftist Socialist friends. Zyromski abstained from attacking Blum and concentrated his fire upon the British government and the French right, but the Communists and the trade-union leaders were outspokenly indignant. Their feeling ran high against Blum, whom they accused of having "taken sanctions against the legal government of Spain."

From the beginning of his activity as premier, Blum maintained the most intimate contact with the working class, far more intimate than Ramsay MacDonald or any German Social Democratic minister had ever considered necessary. He now had ample opportunity to feel the workers' reaction to his Spanish policy. When Blum spoke in memory of Jean Jaurès, the great French Socialist leader, at the end of July, a chorus of cries, "Airplanes for Spain," interrupted his speech. Feeling grew increasingly intense. On September 4, the Spanish town of Irun on the French border fell into Franco's hands after heroic resistance. Because Irun's capture was mainly due to the Republic's lack of ammunition, French working-class resentment against Blum's nonintervention policy reached its highest pitch. In the provinces, the workers were more inclined to back Blum against the Communists, but in Paris passion ran high among the leftist workers. Two days after the fall of Irun, Blum spoke at a mass meeting to justify his policy. He was received with hostility. But by the end of his speech the huge meeting, in which Communists constituted a large proportion of the audience, was as enthusiastic for Blum as ever before. This did not mean that they now agreed with his policy, but few any longer felt that he was a "traitor"; it was patent that he was acting in what he considered the interest of French labor. "You know," Blum said, "I have not changed. Do you think I do not share your feelings? . . . When I read in the papers about the fall of Irun and the agony of the last militiamen, do you think that my heart was not with them too? . . .

And do you think me suddenly incapable of reflection and foresight? Do you think I do not understand what it all means? Believe me, if I have acted as I have done, it is because I knew that it was necessary."

If France had sent supplies to Madrid, he continued, other countries would have sent armaments to Burgos, Franco's capital. "The most immediate consequence would have been a competition in the supply of armaments to both sides. And remember that there are countries where everything is concentrated in the hands of one man, and where the intensity of armaments production and the industrial capacity is far greater than here." Blum admitted that he had hoped other countries would follow the French example and immediately stop exporting arms to Spain. He even went so far as to claim that "there is not a single proof, not a single piece of circumstantial evidence to show that the agreement has been violated since it was subscribed to." This absolution given to Italy and Germany was the point at which the Communists leveled most of their criticism. But for most Frenchmen Blum's main argument was this: "Don't you think that we have, after all, saved Europe from war at a particularly critical moment?"

For obvious diplomatic reasons Blum did not mention the British pressure in favor of nonintervention which had been brought to bear upon him, but most Frenchmen knew, or believed they knew, what London's role had been. The French trade unions, though they remained hostile to nonintervention and continued to demand that the government "reconsider its policy in regard to Spain," cautiously added, "in agreement with the British and other democratic governments."

3.

In Britain, apart from the small Communist party and those under its influence, public opinion for a year and a half was almost unanimously in favor of "nonintervention." Immediately after the outbreak of the Civil War, it is true, Major Attlee moved a resolution at a labor conference in London pledging "all practicable support to our Spanish comrades in their struggle to defend freedom and democracy in Spain." That meant financial aid, which was given wholeheartedly by the British workers, but no political support, which could have consisted only of a struggle against nonintervention. Soon afterwards the Communists took up anti-interventionist slogans, but the trade unions now openly came out in favor of nonintervention.

On August 28, a Labour manifesto denounced Italian, German and Portuguese intervention in Spain, and a few days later "grave concern" was expressed "at the delay in bringing the nonintervention agreement into force." Italy and Germany still delayed placing their signatures on the pact. Despite the fascist nations' refusal to play ball, the National Council of Labour, representing the Labour party, the Parliamentary Labour party (the Labour party group in Parliament) and the Trade Union Congress, formally endorsed nonintervention on September 9, 1936. This action did not, however, prevent the British Labour party and trade union delegates to a joint meeting in Paris late in September of the Labor and Socialist International and the International Federation of Trade Unions from voting for the official resolution, a document directed not only against the violations of the non-intervention policy by Germany and Italy but also against the very principle of nonintervention. The French delegates did the same, although at least some of the Socialist representatives backed Blum's policy at home. The embarrassing position of the two international working-class organizations, whose British and French sections voted at home for one policy and for another abroad, was clearly expressed in the official communiqué of the meeting, published on September 29. It contained a statement that the two Internationals "reaffirmed their declaration of July 28 that in accordance with the existing rules of international law the legal government of Spain should be permitted to obtain the necessary means for its own defense." Yet the same communiqué declared that "the violation of this new international undertaking (the nonintervention agreement) by Germany and Italy must inevitably lead to a reconsideration of the situation by the other powers"—which meant, of course, that for the time being nonintervention was receiving the two labor groups' tacit support.

The British Labour party conference held in Edinburgh early in October of the same year endorsed the trade-union decision in favor of nonintervention. After two Spanish representatives, Jiménez de Asua and Isabel de Palencia, had spoken, a resolution was adopted demanding an investigation into the breaches of the nonintervention agreement ascribed to the Fascist Powers. If it should be found that the agreement "has been definitely violated, the French and British governments, being responsible for the initiation of the nonintervention policy, should take steps forthwith to restore to the Spanish government their right to purchase" arms abroad. Nonintervention was supported during the discussion by the leaders of the big trade unions, Ernest Bevin (Transport Workers), Charles Dukes (Municipal Workers), and George Hicks (Building Trades). Arthur Greenwood and D. R. Grenfell, speaking in behalf of the Party Executive, supported the resolution. Sir Charles Trevelyan and a young Welsh leftist member of Parliament, Aneurin Bevan, led the opposition. Herbert Morrison was known to be hostile to nonintervention, but he realized that against the "bloc vote" [5] of the trade unions opposition was hopeless.

Greenwood maintained that in the long run the Spanish Rebels, not the Spanish government, stood to gain by unrestricted competition in supplying both sides with armaments. The British government, he said, would certainly do very little to come to the aid of the Republicans, since many Conservatives were hostile to the Loyalists, whom they regarded as Communists. France alone could not compete with the combined powerful German and Italian industries. He argued that nonintervention, therefore, was better from the Spanish Republicans' point of view than unrestricted trade in arms.

The Executive carried the day with 1,836,000 to 519,000 votes, but the rank and file began to feel uneasy. Less than three weeks after the Conference, Herbert Morrison openly attacked nonintervention, while Major Attlee and Sir Walter Citrine defended their efforts to make nonintervention watertight.

The divergency of views between the international and the na-

[5] At a Labour party conference, the total vote of a trade union is counted for or against a resolution, according to where the majority of the union stands. The minority opinion is not represented in the vote at all.

tional labor organizations reappeared when the trade union and the Socialist Internationals publicly called upon all labor organizations to work for lifting the embargo against the Spanish government. The resolution unanimously adopted by the two Internationals stated that nonintervention had failed and declared it "the common duty of the working class of all countries organized politically and industrially to secure by their influence upon public opinion and upon their respective governments the conclusion of an international agreement—for which the French and British governments should take the initiative—restoring complete commercial liberty to Republican Spain." In the Foreign Affairs Commission of the French Chamber of Deputies the Socialists nevertheless refused to support a Communist motion calling upon the government to abandon nonintervention. A similar proposal, introduced by Jean Zyromski at a meeting of the Socialist party's National Council in February, 1937, was heavily defeated, while Blum's policy was approved by 4,661 to 732 votes. Outside Paris most workers considered nonintervention a guarantee for peace.

Nonintervention caused a sharp conflict between Communists and Socialists in France. On October 23, 1936, the Soviet government officially announced that it "could not consider itself bound by the agreement for nonintervention to any greater extent than any of the remaining participants." Two months later, the French Communists abstained, for the first time, from voting on a motion of confidence relating to the government's foreign policy. In a public statement they explained that although they disagreed with the government's Spanish policy, they would support the cabinet in all other respects. Léon Blum considered resigning, but decided in the end to stay. The Radicals were outspokenly in favor of nonintervention, and large pacifist groups within the Socialist party continued to back Blum. On the right, Franco was still acclaimed as an anti-Bolshevist champion. A few sincere nationalists, such as Henri de Kerillis, the well-known editor of the nationalist newspaper *Echo de Paris* (which had a close connection with the general staff), began to doubt whether French national interest would not be better safeguarded by a Republican victory. But England's influence in favor of nonintervention remained the key to the situation.

4.

Early in September, 1936, the Spanish Republicans realized that their victory depended as much upon the attitude of the British and French governments as upon their own military effort. Nonintervention was due to a large extent to the belief of the British Conservatives and the French rightists that Communists were in control of the Spanish government. To get them to abandon nonintervention, it was necessary to convince Western Europe that the Spanish Republicans were defending a democratic and capitalist regime, progressive but still essentially middle class.

Since the beginning of the Civil War the Communists had defended just such a policy. The Prieto wing of the Socialists and the middle-class Republicans were in favor of this policy as a matter of course. Now Caballero, and a little later the Anarchists, who had resisted at the beginning, rallied to the moderate program. Caballero became head of a new government on September 4, 1936. The middle-class parties opposed to Franco, the Communists, both wings of the Socialist party and after November, 1936, the Anarchists, were represented in Caballero's government. The premier declared: "This Government was constituted—those forming it previously renouncing the aspiration to defend their own principles and particular tendencies, in order to remain united on one sole aspiration—to defend Spain in her struggle against Fascism." [6]

To wage war effectively, all Popular Front groups now were represented in the government excepting only the P.O.U.M. The Anarchists, opposed to government participation on principle, abandoned their resistance in order to save the Republic from the swiftly advancing columns of General Franco. The entry into the government of the extreme leftist groups did not mean, however, that the social revolution, begun the day the workers were armed, was to continue and to develop. On the contrary, the labor groups

[6] Morrow, *op. cit.*, p. 44.

entered the government to stop the revolutionary movement, and the government was anxious to have all labor groups represented in the cabinet so as to give it the necessary authority for preventing further revolutionary measures. The British Conservatives and French rightists who had forced the French Popular Front to accept their views with regard to Spain, now succeeded in stopping the advance of the revolution in Spain. The Madrid Socialist paper, *El Socialista,* explained this openly on October 5, 1936:

> Our geographic law is not that of immense Russia, by any means, and we have to take into account the attitude of the States that surround us in order to determine our own attitude. Let not everything rest on spiritual force, nor on reason, but on knowing how to renounce four in order to gain a hundred. We still hope that the estimate of the Spanish events made by certain democracies will be changed, and it would be a pity, a tragedy, to compromise these possibilities by pushing the velocity of the Revolution, which at present does not conduct us to any positive solution.[7]

The Spanish Communists were foremost among the groups anxious to obtain British and French Conservative sympathy for Republican Spain. In this attitude they reflected the foreign policy of the Soviet Union. Under Communist pressure the Spanish Revolution was terminated, hardly two months after it had begun. Even the land reform was postponed, only the distribution of estates belonging to known supporters of Franco being sanctioned. In industry the interference of the factory committees set up in the early days of the Civil War was restricted. The P.O.U.M. was almost alone in its protest. Loyal to the original Communist ideas which the Comintern had abandoned in 1934, the P.O.U.M. declared that the war could be won only by a victorious revolution in Loyalist Spain. Such a revolution, the P.O.U.M. leaders predicted, would "arouse the great masses to action. It can even take the army (of Franco) away from its reactionary officers. To accomplish this it is only necessary seriously and courageously to advance the program of the Socialist Revolution." Therefore the P.O.U.M., and with it most Anarchists, relied upon politics rather than military weapons

[7] Morrow, *op. cit.*, p. 45.

to win the war, while the government postponed action on social issues lest it cause disorganization of production during the war. To secure arms and ammunition the middle class partners of the Popular Front had to be kept in line and the good will of Britain and France secured. During the crisis of September, 1936, the P.O.U.M. raised the slogan, "Down with the bourgeois ministers." In the Catalonian government, on the other hand, the P.O.U.M. joined the Socialists and Communists, who had unified their organizations, in participating in the government.

After two months of a disorganized proletarian revolution, Spain was now under Communist-Socialist leadership on the road back to a middle-class Republic. An Anarchist leader, Federica Montseny, declared: "The fate of the world, as well as the outcome of this war, depends upon England." To please the British Conservatives the Communists imposed a moderate course upon the Spanish Revolution.

Early in November Franco's troops conquered Toledo and reached the outskirts of Madrid. The Republican government was transferred to Valencia. Germany and Italy recognized the Junta of Burgos as the legitimate government of Spain. Loyalist Spain seemed doomed.

Two events stemmed the tide. The International Brigades of anti-fascist volunteers from many countries provided the still hardly organized Spanish Army with a backbone to resist Franco's legions. At the same time Russian arms began to reach Madrid. Together they saved the city.

From this moment on, Russian influence upon the Republican government became almost irresistible. By withholding their aid, the Soviets could practically have disarmed Spain. In exchange for indispensable Russian aid, the small Spanish Communist party obtained increased influence. The Communists were the best armed men in Loyalist Spain, and slowly but inevitably they assumed control over the administration, thanks to the pressure of the Soviet Union. Franco had accused the Republicans of being Communists before the Civil War broke out. At that time the Spanish Communist party was only an insignificant sect. Now the revolt of the generals, started allegedly against Communist rule, achieved what it purported to destroy: Communist predominance in Loyalist Spain.

Although still a comparatively small party, the Spanish Communists wielded great influence, thanks to their hold over key positions in the administration, particularly the police. They used their newly gained influence in their struggle against the Spanish Trotskyites. The Communists regarded as such the supporters of the P.O.U.M. and also the Anarchists. The Communist-Trotskyite struggle was carried on with extreme violence and illegal methods. Trotskyites were "purged" according to best Russian methods, especially in Catalonia. The Communists established their own "party prisons" and "party police," and several men suspected of sympathy for Trotsky vanished forever without leaving any traces. Among the Socialists abroad the increasing influence of the Communists and of the Soviet Union created much ill feeling. But as long as the French border was almost hermetically closed, the Soviet Union held the key to Spanish defense. "Nonintervention" gave Russia a monopoly in the support of Spain.

The internal conflicts in the hinterland of Loyalist Spain reached their climax in Catalonia in May, 1937, when P.O.U.M. and Anarchists fought on the streets of Barcelona against the United Socialists and Communists (P.S.U.C.). Backed by the government, the P.S.U.C. defeated the P.O.U.M. The Communists now demanded the dissolution of the P.O.U.M., which they described as a Franco agency. Caballero refused. The Communists thereupon raised a whole series of further demands, most of them directed against Caballero's control over the army. They accused him of being "quite unable to create a regular people's army and to unify the command." The man whom Communist propaganda had formerly dubbed the "Spanish Lenin" was now described by the Communists as unfit to govern, because Caballero believed in uniting all proletarian anti-Franco elements in the country, including the Trotskyite group. Caballero submitted a counterproposal according to which the two main trade-union centers, the Socialists' U.G.T. and the Anarchists' C.N.T., should become the backbone of the government, so as to exclude party quarrels. Strongly influenced by the Communists, who by now controlled the unified Socialist-Communist youth organization, the Socialist party abandoned Caballero. Juan Negrin formed a new government in which the Caballero faction of the Socialist party was no longer represented. Instead, Prieto's center group played a leading part. Since the Communists had adopted a right-wing policy, the center and the right wing of the Socialists were better able to coöperate with them than Caballero's left wing. The return to a middle-class republic was effected, and, as a pro-Communist writer put it, "The wilder economic experiments were liquidated in view of war needs. Certain industries were decollectivized." The executive forces were placed exclusively under state control, the former party armies thus coming under the supervision of the government. The last remnants of the revolutionary period at the beginning of the Civil War were destroyed. The P.O.U.M. was dissolved and its leaders were arrested. Under Communist pressure Republican Spain, though dominated by labor, became a state-controlled progressive, but definitely middle-class, republic.

Caballero organized a campaign against the government, but he was deserted by some of his most intimate friends, among them Del Vayo, who did not want to create difficulties for the government during the war. In October Caballero was ousted as secretary general of the Trade Union Federation (U.G.T.), whose control the right-wing Socialists took over.

In a statement issued on September 21, 1937, the new premier, Dr. Negrin, emphasized that there would be "no nationalization or confiscation of foreign property . . . during or after the Civil War" since the Republic needed the aid of other countries.

5.

While Republican Spain was courting Britain and France, the Western democracies became still more committed to nonintervention.

British Labour had begun to realize the implications of nonintervention. In July, 1937, the National Council of Labour declared that in the light of a year's trial of the nonintervention policy the

Spanish government ought now at last to be given the right to purchase arms abroad. From that moment on, the British Labour party carried on a campaign against nonintervention. A special "Spain Campaign Committee" was set up to propagate the party's demands for the withdrawal of foreign troops from Spain and the restoration to the Spanish government of its freedom to buy arms. In addition, the committee launched a plan for immediate practical help. Money collections in various forms proved extremely successful. Major Attlee visited Spain—an action which some Conservatives severely criticized as a violation of the spirit of nonintervention! But in spite of all labor pressure, the British Conservatives remained unshaken in their adherence to "nonintervention" to the bitter end.

In France, the majority of the Socialist party continued to follow a "double-line" policy of defending nonintervention at home and rejecting it in the councils of the international labor movement. With the war continuing and spreading, a new tendency to justify nonintervention was expressed by certain Socialists. At first they had claimed that nonintervention had been imposed upon them by Britain and the French reactionaries, so that the Socialists had been forced to submit to this pressure in order to save the Popular Front in France. Now nonintervention began to claim merit in itself. At the Socialist party Conference in July, 1937, Blum defended his Spanish policy on the ground that it had saved peace. "I recognize that mistakes have been made, that we have suffered certain disappointment," he said, "but above all, I ask you to reflect on the fact that for a year Europe has been kept free of general war. One day in the future the archives will give up their secrets to you or to your children and will show how in August and September of last year we were threatened with, we were next door to, war. Is nonintervention a lie? Is control a fiction? Yes! Yes! A thousand times yes, if you like. But in spite of this I am not sure that this lie, this fiction, has not enabled us to avoid the catastrophe."

This did not prevent the party congress from adopting unanimously a resolution in which the party associated itself "wholeheartedly" with the demand of the international labor movement to restore complete freedom of action to Republican Spain.

A year later, in June, 1938, the Socialist party reaffirmed its stand. This time it did not demand that nonintervention be abandoned, but expressed the pious wish that it be made effective against the Fascist countries.

The British Labour party had completed its conversion to a policy of collective security. But the French Socialists, while proclaiming their full support for this policy, hesitated whenever a concrete decision was to be made. The tragedy of Munich was foreshadowed in the tragedy of Spain.

It is true that the control of land shipments of arms to Loyalist Spain via France was not particularly severe under the second Léon Blum government, while Paul-Boncour was foreign minister. The subsequent Daladier government continued the same course for a while. The change came on June 13, when Daladier's foreign minister, Bonnet, obtained Chamberlain's support for his efforts to convince the recalcitrant French premier that Italian friendship had to be bought at the price of abandoning Spain. Flandin, a leading pro-Hitler Deputy, backed Bonnet. Once again the frontier was hermetically sealed, although the Spanish Rebel ports and the Portuguese-Spanish frontier remained without effective control over the unabated movement of Italian and German shipments to Franco. The French Communists protested as soon as they found out, the decision to close the frontier completely having been kept a secret by the government, and so did the Socialists. But Spain was doomed. The British and French governments had made up their minds to let things take their course. By now it was too late for Blum to reverse this policy. Socialists and Communists were powerless to change French foreign policy.

Nonintervention was under fire in France for the last time early in 1939, after Mussolini had started his campaign for "Djibuti, Tunisia, Corsica." The Radicals now began to doubt whether they could trust Mussolini's promises to withdraw from Spain once Franco's victory was secured. The importance of the Balearics for the maintenance of communications between France and her colonial empire was widely discussed. With Franco's troops by now almost in sight of Barcelona, Blum made a last effort to save the Spanish Republic. On January 17, 1939, he declared in the Chamber of Deputies: "If I could believe that the nonintervention policy could still be carried out honestly, I should still be in favor of it. But how can one accept an arrangement under which our hands are tied while the others boast of complete freedom of action? The British and French governments must either denounce the nonintervention agreement or else model their actions on that of the other signatories. And the Chamber must make a decision on this point." Blum was supported by Izard, a young Socialist Deputy, a newcomer whose speeches in the Chamber aroused considerable interest. He showed that Mussolini's influence in Spain pushed the fascist Falangists into key positions at the expense of the "real Spanish Nationalists." Thus, even after a withdrawal of the Italian troops, Spain would be controlled by men completely under Italian influence. "Mr. Chamberlain," Izard added, "has provided Mussolini with a tremendous weapon of pressure against us."

When Bonnet answered in the name of the government, on January 26, Barcelona had fallen. The remnants of an army that had bravely fought for a lost cause were pouring across the Pyrenees into a France herself destined to feel within eighteen months the full weight of the Fascist International.

Chapter 20

LABOR'S ROAD TO MUNICH

I.

IT WAS the major tragedy of the left in the Spanish Civil War that the right-wing parties in Western Europe were the first to understand the connection between their own social and political interests and their foreign policy. The so-called nationalists in France and England realized that in the Europe of 1936 they had to choose between the effective defense of either their national or their class interests. Protection of the national interests of Britain and France would have dictated support of the Spanish Republicans, conclusion of an alliance with the Soviet Union, and action against Germany and Italy. Such a foreign policy, however, would have furthered the advance not only of democracy in Europe, but also of those progressive forces which to a British Conservative and a French reactionary were identical with "Bolshevism." The "Nationalists" could not reconcile their national and class interests; and, with rare exceptions, they decided to act in accordance with their social and political leanings and to sacrifice the defense of vital national interests over which they had formerly claimed a monopoly.

With the outbreak of the Spanish Civil War, the right wing parties in France and England charted their political course primarily with a view to the effect which victory of one or the other side might exert over their class interests. They realized that a victory of the Republican government, controlled as it was by leftist groups, by Socialists, Anarchists, and Communists, would strengthen the European leftist forces, particularly in France and perhaps even in Britain. This was sufficient reason for them to sympathize with Franco. The French right opposed sanctions against Italy during the Ethiopian War because it felt that a defeat of the Italian dictator might start a revolution in Italy. Britain, considered the protagonist of sanctions, was violently attacked by the French rightist press, even though England was France's main ally against Germany. The League of Nations itself, formerly held almost sacred in France, was slandered as an institution of warmongers. A French reactionary newspaper, the *Action française* called the League "the plague." Even when "German airmen and technicians appeared on the Iberian Peninsula and Italian pilots and warships established themselves in the Balearic Islands astride the maritime line of communication between the Mediterranean ports of France and French North Africa," [1] the French "Nationalists" remained undisturbed and made Franco's cause their own. They had decided to disregard the danger of "a converging pressure from Central Europe and from the Iberian Peninsula" in case of Franco's victory and to consider only the "anarchy" of the Spanish left against which Franco was fighting in the name of middle-class law and order—or so the French right thought.

In Britain, the Conservatives had to take refuge in a theory especially invented to reconcile their conflicting class and national interests. It was claimed that once the war was over, Spanish national pride would turn passionately and irresistibly against anyone who had intervened in the internal affairs of the proud Spanish people. Spain, they argued, would never submit to a foreign yoke, and those nations which scrupulously kept their nonintervention promise would gain the most after the war, regardless of which side should win. Nonintervention was held to be in Britain's best interest; that it worked in Franco's favor made no difference. The fact that Gibraltar had been held by the British for some 230 years after their intervention in a war between Hapsburgs and Bourbons for the Spanish crown did not disturb those who professed their belief in inevitable Spanish revolts against foreign interventionists. The European right realized that the time had come to abandon its traditional foreign policy role of defending national and

[1] Arnold Toynbee and V. N. Boulter, *Survey of International Affairs,* 1937. Vol. II. "The International Repercussions of the War in Spain" (1936–37), Oxford University Press, 1938. (Royal Institute of International Affairs.)

imperial interests against pacifists and other "traitors." The leftists were far slower in understanding the identity of their own political and social interests with those of their countries. They failed to avail themselves of the same unique opportunity that had favored the Jacobins during the French Revolution, that of defending their own interests along with those of their nation.

Among the leftist parties the Communists were the first to come to an understanding of the new situation in which the struggle against the Fascist International coincided with the defense of the democracies. It is true that many were suspicious of the sudden conversion of the Communist parties to ardent patriotism from their former opposition to "national defense under a capitalist regime" and their previously sacred dogma of "revolutionary defeatism," that is, the duty of the working class to bring about the defeat of its own country in the interest of furthering the revolution. The dependence upon Moscow's wishes of the new party line was so clear that few felt convinced that this would be a lasting conversion. Nevertheless, the new policy greatly strengthened Communist prestige in many countries, and Russia became the leader of anti-fascist policy all over the world.

As members of an international party, ruled from one center under an organizational system which Lenin politely termed "democratic centralism," the Communists could adjust themselves more swiftly and far more easily, to the new international situation than could the autonomous branches of the Labor and Socialist International. The Socialist International's influence upon its branches was slight, even before 1933, and the German defeat impaired what little moral authority the International possessed. Within the Socialist parties, with their large and well-established organizations, tradition and routine were powerful obstacles to any change in policy or tactics. It was Socialist tradition to look suspiciously at "national interests," and pacifism was a strong current in postwar socialism. In France a large section of the politically influential Teachers' Union rejected national defense under any circumstances and put forth the slogan "Better a slave than dead." Religious pacifists under George Lansbury's leadership delayed for some time the evolution of the British labor movement toward collective security. Revolutionary defeatists of the Leninist type had found admission into the French Socialist party—particularly in Paris—and remained loyal to their policy although its original defenders, the Communists, had abandoned it in favor of national patriotism. Both in England and France, but primarily in England, the progressives felt that Germany had been badly treated by the victorious Allies. Many German demands, particularly those based upon the democratic principle of self-determination, were considered justified. For many years after Versailles British laborites and French Socialists had defended Germany's claims for a revision of the Peace Treaty, and this tradition could not be easily wiped out. Everywhere the Socialists, afraid of being branded as warmongers, felt uncomfortable in their new role as defenders of national interests against even the Nationalist parties.

Thus the adjustment of the left to a new point of view in international affairs was hindered and delayed by powerful forces, among which tradition was foremost. Those whose professed mission it was to change the world clung to their traditions and routine far more steadfastly than the so-called Conservatives.

2.

In 1935 the British Labour party made a decisive step towards abandonment of its naïve and contradictory combination of pacifism and loyalty to the League of Nations, in favor of a definite policy of collective security. Until then the League of Nations had appeared to most labor people as a mysterious force which could guarantee that right would prevail without any resort to force. Few realized that League action might involve Britain in a war. Adherence to the principles of the League of Nations, it was thought, could be combined with an absolute pacifist creed. The sanctions against Italy rudely shattered this sweet dream and forced upon the Labour party a choice between League policy and pacifism. Since the government supported the League (by adopting a policy of collective security), Labour could follow the government's lead—a course which reinforced the idea still lingering in the minds of many labor people that the mysteries of foreign policy could be understood fully by the ruling class alone. Under these conditions the supporters of collective security had an easy victory. The pacifists were defeated and George Lansbury resigned as leader of the party.

The Spanish War confronted labor with the task of persisting in a policy of collective security in the face of the government's non-intervention stand. For some time, labor considered this task beyond its powers. The fact that Léon Blum and his French Popular Front government appeared before the world as fathers of non-intervention severely hampered those within the Labour party who recognized that this question involved a crucial test of the party's loyalty to its new foreign policy. Some party leaders, and particularly the heads of the unions, were inclined to overestimate the strength of pro-Franco sentiment among the British people to such a degree that they were reluctant to be alone in opposing the government. Labour needed a whole year to grasp the fact that its own interests were identical with those of the British nation, and that this community of views offered them an excellent opportunity for bringing pressure to bear upon the government.

Even before this stage was reached the party had changed its traditional opposition to armaments. Previously, Labour had opposed any rearmament move and had stood for international disarmament, no matter what the international situation might be. This policy was thrown overboard at the party conference in 1936, when the Party Executive submitted a resolution declaring that the armed strength of the countries loyal to the League of Nations must be conditioned by the fighting power of potential aggressors. The policy of the Labour party, according to this view, should be aimed at maintaining such defense forces as would be necessary and consistent with the country's responsibilities as a member of the League of Nations. "But," the resolution continued, "having regard to the deplorable record of the government, the Labour party declines to accept responsibility for a purely competitive rearmament program." That meant that the party supported rearming in principle, but was not bound to vote for armament credits under a government whose foreign policy it opposed. True, labor's opposition to government policy at that time was very weak, so weak that it came close to actual support, particularly so long as labor accepted the Conservatives' doctrine of nonintervention in Spain. Yet this formula gave the party a pretext which enabled it to continue its time-honored practice of voting against armament credits while it now accepted rearmament in principle. This effort to reconcile the pacifists in the party failed. In the hot debate that ensued, Hugh Dalton, who had introduced the resolution, took the sensible line that in the face of fascist rearmament it was essential for Britain to rearm in defense of democracy. The trade unions, eager to discuss coöperation in armament industries with the government, favored outright support for its rearmament policy. Ernest Bevin, speaking for the Transport Workers' Union, demanded from the conference such a statement of unconditional adherence. The pacifists and the left, led by Sir Stafford Cripps, again attacked the Party Executive, though for different reasons. Nevertheless, the resolution was carried by a three-to-one majority.

The following year witnessed the shift in the party's Spanish policy to outright opposition to the nonintervention policy. Thus, while both government and opposition continued to claim that they supported collective security, the Labour party differed with the actual policy followed by the government as far as Spain was concerned. A statement issued by the National Council of Labour in September, 1937, declared that even a Labour government "in the present state of the world must be strongly equipped to defend this country, to play its full part in collective security, and to resist any intimidation by the Fascist Powers designed to frustrate the fulfillment of our obligations." Even a Labour government would therefore "be unable to reverse the present program of rearmament." This statement prepared the way for the party's full assent to British rearmament notwithstanding Labour's critical attitude toward the foreign policy of the "National" government. By 1937 only Lansbury and his pacifist group opposed the policy of the Party Executive, while Sir Stafford Cripps abstained from opposition. Cripps was elected to the new Executive together with Professor Harold Laski and D. N. Pritt, who were in general agreement with Cripps. The Executive obtained a majority of ten-to-one, the pacifists alone being able to muster only about 250,000 votes.

When Foreign Secretary Anthony Eden resigned from the cabinet in February, 1938, over the issue of appeasement, the government could no longer continue the pretense that it still followed a policy of collective security. The groups within the Conservative party now leading were those who favored coöperation with Nazi Germany and Fascist Italy to create a bulwark against progressive currents which they lumped together under the name "Bolshevism." The Labour party now could fight the government not only over one or two incidents, but over its whole foreign policy. Both the appeasement of Mussolini and the continued comedy of nonintervention were sharply attacked by the party. "The Government," declared a Labour Manifesto in that same month, "has violated the conscience of the nation and forfeited its support." And the Manifesto added: "This is not the time for concessions to the dictators. We need a clear declaration that Britain stands for the enforcement of treaties against lawless force and against aggressive interference in the internal affairs of independent states [an allusion to the Spanish Civil War and to the Hitler ultimatum to the Austrian chancellor, Schuschnigg]. Czechoslovakia in particular should be assured at once that Great Britain and the other League Powers will fulfill their obligations to maintain her integrity and independence. It is in this policy that still lies the only real hope of averting a general European War."

The impending Austrian catastrophe and the Nazi threat to Czechoslovakia were clearly foreseen by British Labour. The party was prepared to take risks to prevent war, but it did not yet believe that war could become a reality. Indeed, it need not have, if Nazi aggression had been nipped in the bud before it succeeded in Austria.

3.

Appeasement tendencies were far more marked in France than in England during the first few months of 1938. All those who had clamored for reconciliation with Fascist Italy felt that they had won the day when sanctions were abandoned. The way was open, they thought, for an accord with the Fascist Powers that would end all danger from the left in France and in the rest of Europe.

Officially, almost everyone in France was still in favor of collective security—but this term obviously meant different things to different parties. The Communists were almost alone in demanding full support for Republican Spain. Within the Socialist party only the small group led by Jean Zyromski supported the Loyalists so far as to demand action that risked involvement of France in war. On the other hand, the Socialists were still apparently unanimous in considering that any attack upon Czechoslovakia should immediately bring France to her ally's aid. At a conference of the Czecho-Slovak Social Democratic Labor party in May, 1937, Louis Lévy conveyed a personal message from Premier Léon Blum asserting that in the event Czechoslovakia suffered military aggression, France would regard that act as an attack upon itself. Everyone in France at that time seemed to agree with Blum's promise. Surely everyone in the Socialist party agreed, for the party congress held in Marseilles in July, 1937, reaffirmed "faith in the idea of indivisible peace by means of collective security." It expressed hope that "Republican France will continue to work unreservedly . . . for the development of pacts providing for guarantees and for mutual assistance. . . ." The French treaty with Czechoslovakia was exactly of this type. True, the danger to Czechoslovakia seemed remote, while the Spanish problem was pending, and this may partly explain the difference in the attitude of the French left toward the two republics. The promise to aid Czechoslovakia did not yet involve that risk of war which support of Republican Spain implied. The more remote the possibility that loyalty to collective security might mean war, the greater was the eagerness to embrace the obligations of that doctrine. A further partial explanation of the left's different attitudes towards the two countries may perhaps be found in the belief that France would be united in supporting Czechoslovakia, while it was split over the Spanish issue.

Yet the hope for national unity with regard to support for Czechoslovakia proved unjustified. Toward the end of 1937, after a visit to Berlin, Pierre Étienne Flandin, a former premier, began to preach what was called a policy of "retrenchment," involving the abandonment of French positions abroad which he professed to believe had become untenable. Flandin found support among some of the most reactionary elements in France eager to come to terms with the Third Reich to strengthen the antiprogressive front in Europe. The Socialists reacted immediately and vehemently, declaring that "if we were to follow M. Flandin's policy of retrenchment, France would disappear not temporarily but forever from the world chess board." This was said during a debate in the Chamber in February, 1938, a few days after the Berchtesgaden ultimatum to Austria. No one knew what to suggest to prevent the dreaded *Anschluss*. Yvon Delbos, who continued to serve as foreign minister under Chautemps, as he had before under Léon Blum, solemnly reaffirmed the French pledge to Czechoslovakia. It was always the next victim of aggression, not the present one, for which the French left mobilized.

By implication, the pledge to Czechoslovakia made it clear that France would not aid Austria. Chamberlain serenely announced in the British House of Commons that small countries ought not to be led to believe that the League could guarantee their independence. Thus, with appeasement forces riding high, the Western Powers abandoned Austria. The road to Vienna was open to Hitler's army.

4.

The Labor and Socialist International and the International Federation of Trade Unions, meeting together shortly after the invasion of Austria, expressed their belief that this event must have dissipated any illusions about Hitler's real intentions which still remained. . . . "The whole of Europe," they declared, "is exposed to a Fascist dictatorship which would reduce it to misery and slavery. This is the situation which has been brought about by a few years of mistakes and fear." Labor demanded that nonintervention in Spain be stopped and that Czechoslovakia's independence be "effectively guaranteed by precise and positive undertakings, primarily by France and Great Britain."

France, as this resolution pointed out, was especially exposed to the fascist threat, from Spain, the Danube, the Balearics, and Africa. Yet, the *Anschluss* actually gave strength to Flandin's policy of retrenchment, rather than to those in France who realized the full danger of Nazism. A campaign to abandon Czechoslovakia, the next prospective victim, was already under way. It was a suggestion which the left rejected vigorously. The *Populaire, l'Humanité,* the trade union daily *Le Peuple,* all emphasized the double significance of Czechoslovakia as the last democracy east of the Rhine and as an indispensable link in the French chain of defense against Nazi Germany. A single but significant voice from the left disturbed the apparent harmony. *Syndicats,* a trade-union weekly directed by René Belin, one of the most influential of the younger secretaries of the Trade Union Federation, adopted an outright pacifist attitude. Originally the paper had been created to combat Communist influence within the unified trade-union movement and to defend "pure," non-political trade unionism, but now the paper concentrated more and more upon the defense of pacifism, in much the same way as the Teachers' Union.

Early in January Léon Blum, realizing that a Nazi move against Austria was impending, attempted to form a national government which he thought would be capable of staving off the danger. His plan fell through when the right-wing parties refused to be openly associated with the Communists in a cabinet. Even after the *Anschluss* their attitude remained unchanged, although this time Blum went so far as to suggest a cabinet representing, as he put it, "the whole of France," with the single exception of the Fascists—those "who have excluded themselves from the national community by conspiring against the republican institutions and by becoming agents of foreign powers."

This was a suggestion entirely foreign to Socialist tradition. To many Socialists it even seemed directed against what they regarded as the most important lesson to be drawn from the experience of the last war: namely, that in a "sacred-union" government comprised of all parties, the left was bound to lose influence and prestige. Yet it was the Socialist left, which had constituted the party's anti-"sacred-union" bloc, but which now understood the seriousness of the situation and the new role which the Socialists must play in international affairs. Jean Zyromski, leader of that section of the left wing which rejected Marceau Pivert's mixture of pacifism and revolutionary defeatism, had come to play an important role inside the party although because he had been defeated at the general elections he remained outside the Chamber of Deputies. He had broken with Pivert, his former ally, over foreign policy, having been one of the first French Socialists to understand that resistance to Nazism must be an essential factor in a general anti-fascist policy. During the Spanish War he was the principal spokesman for those in the party who opposed nonintervention, and he was known as the best liaison officer between Socialists and Communists. When Blum submitted his plan for a national government—which he said would be the first such government to be led by the working class rather than by its enemies, as those of Poincaré and Doumergue had been in the past—Zyromski came to his leader's support. "Spain and Europe are threatened by fascist hegemony while the working class is threatened with expulsion from the national community," he said, "I beg you all to support Léon Blum!" The supporters of Pivert, who were shortly afterwards to leave the party, were the only ones to vote against Blum's proposal; it was thus adopted by a large majority.

Within the Radical party, Édouard Daladier favored Blum's proposal. Yet Blum failed. Hatred of the left was still of more consequence to most rightist deputies than the struggle against Hitler. In vain did Blum argue that the million and a half Communists could not be excluded from the army and the factories in case of a war, and that his own record proved that he would not be dominated by Communist ministers. Paul Reynaud and Henri de Kerillis, "nationalists" of the right, who were nationalists first and conservatives second, also supported the Socialist leader. But in the showdown Flandin carried the day. England, he alleged, would be alienated from France if Communists entered the cabinet. Furthermore, most of the right-wing deputies knew that the Popular Front was by now but a shadow of its former self and they hoped and expected to control the government very soon.

After his plan had been defeated, Blum formed a Socialist-Radical coalition government, although admitting that this was not the government which France really needed. It was obviously not a government consistent with the reduced influence of the left, but Blum apparently hoped that by some miracle the right might change its attitude and effect a transformation of his administration into the national government he desired. Discussing the international situation in his Ministerial Declaration, he suggested: "If Czechoslovakia is threatened—a hypothesis I reject—can we not best stave off this by being in a position to utter our warning in the name of the entire French nation?" Blum's foreign minister this time was no longer Yvon Delbos, whose weakness and dependence upon Britain the left had come to fear, but Paul-Boncour, who had acquired, in spite of his past, a reputation of being more resolute. Blum and Paul-Boncour immediately informed London that France would fight for Czechoslovakia. They did not ask for Britain's advice first, as Delbos had always done, but simply announced their own decision in the belief that Britain would follow the French lead. As a next step, Paul-Boncour endeavored to organize a more effective defense for Czechoslovakia by bringing the Little Entente Powers closer together and encouraging military coöperation among them and with the Soviet Union against German aggression. Also, he "relaxed" the formerly strict control over the transport of arms across the French-Spanish frontier. A former Socialist who had left the party in a friendly fashion to continue as delegate to the League of Nations under a government which the Socialists sharply opposed, Paul-Boncour was a sincere believer in collective security. By no means a "strong man," he relied on his famous oratorical gifts far more than on action. Yet, compared with Yvon Delbos, he was a tremendous asset to the government. When, together with the whole cabinet, he resigned on April 8 after the Senate's rejection of Blum's financial policy, the way was open for a foreign policy of full-fledged appeasement.

The succeeding cabinet, headed by Daladier, openly broke with the Popular Front. Although Blum thought that the Socialists should be represented on the cabinet his party refused; nevertheless he continued to pretend that the Popular Front still lived. Almost desperately, he clung to his belief that the national government which he considered inevitable would be organized under the leadership of the Popular Front, if only Socialist-Radical coöperation could be maintained.

Daladier and Bonnet, the new foreign minister, at first seemed ready to continue the foreign policy of Blum and Paul-Boncour. Daladier announced his "loyalty to all pacts and treaties we have signed." Socialists and Communists voted for the government. The Communists in particular showed enthusiastic confidence in Bonnet when the new foreign minister, immediately after having assumed his new functions, sent for the Czechoslovakian minister, Osusky, and told him that "the position of the French government in relation to Central Europe has not undergone any change."

5.

British labor, in the meantime, had been striving to force Chamberlain into a clear-cut commitment of protection for Czechoslovakia. Although Chamberlain refused, it looked as if labor had been successful when, during the crisis of May 21 and 22, the British ambassador in Berlin, Sir Nevile Henderson, warned Hitler that England would support France if Czechoslovakia were attacked. This warning, together with France's apparent firmness, checked whatever aggressive plans Germany may have had at the time. British and French Socialists hurried to use this success to convince public opinion that war could be averted forever if a firm attitude were maintained against any threat of aggression. A week after the crisis the Executive of the Labor and Socialist International declared:

> A week ago a general European war was averted only by the firm attitude of certain governments. But an acute crisis may arise again at any moment. This recent experience may prove that if peace is to be maintained, a supreme effort must now be made to organize collective defense on a firm basis under the leadership of the Great Powers, members of the League. This must be done if our European heritage of civilization and democracy is to be saved from complete destruction in the ruthless march of Nazi Germany towards world domination.

A first success had been gained by the forces of democracy; whether it was due to their strength or to German lack of preparedness for a decisive test remained to be seen. But when negotiations were opened in June between the Prague government and Konrad Henlein, the leader of the Nazi Sudeten Germans, appeasement appeared in a new form.

6.

After the invasion of Austria, the so-called "activist" front of the German anti-Nazi parties in Czechoslovakia broke down. Of the three German parties which had coöperated in the past with the Czechs in the government, two abandoned the struggle. The small German Agrarian party and most members of the only slightly larger German Christian Social party rushed into Nazi Henlein's fold. The German Social Democrats, biggest of the three parties, alone continued the anti-Nazi struggle among the German-speaking population of Czechoslovakia.

Their task was almost hopeless. The Sudeten people had always been the most nationalistic Germans in the world. Sudetenland was the cradle of National Socialism, and there the first German National Socialist party had been founded long before Hitler. Grave Czech mistakes had created bitter resentment among the Sudeten Germans, and efforts to better the situation were weak and belated. The Sudeten German Social Democrats maintained that some national and social demands of the German-speaking population were justified, especially since the economic crisis hit the export industries concentrated in Sudetenland with particular force. The Czechoslovakian government's pro-agrarian economic policy tended further to reduce exports. Nevertheless, the German Social Democrats believed that the necessary reforms could be achieved by democratic coöperation with the Czechs. At a party conference held at the end of March, 1938, a few weeks after the Austrian *Anschluss*, the party president, Wenzel Jaksch, defined what he called "three realities of Sudeten German policy": first, the state frontiers would remain; second, the democratic constitution of the Czechoslovakian government would remain; third, Prague would remain an economic and administrative center. The party obviously based its policy upon its confidence that France and Britain would never abandon Czechoslovakia.

Henlein, however, was riding high. He had obtained four fifths of the Sudeten German votes, while the Social Democrats in contrast were merely a small minority exposed to the Nazi terror organized on neighboring German soil and using Sudetenland's German employers against German workers. After the Austrian *Anschluss* an almost irresistible wave of Nazi propaganda swept the region. Yet the fact that the Social Democrats continued to exist and to struggle against Nazism after the middle-class parties had withdrawn from the battlefield, strengthened the moral authority of the party. On the first of May surprisingly large Socialist demonstrations were held, and the following weeks confirmed the impression that successful and prolonged Czech resistance against the Third Reich might also break the Nazi stranglehold on the Sudeten Germans. Czechoslovakia's ability to withstand Hitler clearly depended upon the loyalty of its Allies, a fact which none knew better than the Czechs themselves. As Wenzel Jaksch said, in a report to the Executive of the Labor and Socialist International in May, 1938: "We are counting upon an armed peace until the autumn months. Czechoslovakia possesses all the military, moral, and economic conditions for carrying through this burdensome experiment. It can only be compelled to capitulate through the treason of its friends."

On July 25, Mr. Chamberlain announced that he had asked Viscount Runciman to go to Prague as unofficial "advisor and mediator."

France felt uneasy, and the Communist *Humanité* accused Runciman of being pro-German. But, on the whole, the left assumed that since Britain was showing its interest in the settlement of the Czech dispute, Chamberlain was definitely committed to stand by France in support of Czechoslovakia should Germany attack. Even the left, the Communists perhaps excepted, was therefore ready to let Britain take the lead and commit herself even more, as they believed, to the Czechoslovakian cause. In August, when the German mobilization was started, the left immediately appealed to Britain to repeat with even greater vigor the successful stand of May. No doubt existed among Socialists and even Communists that the French government would fulfill its obligation to Czechoslovakia. Georges Bonnet was sometimes criticized in *L'Humanité* for not being sufficiently outspoken to make Berlin realize that the integrity of Czechoslovakia was essential to French security; his lack of aggressiveness was considered to be a question of form rather than of essentials. The only real task, the French left thought, was to keep Britain in line.

A conference of the British trade unions showed that whatever the extent of naïve pacifism formerly existing among British labor, it was by now practically abandoned. Although criticism of the government's foreign policy was voiced, the congress endorsed trade-union coöperation with the government for the acceleration of rearmament. The most powerful opposition to this decision came from the Engineering Union, which suggested that resistance to the government's foreign policy should be carried to the point of refusing coöperation with it. If the Spanish embargo were abandoned, the union's spokesman said, his organization would withdraw all reservations against the speed-up of rearmament.

In the early part of September the crisis neared its climax. Prague, hard pressed by Britain and France to conclude an agreement with the Sudeten German Nazis, submitted its "final proposals." The left approved, although its comments were interspersed with expressions of doubt as to whether the concessions made to the Nazis were not so far-reaching as to endanger Czech national defense. Léon Blum wrote: "British and French pressure in Prague cannot be driven any further. No longer must Paris act in Prague, but in London. No longer must England act in Prague, but in Berlin."

Despite growing fears, confidence persisted that Paris, if it came to a showdown, would protect Czechoslovakia. Even *L'Humanité* said: "The guarantors of Czechoslovakia will not allow the treaties which bind them to Prague to be endangered . . . Since the protective measures have been taken by the French government, Europe knows that France will respect its signature. Then the Anglo-French agreement will take on its full significance." The British, including the left for the most part, failed to understand—as the French had failed to understand—the international significance of Czech internal reforms, but labor did realize that Czechoslovakia was the decisive test of collective security. "The time has come," the National Council of Labour proclaimed, "for a positive and unmistakable lead for collective defense against aggression and to safeguard peace. The British government must leave no doubt in the mind of the German government that it will unite with the French and Soviet governments to resist any attack upon Czechoslovakia."

In Czechoslovakia the Czech Social Democrats protested against the concessions made to "the Sudeten German Nazis, who are hostile to democracy and to the country." In order to strengthen the Czech government against further Franco-British pressure, the party collected more than a million signatures to a petition demanding that no further concessions be made to the Nazis. The Communist *Rude Pravo* declared, "It is a mistake to believe that by granting the Sudeten German demands, peace will be saved. Peace will be maintained only if Czechoslovakia remains strong and sovereign."

On September 12 Hitler delivered a threatening speech at the Nazi party rally in Nuremberg, a declaration which showed that no concessions would be enough to satisfy the Fuehrer. In Prague, Wenzel Jaksch, speaking for the German Social Democratic party in Czechoslovakia, answered: "National equality of status and far-reaching self government can be achieved without war . . . Germany once more goes the disastrous way of power politics, refusing equality of status to other nations and striving after hegemony over other nations. A world full of weapons will rise against the German nation. The Sudeten Germans will be the first victims."

Jaksch was still confident of French and British support. But as a result of the Hitler speech, the right in France now began in earnest its campaign against Czechoslovakia. In almost the same terms as were used in Nazi propaganda, French newspapers described Czechoslovakia as a hotbed of Bolshevism out to force France into a war with Germany for Russia's sake. The reactionaries, recognizing that a war against Germany might create revolutionary dangers in Europe, had made up their minds to sacrifice Czechoslovakia at the risk of isolating France on the Continent. The left, too, began to waver in the face of the apparent explosion of its theory that collective security would exclude recourse to force, since the mere threat would be a sufficient deterrent to any aggressor. Pacifists renewed their attacks upon collective security. The union of postal, telegraph, and telephone workers opened fire on the position of the Trade Union Federation (C.G.T.), which continued to urge firmness. The postal workers opposed the C.G.T. attitude in the name of "proletarian internationalism and of the traditional anti-militarism of the workers." Even if they must carry on alone, the resolution said, "the postal workers will struggle to the end against all wars whatever their pretexts, and whatever the attitude of governments, parties, and even of the Trade Union Federation." Their union was not isolated, for a few days later the Teachers' Union issued a similar statement. *Syndicats,* organ of a group of anti-Communist trade unionists, supported the pacifists. The official trade-union daily, *Le Peuple,* together with *Le Populaire* and the Communist *Humanité,* continued to hold firm for a few days. On September 14 Léon Blum suggested that British and French police be sent to Sudetenland to prevent further incidents.

The following day Chamberlain flew to Berchtesgaden. In London the left failed completely to understand his game. The Labour party's *Daily Herald* wished him "good luck" and spoke of a "bold course" which, it said, "will receive general support." The left believed that the British prime minister made his flight to impress upon Hitler Britain's resolve to fight. "The purpose is not," the *Daily Herald* stated, "and could not be allowed to be the striking of a private bargain." Herbert Morrison continued to warn against an "illusionary peace" which would bring "even more terrible and dangerous wars in the future." Addressing a mass meeting of the International Peace Campaign, Morrison suggested that those Sudeten Germans who wished to live in Germany be exchanged for Germans who wished to live outside Germany, with the frontiers left untouched.

The French left was less unanimous in its judgment—or rather misjudgment—of Chamberlain's move. Blum, holding the same attitude as the *Daily Herald,* expressed his "admiration without any reserve." The Communist *Humanité,* in contrast, protested vociferously against Chamberlain's journey, which it said was bound to increase Hitler's prestige. Gabriel Péri, the Communist expert in foreign affairs, wrote: "It is not peace that will be saved in Berchtesgaden. Peace is inseparable from the protection of Czechoslovakia; and it is to organize Czechoslovakia's sacrifice that the prime minister left for Berchtesgaden." British and French cold-shouldering of the Soviet Union over the Czech issue began to fill Communists everywhere with distrust for Chamberlain and Daladier. The trade-union paper *Le Peuple* was ambiguous. The editor in chief predicted that Chamberlain's journey "will be another defeat for the cause of peace." The following day René Belin, editor of *Syndicats,* later a member of the Pétain Government, wrote in praise of the British prime minister and declared that "a mediocre or even a bad settlement is better than even a victorious war." The trade unions, among which all tendencies of the left were represented, reflected their conflicts.

When the terms of Chamberlain's peace became known, the breakdown of the left quickly became apparent. The British, their strange confidence in Chamberlain's loyalty to collective security rudely shattered—for years, after all, they had attacked his unwillingness to commit himself to collective security—protested violently against the "shameful betrayal." The French left, however, was completely paralyzed by internal dissension. With only one or two exceptions, the Socialists of the "neutral" countries meanwhile became primarily concerned with their countries' staying out of war.

7.

On September 13 the Dutch and Scandinavian governments declared in Geneva that regardless of what happened in Europe they would stay neutral. The Scandinavian governments, led by Socialists, voiced the policy of the labor parties. The Dutch Social Democrats, an opposition party, protested against their government's neutrality decision. J. W. Albarda, the leader of the Dutch Social Democratic party, wrote in a bitter article: "I think we are wrong in attributing the blame for the dark outlook (after Munich) to France and England alone. A heavy part of the responsibility is shared, in my opinion, by the small European powers, in particular by Belgium, Holland, and the four Scandinavian countries." The Scandinavian Socialist press answered that the small countries had been excluded for several years by the Great Powers from any share in determining European affairs and therefore could not be expected to fight wars for which the Great Powers alone were responsible. The fact remained that, although they were pledged to a policy of collective security, the Scandinavian Socialists now supported their governments' determination to remain neutral in a war which might be started by a Great Power attacking a small country.

The Socialist parties in the small European countries had followed the policy of nonintervention without great enthusiasm, but as an unavoidable necessity so long as the democratic Great Powers advocated such a policy. An incident between Belgium and the Spanish Republican government showed, however, that some Socialists in the small neutral countries considered "nonintervention" as justification for a complete lack of interest in the fate of Spanish democracy. A Belgian, Baron de Borchgraeve, was found dead near the battle lines in Madrid. Although the circumstances surrounding his killing and his alleged connection with the Belgian embassy were mysterious, the Belgian Socialist foreign minister, Spaak, proceeded with considerable energy to establish claims against the Spanish government. The Catholic and Liberal members of the government, hostile to the Spanish Republic, applauded the Socialist foreign minister. The Socialist party President, Vandervelde, preferred to resign as vice-premier and minister of public health rather than be associated with such a claim. Indalecio Prieto, Spanish minister for the navy and air force, sent Vandervelde a telegram which expressed the Spanish Socialists' feeling of having been betrayed by their comrades abroad. He said: "You, Comrade Vandervelde, by such a courageous attitude as that which you adopt today, succeed in maintaining unsullied your life as a Socialist; and you give your comrades in Spain consolation for the terrible bitterness caused us by the contradictory and incomprehensible conduct of other eminent personalities of European socialism." Serious conflicts ensued within the Belgian Labor party. De Man and Spaak developed in public speeches the principles of what they called a "National Socialism" based upon the acknowledgement of the breakdown of the International, and the need for working-class action within the limits of isolated countries. Although later the two leaders endeavored to interpret their new theory so as to meet rising criticism, a feeling of uneasiness persisted within the Belgian Labor party.

Throughout the Czechoslovakian crisis, Spaak and De Man defended Belgium's neutrality policy in agreement with the so-called Oslo Bloc, comprising the Scandinavian countries and Holland. When the left wing of the Belgian Labor party drew attention to the fact that the Labor and Socialist International, with which the Belgian Labor party was affiliated, stood for collective security, De Man replied that this was due solely to the influence of political refugees, particularly those from Germany and Austria, upon the decisions of the International. This was a rather unfortunate argument for De Man to adopt, because his former lieutenant, Max Buset, pointed out that all important resolutions of the International had been adopted unanimously—which meant by the delegates of the Belgian Labor party too. Undeterred, the trade unions continued to back Spaak and De Man, for any other course would have disrupted the government coalition and forced the Socialists out of the government. This the union leaders feared above all.

The neutrality policy of the "Oslo-Socialists," supported by the Swiss, and the internal French conflicts paralyzed the Labor and Socialist International. Efforts to organize coöperation at least between the British and the French Socialists failed in spite of many meetings. Although official reports of these conversations always announced that complete unanimity prevailed, they were always careful never to state precisely the policy of the International. The Communist International, too, kept a strange silence. British and French Communists agreed in opposing Chamberlain's appeasement policy, but a joint appeal which these two parties published lacked the signature of the Russian Communist party. Apparently Russia did not wish to go too far in committing itself to any foreign policy, and a manifesto signed by the Communist International or by the Communist party of the Soviet Union would obviously have been binding for the country of Communist dictatorship. Suspicious minds may be inclined to discover in Moscow's silence in September, 1938, inklings of Russia's turn-about in 1939.

England constituted the center of leftist resistance to appeasement. The British Labour party condemned the Anglo-French proposals without reservation. The National Council of Labour spoke of a "shameful betrayal," of concessions made under the "brutal threat of armed force," and added, "With every surrender to violence, peace recedes." The party organized 2,500 mass meetings in London and the provinces against Chamberlain. Since the Communists supported this campaign, the small pacifist group under George Lansbury and the Independent Labour party were the only leftist forces to approve the appeasement policy. Their attitude was of little significance compared to the opposition of the large union organizations, which were unanimous in protesting against the betrayal of collective security. The I.L.P. policy was especially peculiar. During the World War the party had been the heart of pacifist war resistance and many conscientious objectors had joined its ranks. After its break with the Labour party, Communist and later Trotskyite influences penetrated into the I.L.P., which then adopted a policy of "revolutionary defeatism" in line with Lenin's World War slogan. Under the pressure of the 1938 crisis this revolutionary defeatism as put forth by James Maxton, the I.L.P. leader, became identical with whole-hearted support of Chamberlain's appeasement.

Although the Labour party leadership was unanimous in protest against Chamberlain, its opposition remained ineffective. Public opinion was overwhelmingly in favor of the prime minister, who, it was sincerely believed, had saved peace for "our time." Further discouragement was felt by the left because the Labour party had little hope of winning a majority in the near future. Proposals for a British Popular Front, to consist of the Labour party, the anti-Chamberlain Liberals and the Communist party, had been constantly rejected by the Labour party, which refused to ally itself with the Communists and maintained that a Labour-Liberal alliance could hardly agree on domestic policy. Although a Labour-Liberal compromise on domestic issues would indeed have been difficult, foreign policy was so dominant an issue that many Labour leaders, among them Sir Stafford Cripps and Harold Laski, favored such an alliance. But the trade unions refused to give international affairs precedence over their economic claims. As a result the left struggled continuously under the handicap of the split within the anti-Chamberlain forces.

It is true, as the opponents of the Popular Front in England pointed out, that the French Popular Front failed to pursue an anti-fascist foreign policy. But the French Popular Front had been created primarily to resist French fascism. Although its program expressed willingness to practice a policy of collective security, this part of the program had never been the main plank in the Popular Front platform. Faced with the danger of immediate war, many Popular Front groups in France preferred pacifism to international solidarity.

In this respect Paris was different from the rest of the country. On September 25 the building workers in the capital called off a strike in order not to weaken France's stand against the Nazis. But Paris was the center of the Communist movement and the Communist party was clear and outspoken in its criticism of appeasement. "Obeying the injunctions of Hitler," a Communist manifesto said, "Mr. Chamberlain has got the British and French ministers to agree to the dismemberment of Czechoslovakia, the integrity of which is inseparable from French security and the peace of Europe. Repudiating the treaties bearing the signature of France and the undertaking which they solemnly renewed only a few days ago, the Daladier Government has agreed to this new capitulation to international fascism." And the manifesto concluded with what proved a highly accurate prophecy: "After that, Hitler will be able to demand French colonies and Alsace-Lorraine, while Mussolini will ask for Tunisia, Corsica, Nice, and Savoy."

The Socialists were far from agreeing on such a condemnation of appeasement. Léon Blum's articles in *Le Populaire* reflected the party's internal confusion. Paul Faure, the general secretary of the party, and twice a minister in Blum cabinets, strongly opposed France's going to war for Czechoslovakia's sake. The Socialists' duty, he argued, was to follow the policy of the internationalists during the Great War. Internationalism, according to his view, consisted of repeating in 1938 what ought to have been the Socialists' attitude in 1914. Believing that Socialists must always refuse to support war, he failed to see that in the war of 1914 the international working class had little interest in influencing the outcome of the war. Neither side then represented a system which the Socialists could favor. In 1938, when fascism threatened the continued existence of a group of democratic countries, the workers had a vital interest in defeating fascism. Collective security was but an extension to international politics of Socialist anti-fascism.

Faure received powerful support from pacifist trade unionists throughout the country. Among the Socialist electorate were many peasants who, having little interest in foreign affairs, preferred Faure's isolationism to collective security. In Paris, Faure could count on the "revolutionary defeatists" of Marceau Pivert, who followed the line of the British I.L.P. and whose spirit survived even after Pivert's expulsion from the Paris section of the Socialist party.

Jean Zyromski and his left wing, who had opposed nonintervention in Spain, now took the lead in the anti-appeasement struggle. Later events proved that Faure commanded what may have been a majority, and was certainly a very large minority, of the party. Blum, anxious to preserve the unity of the Socialists, adopted an intermediary attitude which also corresponded to his inclinations. His intelligence told him that France ought not to lose in the war of nerves which Hitler obviously was waging. The greater the risk of war, he once had observed, the more determined the democracies must be to accept the challenge. Unfortunately Blum always hesitated to follow his own advice when confronted with the immediate danger of war. Because he somehow believed that Hitler would be satisfied with certain concessions, he failed to understand the dynamics of the Nazi system that were always forcing the Third Reich to larger demands. Convinced that Hitler was but the instrument of big business, he believed—or least hoped—that at some point his masters would force Hitler to stop, since industry might have more to lose than to win by war. Blum never entirely lost hope that some arrangement might be concluded with the dictatorships. He was ready, as he once said, to accept peace even from the hands of a blood-stained dictator.

After the Anglo-French Plan became known, and while British and French ministers discussed it in London, Blum protested not so much against the plan as against the absence of Czech delegates.

"It would be an unbearable action," he wrote, "on the part of the Great Powers toward a small country, if they were to dispose of Czechoslovakia without Czechoslovakia's being represented." On the following day he penned a much quoted sentence:

"Whatever happens, the consequences of the London Plan will be far-reaching both for Europe and France. War has probably been averted. But it has been averted under such conditions that I, who have always struggled for peace, who for many years have dedicated my life to peace, cannot feel any joy and am merely filled with mixed feelings of cowardly relief and shame."

Gabriel Péri answered in *L'Humanité* without referring to Blum: "It is not true that the danger of war is averted. What is true is that Germany's warlike ventures, so far restrained, now can develop freely, since the dam opposing them has been broken." Blum undoubtedly would have agreed with that if only he had followed his reason. But his sentiments, together with the necessity of saving the unity of the Socialist party, prevented him from listening solely to rational considerations. Furthermore, everyone in France felt the pressure of public opinion worked up by almost the entire press to a frenzy of war panic.

Even the Labour party in Britain felt this pressure of public opinion. When Chamberlain announced that a conference would be held in Munich, Major Attlee "welcomed" the prime minister's statement. The *Daily Herald* wrote on the following day, "Relief is natural," but the labor paper hastened to add, "When the details are known, the public opinion of Britain will, we believe, be profoundly shocked that such relief has been purchased at the expense of a further abandonment of a small, brave, and democratic nation."

As soon as the results of Munich became known, the Labour party launched its attack upon the Government. In the House of Commons Major Attlee, Herbert Morrison, Hugh Dalton, Arthur Greenwood, Philip Noel Baker, and Sir Stafford Cripps strongly criticized the Government. Attlee said that "Munich was not a real peace conference. It was an armistice granted in the face of force. . . . We feel humiliation in that there has been no victory for reason and humanity. It has been a victory for brute force. . . . The cause of democracy, which is in our view the cause of civilization, received a terrible defeat." Hugh Dalton protested against the exclusion of the Soviet Union from Munich. Sir Stafford Cripps, who had definitely abandoned his former opposition to collective security, said: "You won't forever satisfy rival imperialisms by handing over to them the smaller nations of the world. The time will come when the clash will be at your own door."

An official Labour party amendment to the vote of confidence expressed the party's opposition to Munich. Couched in the time-honored terms of British parliamentarism, it said:

> That this House, while profoundly relieved that war has been averted for the time being, cannot approve a policy which has led to the sacrifice of Czechoslovakia under threat of armed force, and to the humiliation of our country and its exposure to grave dangers;
>
> And, realizing the intense desire of all peoples for lasting peace, demands an active support of the method of collective security through the League of Nations and the immediate initiation by his Majesty's Government of proposals for the summoning of a world conference to consider the removal of economic and political grievances which imperil peace.

Six pacifist Labour members, led by George Lansbury, refused to vote for this amendment. In addition, four members of the Independent Labour party abstained from voting for the motion of nonconfidence, as did also a considerable number of Conservatives.

The idea that a world conference could redress grievances in a way that would satify the Nazis could hardly be maintained. The proposal's only justification was that it offered the only alternative to mere waiting for the inevitable war. It was more realistic than Chamberlain's appeasement and French labor's enthusiastic reception of the news of Munich. For the French trade unions, though Communist influence was strong, were swept off their feet. The Executive of the Trade Union Federation (C.G.T.), reversing its previous stand, suddenly found reason to "congratulate itself that this agreement should have averted the worst in the immediate future by suspending the war race." The only protest which the unions formulated was directed against the danger that Munich might be the "preface to a four-Power pact" against which democratic opinion everywhere, it was said, had always protested. Léon Jouhaux, the trade-union leader, who might have thought differently, was at the time on his way from America to France.

The Socialist deputies decided, with only seven dissenting votes, to support Daladier's foreign policy. In the Party Executive, Zyromski's influence was considerably stronger. The pro-Munich majority was only fifteen to twelve, with four members abstaining. Anxious to avoid the impression that a gulf existed between deputies and Party Executive, a second vote was taken and this time eighteen members were for Munich and twelve against.

Consequently, Blum made an extremely weak and confused speech stating the Socialist attitude in the Chamber. He repeated that they felt joy and sorrow at the same time and that he considered that the main responsibility for Munich lay with those who had refused to accept his proposal for a national government. "France must now be honest with herself," he pleaded, "and examine all the treaties to which it is a party, frankly denouncing those which it does not intend to fulfill." This was a retrenchment policy, such as Flandin had suggested, with the one important difference that Blum spoke after, not before, the dismemberment of Czechoslovakia, with its accompanying blow to French power and prestige in Central Europe. Finally Blum warned against efforts to exploit Munich for reactionary purposes—a warning which events soon proved to be fully justified. France's diplomatic defeat appeared to many as a victory of the right, which had taken the lead in opposing aid for Czechoslovakia, over the left, which had abandoned collective security much later. Munich was thus the starting point for a triumphal campaign of reactionary forces against labor and democracy on the Continent.

The Communists, a lone Socialist, and a single right-winger were the only deputies to vote against Munich. The Socialists voted for the government when the Munich issue was to be decided and abstained from participating in the vote on plenary powers for Daladier. It was symbolic that this outward expression of the disintegration of the Popular Front occurred over an issue of foreign policy.

On October 1, the German Armies crossed the Czech border and advanced into what had been the territory of the last democracy in Central Europe. On the same day, the German Social Democratic party in Czechoslovakia, the last free German branch of the International, dissolved its organization. Its final manifesto addressed to the German workers now about to be subjected to Nazi rule, somberly declared:

> Perhaps the day will come when they who have sacrificed us will be chosen as new victims. History alone will give a definite judgment on our attitude and theirs. . . .
>
> We lower our standard before the glorious heritage which we have steadfastly maintained, and we retreat from the battlefield hoping that it may be given to a happier generation to serve more successfully our ideal, to which we shall remain faithful to the end.
>
> Long live Socialism!

Chapter 21

INTO THE ABYSS

1.

MUNICH was followed by quickening disintegration in the European labor movement. The gulf between Socialists and Communists, narrowed during the Popular Front period in France, widened once again. The Labor and Socialist International, though not officially dissolved, practically ceased to function as a political agency. Within the French Labor movement there began a bitter struggle between pro- and anti-Munich tendencies. Everywhere reactionary forces advanced. The victory of the Third Reich, the defeat of Western European democracy, the diplomatic neglect of Russia during the entire Munich period and consequent loss of Communist prestige, the crushing blow dealt to collective security and those who stood for it—all this combined to enhance anti-leftist feeling throughout Europe.

The Executive Committee of the Labor and Socialist International meeting in Brussels in October, 1938, published a long statement of protest against Munich. But since it had to be acceptable to anti-Munich British and pro-Munich French Socialists, and inoffensive to the neutral Belgian, Swiss, and Scandinavian labor parties, the protest was directed against the form rather than the substance of "appeasement." Its principal accusations were that the Munich agreement had "been elaborated in great haste, without impartial and expert assistance, by a Conference held in the victor's citadel, which was very different from the International Conference proposed by President Roosevelt. Czechoslovakia was not even given a hearing. No consideration of justice or of the equality of nations was taken into account. The immediate entry of German troops and the handing over of the fortifications was accepted without any measure being taken for the protection of democrats and men of independent mind." Scarcely a fundamental protest against Munich!

After the dissolution of the German Social Democratic party in Czechoslovakia, the Labor and Socialist International also lost its Czech branch, for the Czech party resigned from the International and later proclaimed its own dissolution. Attempting to adopt protective coloration, the party leadership dropped its Jewish members and organized a Czecho-Slovak Workers party which renounced class struggle and internationalism. In Slovakia the emerging totalitarian regime of the Catholic People's party dissolved the Workers party shortly after its foundation. By March, 1939, the final destruction of what remained of the Czechoslovakian Republic also entailed the end of the Workers party, and many of its leaders were arrested by the German Nazis. The Communist party had been dissolved by the authorities shortly after Munich.

The Hungarian Social Democratic party followed the Czech example by excluding Jews from all important functions in the party and in Parliament. As a price for its existence after the victory of the counter-revolution in 1919, the Social Democratic party had had to take part in the Nationalist campaign for a revision of the Hungarian frontiers. Now the party hailed "the realization of self-determination" by which a slice of Czechoslovak territory, the Carpatho-Ukraine, was ceded to Hungary. The Social Democrats, an official statement said, "welcome this historic event with the same feeling of expectation and the same joy which all Hungarian people feel during these days."

The Polish Socialist party (P.P.S.) held a similar attitude toward the annexation of parts of former Czech territory in Silesia. But the P.P.S. realized, what the Polish government apparently did not understand, that the diplomatic defeat of France threatened the very existence of Poland. In a public statement the Polish Socialists deplored the political methods employed at Munich. It was this attitude which later gave the party the right to claim a leading part in the heroic though futile defense of Warsaw against the Nazi Army. The Polish Socialists were the main force that had consistently opposed Colonel Beck's policy, as well as the Fascist ideas of the right-wing opposition.

Altogether very little was left after Munich of free labor organizations east of the Rhine. The advance of Nazism restricted labor to a narrow fringe of territory in Western and Northwestern Europe. After the loss of its Czechoslovakian branch, the Communist International counted only one more European party outside Russia worth mentioning, namely, the Communist party in France.

2.

The first consequence of Munich in French domestic policy was a violent anti-Communist drive, in which the government participated. The Communists had been defeated at Munich, now they had to pay the price of the breakdown of their policy. They had been more responsible than any other party for the creation of the Popular Front, designed to struggle against the rising tide of French fascism. The Communists had taken too much for granted when they assumed that domestic anti-fascism would imply anti-fascism on the international scene as well. Among the Socialists, pacifism was strongly represented. Many Radicals and men from the intermediary groups between Radicals and Socialists, such as Marcel Déat, had turned out to be among the most outspoken opponents of collective security and the most ardent supporters of Munich.

Within the French Socialist party, Munich caused a tremendous crisis. Early in October a Committee of Inquiry into the foreign policy of the party was set up. In this committee the struggle over Munich came to a head. Under the leadership of the party secretary, Paul Faure, one group rejected all mutual assistance agreements, including the Franco-Soviet Pact. Some members practically justified the dismemberment of Czechoslovakia by stressing national self-determination as a principle which should take precedence over every other factor, including democracy. Blum considered the internal situation of the party desperate. It was impossible to achieve an understanding between the Faure group supported by the naïve pacifism that went rampant in France after Munich, and the Jean Zyromski faction, which advocated a strong anti-fascist policy and categorically rejected Munich.

Internal affairs came to the fore early in November, when the forty-hour week, though maintained in principle, was abolished in practice by the government in the interest of rearmament. None of the Popular Front reforms was more cherished by the workers than the "cinq fois huit," the five-day week, with eight working hours each day. When Paul Reynaud, the minister of finance, proclaimed over the radio that "the 'week with two Sundays' has ceased to exist in France," the workers felt that they were being deprived of the most important gain they had obtained through the Popular Front. None of the working-class leaders told their supporters that French production had declined at a dangerous rate, that French security was being threatened by a German armaments industry running almost continuously with a work week up to sixty hours; and that only tremendous efforts of workers and employers alike could save France. Still, as long as unemployment continued to exist in France without the government absorbing it in an expanded rearmament program, it was difficult for the workers to see why their hours of employment should be extended.

Speaking at the congress of the trade unions on November 16, Léon Jouhaux, the trade-union leader, cautiously referred to the idea of a general strike against the government's decree. This threat was obviously made for bargaining purposes. It was mainly due to Communist pressure that it became a reality. For the Communists the strike was primarily a protest against the foreign policy of Daladier and Bonnet. Jouhaux delayed the strike as long as he could, hoping for mediation until the very last moment, but Daladier and Reynaud had made up their minds to smash once and for all what they regarded as illicit trade-union interference with government business. Public opinion, which seemed convinced that trade unions were delaying vital French rearmament measures, supported the government's decision to force the issue and break the strike.

For the first time, Daladier lived up to his reputation as a "strong man." He had not dared to resist the fascist rioters after February 6, 1934, or German Nazism at the time of Munich, but now he mobilized against the unions all forces at his disposal. He "requisitioned" the railroads and public services and organized mass trials of doubtful legality against workers who went on strike before the general strike was scheduled to begin. The workers felt that they were risking their jobs for a mere gesture, since the general strike was restricted to a twenty-four-hour demonstration by the trade-union leadership. This was not a strike to win power, but merely to serve as a warning to the government. In view of the government's ruthless resistance, the risks involved in the strike were greater than the possible gains. As a result, the strike which took place on November 30 was a failure.

Widespread dismissals of striking workers ensued. The Trade Union Confederation (C.G.T.) lost a considerable part of its newly won membership. Internal dissension between the Communist and the anti-Communist trade unionists became more bitter than ever before. René Belin, one of the leaders of the anti-Communist faction, accused the Communists of being responsible for the loss of the strike. Still the disagreements did not prevent the Socialists from joining the Communists in sharp opposition to Daladier.

November 30 witnessed the peak strength of the pro-Munich forces. Coming from Daladier, the argument that exigencies of national defense dictated the smashing of the strike appeared as pure mockery to many workers. They felt that the Third Reich had helped French reactionaries to defeat the French working class. It was no accident that Ribbentrop's visit to Paris and the signature of a Franco-German declaration of friendship were postponed until after the general strike. The defeat of the workers was a prerequisite for this crowning act of Munich policy.

The total collapse of the appeasement program was not long delayed. The Italian demonstrations for Tunisia, Corsica, and Nice on November 30 rudely shattered the confidence of those who sincerely believed that Munich had saved peace at least "in our time." Although the first reports of the Rome demands were played down in the French press on orders of the government, which was anxious not to spoil what it stubbornly believed to be hopeful prospects of a French-Italian understanding, news of the persistent Italian press campaign against France could not be suppressed. When the Socialist Party Congress met at the end of December, Faure's pro-Munich policy had lost most of its old glamour and much of its former support. The Seine Federation, which had hailed Daladier upon his return from Munich, now voted for Léon Blum, who once again had become the spokesman of collective security. When Zyromski joined forces with Blum, Faure's defeat was assured.

Backed by this victory Blum made a last desperate effort to obtain French aid for Loyalist Spain. It came too late. On February 27 the Chamber of Deputies approved official recognition of Franco.

3.

On March 15, 1939, the British House of Commons discussed the news of Germany's march into the post-Munich remains of Czechoslovakia. Chamberlain, obviously disturbed, announced that a planned visit of the president of the Board of Trade to Berlin was "postponed." Nevertheless the prime minister still professed to have faith in the September settlement. "I have no doubt," he said, "that the course we took was right." David Grenfell, speaking for the Labour party, took an opposite view. The latest act of Nazi aggression, he charged, was a direct consequence of Munich. Hugh Dalton, another Labourite, complained that at Munich "the prime minister had been out-maneuvered, hustled, and humbugged by Herr Hitler." But among the Conservatives the spirit of Munich was still unbroken. It needed the wave of bitter protest that shook the country after March 15 to convince Chamberlain and his followers that "appeasement" was on its last legs. In a speech at Birmingham two days later Chamberlain admitted that his policy had failed.

This should have been a day of triumph for the Labour party, which had opposed Munich and the Munich spirit. But the real victor was Winston Churchill, whose warnings against German National Socialism had been much more powerful and had come so much earlier that he, rather than Labour, now represented the spirit of resistance to Hitler in the minds of the people. Labour had missed its great opportunity to lead the nation into the struggle against German Nazism—probably its best opportunity for overcoming the party's dismal defeat of 1931. Labour had once again been too slow. During the coming months, the last few that remained before the outbreak of hostilities, Labour was to let the initiative and the national leadership fall to other men.

On April 3, 1939, after the British pledge to Poland, Arthur Greenwood, the deputy-leader of the Labour party—Major Attlee was ill—expressed the hope that "a much more broadly based scheme of mutual protection and assistance" would be established. The "appeasement" chapter was closed, he said, and the first words of a new chapter, which he would entitle "mutual aid" were being recorded. He asked for an understanding with the Soviet Union. "However they (the members of Parliament) might assess the military value of the U.S.S.R., there could be no question that she might well prove to be the final decisive and smashing factor on the side of keeping the peace in the world." The most forceful demand for an immediate agreement with the Soviet Union came from David Lloyd George. James Maxton, speaking for the Independent Labour party, protested against what he termed "war speeches," and demanded that appeasement be continued. Sir Stafford Cripps described Chamberlain's government as "hardly a fit instrument to rally the world to save democracy and freedom." But whatever might have been the correctness of his assertion, the Labour party's past had not endowed it with sufficient confidence or authority to enter a convincing claim to power.

Events were moving rapidly toward a climax. On April 7 Albania was occupied by Italy, an act which gave a final push to the crumbling house of appeasement. A few weeks later compulsory military training was introduced in Britain. Labour was furious. Not only did conscription run counter to its long-cherished tradition, but the party was incensed that the prime minister had broken his promise not to sponsor conscription in peace time. The Labour leaders, fearing repercussions upon labor standards and union principles, claimed that there was no evidence that the voluntary scheme had failed. Labour assumed leadership of the opposition to conscription, although the Labour leaders declared that they were "prepared to take all necessary steps to provide for the safety of the nation and the fulfillment of its international obligations." George Hicks, a trade-union leader, speaking in the House of Commons, complained, "We have been deceived."

Chamberlain was not very clever in his handling of the opposition, particularly in withholding for too long a time the announcement of his plans. Labor, on the other hand, was demanding a policy of resistance to aggression, while refusing at the same time to help provide the nation with the instrument that most experts thought was indispensable for carrying out such resistance. The French, including the Socialists, had long insisted that England adopt conscription to prevent the possibility that the French Army alone would have to withstand the onslaught of the German forces until a British expeditionary force might be ready, perhaps a year after the outbreak of war. Popular feeling in Britain was opposed to conscription, so much so that even the British Communists voted against the measure, although their French colleagues were enthusiastic supporters of the plan. Still, many people had hoped that despite the popular feeling British Labour would not lose an opportunity to demonstrate its leadership of national resistance to fascism.

Although it fought compulsory military training at home, Labour's campaign for resistance to fascist aggression continued unabated. It began to bear fruit after Hitler's coup against Prague. His threats against Poland strengthened British determination to resist.

4.

The change in British temper reacted strongly upon France. Following the outbreak of the Spanish War, Paris had followed the British lead in appeasing the dictators to avoid being isolated and to win British support for the final stand against Hitler. The point now seemed reached where London had made up its mind to retreat no longer. Paris, though now far more committed to appeasement than was its ally, again followed the example of Britain, which this time was moving in the opposite direction. The left, however, did not profit from this change. Daladier, who had been responsible for Munich, remained in power, just as Chamberlain held on in Britain.

After the final liquidation of the Popular Front, the Radical party moved to the right, becoming in fact a Center party. The Socialist-Communist alliance broke down in the summer of 1939. Communist attacks upon the Socialist party served as the final blow, although Faure's Socialist right wing had in fact been awaiting an opportunity to dissolve an alliance which, after the end of the Popular Front, had little to offer to the Socialists. The defeat of the general strike hastened the split.

Both Socialists and Communists lost heavily in membership. Trade-union membership was reduced to about one half of the record figure of 1936, and the continuous decline threatened to do away with the entire advance made at the time of the sit-down strikes. More important than membership losses were the internal dissensions in the Socialist and trade-union movements, which continued unabated until the outbreak of the war.

In this manner the strength of the French left was constantly being sapped. The great days of the advancing Popular Front were but a pale memory when the outbreak of the war presented European labor with its day of reckoning.

PART VI

Outlook

Chapter 22

THE UNDERGROUND MOVEMENT

I.

AS LONG as the cannons roar on the battlefields of Europe, it may seem idle to speculate on the future of European labor. The great war will determine whether free labor organizations will survive or be resurrected in Europe, or remain smashed for decades to come. A Nazi victory will mean the end of that European labor movement which has contributed so greatly to determining the development of Western democratic civilization. If Hitlerism is defeated, a new opportunity will arise for the progress of free labor.

These predictions are no more than commonplace; and they may lead to the conclusion that the military, not labor, will decide labor's own fate. Yet while the war progresses, it becomes increasingly clear that if Hitler is to be defeated, the victory will be obtained by political as well as military weapons. A revolt of the oppressed nations, an upsurge of the working class in Germany and Austria, resulting at least in a slowing-down of German war production—these will have to combine with the victorious resistance to Nazism by the armies in the field to achieve the complete overthrow of Hitlerism.

In the countries openly carrying on the struggle, labor's contribution to the war is twofold: economic and political. In this struggle of huge mechanized forces, victory depends to an extent never previously foreseen on the work of the factories in the hinterland. Without labor's full devotion to the cause of the war, no country can hope to win. Labor's entry into the British war cabinet was a decisive step toward full development of that country's potential war strength. The inability of the French Popular Front to organize for effective national defense and the hopeless effort of the subsequent French governments to rearm without the coöperation of the working class or even against its opposition were among the main causes of the French defeat. Together with monopolistic resistance to plant expansion, labor difficulties contributed to appreciable delays in the execution of the American rearmament efforts. Labor's economic coöperation is as significant a military asset as the army itself.

A victorious grand strategy in this war, it has been repeatedly pointed out, must envisage a revolutionary strategy designed to arouse internal conflicts in the vast Nazi-dominated realm of Continental Europe. Once the Third Reich is tottering under the heavy blows of its opponents, the coup de grâce will come from the struggle of oppressed countries for national freedom and of labor for social and political emancipation. The working-class organizations in the countries opposing Hitlerism are indispensable links with whatever underground organizations exist inside the Third Reich. Labor's political influence in and upon the democratic countries must be directed toward imposing such a revolutionary strategy upon the anti-Nazi governments.

Is European labor conscious of its great task? Has it outgrown its pressure-group mentality and its laissez faire philosophy? Has it reached that stage of maturity which will enable it to claim the leadership of a victoriously emerging new democratic world?

These questions must be addressed, first of all, to the small dispersed underground groups inside the Third Reich who today are powerless, but who tomorrow may be the leaders of a strong popular movement, if democracy is to be victorious.

These questions must also be answered with regard to the leading democratic country in Europe, Great Britain. British labor holds the key to vital "war secrets," the British war effort and the British war strategy.

2.

Measured in terms of human heroism and suffering, underground labor groups have a long history. Underground labor organizations have existed at one time or another almost everywhere in Europe, since the time when the British trade unions were declared illegal by the General Combination Act of 1799. The Russian labor parties, both Menshevik and Bolshevik, grew up under the terror of czarism. But the fascist totalitarian dictatorships, under which Italian labor has existed since 1926 and German labor since 1933, are essentially different from those old-fashioned authoritarian regimes. Not only has fascist terror surpassed anything ever seen before; for the first time in modern history the Italian and German governments have controlled and "coördinated" every aspect of life, political, social, economic, and private. To the political means of power possessed by the old dictatorships, fascism has added tremendous economic and social instruments of pressure. With overwhelming force unhampered by legal restrictions, the party in control smashed any effort to create organizations independent of fascism. Mere contact between people of opinions hostile to the party in power is considered high treason.

The underground labor organizations of the present war period have been handicapped by profound disappointment and skepticism. They no longer have the invincible self-confidence of the underground organizations of the pre-war era, to whom illegality was but a passing stage in labor's irresistible ascent to power. The modern underground organizations arose out of the defeat of powerful mass organizations seemingly at the threshold of victory. It needed deep conviction, boundless heroism, and—a virtue rare among revolutionaries—unlimited patience to continue underground activity under these circumstances. Whatever could be done was bound to be insignificant compared with the giant displays of strength which the fascist dictatorships were presenting to their subjects. Victory seemed far distant, perhaps beyond the limit of individual life. Yet thousands of workers continued under new conditions and with new methods the eternal struggle of humanity for freedom.

3.

Conditions varied greatly in the three main countries of fascist dictatorship, Italy, Austria and Germany. The underground movements in each started from different points of social and political evolution. Although they had much in common, the forms and histories of these three underground movements were bound to have distinct individual characteristics.

The Italian underground movement was the oldest of the three. After having existed under conditions of semi-legality from October, 1922, until late in 1925, the Italian labor organizations were destroyed by Mussolini's turn towards totalitarian dictatorship. Many labor leaders were forced to flee, others were imprisoned and deported. New nuclei had to be formed out of young workers less familiar with the problems of labor organizations and also more exposed to the influence of fascist propaganda. Contacts between the Socialist party centers and the local sections, and among the local sections themselves, became increasingly difficult as Fascist terror sharpened and the police gained experience in dealing with the underground organizations.

By the spring of 1927 Communist and Socialist organizations had reached a stage where there existed an "almost complete separation of the center from the party rank and file, and the rank and file from the masses." A new anti-fascist organization, Giustizia e Liberta, arose to unite activist elements of the various anti-government groups. When Mussolini's deflationary policy created general dissatisfaction and caused strikes and wage movements, Giustizia e Liberta developed extensive activity. It organized propaganda flights over Milan and Rome, freed political prisoners on the Lipari Islands, and spread propaganda material all over the country.

But the police finally succeeded in discovering the new organization's underground apparatus and imprisoned its leaders. With this loss, the organization rapidly declined. From 1932 to 1935–36 the underground movements in Italy were practically paralyzed. The outbreak of the Ethiopian War, bringing with it price increases for foodstuffs and unrest in the factories, created new opportunities for anti-fascist propaganda and action.

By this time the underground movement was a completely new organization. It consisted chiefly of young men, most of them intellectuals and students, who had not lived through the pre-Fascist era of the labor organizations. They did not regard their movement as a continuation of the old Socialist or Communist parties, but as a new departure. Large parts of their public had grown up under Fascist conditions; for them the old slogans of socialism or communism had little meaning. In their struggle against a state-controlled society, socialism meant first of all a movement for liberty against an all-powerful government. They stressed personal and civil liberties rather than Socialist planning.

But there were still many workers in Italy who had taken part in the struggles of the pre-fascist era and who were still thinking in terms of traditional socialism. Older than the members of the underground organizations, they were less inclined to take part in illegal activities. But they were stronger in numbers than the underground workers, and had closer contacts with the factories. Thousands of Italian workers living abroad, particularly in France, were organized by the Italian labor parties set up in the democratic countries. When these workers who had been educated in traditional Socialist thinking returned to Italy, they helped in establishing contacts between the underground movements and the large masses of the working class.

Out of the contact between the new ideas of the underground movements and the experience and tradition represented by the older workers, a new type of Socialist thinking and Socialist action has thus arisen. Its effectiveness will depend primarily upon the great political and social decisions to come in Europe.

4.

After the defeat of February, 1934, the Austrian labor movement immediately began to organize underground groups that were unique in the history of this type of movement: they were mass organizations. In spite of its military victory the Dollfuss regime was unable to inspire that awe and discouragement among its opponents that was one of the strongest weapons of the German Nazis. The fact that workers had offered resistance, though unsuccessfully, to Dollfuss' troops, gave the Austrian underground movements self-confidence, while the capitulation in Germany killed the spirit of the Reich's working class. Utopian hopes of a "revolutionary October" modeled on the Russian revolution were alive among large groups of underground workers, many of whom looked toward the example of the Soviet Union for inspiration and guidance, after the disappointing end of democratic methods. The Communists made rapid headway at the expense of the Social Democrats.

Weak as it was, the Dollfuss regime succeeded in surviving the death of its creator and the Nazi onslaught of July, 1934. It was then that the hope for a swift revolution was abandoned by the underground movements. They began to realize that the long and arduous task of organization lay ahead of them.

The principal Socialist organization was the "Revolutionary Socialists" (R.S.). They coöperated with the "Delegation Abroad," which the leaders of the unsuccessful February struggle, Otto Bauer and Julius Deutsch, had set up in Brno, Czechoslovakia, close to the Austrian border. Bauer acknowledged from the beginning that actual leadership of the movement had to be vested in men living inside Austria, and that his role was that of an adviser and representative abroad. In spite of this—perhaps, because of this—he continued to exert great influence upon the R.S.

The R.S. organized a Central Committee in Vienna, arranged for distribution of the weekly *Arbeiter-Zeitung*, with a circulation of up to 50,000 copies, and succeeded in absorbing all the other Socialist underground groups that had sprung up independently after February, 1934. Following the French example, they concluded an agreement on united action with the Communist underground movement, but this failed to work satisfactorily. Adhering to the new Comintern line the Communists were eager to find allies among the most reactionary groups in Austria, to unite all in a powerful anti-Nazi league. The R.S. refused to coöperate with fascists and monarchists. While the Communists held the lead among the underground movements immediately after February, 1934, the R.S. gradually succeeded by effective organization in constructing an underground apparatus superior to anything previously known.

Two conferences were held in September and December, 1934, to organize the R.S. movement in Vienna and the entire country.

The organization was firmly established, but the police became constantly more effective in unearthing R.S. groups. Slowly the R.S. were forced to abandon their previous semi-open mass action and to concentrate upon other forms of activity, primarily education. By creating factory nuclei and coöperating with the "illegal" trade unions that had been set up in the meantime, the R.S. maintained contacts with the working class. They constituted a real party, not merely the nucleus of a party like the Italian and German underground organizations.

By the time Schuschnigg was forced to look for allies in Austria in his struggle against Hitler Germany, the R.S. and the "illegal" trade unions coöperating with them were in control of the Austrian labor movement. The fascist unions were empty shells, government-appointed leaders without followers. Had coöperation been established in time between Schuschnigg and labor, Austria might at least have offered resistance to the annexation—although such resistance without support from the outside world would of course have been doomed to failure. Schuschnigg's delay in revising Dollfuss' fatal mistake of February, 1934, rendered futile all efforts to organize the defense against the Nazi juggernaut.

Under Hitler's rule the Austrian underground movements shared the fate of their German counterparts. The best known, and therefore most exposed, Austrian opposition leaders of the Dollfuss-Schuschnigg era went into exile. The mass organizations were reduced to mere nuclei. Under Czechoslovak pressure, the "Delegation Abroad" of the R.S. was transferred to Paris, so far away from the country as to make impossible the exertion of the continuous and intimate influence of the preceding few years. As a result the Austrian movement was partly assimilated by the German underground organizations. Yet the Austrian Socialists refused to abandon their independent status in favor of a joint German-Austrian organization as long as no united German Socialist movement existed. Instead, the Austrian Socialists concluded a working agreement with certain German Socialist groups, in particular the New Beginning group. The Sopade, the German Socialist Party Executive abroad, refused to subscribe to this agreement.

5.

Until the very last moment, the German left had not believed that Hitler would be able to establish a totalitarian dictatorship. The Communists, though persecuted earlier than the other leftist groups, expected the failure and breakdown of Hitler's regime in the near future. For a brief interlude many Socialist leaders thought that by abandoning the internationalist aspect of the Socialist program and activity, the organizations might be saved, but after Hitler destroyed the trade unions and dissolved the Social Democratic party, the only remaining alternative was to build underground organizations.

At first the Socialist and Communist underground groups were fairly large organizations in which thousands of workers and intellectuals played active roles. The Communists, having had more experience in underground work and being less compromised in the eyes of many workers by the inglorious breakdown of German democracy, held a certain advantage over the Socialists. Communist confidence in an approaching revolution led them to sacrifice their members recklessly, for they thought the revolution would soon free them again. Open mass action and the wide circulation of illegal newspapers cost the Communists heavy imprisonments, but for a while they led the leftist underground movement. The Socialists were slower in setting up their clandestine groups, consisting of five men, of whom only one was supposed to know one member of another group. The Socialist Party Executive had neglected to prepare such groups and even resisted the emergence of an activist group which was beginning preparations for underground work during Von Papen's and Schleicher's chancellorships. After Hitler's victory the Socialist organizations were split into several underground groups, the most important of which were the official Party Executive—called Sopade after the German initials—whose headquarters were first in Prague and later in Paris, and the New Beginning group. Many other leftist groups existed apart from these and some still continue to function.

New Beginning emerged when members of the Socialist Youth

organization united with former Communists opposing the leadership of the Communist party. They created a new group that would seek to effect a united labor movement in the future. The first task of New Beginning was, according to its leaders, to educate and train the members themselves so as to enable them to take the lead of a German revolution whenever time should be ripe for it. While the Communists were working under the assumption that such a revolution was in sight, New Beginning believed that fascism had come to stay. There was no use, therefore, in wasting precious lives and energies in actions that could end only in catastrophe. The main task, they felt, was to train the Socialists themselves. As a result New Beginning tended to isolate itself from the masses of the working class.

Other underground movements, particularly of the Communists, were inclined at first to look askance at the isolationist tendencies of the New Beginning groups. By 1936, however, little remained of most of their original organizations, especially of those which had used mass action methods. The dreaded Gestapo had destroyed many groups and had arrested entire leadership committees. Hitler's diplomatic successes, the lack of resistance on the part of the democratic powers, and the disappearance of unemployment under the Nazi economic dictatorship discouraged many anti-Nazis. On the other hand, the amelioration of the economic situation increased the self-confidence of the workers. Despite the terror, the fear of losing one's job was no longer so powerful a brake on labor action as it had been during the period of mass unemployment. Passive resistance in the factories, coördinated movements to obtain wage increases occurred here and there.

On this basis, new underground groups came into being. Some were heirs of the older organizations, but consisted largely of new men. They were very small groups, few men daring to defy the Nazi terror machine. Large groups had little chance of avoiding detection. With Hitler marching from triumph to triumph, the underground men had to have almost superhuman confidence in their anti-fascist creed. They had to abandon private life when private contacts endangered their political activities. The largest part of their work consisted of constantly circumventing the police danger. "To make a single telephone call," an underground worker wrote, "would involve hours of complicated arrangements. To meet somebody for a few minutes' talk could take a day's preparation. For two or three to meet together at the same time would call attention to their subversive activity. The entire energy of highly qualified people was engrossed in keeping contact alive among only a few dozen friends in the same city or town. Contacts with other towns in the same district had to be broken off. Frequently there was no knowledge in one village of local resistance which cropped out in the next. It was sometimes only after months, and then through a fog of gossip, that the events in one's own city came to be known. It may well be that during this period thousands of little resistance groups were scattered through Germany; but none of the stronger organizations had more than a few hundred dissociated persons."

To exert influence upon the workers in the factories, these small underground groups had to turn toward the larger body of the former Social Democrats or Communists who had not given up their political opinions but who refused to take part in underground work. Former lower-rank trade-union officials or party workers who still enjoyed the confidence of their fellow workers were the bridge between the underground movements and the working class itself. They kept the underground corps informed about occurrences in the factories, and reported on the temper of the workers. In turn they were anxious to receive information from the underground workers about events kept secret or misinterpreted by Nazi propaganda. On the basis of personal friendships the former officials of the legal labor movements transmitted the slogans of the underground to the workers in the factories. In times of political hopelessness this bridge between the underground movements and the working class would crumble and all but isolate the underground movement from the large masses of the working class. When the outlook became better from the point of view of the anti-fascists, the former trade-union sub-leaders were again eager to meet and listen to the representatives of the underground groups.

The Munich crisis was the great turning point in the pre-war history of the anti-Nazi movements inside Germany. If the Austrian *Anschluss* had been welcomed by most Germans, the realization that Hitler was prepared to go to war over the Sudeten German issue came as a shock to many. Anti-Nazi currents were strengthened, and the underground movements made progress. The brutal pogroms of November, 1938, widened the gulf between the Nazi party and some sections of the German people.

The old Socialist-Communist division had lost most of its significance for the underground movement. The problems that were discussed among those engaged in anti-Nazi activities had little in common with the traditional arguments separating Socialists and Communists. The old arguments over reformist and revolutionary methods no longer applied to the conditions of a fascist country, where reforms could be achieved only by revolutionary methods. Technical questions of propaganda were far more important for most of the underground men than discussions about the respective share of the different labor parties in the guilt for Hitler's victory. The influence of foreign centers that might have strengthened the division between Socialist and Communist underground groups dwindled, as contacts with the outside world became increasingly difficult. If, nevertheless, no fusion between the various underground groups was effected, it was mainly due to their reluctance to establish new contacts which they did not fully control. The risk involved seemed too great and the advantages of a fusion too small to warrant the experiment. Moreover, no one could speak with authority for the many groups that worked without contact with other groups, isolated in cities and villages all over Germany. A fusion would have been a merger of committees abroad, rather than of the underground groups in Germany itself, and the Committees abroad were precisely those which preserved the old party spirit and the old divisions.

The German-Russian Pact drove a wedge between those groups which defended it and the great majority for whom it was betrayal, shameless and unexplained, of the workers' cause by the Soviet government. The Communists endeavored to continue their activity, but they soon discovered that they could have no slogans which would not place them in the unenviable position of either backing

Hitler or opposing the Soviet Union. The mere slogan of "immediate peace"—in accordance with the Comintern line—meant support of Hitler's efforts to profit from his initial successes in the war by forcing England and France to capitulate. After a long period of confusion, the remnants of the Communist underground organization worked out a new policy based on an alleged division between Nazis favoring the Soviet Pact and those opposing it.

Walter Ulbricht, since 1935 head of the Central Committee of the German Communist party in Moscow, wrote an article opposing the German Socialists' pro-Allied policy in which he said:

If Hilferding and the other former Social Democratic leaders direct their war propaganda against the German-Soviet Pact, they do so because the English plan to bring about war between Germany and the Soviet Union will succeed the less, the more deeply rooted is the friendship between the German people and the Soviet people in the toiling masses. It is for this reason that not only the Communists but also many Social Democratic and National Socialist workers regard it as their duty not to allow the Pact to be broken under any circumstances. Whoever intrigues against the friendship of the German and the Soviet peoples is an enemy of the German people and is being branded as an accomplice of English imperialism. Among the toiling people of Germany the efforts increase to unearth the supporters of the Thyssen clique, these enemies of the Soviet-German Pact. In many cases the demand was raised to remove those enemies from the Army and the State apparatus and to confiscate their property.[1]

Communist duty obviously consisted in fighting the so-called Thyssen clique among the Nazis, while the rest of the Nazi party, including apparently Hitler and Ribbentrop, had ceased for a while at least to be an enemy of the working class.

To the non-Communist underground movements the outbreak of the war brought tremendous encouragement in spite of the Communist turn-about. For the first time since his advent to power Hitler was being faced with armed resistance. Although critical of the Allied leadership, its intentions and its methods of waging the war, the non-Communist underground groups realized that their own fate and that of a German revolution were inseparably connected with that of the French and British democracies. A victori-

[1] This article is referred to in Paul Hagen, *Will Germany Crack?* New York, Harpers, 1942, p. 223 f.

ous German revolution might be forced to resist Allied plans for splitting up Germany or imposing unbearable peace conditions. Until the downfall of the Hitler system, however, the Allied armies were defending the freedom of Western Europe and that of Germany as well.

6.

Little reliable information is available on the fate and the development of the underground organizations after the outbreak of the war. But what is reported on the preceding pages may help to answer the vital question regarding the political maturity of the underground groups.

As a moral and intellectual elite, the members of the underground groups are bound to be superior in their political maturity to the average German worker, and a judgment may be misleading if based alone upon the state of mind of the men actively engaged in anti-Nazi work. However, even for the larger number of sympathizers of underground groups, events have done a great deal to clear away the dead wood of the past. These sympathizers are fairly numerous, and together with the underground workers might constitute the leadership of the future German working-class organizations.

Both Socialists and Communists have revised much of their former creed. The Socialists admit, as a matter of course, that their struggle is a revolutionary one, to be fought regardless of Nazi law and aimed at the overthrow of the Nazi constitution. Having gone through the experience of a hostile totalitarian regime, the Communists have come to recognize the value of democratic liberties. The repeated twisting of Soviet Russia's foreign policy has done a great deal to destroy Communist prestige, which was considerably enhanced during the Popular Front period; Russia's entry into the war may have done much to reëstablish it. Particularly since the war has broken off communications with organizational centers abroad which were anxious to preserve old set-ups and, accordingly, old splits, the terms Socialist and Communist have lost most of their application to countries such as Germany.

Return to a democratic system with its stress on human individuality has become the generally accepted desire of anti-Nazis, but all agree that the Weimar Republic is gone forever. Not only is it recognized that the weakness of the Republic in the face of its enemies was suicidal; the coöperation of democratic labor elements with protagonists of the former regime, the grafting of democratic reforms upon a semi-feudal social and administrative structure—both characteristic of the Weimar Republic—have become obviously impossible for any future contingency. Unless foreign troops, directly or indirectly, control Germany, the German defeat and the overthrow of the Nazi dictatorship will realize, for the first time, the old Radical dreams—a complete break with one system and the opening of a new era.

The task of reconstruction will not allow pressure-group activities on the part of the working class. Unless the victorious Allies take over the administration of Germany, the country will be confronted with a problem unique in modern history, which it will be labor's foremost duty to solve.

One of the greatest bulwarks of a fascist dictatorship is the total destruction of alternative authorities. With army, administration, judiciary, and all social organizations under Nazi control, a breakdown of Nazi authority means that the country is left an amorphous mass. There is no alternative government waiting for its day, as under the British parliamentary system; no organized opposition exists with a nationally known leader who could take over from the Nazi regime; even within the smallest community, the Nazi system has eradicated the last trace of independently organized social life.

A breakdown of the Nazi system is unlikely to be a partial process. If Nazism is defeated, the entire huge machinery built up by the party and controlled by it, will in all probability fall into ruins. With the army, the administration, and all social organizations under Nazi control, a Nazi defeat would destroy all authority in the country with the possible exception of certain church groups. No analogy for such a complete dissolution of a party and of an organized state can be found in the life of a liberal country. Totalitarianism is not merely a highly centralized political machine comparable to that of an American city, but essentially different from anything known in free countries.

However, if the Nazi leveling process has succeeded in smashing all non-Nazi strata of society and has transformed citizens into one uniform mass of politically impotent subjects, it has not been able to destroy social groups as such. Although organized workers are not permitted to meet or to discuss their problems and organize for the defense of their interests, they still continue to associate every day in the factory. They cannot form free trade unions and freely elect their leaders; but the factory itself shapes working-class groups, and daily contact creates leaders. The factory thus may be the nucleus of a future organized society in a democratic Germany.

In a certain sense, this is a situation similar to that which gave birth to the Russian soviets. Since the working-class organizations were too small to control the vast territory of Russia, the revolutionaries of 1905—and after them those of 1917—felt the need for a system which made the whole of the working class, organized and unorganized, part of the government machine. This was the origin of the soviet idea. The German factory may fill that role in tomorrow's Germany. The soviet idea is not necessarily dictatorial; between March and November, 1917, soviets were the backbone of Russian democracy. A German government based upon soviets may be a democratic government; and in view of the popular revulsion against a totalitarian regime that ended in war and defeat, such a future German government will almost certainly not be totalitarian.

With the factories as centers of society, the German working class may be the main bulwark of a new regime. The Nazis, who set out allegedly to resist the progressive "proletarianization" of the German middle class and to reverse the process, have created the largest proletarian class of any nation in the world. Faced with a restricted labor supply in their drive for swift rearmament and anxious to expand their factories, the Nazis "rationalized" trades and distribution with the declared intention of forcing independent businessmen into the ranks of the working class. Therefore no German social regime can hope to maintain itself that does not take into full account the fact that the industrial working class now represents probably a clear majority of the German population. A future non-Nazi Germany will have a working-class complexion, whatever that may mean in terms of social institutions.

Again as in 1918, though under vastly different conditions, labor will thus be called upon to lead the nation. This time no reliance upon the voluntary coöperation of elements which constituted the old regime will be possible; the division between past and future will be clear cut. No hope can be placed upon the initiative of others, for "the others" will be less able to act than labor. There can be no effort to maintain essential institutions of the past and to use them for democratic and socially progressive policies—for Nazi institutions were expressly devised for anti-democratic and militaristic objectives. No trust can be placed in the automatic processes of capitalism, for no really capitalistic society exists in Germany. A return to a freely competitive capitalist system under post-war conditions of hunger, misery and mass unemployment will be deliberate suicide for any group that tries it.

No way is thus left for labor to avoid its responsibility if Germany loses the war. Neither pressure-group nor laissez faire policies can possibly be applied to the post-war situation. The downfall of fascism is bound to cause gigantic problems; a new society has to be created out of an almost completely unstratified agglomeration of human beings. Ineluctably, labor will be confronted with a task that will test its constructive abilities to the limit.

Chapter 23

A NEW OPPORTUNITY

1.

"THE *history of all countries shows that the working class, exclusively by its own effort, is able to develop only trade-union consciousness; i. e., it may itself realize the necessity for combining in unions, for fighting against the employers, and for striving to compel the government to press necessary labor legislation, etc. The theory of Socialism, however, grew out of the philosophic, historical and economic theories that were elaborated by the educated representatives of the propertied classes, the intellectuals. According to their social status, the founders of modern scientific Socialism, Marx and Engels, themselves belonged to the bourgeois intelligentsia. Similarly, in Russia, the theoretical doctrine of Social Democracy arose quite independently of the spontaneous growth of the labor movement; it arose as a natural and inevitable outcome of the development of ideas among the revolutionary socialist intelligentsia. . . .*" So Lenin wrote in a famous pamphlet, *What Is to Be Done?* [1]

In accordance with this theory Lenin based his system of organization upon a group of leaders who could direct the working class to synthesize its everyday activity with a struggle for power looking towards the ultimate transformation of society. His efforts were successful in Russia, with its poorly organized industrial proletariat, but they failed wherever the Bolsheviks clashed with existing well-organized labor movements. The defeat of the Comintern's revolutionary hopes after World War I ended in the passing of

[1] Lenin, *What Is to Be Done? Burning Questions of Our Movement.* Marxist Library, Vol. XIV. New York, International Publishers, 1929.

control of the Communist movement outside Russia to the radicals, who had already been defeated in the Socialist parties.

Outside of Russia the progress of labor from the status of pressure group to political party could succeed only to the extent that the masses themselves gained understanding of their own tasks; that could not be accomplished by dictatorial leadership. For in Western and Central Europe little could be achieved by labor parties without the understanding and free coöperation of the entire working class. Only improved insight into the situations confronting them could induce the workers to abandon their narrow trade-unionist outlook in favor of broad constructive policies which could both serve the entire nation and create the conditions necessary for labor's further social advance.

Such an evolutionary process was bound to be slow. Groping through a dense fog of tradition, romantic radical slogans, laissez faire legacies, and collective inertia, the Socialists sought to develop independent policies for the whole range of national problems and thereby to enable labor to fulfill its role as a major national party. They were still far from this objective when the great crisis, beginning in 1929, and the rise of Nazism put the movement to a decisive test. Has the process since that time given labor in the few remaining democratic countries the wisdom and experience to fulfill its great role, should a defeat of Nazism again present the working class with an opportunity for constructive action?

2.

British Labour, the only important free labor organization left in Europe, has undergone a rapid change since its great electoral defeat in 1931. It has been forced to abandon its pleasant dream of the "inevitability of gradualness," the automatic transition of the capitalistic society into a Socialist order—that dream expressed so characteristically in MacDonald's talk of patient waiting until the corn should no longer be green. Fascist practice in Germany has demonstrated—to quote a group of Socialist intellectuals in the Labour party—that "the next step towards an integrated economy, which can conquer mass unemployment and overcome recurrent economic crises, need not automatically occur as a consequence of the efforts of the labor movement, but can be forced on society by brutal and reactionary means, in the course of which the industrial and political instruments of working class struggle are smashed to pieces." [2] The conclusion to be drawn from these facts was unpleasant but inescapable: labor can no longer confidently rely on its old faith that socialism is the inevitable heir of capitalism. No longer is it possible to maintain that labor has only to concern itself with the day-to-day industrial and social struggle within the limits of the capitalist institutions, and that socialism will ultimately be realized by the sum total of the achievements obtained in these struggles. Labor has been brought to understand that it has either to accept the existing social system and adjust working-class action to the laws of capitalist economy—or consciously engage in constructive action transforming the very basis of society.

An expression of this growing recognition can be found in the proceedings of the Labour party conference held in Bournemouth in May, 1940, shortly after the resignation of Chamberlain and the Labour party's decision to join the new cabinet headed by Winston Churchill.

On behalf of the Party Executive, Harold Laski submitted to the conference a statement on Socialist war policy. He described this policy as an attempt to recover the dynamic of democracy by a method based on socialism. "Only bold Socialist planning of the foundations of our system," he said, "can give us the faith and power to meet the claims of those who will bring us victory. They (the soldiers) are entitled now to the assurance that they will not make their sacrifice in vain."

The Labour party's policy was threefold: first, planning for the war itself; second, meeting the conditions that would arise when victory had been won; and third, arranging the long-term program that would be necessary after demobilization had begun. The statement explained that the party's demand for efficient war planning was the reason for the entrance of its leaders into the government.

[2] See *"U.S.S.R.?"—Our estimate of its significance for the British Labour Movement*. Published by the Socialist Charity Group, Greenford, Middlesex. See also the extremely valuable *Labour Discussion Notes* issued by the same group (M. Chance, Greenford, Middlesex).

"Our message to them is that in the degree that they use the full resources of their trade union knowledge and experience in the planning of the war, will they be useful," the party declaration continued.

"We must remember that Britain has been conquered only twice in its history. The first time was by William the Norman in 1066 and the second by Montagu the Norman in 1931 [an allusion to Montagu Norman, governor of the Bank of England, and his part in the events leading to the defeat of the second Labour government in 1931]. We take the view that the reign of Montagu the Norman should now ebb peacefully to its close. . . ."

"We serve notice on the Government today," Harold Laski declared amid loud cheers, "that never again as a movement are we willing to endure a society in which there are three million unemployed. We serve notice on them and our leaders that never again will we endure a society in which whole areas of our civilization are distressed areas." The workers must share equally in gain as in toil, Laski demanded, adding that the grim months of the war should be used to move nearer the goal of social democracy.

This policy, unanimously endorsed by the party conference, was clear indication that the movement was beginning to realize that social change could only be achieved as a result of conscious efforts to bring about change.

3.

When labor thoroughly understands the lessons of the rise of Nazism and of this Second Great War, its evolution to a fully developed political party will be completed. Comprehension of the new problems began after the defeat of 1931, when the labor movement abandoned its naïve laissez faire creed and sought to develop an economic policy which could serve as basis for social demands. The next decisive step followed in the Lansbury crisis, when the utopian belief in an inner harmony between loyalty to pacifism and the League of Nations was sacrificed in favor of a collective effort to resist aggression. No longer were foreign affairs outside what Keir Hardie called "the real work of the party," and labor began to realize the considerable extent of its own particular role in the democratic struggle for self-preservation. Labor's stand against the policy of Munich, and the "phony war" of Chamberlain, its insistence upon basic reforms to harness the political strength of the country to its war task, the measures of economic planning introduced by the Churchill-Labour coalition—all these bear testimony to the new spirit of the British working class.

The real test, however, is still to come. In the countries subject to fascism, the old labor organizations have been destroyed and little more than sentimental ties—honorable and sometimes powerful—connect the present with the large mass organizations of the past. The old forms have disappeared. When labor regains power at some future day, new men will appear on the political scene, free from any responsibility whatsoever for labor's earlier great defeat. Thus, the prospect for constructive action undertaken in a fresh spirit and unhampered by the past is bright.

British Labour has fully maintained the continuity of its organized existence. The break with the past is therefore by no means as complete as in the case of the underground groups. Tradition, even that of the MacDonald period, is still alive in individuals and institutions. The present leadership consists of men who have grown up in the atmosphere of the MacDonald era. It is understandable why certain opposition groups are somewhat skeptical about the permanency of the new spirit which has manifested itself in the party since the outbreak of the war.

It is true that many symptoms disturbingly reminiscent of the past continue to exist. The new spirit which conceives of the war as a crusade for political and social democracy has been superseded in some labor quarters by a sort of conventional patriotism that is by no means free of jingoism; labor groups still welcome the leadership of conservative nationalist forces; the alliance with middle-class groups, indispensable and wholesome as it may be, is still too frequently pictured as involving the need for sacrificing labor's right to free initiative. While all this is undoubtedly true, the social transformation of Britain as a consequence of the war has made so much headway that the traditions of the laissez faire and of the pressure-group period have been decisively weakened.

Although it is impossible for any human being to foresee the shape of the world to come after the destruction of Hitlerism, it can be predicted with assurance that it will be so different from the pre-1939 world that no one will be able to dream of a return to "pre-war normalcy" as so many did after the First World War. A far more profound reconstruction of Europe will be more desperately imperative than it was after the First World War. Strong as the forces of tradition within British labor undoubtedly are, when confronted with the problems of the post-war world, the British working class will be forced by the new facts of social life and the arising new problems to forge ahead. A task that can be mastered only by constructive action will present itself to British labor and its associates on the Continent. The opportunity will be there. History alone will show whether labor will live up to its mission in a new Europe.

4.

A few words might be permitted at this point on the probable future position of American labor. A defeat of the Axis powers—the only assumption which makes speculation about the future a useful guide for action—will inevitably increase American influence on world affairs. At the present moment, the American trade unions with their approximately ten million members represent the strongest freely organized labor force in the world. American labor then will have a tremendous opportunity to influence world trends and its responsibility will correspond to this opportunity. What is the probability that American labor will be aware of this responsibility and able to acquit itself honorably of its task?

At the end of the last war, American labor representatives coöperated with their European colleagues in preparing labor's demands for the peace conference. Similar coöperation seems not improbable for the final stages of this war. The split of the American unions into C.I.O. and A.F. of L. and further divisions that do not seem impossible in view of John L. Lewis' conflict with the bulk of the C.I.O., render coöperation with European labor somewhat difficult. The A.F. of L. is affiliated with the International Federation of Trade Unions, while the C.I.O. has no organized ties with European labor organizations. In the past this tended to create a certain number of difficulties for European-American trade-union coöperation, but in view of the general rapprochement between A.F. of L. and C.I.O., it is probable that problems of organization would no longer stand in the way of effective international action.

Far more serious is the resistance which some of the "old-fashioned" American labor leaders have opposed to actions in what they regarded as the "political field." If this tendency still persists —and it is probable that it does—then it will present a twofold problem.

American labor pressure-group policies will continue to impede the smooth functioning of the democratic machinery. This does not mean that a serious Fascist menace is bound to arise in the United States. America will not necessarily follow the European pattern, as Britain did not follow the Continental trend to any great extent. National integration in the United States may prove much stronger in relation to the disintegrating force of social conflicts in a period when class forces are in balance. Even if this be so, the problem of maintaining national integration in spite of possible acute social conflicts and under the conditions of a balance of class forces will undoubtedly arise. Whether it can be solved without a severe crisis of American democracy will depend to a large extent upon the political insight of American labor.

American labor's political maturity will also determine the degree of influence which the American unions might be able to exert upon the development of the post-war world. Undoubtedly, the progressive forces in Europe will depend a great deal upon help from American labor, particularly if American conservatives should on their part try to influence European developments. Similarly, European democrats might hope for American labor support against Communist efforts to dominate revolutionary post-war developments. But if American labor follows a narrow pressure-group policy, it will deprive itself of much of its possible influence upon major American policies and, at the same time, will show little inclination to concern itself seriously with the problems of European labor's organizations.

Some pressure in favor of more general and political action might possibly be brought to bear upon the American unions by some former European labor leaders who have found refuge on American soil and, more effectively, by British labor. It might well be that the American unions will show willingness to coöperate in preparing political statements, but the wide divergence between the views of many American labor leaders and their colleagues from Europe might prove a serious stumbling block for a joint declaration on labor's post-war aims. Willingly or unwillingly, the European labor groups will be compelled to rely the more heavily upon Russian support the less understanding American labor shows for the political aims of the British and the Continental working class. Moreover, it is doubtful, at the present moment, whether any political statements to which the American unions might subscribe will be followed by any serious action to support them in the United States.

World politics in general and labor politics in particular will be determined, in the case of an Axis defeat, in the Washington-London-Moscow triangle. The primary aim of European labor is likely to be freedom from outside interference, be it Moscow's pressure in favor of communism, or conservative interference to prevent social changes in Europe. If American labor should remain a prisoner of pressure-group thinking, an indispensable part in the triangle of pull and stress will be missing, and Russian attraction might become extremely powerful.

Thus, the measure of political maturity which the American unions will possess at the end of the war might well contribute to determine positively or negatively the future course of European labor.

BIBLIOGRAPHICAL NOTES

THE MAIN source used in preparing this book was the voluminous literature produced by the European labor organizations themselves. In addition to the daily press organs of the European Socialist and Communist parties, the proceedings of party congresses and trade-union conferences, valuable material is found in hundreds of pamphlets published at one time or another. A few have been quoted in the text itself and in the footnotes.

A great many magazines were connected in various forms with the labor organizations. They contain interesting material on the discussions within the movements themselves. More factual information is available in the *International Press Correspondence,* presenting the communist point of view, and in *International Information,* a weekly news sheet published by the Secretariat of the Labor and Socialist International. This deals primarily with events within the social-democratic movements. In addition, the International Federation of Trade Unions published its weekly news releases.

The following list contains only a small fraction of the literature used and refers almost exclusively to books which might be of special interest to the general reader. For more detailed information the reader will have to go back to the sources mentioned in the two preceding paragraphs. A few items not contained in this bibliographic note are referred to in footnotes.

The following list is arranged according to the chapters of the book.

The main source of information on the post-war splits of the labor movement are the reports of the proceedings of various international congresses held after the war, in particular the reports of the Viennese Union and of the Labor and Socialist International. For a full understanding, it is also necessary to refer to the pre-war congresses, especially those of Stuttgart, Copenhagen, and Basel. The best available source in the English language is Merle Fainsod, *International Socialism and the World War.* Cambridge, Mass., Harvard University Press, 1935.

For the early history of the German Republic, see Arthur Rosenberg, *A History of the German Republic.* London, Methuen, 1936. Also, by the same author, *The Birth of the German Republic, 1871–1918.* London, Milford, 1931.

The best history of the origin of the Austrian Republic is Otto Bauer, *Die österreichische Revolution.* Wien, Wiener Volksbuchhandlung, 1923 (English translation: *The Austrian Revolution.* London, Parsons, 1925). Also consult Friedrich Adler, *Vor dem Ausnahmsgericht; die Verhandlungen vor dem § 14 Gericht am 18. und 19. Mai 1917. Nach dem stenographischen Protokoll.* Berlin, Paul Cassierer, 1919. (English translation: *J'accuse; an Address in Court.* New York, the Socialist Publication Society).

For Hungary, see Wilhelm Böhm, *Im Kreuzfeuer zweier Revolutionen.* München, Verlag für Kulturpolitik, 1924.

The most concise history of the British labor movement is G. D. H. Cole, *A Short History of the British Working Class Movement, 1789 to 1937.* London, Allen and Unwin, 1938. New York, Macmillan, 1937. Allen Hutt's, *The Post-War History of the British Working Class.* New York, Coward-McCann, 1938, represents a more pro-Communist point of view. Certain aspects are well treated in Carl F. Brand, *British Labour's Rise to Power: Eight Studies.* Stanford University, Calif., Stanford University Press; London, H. Milford, Oxford University Press, 1941.

Of the literature on France, I have used particularly David I. Saposs, *The Labor Movement in Post-War France,* New York, Columbia University Press, 1931; Marjorie Ruth Clark, *A History of the French Labor Movement (1910–1928),* Berkeley, California, University of California Press, 1930; Paul Louis, *Histoire du socialisme en France de la Révolution à nos jours,* 3 edition, Paris, Rivière, 1936.

On the Kapp *Putsch,* see Wilfrid Harris Crook, *The General Strike; a Study of Labor's Tragic Weapon in Theory and Practice.* Chapel Hill, The University of North Carolina Press, 1931.

The history of the international trade-union movement during the period between the two wars is dealt with in Lewis L. Lorwin's excellent book, *Labor and Internationalism.* New York, Macmillan, 1929. See also H. A. Marquand and others, *Organized Labor in Four Continents.* London and New York. Longmans, Green & Co., 1939. This is a particularly good source for the coal conflict in Great Britain.

Some aspects of the later evolution of the British Labour party are treated in Dean E. McHenry, *The Labour Party in Transition. 1931–1938.* London, Routledge, 1938.

On the later part of the history of France, I used Alexander Werth, *France in Ferment,* London, Jarrolds, 1934; and by the same author, *The Destiny of France,* London, Hamilton, 1937.

For Sweden, see in particular *Democratic Sweden,* a volume of studies prepared by members of the New Fabian Research Bureau, edited by Margaret Cole and Charles Smith. London, Routledge, 1938; *The An-*

nals of the American Academy of Political and Social Sciences. Social Problems and Politics in Sweden, Philadelphia, May, 1938; a valuable study is Brinley Thomas', *Monetary Policy and Crises; a Study of Swedish Experience,* London, Routledge, 1936; Rudolf Heberle, *Zur Geschichte der Arbeiterbewegung in Schweden,* Jena, G. Fischer, 1925; Nils Herlitz, *Sweden; a Modern Democracy on Ancient Foundations,* Minneapolis, the University of Minnesota Press, London, Oxford University Press, 1939; G. Henrickson Holmberg, "Die Entwicklungsgeschichte der Arbeiterbewegung in Schweden," *Archiv für die Geschichte des Sozialismus und der Arbeiterbewegung,* Vol. 6, 1916, Leipzig, presents useful background material.

Of the voluminous literature on Fascist Italy, I mention in particular the following: G. A. Borgese, *Goliat, The March of Fascism,* New York, Viking Press, 1937; Carl T. Schmidt, *The Corporate State in Action; Italy under Fascism,* New York—Toronto, Oxford University Press, 1939; Gaetano Salvemini, *The Fascist Dictatorship in Italy,* New York, Holt, 1927; also by the same author *Under the Axe of Fascism,* New York, Viking Press, 1936; Ignazio Silone, *Der Faschismus, seine Entstehung und seine Entwicklung.* Zürich, Europa Verlag, 1934; A. Rossi, *The Rise of Italian Fascism, 1918–1922,* London, Methuen, 1938.

The later history of Austrian labor is discussed in Pertinax (pseudonym for Otto Leichter), *Oesterreich, 1934,* Zürich, Europa Verlag, 1934; also by the same author under the pseudonym Georg Wieser, *Ein Staat stirbt, Österreich 1934–1938,* Paris, Les Éditions Nouvelles Internationales, 1938. See also G. E. R. Gedye, *Betrayal in Central Europe; Austria and Czechoslovakia: the Fallen Bastions,* New York, Harper, 1939. For the story of July 15, 1927, see Crook, *op. cit.,* p. 586 ff.; also Oskar Pollak in *International Information,* published by the Secretariat of the Labor and Socialist International, Zurich, 1927.

A detailed report of the Proceedings of the International Socialist Conference is contained in *International Information,* Zurich, 1933.

Hendrik de Man's ideas on the labor plan are developed in *Die sozialistische Idee,* Jena, Diederichs, 1933, and in his *Planned Socialism: the Plan du Travail of the Belgian Labour Party,* London. Gollancz, 1935; New Fabian Research Bureau, London, Publication No. 25. See also Hendrick de Man, *The Psychology of Socialism,* New York, Holt, 1927.

The best available history of the Communist International is Arthur Rosenberg, *A History of Bolshevism from Marx to the First Five Years' Plan.* London, Oxford University Press, 1934. F. Borkenau, *World Communism; a History of the Communist International,* New York, Norton, 1939, is somewhat partisan in some chapters.

It is almost impossible to find an unbiased treatment of the war in Spain. Different points of view are expressed in the following three books: Franz Borkenau, *The Spanish Cockpit; an Eye-witness Account of the Political and Social Conflicts of the Spanish Civil War,* London, Faber and Faber, 1937; Frank Jellinek, *The Civil War in Spain,* London. Gollancz, 1938; Felix Morrow, *Revolution and Counter-Revolution in Spain,* New York. Pioneer Publishers, 1938. In a place by itself belongs Julio Alvarez del Vayo's *Freedom's Battle,* New York, A. A. Knopf, 1940, the moving report of one of the leaders of Republican Spain. The French policy toward the Spanish war is discussed extensively in Alexander Werth's above-mentioned books.

Apart from the extensive references in a great many magazines, I mention particularly Otto Bauer, *Die Illegale Partei.* Paris. Editions Der Sozialistische Kampf, 1938. See also *Italy against Fascism.* Quaderni Italiani. New York. September, 1942.

INDEX